A Guide to Consulting Services for Emerging Healthcare Organizations

A Guide to Consulting Services for Emerging Healthcare Organizations

ROBERT JAMES CIMASI, CBI, CBC

WILEY

John Wiley & Sons, Inc.
New York • Chichester • Weinheim • Brisbane • Singapore • Toronto

Copyright © 1999 by John Wiley & Sons, Inc. All rights reserved.

Published simultaneously in Canada.

This publication is designed to provide accurate and authoritative information in regard to the subject matter covered. It is sold with the understanding that the publisher is not engaged in rendering legal, accounting, or other professional services. If legal advice or other expert assistance is required, the services of a competent professional person should be sought.

Library of Congress Cataloging-in-Publication Data:

Cimasi, Robert James.
    A guide to consulting services for emerging healthcare
organizations / Robert James Cimasi.
        p.   cm.
    Includes bibliographical references and index.
    ISBN 0-471-31625-3 (cloth : alk. paper)
    1. Hospital management companies—United States.   2. Physician
management companies—United States.   I. Title.
    [DNLM: 1. Managed Care Programs—organization & administration—
United States.   2. Health Planning Technical Assistance.
3. Consultants.   W 130 AA1 C573g 1999]
RA971.C585   1999
362.1'0425—dc21
DNLM/DLC
for Library of Congress   98-52741

Printed in the United States of America.

10 9 8 7 6 5 4 3 2 1

To my wife
Laura M. Baumstark, CAE

About the Author

Robert James Cimasi, CBI, CBC is president and founder of Health Capital Consultants (HHC). HCC is a nationally recognized healthcare consulting firm with offices in eight states, specializing in physician/practice integration, senior management consulting, mergers and acquisitions, intermediary services, valuation consulting, financial analysis, industry research and library services, information systems/technology services, and litigation support for healthcare providers and their advisors. Mr. Cimasi has worked with a diverse range of healthcare clients in over 30 states. Mr. Cimasi holds the Certified Business Intermediary and Certified Business Counselor designations and is a member of the American Association of Healthcare Consultants (AAHC), American Hospital Association (AHA), Healthcare Financial Management Association (HFMA), Institute of Business Appraisers (IBA), Institute of Certified Business Counselors (CBC), International Business Brokers Association (IBBA), Medical Group Management Association (MGMA), National Association for Health Care Consultants (NAHCC), National Health Lawyers Association (NHLA), Practice Valuation Study Group (PVSG), and St. Louis Society of Association Executives (SLAE). Mr. Cimasi is a nationally known speaker on healthcare topics and has written extensively in the field. His writings include "Physician Integration Organization, Sample Business Plan" in *Physician's Managed Care Success Manual* by Scott Becker (Mosby, 1999) and chapters on medical practice valuation in *The Handbook of Business Valuation* (John Wiley & Sons) and *Valuing Professional Practices and Licenses: A Guide for the Matrimonial Practitioner, 1997 Supplement* (Aspen Law & Business). Mr Cimasi is the coauthor of the AICPA's advanced business valuation course "Health Care Industry and Medical Practice Valuation." He is currently developing medical practice valuation software with John Wiley & Sons.

Contents

Exhibits, Figures, and Tables   **xiii**

Foreword   **xvii**

Preface   **xix**

Acknowledgments   **xxi**

1. Introduction   **1**

Who and What?   2
When?   4
Why?   5
Where?   6
How?   9

2. Healthcare Industry Trends and Consolidation Forces   **10**

Introduction   10
The Healthcare Reimbursement Environment   11
The Healthcare Regulatory Environment   17
The New Healthcare Paradigm   24

3. Emerging Healthcare Organization (EHO) Models   **36**

Introduction   36
Independent Practice Associations (IPAs)   36
Physician Practice Management Companies (PPMCs)   42
Physician Hospital Organizations (PHOs)   51
Management Services Organizations (MSOs)   56
Group Practice Without Walls (GPWW) Model   75
Fully Integrated Medical Groups (FIMGs)   78
Integrated Delivery Systems (IDSs)   81

4. General Consulting Methods   91

Introduction   91
"Our Product Is Our Process"   92
Consulting Skills   92
The Six Ps: Proper Prior Planning Prevents Poor Performance   93
Vision, Strategic Initiatives, and Tactical Plans   97
The Phases of the Consulting Engagement   98
The Four Phases of Physician Integration   100
Record Management, Memorializing, and Archiving   100
The Engagement Process   102
Professional Fees   104

5. Overview of an EHO Start-Up Program Stressing Physician Advocacy   106

Introduction   106
The Do's and Don'ts of Physician Integration   107
Conceptual Framework   111
Factors Driving the Approach   112
Integration Program Planning   113
Designated Market Assessment   121
Other Factors Affecting the Program   127
Assessment of Potential Affiliate Physician Providers in the Area   127
Determination of Consensus on Integration Model to Use   128
Regulatory Issues   128
Centralized Services   131

6. Physician Integration/Affiliation and Practice Acquisition Programs: A Development Plan and Agenda   137

Program Background   137
Program Planning and Description   143
Integration/Affiliation Models   157
Implementation of Program   164
Conclusions and Recommendations   178

7. Management Status Assessment and Operational Review   180

The Process   180
Management Status Assessment   181
Operational Review   182
Management Information Systems (MIS)   185
Medical Records Management   186

Communications   186
Summary   227

**8. Due Diligence Engagement: Evaluating the Potential
     for Success of an Investment in a Primary Care
     Physician Practice-Management Company   229**

Overview of the Proposed Venture   229
Background of the PPMC   232
The Climate of Primary Care Medicine Today   233
Primary Care Clinic Models Selected   238
Geographic Target Markets Selected   240
Business Plan: Financial Projections and Analysis   241
Business Plan: Growth and Physician Recruitment Strategies   267
Summary of Findings and Conclusions   272
Contingent and Limiting Conditions   275

Appendixes   277

General Research
Appendix 1   Analysis of Cases by Medical Specialty of Provider and Major
             Diagnostic Category (MDC)   280
Appendix 2   Analysis of DRG Demand by MDC Summary Report   284
Appendix 3   Area Hospital Assessment Worksheet   286
Appendix 4   Employment Survey   288
Appendix 5   Major Employer Worksheet   290
Appendix 6   Managed Care Organization/Insurance Worksheet   292
Appendix 7   Economic Environment Worksheet   296
Appendix 8   Medical Practice Selection Matrix   298

Specific Research
Appendix 9   Due Diligence Checklist   300
Appendix 10 Equipment Inventory Worksheet   309
Appendix 11 Sample Medical Practice Documents and Materials
             Request Form   318
Appendix 12 Medical Practice Worksheet   320
Appendix 13 Medical Practice Workbook   331
Appendix 14 Sample Income Distribution Plan   354

Formation of EHO
Appendix 15 Analysis of Compensation Package   355
Appendix 16 Exit Strategies Worksheet   360
Appendix 17 Governance Checklist   363
Appendix 18 Operational Compliance Worksheet   367
Appendix 19 Capital Contribution Worksheet   370
Appendix 20 Physician Contact/Interview Summary   373

Appendix 21   Voting Checklist   375
Appendix 22   Exit Strategies   382
Appendix 23   Database Fields Sample   384

Centralization of Services
Appendix 24   Employee Insurance/Resource Worksheet   386
Appendix 25   Insurance Benefits Assessment   388
Appendix 26   Employer and Employee Insurance Expenses   389
Appendix 27   Summary of Practice Services Worksheet   391

Operational Review
Appendix 28   Sample Management Status Assessment and Operational
               Review: Practice Contracts Summary   393
Appendix 29   Sample Management Status Assessment and Operational
               Review: Synopsis/Timeline of Recommendations   395
Appendix 30   Sample Management Status Assessment and Operational
               Review: Summary of Issues and Concerns   397
Appendix 31   Sample Management Status Assessment and Operational
               Review: Format for Specific Recommendations   399
Appendix 32   Sample Management Status Assessment and Operational
               Review: Medical Practice Site Visit Summary   401

Management Information System
Appendix 33   Information System Vendor Key Business Selection Criteria 403
Appendix 34   Medical Management Software: Annual Maintenance Cost
               Comparison   404
Appendix 35   Medical Management Software: Pricing Comparison   406
Appendix 36   Practice Management Information Systems Request
               for Information   408

Healthcare Executive Search
Appendix 37   Healthcare Executive Search Overview of Conducting a
               Search for Healthcare Executives   424

Miscellaneous
Appendix 38   Confidentiality and Stand Still Agreement   442
Appendix 39   Letter of Intent A: Employment with Practice Acquisition 445
Appendix 40   Letter of Intent B: Option A = Employment and
               Option B = Affiliation   449
Appendix 41   Letter of Intent C: Employment—No Practice Acquisition   453
Appendix 42   Letter of Intent D: Affiliation Arrangement   457
Appendix 43   Consulting Engagement Pre-Engagement Acceptance
               Form   460

Bibliography   **465**

Glossary of Healthcare Terms   **489**

Index   **497**

Exhibits, Figures, and Tables

1. Introduction

Table: EHOs   8

2. Healthcare Industry Trends and Consolidation Forces

Exhibit 2-1. The Shifting Universe of Healthcare Delivery   24
Exhibit 2-2. The Change in Priorities   25
Exhibit 2-3. Key Factors in the Evolution of the Industry—
   Generations of Managed Care   27
Exhibit 2-4. What Winners Will Look Like   28
Exhibit 2-5. Market Evolution   29
Exhibit 2-6. Representative Cities in Various Stages of Market
   Consolidation   30
Table: Growth in Physician Supply 1960–2005   30
Table: Distribution of Physicians in Office-Based Practices   31
Table: Distribution of General/Family Physician Practices   31
Exhibit 2-7. EHO Models   35

3. Emerging Healthcare Organization (EHO) Models

Exhibit 3-1. Independent Practice Association (IPA)   37
Table: Reported IPA Merger and Acquisitions Activity, 1996–97   43
Exhibit 3-2. Number of Physician–Group Acquisitions by PPMCs   44
Exhibit 3-3. PPMC Organizational Structure   45
Exhibit 3-4. Equity Model   46
Exhibit 3-5. Profit and Revenue Models   48
Exhibit 3-6. PHO Ownership Structure Model A   51
Exhibit 3-7. PHO Ownership Structure Model B   52

Exhibit 3-8. PHO Ownership Structure Model C   52
Exhibit 3-9. Pyramid of MSO Goods and Services   58
Exhibit 3-10. Hospital/System Owned MSO   60
Exhibit 3-11. Joint Venture Hospital Physician–Owned MSO   61
Exhibit 3-12. Physician Investor–Owned MSO   62
Table: Advantages of MSOs   68–69
Table: Disadvantages of MSOs   69
Exhibit 3-13. Group Practice Without Walls   76
Exhibit 3-14. Fully Integrated Medical Group   80
Exhibit 3-15. Integrated Delivery System   83

4. General Consulting Methods

Exhibit 4-1. Hierarchy of Organizational Tools   93
Table: Process Outline   95
Table: Timetable of Events   96–97
Exhibit 4-2. Vision Statement   98
Exhibit 4-3. Four Phases of Physician Integration   101
Table: Fee Options Discussion Matrix   105

5. Overview of an EHO Start-Up Program Stressing Physician Advocacy

Exhibit 5-1. Four Phases of Physician Integration   114
Exhibit 5-2. Autonomy/Leverage Diagram   117

6. Physician Integration / Affiliation and Practice Acquisition Programs: A Development

Table: Hospitals' Overall Per-Physician Acquisition Costs for Primary Care
   Physician Practices   142
Exhibit 6-1. Program Structure   144
Exhibit 6-2. Organization-Driven Approach   146
Exhibit 6-3. Physician-Driven Approach   147
Exhibit 6-4. Physician Practice Management Company (PPMC)-
   Driven Approach   148
Exhibit 6-5. Four Phases of Physician Integration   149
Exhibit 6-6. Practice Acquisition/Valuation Process Flow Model   152
Table: Process Outline   154–155
Table: Timetable of Events   156
Exhibit 6-7. Evolution and Continuum of Physician Integration   159
Table: Selection Rating System Matrix   168
Table: Capitation Income Distribution Plan Options   175
Table: Billing/Collections and Claims Resolution Services   178

8. Due Diligence Engagement: Evaluating the Potential for Success of an Investment in a Primary Care Physician Practice-Management Company

Exhibit 8-1. PPMC Comparison of Production and Costs: Subject Pro Forma with Industry Norms   243–245

Exhibit 8-2. PPMC Comparison of 1995 Projections with MGMA Norms   246–247

Exhibit 8-3. PPMC Ratio Analysis: Comparison of Subject Pro Forma with 1994–95 FSSB   248–265

Table: Typical Physician Interview/Site Visit Expenses   269

Foreword

Like no other field, the healthcare industry shifts and its alliances change on an extremely rapid basis. Providing high-quality consulting services in an evolving healthcare marketplace requires both strategic and tactical knowledge and tools, as well as financial intelligence and military-like planning and action. It requires dogged determination and an ability to shift position and plans as the national and local marketplace evolves. Successful consultants have a thorough understanding of the changing healthcare delivery system, a great comfort with and broad knowledge of healthcare topics, and the means and tools by which to deliver advice and counsel.

For years, Bob Cimasi has utilized a method of consulting focused on client-decision analysis. He honed his firm's ability to provide clients with the necessary information and tools to make decisions. In this manual, he shares those tools with other consulting colleagues. Cimasi's methodology is presented to clients and staff alike with his often stated aphorism: "The process is the product."

Cimasi brings to this book the necessary tools to simultaneously juggle multiple projects on behalf of a client while consistently ensuring that the client understands the risks and purpose of each aspect of the engagement as well as the required tasks to be performed and decisions to be made. To the readers of this manual and to his clients, he provides a full range of decisional possibilities.

Consultants have been known to simply provide the easy and least risky of choices to their clients. In that way if things go well they have "ruffled no feathers." If things are not going well, consultants are able to profess that they only provided the standard answers and plans generally employed by most consultants in evolving healthcare organizations. In contrast, Cimasi believes that the client ought to make tough choices. He is not afraid to give the client the full range of options and to provide the client with data and decision-making tools by which to judge the risky and less risky options. He also believes that the consultant should not be frightened to advocate hard and difficult positions on behalf of the client, that is, to be willing to lay oneself on the line for the good and goal of the client.

A consultant can use this book in a variety of ways. First, the consultant should browse through the entire manual. Then, he or she should take the time to read completely those chapters and sections that are of specific interest to his or her own practice and efforts. Finally, the consultant can extrapolate parts of the book that can be implemented in his or her own specific strategies. In addition, the book can be used as a regular reference manual to return to time and again.

The manual provides comprehensive thoughts regarding healthcare and the marketplace. It also provides basic tools, contracts, checklists, and explanations of strategic initiatives that are being adopted from market to market. By using this book, consultants will have a better ability to implement their plans and the plans of their clients than previously possible.

Bob Cimasi is an extremely talented and gifted practitioner. In this manual he brings together a wealth of information and hard-won experience. If you make use of the variety of tools in this manual and bring the determination that Bob has brought to healthcare consulting, you cannot help but enhance your abilities and skills and immensely improve your practice and the quality of services that you deliver to your clients.

Scott Becker, esq.
Ross & Hardies
February, 1999

Preface

I began my career in healthcare consulting by appraising and selling solo or small group medical practices and working with physicians who wished to merge or retire. In turn these M&A-based solutions led to a more diverse consulting business, including medical practice operational and financial management, physician manpower planning, and managed care contracting services. Each of these consulting services requires a broad knowledge of the universe of healthcare delivery within which the subject provider entity operates.

Consolidation in the healthcare industry has led to larger players controlling local and national markets. Emerging Healthcare Organizations (EHOs) are the latest manifestations of two decades of integration efforts in healthcare. As such, they represent the organizational structures through which independent and small providers can compete and prosper in the current market. For physicians and independent providers to survive today requires integration. The opportunities for both providers and consultants are enormous, but in order to take advantage of them requires a serious commitment from both parties.

The healthcare industry is a vast and diverse part of the American economy which is undergoing a sustained and dramatic transformation. To have an understanding of the industry requires a strong knowledge of general business and economic principles as well as a continuing commitment to staying informed. While the healthcare financial and management literature has grown exponentially in the last ten years, its very availability and volume presents a challenge to all of us as professionals working at the forefront of this competitive industry. Simply stated, "How do we find the time to sort through an ocean of information and data, select what is relevant, analyze it, and report it to our clients?"

In starting Health Capital Consultants (HCC), I made a commitment to my career to address that challenge by developing a serious research library as the core of the firm. This effort has assisted us in our efforts to provide cutting edge, well-researched services to our clients in a timely and cost-effective manner.

Part of my motivation in starting HCC was to be able to act as an advocate for those providers without the internal resources to adapt to change quickly enough to effectively compete in today's intensely competitive and dynamically *turbulent* market.

I hope this book will provide technical, practical, hands-on information and practice aids relating to providing quality services to these new client EHOs.

Acknowledgments

I would like to acknowledge the assistance and support of a number of Health Capital Consultants (HCC) staff and colleagues who have helped to bring this effort to fruition. First, my brother, Charles Cimasi, who has worked with me in the consulting field for years and who has strongly influenced my practice philosophy. Tim Alexander, HCC's librarian, was a great help in conducting research for the book and in coordinating the efforts of all those working on the project. Other researchers who assisted in the production of the book are Eric Armbrecht, Kristine Regehr, Ken Clarke, Maggie Pautler, Tracey Medus Aegerter, Gay Lynn Montgomery, and Evelyn Colwell. Many thanks to Todd Zigrang, Paul Wicker, John Hillan, and Jamie Robertson, all senior consultants with HCC, who have excelled throughout numerous engagements with our clients and who assisted in the development and field testing of many of the materials and tools included in this book. The administrative support team at HCC was terrific throughout. David Fulk worked closely as my personal editor during the writing of the book and added greatly to the quality of the final product.

A final word of thanks to HCC's many past and current clients. They are the ultimate source of the experiences that this book comprises. At the beginning and at the end of each day they are the reason we seek to improve our efforts.

## Chapter 1

Introduction

Healthcare consultants and advisors who have traditionally worked with client physicians in solo practices and small groups are seeing their potential client base decline as the healthcare industry consolidates and greater numbers of providers form new and larger organizations. This book will address how these new organizations differ from one another and from traditional practice settings, as well as the consulting services involved in their start-up and administration. The book is designed as an introduction to the national healthcare market; as a reference for the new organizational forms in healthcare, called Emerging Healthcare Organizations (EHOs); and as a detailed description of many of the central types of consulting services these organizations require.

The book is divided into four parts:

1. The first part, consisting of Chapter 2, "History and Evolution of the Healthcare Organizational Structures and Integration," provides a detailed description of the market forces in the healthcare industry that act as catalysts to the consolidation and integration of providers. The section is divided into the broad categories of reimbursement, regulation, the new healthcare paradigm, and Emerging Healthcare Organizations.

2. The second part, Chapter 3, "Emerging Healthcare Organization (EHO) Models," focuses on the six main types of EHOs. The purpose, structure, and function of each EHO model are described, providing a detailed reference for readers.

3. The next part of the book includes several chapters covering the range of consulting services that EHOs require. There are three broad types of these services: start-up consulting, recruiting and affiliation programs, and management and operational reviews.

4. The fourth and last part consists of appendices, including forms, tools, further sources of information, and indices.

Thus, this work is a comprehensive resource for consultants as well as a valuable reference tool for those who provide consulting services to EHOs.

The following quote can serve as a guide throughout this work.

> **The Editor's Creed**
> *I keep six honest serving men*
> *(They taught me all I knew)*
> *Their names are What and Why and When*
> *And How and Where and Who.*
>
> *—Kipling*

WHO AND WHAT?

The healthcare consulting industry is a relatively new one. However, the changes occurring in American healthcare in the last 20 years, combined with the sheer size of the industry, have spawned a growing number and variety of healthcare consulting firms.

This expanding market for consulting services has led many management and financial consulting firms to expand their services to include healthcare consulting. Accounting firms, traditionally the financial advisors for small medical practices, are also moving into the healthcare consulting marketplace. However, the changing nature of medical practice is reducing the number of solo and small-group practices as physicians aggregate into larger practices and other organizational forms, loosely termed Emerging Healthcare Organizations (EHOs). These organizations require different levels of expertise and services from small medical practices. Therefore, for general accounting, financial, and management consulting firms to expand into the healthcare consulting field requires a commitment to becoming informed about the current healthcare market and organizational structures.

Marcus Welby Is Dead

Increasing numbers of providers no longer practice in solo physician practices or in traditional organizations like independent hospitals and small group practices. This work is about traditional healthcare providers that are forming new organizations and delivery systems through the combination of providers and facilities into EHOs that follow the needs and demands of the market. In business, form follows function, regardless of the industry. Therefore, the EHOs examined in this work are categorized by their business functions.

EHOs are Resistors, Cost-Containers, or Integrators   Implementing a defensive strategy against managed care organizations, resistor EHOs—including Independent Practice Associations (IPAs) and Physician Hospital Organizations (PHOs)—have attempted to maintain the status quo. As the market demands more change than resistor EHOs can handle, cost-containers have emerged with tactics to create economies of scale and create more negotiating leverage. Cost-containers are Physician Practice Management Companies (PPMCs) and Management Services Organizations (MSOs). While most markets currently favor cost-containers, there is a movement toward integrators. Integrator EHOs focus on population-based health management to deliver profits rather than just cost-containment. (Don't think that cost-containment has been forgotten by integrators, though!) To accomplish this, integrator EHOs, such as Fully Integrated Medical Groups (FIMGs) and Integrated Delivery Systems (IDSs) control (generally through ownership) the influential organizations or have influence with the people who can change care processes. Their business function is related to market maturity as well as strategy. Refer to Chapter 3 for detailed descriptions of these EHO models.

Introduction to the New Healthcare Paradigm

The delivery of healthcare in the United States is undergoing volatile change. Increasing healthcare costs and the rise of managed care (where nonproviders intervene in the management of care to decrease utilization) have stimulated industry consolidation through mergers, acquisitions, alliances, and network formation. These forces have also led to a shifting of the risk of paying for the healthcare needs of a population from the payors to the providers, which has forced significant organizational and management changes. Consolidation or integration in healthcare may be of two classes. *Vertical integration* refers to the consolidation of different types of provider organizations into one organization capable of providing a greater range of services. A vertically integrated delivery system may be viewed as the ultimate integration effort capable of providing the entire continuum of care required by a population. *Horizontal integration* is the consolidation of similar types of providers, such as physicians or hospitals. Many organizations are involved in both types of integration. For example, some hospitals are integrating both horizontally (with other hospitals) and vertically (with other healthcare organizations in a geographic area).

Insurers and providers have formed Health Maintenance Organizations (HMOs) in an attempt to manage both the care of the population they insure and the costs of this care. The tradition of a solo physician medical practice that accepts fee-for-service reimbursement is giving way to group practices and networks that negotiate managed care contracts and accept per-capita payment arrangements. This trend toward per-capita payments, or capitation, is driving much of the change in healthcare delivery today.

The "Death of Marcus Welby" metaphor for medical care means that not only do physicians practice in very different settings today, but that the traditional management systems of medical practices no longer meet the demands of the market. The type of financial statements used by solo physicians ten years ago are not relevant to the management of costs and reporting of outcomes. Every aspect of the management of a medical practice, from medical records to billing to quality management, is subject to redesign. Each emerging organizational structure has characteristics that influence how best to approach a redesign effort.

As the consulting and financial advice needs of a medical practice change in response to the new marketplace and reimbursement structure, those who advise medical practices must change their approach as well. Accounting is a major area for redesign. Determining the costs for a given patient's episode of care is the key to successfully managing the risk involved in *capitation*, where providers are paid for each insured enrollee regardless of the amount or cost of the care they provided.

More and more healthcare payors and consumers are asking providers to demonstrate medical results and quality as a basis for managed care contracts, and even for payment. This is seen in contracts involving *withholds*, where a percentage of payments are conditioned on meeting certain contract criteria, which may include quality measures such as guaranteeing that a percent of patients are screened for cancer each year. *Outcomes* are the documented aggregate medical results of patient treatment. The costs of collecting and analyzing data on outcomes are prohibitive for providers with a small volume of patients, which further motivates them to integrate and consolidate.

WHEN?

People often discuss healthcare reform in relation to President Clinton's proposed healthcare reform program. In truth, healthcare reform began with the introduction of Medicare and Medicaid in 1965. The government, as the largest payor of healthcare benefits, continues to attempt to control healthcare spending, and its reimbursement policies (described below) mark many of the milestones leading up to the current trends in healthcare delivery. However, the current consolidation and integration environment began with the rise of managed care in the 1980s, when the private sector became involved in controlling insurance costs.

As an aside, the federal government endorsed managed care as a means to control cost with the HMO Act of 1973.

WHY?

Government regulation has had an enormous influence on the healthcare industry. Regulation often brings about profound change, creating financial hardship for some and opportunity for others. All changes to law create work for advisors and consultants who are hired to assist those affected by the laws.

The government's healthcare programs for the poor and elderly, Medicaid and Medicare, have led to the government being the largest single payor in healthcare. The emergence of this government bureaucracy has resulted in much of the standardization and "unitization" of medical care (the use of measurement as a tool in both clinical and operational management) found in healthcare today. The federal government, through encouragement of taxpayers, wants to know exactly what it's buying, including healthcare.

Medicare and Medicaid originally paid for hospital services using a *cost-plus* reimbursement basis, where hospitals were paid for all of their costs and more. The rising costs associated with this system led to the introduction by the federal government of a *prospective pricing system* for hospital payment, where hospitals are reimbursed an average, qualified amount for each patient treated with the same type of diagnosis specified by a Diagnosis Related Group (DRG). The government is currently developing prospective pricing systems for reimbursement for home healthcare, skilled nursing facilities, and rehabilitation facilities. There are also plans for a prospective pricing system for long-term hospital care. Since the government is the single largest payor for healthcare services, these changes exert enormous pressure on providers to reduce costs. To do so, providers are employing more sophisticated management systems and consolidation strategies.

In 1989, the CPR, or Customary, Prevailing, and Reasonable payment standard for physician services, was replaced by the Resource Based Relative Value Scale (RBRVS). Whereas the CPR system was based on physicians' historical charges, the RBRVS system is based on the resources required for a medical procedure, including components for physician's work, malpractice insurance costs, and overhead, all of which are adjusted geographically. These changes in payment levels, implemented incrementally between 1991 and 1996, represent another significant restraint on healthcare cost growth by the government.

While prospective pricing and resource-based payment represent major cost constraints by the government, managed care is the private sector's response to high insurance costs. The new Medicare Choice or Part C programs, the latest governmental managed care initiatives, further constrict payments to providers and expand the influence of managed care. Refer to Chapter 2 for a more detailed description of these changes in governmental reimbursement. The current consolidation and reorganization efforts in healthcare are a direct reaction to these fundamental changes in both governmental and private healthcare payment levels and mechanisms.

The major catalyst for the development of EHOs is the arrival of managed care, which in turn came about due to the rising costs resulting from a healthcare market which had been supply driven, governed by inelastic demand. The healthcare industry today is subject to similar market pressures as other industries. The natural progression from the establishment of managed care organizations in a market to increasing pressure to accept capitated contracts requires that providers consolidate and improve their management systems and expertise to allow for management of the financial risk inherent in capitation.

WHERE?

Market Evolution

Healthcare markets evolve as providers consolidate, managed care plans are introduced, and numerous other factors come into play. This evolution can be classified into a number of market stages. Larger, more metropolitan markets generally are more competitive than smaller, rural markets and therefore urban healthcare delivery systems are usually more integrated. Large markets have historically had larger provider groups, which are attractive targets for those organizations seeking to form consolidated provider organizations. It is typical for the largest groups to affiliate with healthcare systems first and for the smallest practices and independent physicians to consolidate at a later market stage. Hospital management companies, PPMCs, and Managed Care Organizations (MCOs), including public companies, have acquired large numbers of hospitals and physician practices and have been very influential in the evolution of many urban markets. This strategy, called a *roll-up*, is where an organization, usually a PPMC, aggregates physicians into a single operational and/or contracting entity to create a market presence quickly. Consolidation often spurs further consolidation as competition increases.

EHO Statistics

The organizational structure of the healthcare industry is rapidly changing to include an abundance of Emerging Healthcare Organizations (EHOs). Adding to the alphabet soup of healthcare organization names are the different types of EHOs: Independent Practice Associations (IPAs), Physician Practice Management Companies (PPMCs), Physician Hospital Organizations (PHOs), Management Service Organizations (MSOs), group practices and Fully Integrated Medical Groups (FIMGs), Group Practices without Walls (GPWW), and Integrated Delivery Systems (IDSs). The growth of these organizations can be seen in terms of their numbers, size, and influence. Emerging organizations are altering the healthcare industry by replacing the traditional solo practitioner and small-group practice models. In fact, the solo practitioner is an almost completely outdated mode of delivery because of the level of competition in today's market.

In order to convey the scope of the development of EHOs, statistical references are needed. The difficulty arises when trying to provide consistent definitions. When trying to distinguish between these organizations, the descriptions are often too blurred or fluid to allow precise categorization. Different areas, systems, and individuals define these organizations differently. In every source that provides statistical data regarding these organizations, each cites a particular definition or description. It is extremely difficult to provide accurate statistics, not only because of the variance in how these organizations are defined but because of the rapid changes that are occurring involving the names, ownership, locations, and functions of each organization.

Consequently, at times, different sources are used to provide an overall idea of the numbers of these different organizations.

Providers

As of May 13, 1996, the total number of nonfederal physicians (including osteopaths) documented in the American Medical Association's Physician Masterfile is 723,000.[1] This number shows the size of the potential membership for EHOs. Out of all physicians in the United States,

---

[1]*Directory of Physicians in the United States*, 35th ed. American Medical Association, 1996.

487,000 are board-certified physicians through the American Board of Medical Specialists (ABMS).[2]

In 1994, the American Medical Association (AMA) surveyed 19,787 group practices including 210,811 physicians.[3] In 1988, 25 percent of the nation's physicians practiced in groups of five or more. Consolidation increased this figure to 34 percent by 1996.[4]

According to recent government statistics, there are 6,500 hospitals which participate in the Medicare program.[5] This may be compared with 6,201 hospitals identified in 1996 by the National Information Center for Health Services Administration[6] or the 5,134 nonfederal, short-term general and other special hospitals counted by the American Hospital Association in 1996, down from 5,292 in 1992.[7]

EHOs

	Hospital Statistics, 1998 Ed.[8]	Directory of Physician Groups and Networks[9]
IPAs	1,223	1,264
GPWWs	381	—
PHOs	560 (Closed), 1,147 (Open)	799
MSOs	1,139	475
Integrated Salary Model	1,016	—
Equity Model	183	—
Foundation	673	—

[2]*ABMS Medical Specialists Plus*. Marquis Who's Who in cooperation with the American Board of Medical Specialists, January 1997. Users Guide p. IX.

[3]1994/1995 survey in *Medical Groups in the U.S.: A Survey of Practice Characteristics*, 1996 Edition. American Medical Association, 1996, pp. 5, 7.

[4]Socioeconomic Characteristics of Medical Practice 1997, p. 28. American Medical Association, 1997.

[5]*Profiles of U.S. Hospitals*. HCIA, 1998, p. v.

[6]Hospital Statistics by Health Care Information Source (http://www.nichsa.org/faq/default.html). National Information Center for Health Services Administration, 1996.

[7]*Hospital Statistics*, 1998 Edition. Healthcare InfoSource, Inc., a subsidiary of the American Hospital Association, 1998, p. 8.

[8]Ibid.

[9]Information from the Center for Healthcare Information, publishers of the *1998 Directory of Physician Groups & Networks* (obtained via fax).

Sherlock Company, which tracks the PPMC market, listed 164 PPMCs in 1998, including 26,386 physicians.[10] As of July 15, 1998, 32 of these were publicly traded.[11]

No statistics have been identified on the number of Integrated Delivery Systems (IDSs) in existence. However, the American Hospital Association counts 2,058 hospitals in a system and 1,343 hospitals in a network.[12]

HOW?

The integration process that results in the formation of an EHO is a complex transformation involving numerous legal, organizational, political, business, and management issues that the participants and their consultants, attorneys, and other advisors working as a team must address. With the increasing number of EHOs being formed, there are new opportunities for the informed consultant to assist providers in the creation and administration of these new organizations. This book is designed as a comprehensive resource for these consultants.

---

[10]*PPMC Yearbook*. Sherlock Company, 1998, pp. 3–4.

[11]*PPMC*. Sherlock Company. August, 1998, A, B, C, and D.

[12]*Hospital Statistics*, 1998 Edition. Healthcare InfoSource, Inc., a subsidiary of the American Hospital Association, 1998, p. 8.

## Chapter 2

Healthcare Industry Trends and Consolidation Forces

INTRODUCTION

This chapter primarily describes *why* the history of the healthcare industry has created demand for consulting services. *When* companies need consulting services and *where* they are located is a function of a healthcare market's history.

Why? Healthcare organizations need consulting services because of the dramatic changes occurring in the industry. Despite market forces calling for reorganization, administrators have hospitals, health systems, and group practices to run and physicians have patients to see. Already overextended, they have little time for developing and implementing new strategies to ensure their survivability. Enter the consultant. As an outside party, consultants bring a new perspective, experience, and dedicated time to transform an organization.

When? The time is now.

Where? There are no stable markets in the United States; there are only those which are more developed and less developed in terms of its response to managed care. The greatest need for consulting services lies in markets experiencing the sharpest increases in managed care penetration. It is most likely that providers are considering the development of an EHO in response to the market.

THE HEALTHCARE REIMBURSEMENT ENVIRONMENT

Payment reform in the healthcare industry has been spurred by the government's perception of the industry as failing to contain costs. Cost containment reforms significantly affect medical practice patterns and revenues.

The implementation of the Resource Based Relative Value Scale (RBRVS), a relative value scale that is based on the necessary resources used to perform a medical service (i.e., overhead, malpractice insurance costs, and physicians' work), represents a major change to the reimbursement scenario for physician services. The transition from fee-for-service (reimbursement on the basis of services rendered) to a capitated basis (where payment is based on the provision of all care to a defined population) will cause providers to further alter delivery of care, with the result that the revenue stream of physician groups may be significantly altered.

Managed Care Organizations (MCOs)—organizations that provide managed healthcare services—are moving rapidly to share financial risk with providers, forcing them to be accountable for the delivery, cost, and quality of services. The incentive to control costs positions managed care as a rational component in today's healthcare system. Capitation—payment for healthcare services where the physician/provider receives a fixed amount per enrollee for a fixed period of time for specified services—further shifts the financial risk from the insurer to the provider, thus removing the fee-for-service incentive to perform more work than necessary.

Fee-for-Service to Managed Care

The fee-for-service system was prevalent in the healthcare industry for several years. Fee-for-service is a method of paying providers for individual medical services as they are rendered. The patient's bill varies by the number of services or procedures actually received. The patient is billed at the time of service.

Although traditional indemnity plans, where policyholders are insured against specific types and levels of losses, were the dominant force in healthcare insurance through the 1980s, they continue to lose ground. Only 28 percent of employees were enrolled in conventional fee-for-service plans in 1995. At that time, Towers Perrin, a benefits consulting firm, projected that this figure would fall to 10 percent in 1997.[1]

---

[1]*The Guide to the Managed Care Industry.* HCIA, 1998, p. xi.

Managed care is a broad term that encompasses the type of care provided by Health Maintenance Organizations (HMOs),[2] Preferred Provider Organizations (PPOs),[3] and other health plans that assume insurance risk and practice selective contracting (i.e., limiting enrollees to a panel of providers).

Because MCOs assume risk, they focus on managing care as well as managing costs. MCOs hold providers accountable for offering quality services at predetermined levels of reimbursement. In addition to HMOs and PPOs, managed care is dispensed by traditional indemnity insurance companies and the government. The Blue Cross and Blue Shield Association—easily the most recognizable indemnity insurer in the United States—has become far and away the largest managed care insurer, with over 37.5 million managed care enrollees—more than one quarter of all people enrolled in managed care in the country.[4]

MCOs manage costs by holding providers accountable for providing care to a population through:

- Clinical practice standardization
- Selective contracting
- Low-cost settings
- Reduced discretionary hospital admissions
- Effective staff use

These mechanisms ensure that financial risk is shared by the MCOs and the providers, forcing them both to be accountable for the delivery, cost, and quality of services.

Unlike traditional indemnity plans, to be profitable, MCOs must ensure that the premiums they collect are greater than their expenses. While indemnity programs rely on grouping together a large number of people for insurance purposes and charging higher premiums to stay abreast of rising costs, MCOs must operate cost-effectively because they assume risk.

---

[2]HMO: any organization that, through an organized system of healthcare, provides or ensures the delivery of an agreed-upon set of comprehensive health maintenance and treatment services for an enrolled group of persons under a capitation or a prepaid fixed sum arrangement.

[3]PPO: an entity through which healthcare providers contract with insurers to provide care based on a fee schedule. Plan members are encouraged to use the services of "preferred providers." If plan members use a provider other than one in the plan, the insured might be liable for a certain share of those charges.

[4]*The Guide to the Managed Care Industry.* HCIA, 1998, p. xi.

At the end of 1996, an estimated 160 million people—over 60 percent of the U.S. population—were insured by some kind of managed care plan. This is more than a 40 percent increase from 1995, when 112 million people were insured by MCOs.[5]

Medicaid managed care enrollments have risen since 1981, when the Health Care Financing Administration (HCFA) ruled to allow states more freedom in managing Medicaid funds. Between 1990 and 1996, the number of Medicaid beneficiaries enrolled in managed care plans rose from 2.1 percent to almost 11 percent.[6]

Capitation and RBRVS

With the advent of managed care, a capitation payment environment has emerged. This system consists of per capita payment for healthcare services based on the number of enrollees, regardless of the number who actually receive service. Groups contract to provide a specific menu of health services to a defined population over a set period of time. The medical group usually receives, in advance, a negotiated monthly payment from an HMO. This payment is the same regardless of the amount of service rendered by the group.

A recent study showed that 92 percent of physicians have at least one managed care contract and that 44 percent of the average physician's revenue comes from a managed care plan. The same survey showed that the mean portion of revenue from capitation is 7 percent.[7]

Congress continues to consider federal healthcare reform measures, especially relating to reforming the public insurance market. Many of these measures center on managed care practices. This is important, because any reforms can obviously affect physician revenue streams.

The Resource Based Relative Value Scale (RBRVS) system was intended to bring medical practice more in line with a prospective payment system where payments are made based on set fees for types of procedures or diagnoses. Medicare payments are based on the relative value assigned to each procedure's work, practice expense, and malpractice costs, with payment adjusted by a geographic and a universal conversion factor. Every physician uses the same payment schedule under the Medicare program.

---

[5]Ibid.

[6]*Medicaid Managed Care Enrollment Report.* HCFA, 1995. Major Issues in Medicare Managed Care: Briefing Materials. PPRC, February 1997, p. 6.

[7]Physician Marketplace Statistics 97/98. American Medical Association, 1998, pp. 116–119.

Officials involved in its development viewed the RBRVS payment schedule as the best way of preserving physicians' clinical autonomy and maintaining patient access to quality medical care.

Congress established the Physician Payment Review Commission[8] in 1985, charging it with advising Congress on methods of reforming payment to physicians under the Medicare program. This responsibility now includes:

- Advising the Congress on setting standards for expenditure growth and updating fees
- Commenting on reports by the Secretary of the U.S. Department of Health and Human Services on issues related to utilization of medical services, access, and policy
- Sponsoring health services research

The 1997 Physician Payment Review Commission's Annual Report to Congress reported that Medicare payments per service had been reduced 2.1 percent between 1995 and 1996 due to policy changes recommended by the commission. Such recommendations are made annually to Congress and affect the annual updates to the relative values and conversion factors used to determine payments.

Healthcare Industry Symptoms Driving Payment Reform

The idea of payment reform has been spurred by the perceived failure of healthcare industry cost containment. This perception has been driven by:

- Lack of accountability for cost
- Supply-driven market with inelastic demand
- Excess capacity of providers and specialty imbalance
- Cost-plus reimbursement
- Unsustainably high profit margins of industry and profession

The transition from the passage of Title XVIII of the Social Security Act of 1965 until the passage of the Balanced Budget Act of 1997 (BBA 97) included the following stages.

- The Omnibus Budget Reconciliation Act (OBRA) of 1981 allowed states to apply to HCFA for program waivers, enabling them to utilize

---

[8]Merged with the Prospective Payment Assessment Commission into the Medicare Payment Advisory Commission.

different payment and delivery systems for Medicaid including managed care plans.

- OBRA 1985 directed the development of RBRVS by commissioning the Hsiao/Harvard Studies.

- OBRA 1986 reduced payments for cataract surgery and anesthesiology, setting out the concept of "inherent reasonableness" for the first time.

- OBRA 1987 provided payment reductions for twelve additional groups of "overvalued" procedures.

- OBRA 1989 established volume performance rates, replaced the Customary, Prevailing, and Reasonable (CPR) payment standard with a fee schedule based on relative values (RV), and replaced the Maximum Actual Allowable Charge (MAAC) restriction on nonparticipating MDs with a new limiting charge. States shrink caps.

- OBRA 1990 (Public Law 101-508) made revisions to OBRA 1989 RVs, asserted "budget neutrality," and set transition rules.

- Final rules and schedules for RBRVS were published by the HCFA in the U.S. Federal Register on November 25, 1991, and took effect on January 1, 1992.

- OBRA 1993 rewarded primary care and exempted "clinics without walls," entities legally combining independent physicians or medical practices in order to create centralized management and decision-making structures and to share services such as administrative, billing, and purchasing costs, resulting in an organization with multiple sites, allowing physicians and medical practices to retain their independence by maintaining their private office and practice styles. Under this arrangement, assets are not merged.

- The Balanced Budget Act of 1997 (BBA 1997) authorized Provider Sponsored Organizations (PSOs)—entities in which providers own a majority interest—to contract directly with Medicare. PSOs will bear the full financial risk for the provision of services covered by Medicare by accepting capitated payment for enrollees. HCFA has developed solvency standards for PSO licensing.

- BBA 1997 also expanded Medicare managed care options to include coordinated care plans that range from HMOs and PPOs to PSOs. Other benefit categories include Medical Savings Accounts (MSAs) and traditional fee-for-service plans. The current HMO risk-contracting program will be replaced with up to eight types of health plans, ranging from provider-sponsored Medicare + Choice coordinated care to private fee-for-service opt-out (no Medicare or Medicare + Choice reimbursement).

All of this legislation, and especially the implementation of RBRVS, has played a significant part in changing reimbursement patterns and practice revenues.

Will RBRVS Be Abandoned?

Healthcare payment reform is gaining momentum, with focus shifting from the federal to the state level. With continued cost-containment pressure, RBRVS is likely to be replaced by capitated plans, at least in those areas where excess provider capacity has been squeezed out of the system.

The change from a fee-for-service basis to a capitated basis may have a more significant impact on medical practices than RBRVS, due to the shifting of "risk" from the payor to the provider.

The Transition from Fee-for-Service to Capitation

The transition from a fee-for-service form of reimbursement to capitation will cause healthcare providers to alter their ways of delivering care. The transition to capitation may offer several benefits to providers by:

- Preventing overutilization
- Decreasing staffing costs
- Providing for immediate access to reimbursement
- Giving freedom from insurance utilization controls and preauthorization requirements
- Being considered attractive to payors
- Increasing information sharing

Capitation also has several restrictions that should be considered.

- Fixed reimbursement requires significant and consistent utilization management.
- Quality of care may be compromised in certain cases because of inadequate treatment or extended waiting times.
- Establishing parameters and administrative guidelines can be complicated.
- The demographics of small populations can inhibit cost containment for physicians.

Physician Payment and the Provider Sponsored Organization (PSO)

Congress opened the door for PSOs to contract with Medicare through the Balanced Budget Act of 1997. Capitation payments to physicians, hospitals, and other providers may increase dramatically if PSOs successfully enter the market. PSOs include hospitals and physicians who contract directly with purchasers on a capitated basis, sidestepping insurance companies. Providers are in favor of the PSO, claiming more money could go to patient care by eliminating the middlemen (insurance companies), but insurers warn about the possibility of bankruptcy and putting patients at risk if providers are unable to provide their promised care. Insurers want PSOs to meet the same state solvency requirements as HMOs. Federal solvency standards include preliminary net worth requirements of $1.5 million, including, $750,000 in cash or cash equivalent, to apply for licensure. HCFA began accepting PSO applications in the summer of 1998.

Healthcare reimbursement has undergone many changes in the past several years. Perhaps the most important changes have been the increased prevalence of managed care payment arrangements and the shift from fee-for-service care to capitation. The implementation of RBRVS has played a large part in this transition.

THE HEALTHCARE REGULATORY ENVIRONMENT

Increasing government scrutiny of the business of medicine has led to tightened restrictions on nonprofit institutions, a crackdown on fraud and abuse, and an increase in antitrust and anti-kickback (or self-referral) investigations. The healthcare regulatory environment poses many serious considerations for EHOs. The specific considerations facing particular EHO models are discussed further in the individual model descriptions.

Healthcare providers face severe sanctions for sharing the profits of collective economic activity because the government believes that financial rewards for patient referrals might drive up healthcare costs, particularly federally funded ones, by encouraging practitioners to prescribe unnecessary or inordinately expensive care.

The need to survive in today's competitive economy and healthcare environment has forced facilities and individual providers to form new relationships in order to secure market position and compete efficiently.

Because the penalties for running afoul of the Medicare and Medicaid fraud and abuse laws are substantial, healthcare financial managers must be aware of what conduct is prohibited and what is permissible.

Anti-Kickback and Medicare Fraud and Abuse

The Ethics in Patient Referrals Act of 1989, the so-called Stark Bill, prohibits a physician from making a referral for clinical laboratory services that are reimbursable under Medicare to an entity with which the physician or an immediate family member has a financial relationship or compensation arrangement. Nor can the entity present a claim to Medicare or bill any individual or other entity for such clinical laboratory services. Sanctions for violating this law include denial of Medicare reimbursement, refund of any amounts collected in violation of the law, and significant civil monetary penalties for each item or service provided pursuant to a prohibited referral plus twice the amount billed for the item or service.

In August 1993, the federal self-referral prohibition was expanded as part of the Omnibus Budget Reconciliation Act of 1993 (OBRA 1993). OBRA '93 changed the self-referral prohibition in several ways. Significantly, the Medicare self-referral prohibition was broadened not to all payors, but only to Medicaid services.

Self-referral was banned for additional "designated health services," including:

- Physical therapy
- Occupational therapy
- Radiology or other diagnostic services
- Radiation therapy
- Durable medical equipment
- Parenteral and enteral nutrients, equipment, and supplies
- Prosthetics, orthotics, and prosthetic devices
- Home health services
- Outpatient prescription drugs
- Inpatient and outpatient hospital services

The self-referral ban prohibits physicians who have a "financial relationship" with an entity from referring their patients to the entity for "designated health services" that are covered by either Medicare or Medicaid.

An indirect sanction for violation of the fraud and abuse laws is that illegal payments are not tax-deductible. Many arrangements under the fraud and abuse laws also raise issues under the tax laws governing exempt organizations. Under Internal Revenue Code (IRC) Section 501(c)(3), tax-exempt organizations must be organized and operated exclusively for charitable, religious, or educational purposes. The tax laws contain prohibitions against "private inurement" and "private benefit" for tax-exempt entities. Under this rule, certain "insiders" of a tax-exempt entity, including directors/trustees, officers, and certain physicians, may not engage in a non-fair-market-value transaction with the tax-exempt entity. If the entity allows such inurement and the private benefit conferred on an individual is not merely incidental to the exempt activities of the organization, the IRS may revoke the organization's exempt status.

The primary concern is that the private benefit and private inurement standards are fulfilled, along with other structural and community benefit requirements. Some of the relevant issues are:

- Presence of insider interests and/or involvement
- Control and profit allocation status of the exempt organization after the transaction
- Above-average post-transaction compensation
- Purchase price above fair market value
- Inaccurate discount rate or annual revenue growth rate
- Fraud and abuse violations

The 1994 Hermann Hospital (Texas) case established new guidelines restricting salaries, retention incentives, and some recruitment incentives. Also in 1994, the IRS gave notice of its heightened enforcement activity by revoking LAC Facilities' tax-exempt status due to a finding that it was operating for the benefit of (to the "inurement" of) its shareholders during its sale.

Market Perceptions of Regulation, Cost Containment, and Reform Drive Value

Regulatory, cost-containment, and "reform"-related topics dominate both the industry and general trade press, fostering market uncertainty and a general perception of greater risk to providers and prospective purchasers/ investors.

Regulatory "hassles" continue to dramatically affect the formation and operation of healthcare practices. Some examples follow.

Fraud and Abuse: Ethics in Patient Referrals Act—Stark I and Stark II
The Stark laws Changed referral patterns and ownership of ancillary service provider entities.

The Thornton Letter D. McCarty Thornton, representing the Office of the Inspector General of HHS, stated that payments by acquirers of medical practices for goodwill, value of ongoing business units, convenants not to compete, exclusive dealing arrangements, patient lists, and patient records would be "suspect." Practice valuation, according to Thornton, should exclude any amounts that "reflect, facilitate or otherwise relate to the continuing treatment of the former practice's patients."

Clinical Laboratory Improvement Act of 1988 (CLIA)   CLIA raised the cost of lab services and caused many practices to abandon lab revenue streams.

Resource Based Relative Value Scales (RBRVS)   The introduction of RBRVS altered reimbursement of fees.

Utilization and Peer Review by Insurance Carriers, Medicare   Utilization and peer review increase the cost of billing, record keeping, and claims resolution, and sometimes result in economic credentialing.[9]

Occupational Safety and Health Administration (OSHA)   OSHA laws require additional operational expense.

Americans with Disabilities Act (ADA)   ADA requires additional capital investment in premises/facilities and impacted practice staffing policies.

IRS Enforcement   1099 (Independent Contractor) versus W2 (Employee) status and pension plan scrutiny have altered the traditional basis of associateship relationships.

Court Decisions   Court decisions based on regulatory edicts related to fraud and abuse enforcement—e.g., the precedent of Polk County Memorial v. Peters (Fed-Eastern District of Texas)—have been considered especially dangerous to the preservation of contractual provider relationships.

Chronology of Key Healthcare Milestones

1972—Medicare Anti-Kickback Statute Section 1128B[b] of Social Security Act (42 U.S.C. 1320a-7b[b]) provides felony criminal penalties (five years/$25,000 fine) for knowingly and willfully offering, paying, solicit-

---

[9]*Economic credentialing* describes the practice of Managed Care Organizations sanctioning physicians who don't adhere to their cost-containment strategies or treatment protocols by not including them on future panels or even by dismissing them from current panels.

ing, or receiving remuneration in order to induce business reimbursed under Medicare or state healthcare programs.

1986—General Counsel Memorandum (GCM) 39498 (4/24/86)—reasonable compensation for physician recruitment—provides that the value of the incentive must bear a discernible direct relationship to the value of the physician to the hospital.

1987—Under the Medicare and Medicaid Patient and Program Protection Act of 1987 (MMPPA) (Public Law 100-93), Section 2, OIG could exclude a provider from future Medicare participation as a civil alternative to criminal enforcement.

1987—Section 14 of Public Law 100-93 requires promulgation of regulations specifying those practices that will not be subject to criminal or civil enforcement of MMPPA. (Known as "safe harbors.")

1989—Ethics in Patient Referral Act of 1989 ("Stark Bill").

1989—The "Stark Referral Ban," part of the Omnibus Budget Reconciliation Act (OBRA) of 1989, prohibits a physician from referring Medicare patients to clinical labs with which the physician or a family member has a financial relationship.

1989—Initial proposed "safe harbor" regulations published in Federal register by OIG of HHS (1/23/89). Solicits comment.

1990—OBRA 1990 prohibits payment of federal matching funds to state Medicaid programs for physician services unless the physician meets certain requirements and prohibits the unbundling of services by hospitals.

1991—Final "safe harbor" regulations published in Federal Register by OIG of HHS (7/29/91).

1991—"Hansletter Decision" (9/91). HHS rules MDs in laboratory limited partnership violated the law and bars them from future Medicare participation.

1991—IRS General Counsel Memorandum (GCM) 39862 (11/22/91) reverses prior position and rules that hospital sale of partial income stream jeopardized tax-exempt status, in part because payments were in violation of anti-kickback laws.

1992—OIG releases Special Fraud Alert addressing financial incentives offered by hospitals and other healthcare facilities to recruit and retain physicians (5/7/92).

1992—"Safe harbors" regulation is published, protecting certain limited managed care activities from the reach of the anti-kickback statute.

1993—Comprehensive Physician Ownership and Referral Act of 1993 ("Stark II") seeks to extend coverage of present anti-kickback law by prohibiting all self-referral practices and expanding scope of services for self-referral prohibitions. Law to take effect 1/1/95. Original Stark law applied only to Medicare referrals for clinical lab services (1/5/93).

1993—Seven new "safe harbor" provisions. Department of HHS eliminates 60-40 rule for entities serving rural areas as defined by OMB and used by Office of the Census. Also, protection for payments/benefits offered by rural entities for recruiting, protection of payments to physician investors in ambulatory surgical centers for self-referrals, greater group practice physician investor protections, and protection for Cooperative Hospital Service organizations (CHSO) (9/21/93).

1993—Congress expands the Stark law, requiring most healthcare providers to reexamine their financial relationship with physicians (Stark II) (8/93). Allows the HCFA to establish additional regulations necessary to protect against program abuse.

1995—IRS issues MD recruitment/acquisition guidelines in *Herman Hospital* case (Texas).

1995—Stark II. As of January 1, 1995, prohibited designated services are expanded to include physician and occupational therapy services, durable medical equipment, and inpatient and outpatient hospital services.

1995—As of August 14, 1995, the DHHS issues final regulations interpreting the self-referral prohibitions of Stark I (42 C.F.R. Part 411).

1996—The Health Insurance Portability and Accountability Act of 1996 is signed into law August 21. The Health Insurance Reform Law (PL 104-191) includes minimum federal standards for portability of insurance between jobs, renewability, issuance, non-discrimination, long-term care, data requirements, and standards of consumer protection. The law as enacted July 1, 1997, and enforcement began January 1, 1998.

1996—On August 28, the Federal Trade Commission and the Department of Justice issue revised "Statements of Antitrust Enforcement Policy in Healthcare." Specifically modified are the statements on Physician Joint Networks and Multi-Provider Networks, expanding the rule of reason and thereby loosening antitrust guidelines for these groups.

1996—The Health Insurance Portability and Accountability Act (HIPAA), signed into law August 21, 1996, is designed to guarantee coverage for most individuals who lose coverage due to termination or change in employment. Insurance companies will be prevented from denying coverage based on the health status of an individual and must renew policies as long as the premium is paid.

1997—The Balanced Budget Act (BBA) of 1997 calls for balancing the federal budget in 2002, through a combination of $270 billion in spending reductions and $115 billion in tax cuts over five years, including:

- $115 billion in Medicare savings
- $14.6 billion in Medicaid savings
- $24 billion in children's health spending

The act also repeals the Boren Amendment, which required states to reimburse hospitals and nursing homes at Medicare rates. This will allow states to accelerate their plans to move elderly and disabled Medicaid beneficiaries to managed care without applying for Section 1915 (b) waivers.

The act replaced the three conversion factors for Medicare reimbursement with a single conversion factor starting in January 1998. This represents an 8.4 percent increase for nonprimary, nonsurgical services, a 2.6 percent increase for primary services, and a 10.4 percent decrease for surgical services.

BBA '97 allows Provider Sponsored Organizations (PSOs) to contract directly with Medicare. PSOs are entities in which providers (physicians and/or hospitals) own a majority interest. Federal solvency standards will be developed by the Health Care Financing Administration. Payment will be on a capitated basis, with PSOs receiving a monthly capitation payment for each member.

A new category of benefits called Medicare Part C (or "Medicare + Choice") was created starting in November 1998 and comprises a number of new benefit categories and coordinated care plans.

1998—The Clinton administration's fiscal 1998 budget establishes federal oversight of PSOs offering Medicare managed care plans for the first two years. After a two-year period of federal oversight, states will assume regulatory authority if their standards meet or exceed those of the federal government. Dispute over appropriate solvency standards for PSOs and over who should set them has pitted provider groups such as the American Hospital Association and the American Medical Association against managed care organizations, insurers, and their state regulators.

There is a long history of regulation in the healthcare industry, but the current trend is toward allowing market forces to work on decreasing cost and increasing quality and access. PSOs and several demonstration projects at HCFA are evidence of this trend. Nonetheless, the government, as the single largest payor of healthcare, has a financial interest in the industry's efficiency and efficacy. Thus, regulation will continue and likely focus on fraud and abuse, antitrust, non-profit organizations, and anti-kickback or self-referral.

THE NEW HEALTHCARE PARADIGM

Healthcare is delivered differently than in the past, when the hospital was the focal point of the system and patients had easy access to any physician. The system was characterized by indemnity insurance provided through employers or purchased independently by patients, and had developed, after healthcare costs began to rise, some techniques for controlling the utilization of services and supplies. Although the healthcare industry in some cities remains in this market stage, managed care has caused change and evolution in other regions to other market stages. In these cities, the industry matures to a point where appropriateness of care is evaluated, a "continuum of care" is emphasized (where patients make smooth transitions from doctor to hospital to rehabilitation or home care), and clinical outcomes are the measurement of value.

"Hospital-Centric" to "Covered Life–Centric"

The previously common practice of paying a physician directly for a service provided is now becoming rare. This was typical in the "hospital-centric" paradigm of healthcare delivery. Procedures were performed

EXHIBIT 2-1

The Shifting Universe of Healthcare Delivery

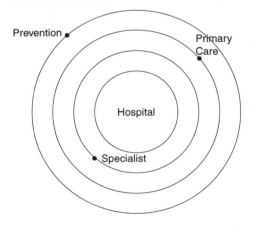

Ptolemy believed the planets
revolve around the Earth.

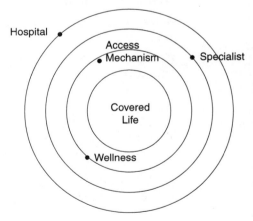

Copernicus and Galileo discovered
that the planets (Earth included)
revolve around the sun.

without much regard for cost, consultations with specialists were frequent, and offering preventive advice was not a common practice. These conditions imply that the healthcare delivery system orbited hospitals, and that when it came to accessing care through the fee-for-service system, the price tag for services was incidental. (See Exhibit 2-1.)

The center of today's delivery paradigm is covered lives; that is, individuals covered by some form of managed care insurance plan. Refer to Exhibit 2-2.

Managed Care Plans

Managed care plans have challenged the traditional providers' hold on patient loyalty and referral patterns. As a result of the demand for cost containment, there has been a rapid growth in the number of patients covered by managed care. Health Maintenance Organizations (HMOs) and Preferred Provider Organizations (PPOs) have sought to combine the role of the insurance company, utilization review organization, and medical services provider in order to offer prepaid medical plans to subscribers, thereby forcing cost containment by integrating operational and financial functions.

HMOs passed a milestone in 1995, as enrollment among large employers nationwide rose from 27 percent of all eligible employees in 1994 to 31 percent, exceeding indemnity plan enrollment for the first time.

EXHIBIT 2-2

The Change in Priorities

The Change In Priorities	
FROM	**TO**
Hospital Specialty Care Centered	Covered Life Driven Delivery System
Micro Management	Provider Self-Management
Individual Provider Performance	System Performance
Coordinating Services	Actively Managing Quality
Treating Illness	Maintaining Wellness
Acute Inpatient Patient Care	Continuum of Care\Outpatient Driven
More Selective Contracting	Open Specialty Panels
Insurer Bears Risk	Providers Bear Risk

Physician participation in managed care has also increased: The percentage of (nonfederal) physicians in practices with managed care contracts increased from 88.1 percent in 1996 to 92.3 percent in 1997.[10]

Driven by the bottom-line worries of employers, cost containment is now a monumental concern. In an HMO, primary and preventive care is often readily accessible to patients, and access to specialists is likely to be controlled by a primary care "gatekeeper" physician. Under a capitation payment system, providers accept a fixed amount of payment per subscriber (e.g., member in an HMO) for a given period of time, in return for providing specified services. Capitation shifts the risk from the payor to the physician and the practice.

The capitation reimbursement system makes not seeing patients a viable cost-reduction strategy, so a strong focus on preventive care is effective. In addition, much depends on the health, habits, and expectations of subscribers. Physicians must be aware of the health demographics of the patients they contract to serve. They must also employ significant and consistent utilization management in order to profit. Refer to Exhibit 2-3 for an illustration of the evolution of managed care systems.

Capitation leads to an emphasis on coordination—that is, establishing communication links between providers along the continuum of healthcare (doctors, hospitals, nursing homes, etc.). These links help ensure that patient care isn't interrupted between caregivers, which enhances quality, and patients don't have to be asked about basic information at every point. Eventually, integrated healthcare networks evolve. (See Exhibit 2-4.)

Market Evolution Factors Driving a Shift to Very Large Purchasers and Very Large Provider Networks

In this era of increased competition in healthcare, purchasers have exerted pressure on the healthcare system to lower costs to achieve economies of scale, and to improve the quality and outcomes of healthcare (refer to Exhibit 2-5). Large employers conduct research on providers and negotiate with insurers for lower-cost managed care products. Purchaser coalitions have begun to engage in collective purchasing to demand greater value and accountability from the healthcare system.

Corporate Employer Alliances and Healthcare Provider Networks are being formed and driven by corporate healthcare buyers who want one-stop healthcare shopping with cost containment and quality outcome measurement.

---

[10]*Physician Marketplace Statistics 1997/98*. American Medical Association, 1997, p. 116; *Physician Marketplace Statistics 1996*. American Medical Association, 1996, p. 133.

EXHIBIT 2-3

Key Factors in the Evolution of the Industry—Generations of Managed Care

1st	2nd	3rd	4th
Managed Access	**Managed Benefits**	**Managed Care**	**Managed Outcome**
Utilization review firms using limitations on benefits to contain costs and/or HMOs introducing administrative barriers:	Utilization review with discounted fee-for-service networks:	Utilization review with quality-based network:	An integrated managed healthcare system *requires*:
• Precertification required	• Emphasis on managing benefits	• Greater emphasis on treatment planning and quality management	• A system integrator offering a spectrum of operational clinical, financial systems—meets the needs of all buyer markets, benefit payors and beneficiaries
• Significant copays	• Precertification primary and treatment planning secondary	• Focus on most appropriate care in most appropriate setting	• Locally responsive delivery systems and services based on national standards and capabilities
• Emphasis on managing/restricting patient access	• Cost containment emphasized over clinical management	• Patients managed through a continuum of care	• Mutually beneficial *partnerships* with the physician community
• Reliance primarily on non-clinical reviewers	• Traditional treatment models employed	• Clinical management of network; provider–case manager collegiality	• Effective use of technology to measure/report and enhance quality and outcomes
• Physicians totally outside system	• Physicians "included," but their care delivery "inspected"	• Shift toward improving access and benefits to reduce costs	• Full accountability for service/savings through financial guarantees
			• Proof of value for customers

EXHIBIT 2-4

What Winners Will Look Like

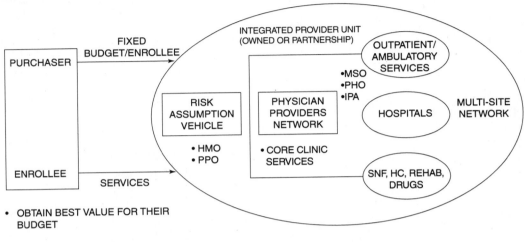

- OBTAIN BEST VALUE FOR THEIR BUDGET
- ENCOURAGE PROVIDER SELF-MANAGEMENT/CQI

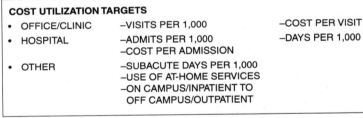

COST UTILIZATION TARGETS		
• OFFICE/CLINIC	–VISITS PER 1,000	–COST PER VISIT
• HOSPITAL	–ADMITS PER 1,000 –COST PER ADMISSION	–DAYS PER 1,000
• OTHER	–SUBACUTE DAYS PER 1,000 –USE OF AT-HOME SERVICES –ON CAMPUS/INPATIENT TO OFF CAMPUS/OUTPATIENT	

Markets Continue to Evolve through Several Stages toward Greater Consolidation

The growing acceptance of managed care as a healthcare delivery system is exhibited by ongoing enrollment trends. HMO enrollment grew 40 percent in just five years between 1990 and 1995.[11] Such enrollment growth will continue as public and private payors transfer more people into managed care programs. Refer to Exhibit 2-6 for a listing of cities in different market stages.

Enrollment in managed care plans has come primarily from the commercial market, but payors are now interested in smaller group, Medicare,

[11]*Statistical Abstract of the United States,* 117th ed. U.S. Bureau of the Census, 1997, Table 173, p. 121.

EXHIBIT 2-5

Market Evolution

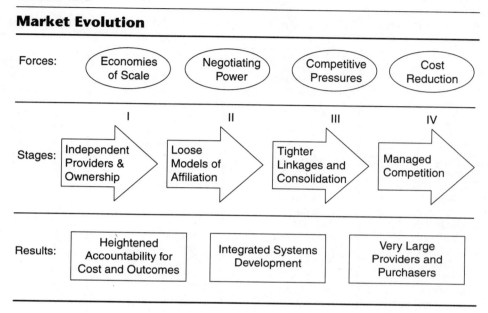

and Medicaid populations. Medicare enrollment in HMOs increased from 8.7 percent of beneficiaries in 1994 to 12.7 percent in 1996.[12]

Generally, as markets mature, revenue per member per month (pmpm) declines significantly and payors drive medical costs down. However, despite increased enrollment figures, recent years have seen HMO medical costs rising while premiums decrease. The result has been intense pressure on profit margins.

Trends in Physician Supply, Distribution, and Specialization

Trends in Physician Supply. Total MD/population ratios have increased over a thirty-year span, with a projected increase continuing throughout the twenty-first century. With the rapid increase in MD supply, the patient base per MD is declining, resulting in increased competition. In concept, this might make it more attractive to acquire an existing practice that already has a patient base than to start a new practice. However, this concept is challenged by the issue of whether the patients still "adhere" to practices or to payors (e.g., insurance plans).

---

[12]*Annual Report to Congress.* Physician Payment Review Commission, 1997, p. 33.

EXHIBIT 2-6

Representative Cities in Various Stages of Market Consolidation

Stage 1 Unstructured	Stage II Loose Framework	Stage III Consolidation	Stage IV Managed Competition
Omaha	Miami	Orange, CA	Minneapolis/St. Paul
Nassau	Louisville	Milwaukee	San Diego
Galveston	Ft. Worth	San Francisco/	Los Angeles
Syracuse	Dallas	Oakland	Worcester
Little Rock	Tampa	Portland	
Gainesville	Cincinnati	Sacramento	
Chapel Hill	Columbus	San Jose	
(Triangle)	Atlanta	Denver	
Birmingham	Orlando	Detroit	
Charleston, SC	Jacksonville	Boston	
Harrisburg	Cleveland	Salt Lake City	
Middlesex, NJ	St. Louis	Riverside/San	
Newark	Hartford	Bernardino	
Shreveport	New York City	Madison	
Winston-Salem	Kansas City	Tuscon	
Columbia, MO	Ann Arbor	Seattle	
Augusta	Baltimore	Phoenix	
Greenville, NC	New Orleans	Washington, DC	
Morgantown	Indianapolis	Providence	
Charlottesville	San Antonio	Houston	
Iowa City	Toledo	Fort Lauderdale	
	Richmond	Chicago	
	Lexington	Albany	
	Oklahoma City		
	Pittsburgh		
	Nashville		
	Philadelphia		
	New Haven		

Growth in Physician Supply 1960–2005

Year	Total Physician Population	Physician/Population Ratio
1960*	260,000	1:703
1980*	467,000	1:494
1994*	539,000	1:481
2005**	659,000	1:432

*Physician Characteristics and Distribution in the US, 1997/98 ed., AMA, p. 34.

**Statistical Abstract of the United States 1997, 117th ed., U.S. Dept. of Commerce, pp. 9, 413.

Trends in Physician Distribution. Greater access to larger patient bases with the resulting higher compensation, as well as greater possibilities for lifestyle choices and coverage, may have driven the increasing movement of physicians to urban locations.

Distribution of Physicians in Office-Based Practices

Year	Metropolitan	Non-Metropolitan
1970	82.6%[a]	17.4%[a]
1980	84.4%[b]	15.6%[b]
1990	86.0%[b]	14.0%[b]
1993	86.7%[b]	13.3%[b]
1996	87.8%[c]	12.2%[c]

[a](*Physician Characteristics and Distribution*, AMA, 1987, p. 28)
[b](*Physician Characteristics and Distribution*, AMA, 1994, p. 32)
[c](*Physician Characteristics and Distribution*, AMA, 1997, p. 32)

Distribution of General/Family Physician Practices

Year	Metropolitan	Non-Metropolitan
1970	67.6%[a]	32.4%[a]
1980	68.8%[b]	31.2%[b]
1990	71.4%[b]	28.6%[b]
1993	72.1%[b]	27.9%[b]
1996	74.7%[c]	25.3%[c]

[a](*Physician Characteristics and Distribution*, AMA, 1987, p. 28)
[b](*Physician Characteristics and Distribution*, AMA, 1994, p. 32)
[c](*Physician Characteristics and Distribution*, AMA, 1997, p. 32)

Trends in the Specialization of Professional Practices. The trend of physician practice has moved toward specialization and away from primary care since 1965, when 48.8 percent of MDs were in primary care, compared with 34 percent of MDs in primary care in 1996.[13]

The rise of managed care has prompted the increased role of the "gatekeeper" in some markets, and the rapid consolidation of healthcare providers into integrated delivery systems and other EHOs.

An integrated delivery system is a combination of hospitals, medical services, physicians, and other providers that provide coordinated, continuing ambulatory and tertiary care to a defined population or group

---

[13]Physician Characteristics and Distribution in the U.S., 1987 and 1997/98. American Medical Association, 1987, p. 19, 1997, p. 283.

of enrollees. Because of the gatekeeper's increasing importance in some markets, a premium in "value" has been placed on primary care physicians (PCPs).

Internal Medicine is the largest primary care specialty (60 percent are generalists), with Pediatrics second and General/Family Practice third. These specialties have become more attractive and practices in those specialties are often highly sought after as patient care gatekeepers into the managed care–oriented delivery systems.

Despite this and a recent trend toward "right-sizing" (i.e., the reduction in numbers of specialists allowed within managed care networks or panels), the trend toward specialization continues. In fact, in a growing number of markets, the gatekeeper system has failed and is being replaced with *open access, specialty-driven panels*, which are marketed through point-of-service (POS) or other capitated reimbursement models that downplay the importance of PCPs and replace them with other access mechanisms. In these markets it is believed that the PCP may actually be an endangered species that will be replaced by paraprofessionals, as discussed below.

Changes in the Professional Practice Competitive Environment

Physicians are not just competing with physicians. The emergence of competing providers from allied health professions—physician extenders and paraprofessionals—as lower cost providers has increased competitive pressures on physician practices. Physician extenders or paraprofessionals can either compete or add practice revenues. The integration of paraprofessionals is on the rise. Paraprofessionals can have the effect of increasing practice productivity and revenue.

Competing Providers—Allied Health Professions

- Psychiatrists *versus* psychologists *versus* licensed psychotherapists
- Ophthalmologists *versus* optometrists *versus* opticians
- Orthopedists *versus* osteopaths *versus* chiropractors
- Physician's Assistants (PAs)[14]
- Nurse practitioners (NP)

---

[14]*Perceptions of Marketplace Demand: Results of National Survey of '97 Physician Assistant Graduates.* Perspectives on Physician Assistant Education, Vol. 9, #14, Autumn 98, pp. 192–196; *Monthly Labor Review,* Department of Labor, Nov. 1997, Vol. 120, #11, p. 65. Jim Cawley reported 2.32 position offers for each PA graduate in 1997. The U.S. Labor Department predicts that the number of PA positions will grow 47 percent by 2006.

- Nurse midwives and certified nurse midwives (CNM)
- Certified registered nurse anesthetists (CRNA)

The center of the healthcare delivery system has traditionally been the hospital. Today's environment, however, places covered lives at the center of the delivery system. This has major implications for prevention, access, referrals, risk, and physician supply. In addition to these issues, changes in the professional practice competitive environment and the effect on revenue has also been discussed in this section.

Emerging Healthcare Organizations (EHOs)

The business objective in healthcare now is control over covered lives. EHOs are generally formed to pursue this goal.

> An emerging healthcare organization is an organizational form consisting of hospital(s), physician(s), and/or health plan(s) that have consolidated, merged, integrated or affiliated in response to managed care and integration forces in their market.[15]

The critical element to this broad definition is the reason for an EHO's existence. Market forces, primarily demands for lower prices and/or improved outcomes, catalyze EHO development and operations.

EHOs are vehicles for physician integration. In a cost-sensitive managed care environment or a more progressive outcome-focused one, it is critical for payors and others who bear risk for health services to have strong relationships with physicians. The rationale is simple: Physicians direct care, thereby giving them considerable control over healthcare expenditures and medical outcomes.

Classification.   EHOs take numerous forms to fill many functions in today's marketplace. To simplify the complex situation, this book focuses on six major EHOs:

1. Independent Practice Associations (IPAs)
2. Physician Hospital Organizations (PHOs)
3. Physician Practice Management Companies (PPMCs)
4. Management Services Organizations (MSOs)

---

[15]*Capital Survey of Emerging Healthcare Organizations,* Second Annual Report 1996, Integrated Healthcare Report, Medical Group Management Association, and Ziegler Securities, 1996, p. 1.

5. Fully Integrated Medical Groups (FIMGs)

6. Integrated Delivery Systems (IDSs)

In addition to these models, the next chapter includes a section on Group Practices without Walls (GPWWs), a less prevalent model, but one which is important in the history of EHOs.

Type of Integration. By definition, EHOs are integrated businesses. However, integration comes in two forms: horizontal and vertical. Horizontal integration is "the acquisition and consolidation of like organizations or business ventures under a single corporate management, in order to produce synergy, reduce redundancies and duplication of efforts or products, and achieve economies of scale while increasing market share."[16] When hospitals join together and create hospital systems or when physicians join forces to form organizations that primarily offer physician services, horizontal integration is at work.

Vertical integration involves the joining of organizations that are fundamentally different in their product and/or services offerings. It is "the aggregation of dissimilar but related business units, companies, or organizations under a single ownership or management in order to provide a full range of related products and services."[17] The evolution of many healthcare markets is being driven by a vision for fully integrated organizations.

A Framework for Understanding EHOs. A framework for the emerging enterprises in the business of healthcare is shown in Exhibit 2-7. Its rows classify each EHO by its function and level of integration (least integrated at the top) and the columns denote integration type (horizontal versus vertical). In less technical terms, it is a two-by-three matrix where the short axis represents the type of integration and the long axis represents the type of business operations.

Each of the three levels can be identified according to their business strategy:

1. *Resistors (IPAs and PHOs):* Organizations designed to maintain the status quo, fend off managed care, or slowly learn how to successfully operate in a managed care environment.

---

[16]Peter Boland. *The Capitation Sourcebook.* Boland Healthcare, 1996, p. 618.

[17]Ibid, p. 629.

EXHIBIT 2-7

EHO Models

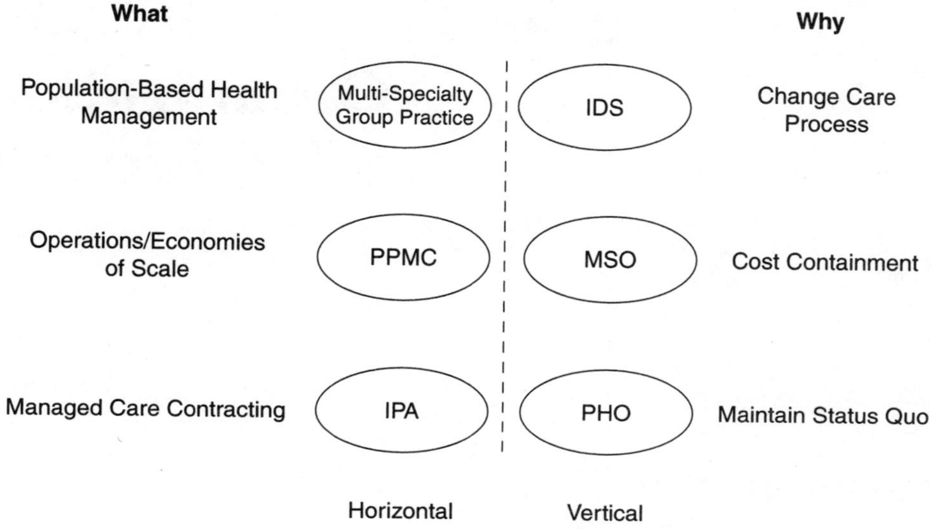

What			Why
Population-Based Health Management	Multi-Specialty Group Practice	IDS	Change Care Process
Operations/Economies of Scale	PPMC	MSO	Cost Containment
Managed Care Contracting	IPA	PHO	Maintain Status Quo
	Horizontal	Vertical	

2. *Cost Containers (PPMCs and MSOs):* Organizations that are capable of controlling healthcare costs through economies of scale. Their ability to contract effectively with managed care organizations and systematically reduce utilization of services is limited, however.

3. *True Integrators (FIMGs and IDSs):* These are organizations that are so financially integrated through risk contracting or ownership that true integration of care processes is possible. There are very few true integrators operating in the United States, but many EHOs see themselves as evolving toward true integration.

More information about each model appears in the following chapter.

## Chapter 3

Emerging Healthcare Organization (EHO) Models

INTRODUCTION

This chapter describes *what* response providers are making to changes in the healthcare market.

What?   This section describes the organizations that healthcare providers are building in response to the market changes. Collectively, they are called Emerging Healthcare Organizations (EHOs) and they are part of the changes in the way employers and individuals buy health insurance, payors reimburse services, physicians and hospitals interact, community health issues are addressed, etc.

INDEPENDENT PRACTICE ASSOCIATIONS (IPAs)

Definition

Individual Practice Associations or Independent Practice Associations (IPAs) are legal entities of independent physicians that contract with health insurance companies to provide medical services. IPAs are generally not-for-profit, although that is not a requirement. Individual physicians operate under their own tax IDs, Medicare provider numbers, etc., and generally do not share administrative overhead or centralized systems such as billing and claims-processing information systems. Although some IPAs include investment by hospitals, this section focuses on the horizontally integrated IPA which excludes hospitals and other non-physician-controlled businesses. Refer to Exhibit 3-1 for an illustration of the organizational form of an IPA.

It is important to distinguish an IPA from an IPA-model HMO. Although many people freely use the term IPA to describe both, they are quite different. An IPA-model HMO is a managed care product with an open panel where patients have a wide choice in their physicians. In this case, the managed care company has assembled the so-called IPA as a provider panel. The *true* IPA is organized by physicians in an effort to protect the interests of its member physicians. The true IPA may have contracts with multiple managed care organizations that offer various types of products, including (but not limited to) IPA-model HMOs. This section describes characteristics of the true IPA.

History

The IPA has been in existence for several decades. The HMO Act of 1973 codified the IPA by including it as one of two federally qualified HMO-models that employers with more than 25 employees must offer. The other option was a closed panel HMO. While the important distinction between a IPA-model HMO and true IPA was made above, their histories

Exhibit 3-1

Independent Practice Association (IPA)

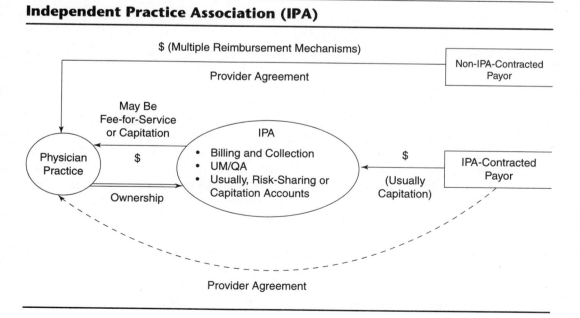

are congruent. True IPA developed independently and joined with HMOs contractually to create true IPAs.

Over the past decade, the IPA has become the leading model of physician organization used by private-practice physicians for contracting with HMOs, Preferred Provider Organizations (PPOs), and other managed care organizations. Over 1,200 IPAs have been identified by the American Hospital Association (AHA), but because they are forming so quickly, the actual number may be twice this many. In 1997, 50 percent of physicians participated in managed care contracts via IPAs, and for the average physician these contracts represent about 20 percent of their revenues. However, some specialists in high managed care penetration markets earn up to 70 percent of their revenues through an IPA contract.

Business Objectives of IPAs

The IPA is often the first step physicians take into the murky waters of integration. Such a step is often made because of a catalyst, such as a managed care organization implementing a new fee schedule that requires deep discounts from historical levels. When independent physicians initially come together to discuss options, characteristics of the IPA are generally outlined. Physicians build IPAs because its members seek to (1) preserve clinical autonomy, (2) avoid joining a group practice, (3) gain negotiating leverage with payors, and (4) retain market share.

Historically, physicians have used (and still use) the IPA as a defensive strategy against managed care. The IPA provides a vehicle for independent practices to maintain relationships with a large number of payors, thereby decreasing the likelihood that patients will leave the practice due to a change in insurance carrier. But newer IPAs like HealthFirst Network of Pensacola, Florida, accept financial risk and assume medical management responsibilities to maximize both reimbursement and autonomy.

HealthFirst is a 100-percent physician-owned IPA that began in 1985 as a messenger-model IPA. (A messenger model requires that every contract be reviewed by the IPA's membership before signing, and there is no a priori requirement to sign any contract negotiated by the IPA. The weakness of the messenger model is that payors can destroy any leverage of an IPA by directly negotiating with selected members.) From 1985 to 1995, the organization grew to cover 30,000 HMO members. In 1995, the pivotal year for the company, HealthFirst signed its first professional services capitation contract. Included in this contract was delegation of all administrative services associated with a professional services capitation agreement: claims, referral and authorization, credentialing, and utilization management. The successful negotiation was due, in part, to

HealthFirst's abandonment of the messenger model for an attorney-in-fact, which gave the IPA a right to negotiate contracts under the trust that its member physicians would accept the terms. In addition to creating the operations infrastructure, HealthFirst has increased its covered lives to 53,000 HMO enrollees (approximately 75 percent of the market's total HMO enrollees) and 97,000 PPO lives.

Functionality

IPAs vary in their functions. Some are nondelegated, meaning they serve only as contract negotiators. Fully delegated IPAs like HealthFirst accept full financial risk for medical (at least professional) services and handle administrative and medical management associated with the managed care contract. Limited benchmarking information is available from the IPA Association of America.

In fully delegated IPAs, the IPA negotiates with managed care organizations for a capitation rate inclusive of all physician services. The IPA in turn reimburses the member physicians, although not necessarily using capitation. The IPA and its member physicians are at risk for at least some portion of the medical costs, in that if capitation payment is lower than the required reimbursement to physicians, the member physicians must accept lower income.

Advantages

- Vehicle for physicians to participate in risk contracting
- Low capital requirements
- Good first step into managed care for many physicians
- Physicians maintain professional and business autonomy
- May provide access to high-tech information systems for financial management, claims processing, and utilization review
- Provides leverage in negotiations with payers and hospitals
- Medical management can reduce utilization to levels of well-established integrated group practices

Disadvantages

- May be difficult to create same efficiencies as integrated group practices
- Often specialist-dominated
- Does not address expense side of physician practice management

- Although it may negotiate capitation rates, there are antitrust concerns regarding discounted fee for service contracting
- Special care must be taken to avoid aggregation and disqualification of participating physicians' pension plans

Assessment of an IPA

Since the IPA is basically a business intermediary that connects independent physicians (generally in small group practices) with managed care payors, its value lies in its contractual relationships. To be more specific, value lies in the strength and appropriateness of its relationships for tomorrow's marketplace. Thus, the assessment of an IPA involves an investigation into its structure, sponsorship, function, specialty composition, and contracts. Since there is such great variation within each of these components, it is important to use the following questions as a guide for understanding each IPA's business and, subsequently, its value.

Structure. The more common business structures for IPAs are general business corporations, professional corporations with sole or multiple shareholders, professional partnerships, and nonprofit corporations with one or more statutory corporate members. Regardless of the IPA's structure, the primary questions are:

- Is the structure appropriate for the current business functions and for those planned for the future?
- Are the IPA members locked in to the IPA, or can members easily abandon the business?
- Is the structure legal? For example, some states prohibit the corporate practice of medicine, which means the IPA must have a structure that accommodates this law.
- As with any business, when the structure is weak or inappropriate, risk increases.

Sponsorship. Many analysts estimated that starting an IPA today costs $70,000 to $150,000 or more. Physicians often discover that they cannot raise the necessary capital among themselves to launch the business. In the early days of IPA development, hospitals, HMOs, and medical societies sponsored IPAs. More recently, Physician Practice Management Companies (PPMCs), Management Service Organizations (MSOs), Physician Hospital Organizations (PHOs), and hospital companies have become sponsors. Sponsors have great influence over the strategy and stability of the IPA. Thus, one must examine the IPA sponsors, because their stability is directly related to that of the IPA.

Specialty Mix. The business strategy of the IPA is reflected in its physician mix. IPAs are multi-specialty, primary care, or single specialty. The advantage of one of these models over another depends on the market's current demands. The growth of primary care IPAs came about with the emergence of gatekeeper HMOs. Single-specialty IPAs are becoming popular now because health plans have an interest in disease management and consumers are demanding the option to see specialists for treatment of certain diseases. It's the physician mix that determines what products the IPA offers; thus, it is important to evaluate the specialty mix in the context of the market.

Functions

There are two types of contracts that are critical to the long-term survival of an IPA: provider and managed care contracts. Since provider contracts are the basis of an IPA's products, the strength of contracts with key physicians must be examined for stability and profitability. The physician enterprise is currently undergoing great consolidation and IPAs are subject to losing key members to other IPAs, hospitals, PPMCs, or other provider organizations.

PPMCs and the IPA

The IPA is an important component of PhyCor (NASDQ: PHYC), one of the nation's largest publicly traded PPMCs. Revenue from its 90 IPA businesses (19,000 physicians in 28 markets) accounts for approximately 16 percent of its total revenue.

PhyCor has increased its focus on the development of IPAs to enable the company to provide services to a broader range of physician organizations, to enhance the operating performance of existing clinics, and to further develop physician relationships. It develops IPAs that include affiliated clinic physicians to enhance the clinics' attractiveness as providers to managed care organizations.

PhyCor has grown its IPA business through both acquisition and internal development. In 1996 and 1997, the company acquired 6,972 physicians in two transactions. This represents 37 percent of all IPA physicians involved in a merger or acquisition during this period.

Reported Merger and Acquisition Activity

There were 22 reported IPA mergers/acquisitions in 1996 and 1997. The chart below shows the distribution of these deals by quarter. Only 45 percent reported the transaction price. The chart lists all reported transactions. Notice the great variation in price, number of physicians, and number of managed care enrollees. A more detailed investigation of these transactions reveals great variance in the structure, sponsorship, specialty mix, functions, and contracts of these IPAs.

PHYSICIAN PRACTICE MANAGEMENT COMPANIES (PPMCs)

Definition

Physician Practice Management Companies (PPMCs) are management firms that specialize in the management of large group practices or IPAs through ownership, management agreement, or both. PPMCs generally own the physician practices with which they affiliate via subsidiaries. In the last five years, PPMCs have acquired increasing numbers of physician practices. Refer to Exhibit 3-2 for an illustration of the growth of practice acquisitions by PPMCs.

Although PPMCs have been classified as simply publicly traded MSOs, there is a more refined definition. First, to be classified as a PPMC, an organization must be physician-dominated. The term "physician-dominated" refers to the primary strategy of the organization. A company that manages physician practices but is owned by a hospital is not a PPMC for the purposes of this book. Secondly, a PPMC need not be publicly traded.

Recently, large PPMCs have branched out into other nonmedical practice businesses, such as pharmaceutical benefits management (e.g., Caremark, acquired by MedPartners) and disease management. Some PPMCs even own HMOs. This can cause the differences between EHO models to become quite blurred.

Objectives of the Model

The emergence of PPMCs is the result of consolidation in the healthcare industry. As the institutional and insurance players (i.e., hospitals and HMOs) became larger, the need for access to capital became greater for physicians. In recent times, capital has become as influential, if not more influential, in directing patient care as the authority of a medical degree. PPMCs offer access to the capital markets that physicians have

Reported IPA Merger and Acquisitions Activity, 1996–97

Date	Target	State	Acquirer	Physicians	Price	Price/Physician	Managed Care Lives
1/11/96	Senior Summit Plan	CA	HealthCap, Inc	33	N/A	N/A	1,000
1/31/96	Century IPA	CA	FPA Medical Mgt	200	$7,177,331	$35,887	N/A
1/31/96	Foundation Health IPA	CA	FPA Medical Mgt	93	$10,063,654	$108,211	N/A
1/31/96	VIP IPA	CA	FPA Medical Mgt	190	$6,159,015	$32,416	N/A
4/15/96	Physicians First, Inc.	FL	FPA Medical Mgt	125	$25,000,000	$200,000	90,000
7/1/96	Foundation Health Arizona IPA	AZ	FPA Medical Mgt	19	$4,000,000	$210,526	14,000
7/1/96	Foundation Health Florida IPA	FL	FPA Medical Mgt	44	$16,000,000	$363,636	6,000
8/28/96	SPACO Mgt Co	TX	PhyCor, Inc.	972	N/A	N/A	32,000
9/11/96	Wake Primary Care Phys	NC	FPA Medical Mgt	70	N/A	N/A	11,000
10/4/96	Brooklyn Medical Systems	NY	PhyMatrix	600	N/A	N/A	N/A
11/11/96	AHI Healthcare Systems	CA	FPA Medical Mgt	8200	$130,000,000	$15,854	200,000
11/15/96	MedTrust, Inc	VA	Doctors Health Sys	450	$377,500	$839	N/A
2/17/97	Three Chicago IPAs	IL	Chicago Physicians	150	N/A	N/A	N/A
4/7/97	Breathco, Inc.	FL	PhyMatrix	100	N/A	N/A	400,000
4/13/97	Florida IPA	FL	PhyCor, Inc.	6000	N/A	N/A	35,000
5/15/97	Four IPAs	TX	Strategic Medical Sys	315	N/A	N/A	N/A
5/20/97	Piedmont IPA	NC	MedPartners	172	N/A	N/A	N/A
8.18/97	Cardinal IPA	NC	MedPartners	323	N/A	N/A	15,543
11/15/97	Corpus Christi Network	TX	Strategic Medical Sys	226	N/A	N/A	N/A
11/15/97	Nacogdoches Area Physicians	TX	Strategic Medical Sys	91	N/A	N/A	N/A
12/1/97	Urology Consultants	FL	PhyMatrix	120	$3,480,000	$29,000	700,000
12/15/97	MidSouth Physicians Alliance	TN	Physican Health Corp	N/A	$4,278,000	N/A	N/A

Source: The Health Care M&A Report, Irving Levin Associates, Inc. 1996–1998

EXHIBIT 3-2

Number of Physician–Group Acquisitions by PPMCs

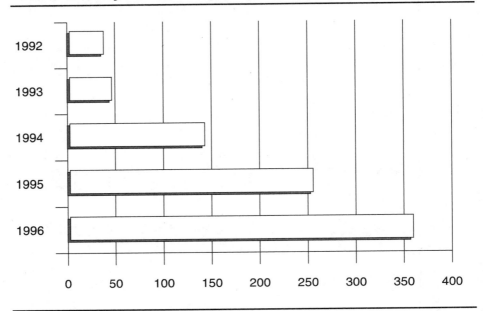

not historically had. With capital, physicians in PPMCs have been able to build surgery centers, expand service lines, and bolster contracting leverage with managed care organizations, hospitals, and health systems.

> The PPMC industry is the embodiment of a classic reaction response to perceived uncertainty and opportunity, and has been driven by the classic human instigators—fear and greed.[1]

Physicians have joined PPMCs to regain control of their businesses or cash in on them—or possibly both. By offering cash and stock for affiliation agreements, PPMCs have attracted entrepreneurial physicians and moved local markets. The infiltration of a PPMC such as PhyCor (NASDAQ: PHYC) into a market often causes hospitals, managed care organizations, and physicians to mobilize and respond. There is evidence in many markets that PPMCs catalyze the development of other EHOs, particularly hospital-sponsored MSOs. This is because in markets with an oversupply of beds, hospitals have the most to lose if the medical staff organizes and obtains control of global capitation dollars. In this scenario,

---

[1]"External Capital Sources for PPMCs," PPMC. March 1997, p. II.

hospitals may have to compete based on price in negotiations with physicians. Hospitals are generally not familiar with the situation of negotiating with physicians for survival.

History

As of September 1998, 32 PPMCs were publicly traded. Sherlock Company, a firm that tracks physician practice management companies, identified 125 private PPMCs across the nation. The publicly traded industry has undergone large swings in its market capitalization.

Organizational Structure

PPMCs are categorized according to their affiliation design and physician specialty mix. Exhibit 3-3 shows the placement of four PPMCs on an organizational structure chart, with 12 possible combinations of affiliation design and physician specialty mix.

EXHIBIT 3-3

PPMC Organizational Structure

Physician Mix

Affiliation Design		Hospital Based	Multi-Specialty	Primary Care	Single Specialty
	Equity		PhyCor		
	Management Company		FPA		
	Physician Contractor	Coastal			Pediatrix

PPMC affiliation comes in three varieties: equity, management company, and physician contractor. Each of these three affiliation designs may have a different mix of specialties, as depicted in Exhibit 3-3. Multi-specialty models are the most common, but single-specialty models have been the most successful recently.

Equity.   Affiliation via equity requires two major events for the transaction to take place:

1. The PPMC purchases the clinic's tangible assets, generally excluding real estate. PPMCs pay cash and stock for the tangible assets. The ratio of stock to cash has been on the decline due to weak performance of PPMC stocks. Hence, many physicians recently entering deals with PPMCs have required more cash to hedge the risks associated with stock performance.

2. A long-term (25 to 40 years) management services agreement between the PPMC and the clinic is signed. A local subsidiary of the PPMC is often formed, and a long-term management services agreement between the local subsidiary and the clinic is created at the same time.

Management Company.   Exhibit 3-4 shows the most widely used model for developing a PPMC, "The PhyCor Model." The local sub-

Exhibit 3-4

Equity Model

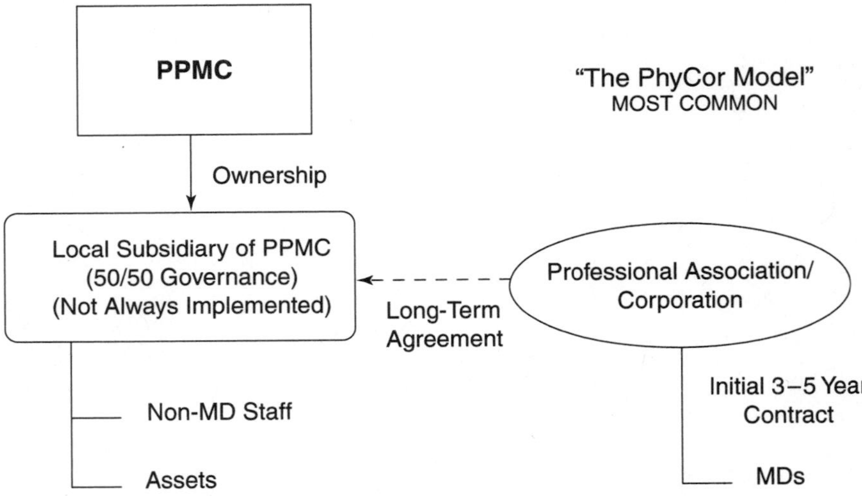

sidiary generally has a governance board, with representation shared equally by the PPMC and the affiliated clinic.

The management model for affiliation with a PPMC involves physicians being part of an IPA that is owned by or contracts with the PPMC for management services. Physicians maintain their independent practices, as the PPMC does not acquire any assets of the medical practices or enter into any long-term agreements. Short-term agreements for managed care contracting are executed.

Physician Contractor. The third form of affiliation is the physician contractor model. In this case, the PPMC primarily provides services to hospitals and contracts with independent physicians to render services specified in the PPMC/hospital contract. The PPMC/hospital contracts are short term, usually around three years. Physician compensation is generally based on salary plus bonus. Coastal (NYSE: DR) utilizes such a model in its emergency medicine management services, as does Pediatrix (NASDAQ: PDX) in its neonatology services.

Functionality

Revenue moves through a PPMC to a physician by one of two methods: a profit model or a revenue model. Exhibit 3-5 illustrates these models.

Profit Model. In the profit model, the PPMC receives full reimbursement for the practice-related services and products consumed by the physicians. On average, 17 percent of the amount remaining (or approximately 8.5 percent of total net revenue, assuming overhead of 50 percent) is held by the PPMC as profit. The physician group receives the difference. The profit model aligns the incentives of the PPMC and physician group to keep costs down. Despite this model's high prevalence in the market, it has been deemed "suspect" by the Department of Health and Human Services (HHS): Any practice management contract in which the PPMC is both reimbursed for its costs and paid a fee based on a percentage of net practice revenue most likely violates federal anti-kickback rules.[2] Whether or not companies will be investigated remains to be seen.

Revenue Model. The revenue model is much simpler than the profit model, and the above HHS advisory opinion does not apply. Net revenues are divided according to a predetermined percentage. For example,

---

[2]*Advisory Opinion 98-4*. Office of the Inspector General: U.S. Department of Health and Human Services, April 15, 1998, pp. 1–7. www.HHSGov/progorg/oig

EXHIBIT 3-5

Profit and Revenue Models

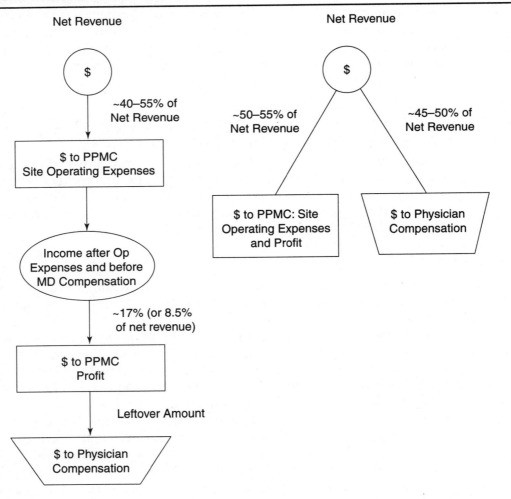

the PPMC may receive 55 percent of the net revenue while the physician group receives 45 percent. Incentives remain unaligned in this model, since there are no incentives for the physicians to manage costs locally or for the PPMC to be attentive to the needs of the physician group.

Advantages

- Management infrastructure and experience
- Access to capital

- Expansion of existing business
- Overhead economies
- Relationships with managed care companies
- Operational knowledge from multiple geographic regions
- Physician-driven culture
- Opportunity for equity ownership in a larger company

The sole purpose of a PPMC is the management of physicians' practices. A PPMC has the management expertise that small physician groups cannot afford and hospitals or managed care organizations do not possess. Many hospital administrators erroneously think that the management of a medical practice is similar to or easier than the management of a hospital. This is simply not true. A medical practice and a hospital face different operational issues and work on very different profit margins. One of the primary reasons that many hospital-sponsored MSOs fail is because they are run like a hospital or by departments of the hospital.

In theory, PPMCs can provide economies of scale by bringing together large numbers of physicians to purchase services and products. Many PPMCs have not realized the economies of scale that they were expecting. This failure is likely due to the geographical diversity and different needs of the various specialties included in these PPMCs. Many single-specialty PPMCs have been able to achieve economies of scale, however.

By offering an equity position to physicians, PPMCs may provide a greater sense of ownership. A culture of ownership more easily aligns incentives.

Disadvantages

- For-profit character
- Volatile market conditions
- Inability to maintain earnings momentum has dramatic impact on market value of business
- Uncertain ability to add value to physician practices
- Loss of independence

For the publicly traded PPMCs, there are constant pressures to meet stockholder demands. Whether these pressures affect daily behaviors related to patient care is unknown, but having one's retirement tied to the stock performance of one's own company is a situation not many physicians are experienced with. Regardless of this disadvantage, many PPMCs have taken a national focus and forgotten that healthcare is a local business.

In many markets, it is difficult for PPMCs to increase their market share of physician services to a level that is influential in managed care contract negotiations.

Future

Based on the last 12 months before this book was written, the outlook for PPMCs is bleak. However, there is evidence suggesting that single-specialty PPMCs have a favorable position in the market.

CASE STUDY: COASTAL PHYSICIAN GROUP

In December 1993, Coastal Physician Group (formerly Coastal Healthcare) was riding the wave of the emerging PPMC sector of healthcare. Its stock price was near $40 and it was the talk of managed care organizations and hospital systems that recognized the potential threat of organized physicians with access to large amounts of capital.

Historically, Coastal utilized the physician contractor model by contracting with hospitals to manage emergency departments. When it went public in June 1991, its strategy changed to a focus on primary care and multispecialty sites. The company purchased a number of physician groups in the South, following a standard equity model. Wall Street viewed the strategy shift favorably, as evidenced by Coastal's elevated stock price.

However, Coastal made a major strategic error. They owned several practices in Florida whose sole contracts were with Humana, a market strongman in the state. Coastal purchased a Florida HMO in late 1995, and Humana changed its view of Coastal from a service vendor to a direct competitor. Humana withdrew enrollees from Coastal clinics and restructured its agreements with Coastal physicians. Since 90 percent of Coastal's South Florida business came from Humana contracts, profitability dropped as significant amounts of money were lost on the South Florida operations. The downward spiral of Coastal's stock price began. By the end of 1995 it had fallen to $12, and the fall continued for the next three years. The company has endured a proxy battle and has spent much of its time solving banking problems rather than focusing on the management of the physician practices.

As the internal situation at Coastal became turbulent, competition in the PPMC market heated up as well. PhyCor, MedPartners, and other competitors have made it more difficult for Coastal to overcome its financial woes. Recently, Coastal has rededicated itself to its original business of emergency department management. The company has sold its New York and North Carolina HMOs and is considering the sale of its remaining managed care operation in Florida.

As of August 6, 1998, Coastal's stock price was $0.75. Physicians who sold their practices in exchange for stock are probably lamenting that decision.

PHYSICIAN HOSPITAL ORGANIZATIONS (PHOs)

Definition

A Physician Hospital Organization (PHO) unites a hospital or group of hospitals with a physician organization through a contractual relationship. The PHO is usually owned by the physicians and hospital and, in many cases, is a nonprofit organization. The ownership arrangement usually takes one of three forms (see Exhibits 3-6, 3-7, and 3-8). In Exhibit 3-6, individual physicians own shares of a physician organization that enters a joint venture with a hospital called a PHO. Exhibit 3-7 shows a situation where the physicians directly own shares in the PHO, rather than through an intermediary physician organization. An alternative PHO, as illustrated in Exhibit 3-8, shows no physician ownership, but 100-percent ownership by the hospital and participation agreements with physicians.

EXHIBIT 3-6

PHO Ownership Structure Model A

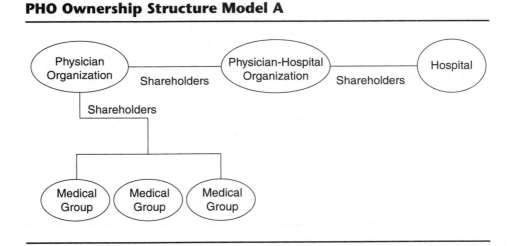

EXHIBIT 3-7

PHO Ownership Structure Model B

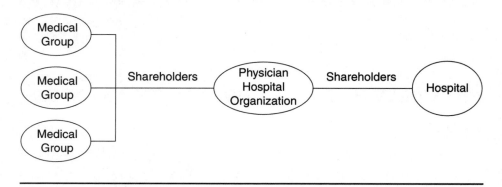

EXHIBIT 3-8

PHO Ownership Structure Model C

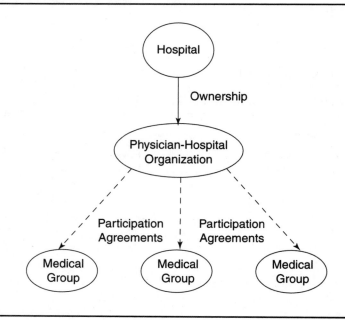

Objectives of the Model

The objective of forming or joining a PHO is different for hospitals and physicians. Hospitals may seek to expand their control of the range of health services and improve relations with physicians. Physicians may be looking for some security under the shelter of a capital-rich hospital. However, there is one common objective for all parties, which is improved leverage in negotiating managed care contracts.

There are two basic models for a PHO's contract negotiation. The PHO may implement a messenger, whereby it analyzes each contract offered by a payor (employer groups, managed care organizations, etc.) and transmits its analysis and the contract to each physician and hospital. Each physician and hospital then decides independently whether or not to accept the contract. A preferred model is one in which the physicians and hospitals establish contract criteria prior to negotiations. With such criteria in place, the PHO can negotiate with payors under the assurance that if agreement criteria are met during a defined negotiation period (e.g., 120 days) then both physician and hospital members are bound by the terms.

A successfully negotiated PHO contract generally defines two relationships—one between physicians and the payor and another between the hospital and the payor—instead of one relationship between the PHO and the payor, as one might imagine.

If the PHO cannot reach an agreement with the payor during the negotiation period, the payor is free to negotiate with each physician individually. This "back door" strategy is often executed by managed care organizations that feel they can negotiate better rates with individual providers, do not need the hospital in the PHO, or do not need all the PHO physicians in their network.

Start-Up and Operational Costs

PHOs are relatively easy to establish, due to low capitalization requirements. The capitalization of a PHO correlates with the amount of medical management functions that it needs. Initial capitalization is determined by many methods, but most PHOs strive toward equal ownership between the hospital and physicians. It is common for the hospital to fully fund the start-up of the PHO, although that is not a desirable scenario. The hospital should never be the sole source of financing, nor should it have a disproportionate share of profits or losses.

According to a recent survey, the median organizational capital requirement for a PHO is $220,000. These costs range from $95,000 (at the 25th percentile) to $709,000 (at the 75th percentile). The areas of highest capital requirement are operating cash requirements, with a median expenditure of $150,000; organizational/development costs, with a median expenditure of $75,000; management information systems (MIS), with a median expenditure of $50,000; and fixtures, furnishings, and minor medical equipment, with a median expenditure of $28,000.

The median reported total future capital requirements for the PHO is $613,000. The total reported future costs range from $130,000 at the 25th percentile to $3,500,000 at the 75th percentile. The area of highest capital projections are medical practice acquisitions, with a median expenditure of $3,500,000 for those PHOs reporting planned acquisitions; additional operating cash, with a median expenditure of $175,000; consulting, legal, accounting, with a median expenditure of $75,000; management information systems (MIS), with a median expenditure of $40,000; and fixtures, furnishings, and minor medical equipment, with a median expenditure of $20,000.[3]

Organizational Structure

Since the PHO is an independent entity, the individual physicians' existing practice organizations generally choose to remain physically separate. Thus, aside from the medical management, utilization review, quality improvement, and related standards that the PHO may need to impose for contracting purposes, practice autonomy of the constituent providers can be largely maintained. As IPAs are considered the first step in horizontal integration, the PHO is the first step in vertical integration.

Another dichotomy beyond contracting exists among PHOs: *open* versus *closed*. These terms refer to the design of the provider panel. An open PHO is one that any member of a hospital's medical staff may join. A minimum credentialing requirement generally exists (which is sometimes equivalent to obtaining admitting privileges). Since specialists have more to lose than primary care physicians by not consolidating contracting efforts, open PHOs are often specialty-dominated. Many open PHOs are established with the vision of one day becoming a *closed panel*, where non-cost-effective providers are removed from the organization; but few PHOs have made such a transition. Some PHOs begin as closed panels and limit membership to a defined group of physicians. PHOs that begin as closed panels have a higher percentage of primary care physicians in the membership and governance. While this increases the attractiveness of the PHOs to those seeking managed care contracts,

---

[3]*Capital Survey of Emerging Healthcare Organizations, Second Annual Report 1996, Based on 1995 Data*. Integrated Healthcare Report, Medical Group Management Association, and Ziegler Securities, 1996, p. 29.

closed panel PHOs are often difficult to implement due to political conflicts between the hospital and medical staff. For example, specialists
have been allies of hospitals, and since closed-panel PHOs disproportion-
ately favor primary care, hospital administrators often choose to not exclude specialists based on their historical relationships with them.

Functionality

When PHOs can meet their objective of securing capitation contracts,
they undertake a new functionality: medical management. Most providers seek risk contracts because they feel they can better bear the responsibility of medical management than a managed care company, and
thereby reap the financial rewards. However, medical management is
not an easy proposition, and most PHOs are unprepared for the time, effort, and systems required to establish an effective program.

Advantages

Advantages of PHOs include their ability to offer payors one-stop shopping, their streamlined administrative functions, their ease in providing
patient referrals, their efficiency of contracting, and their ability to provide regional care with regional pricing.[4]

Due to managed care strategies aimed at decreasing utilization of inpatient services, hospitals have more to lose than physicians (especially
those in primary care) when managed care companies secure control of
the delivery system. By partnering with physicians, hospitals reduce
their risk of having to accept unreasonably low fees or of being shut out
of a managed care panel. The advantages of the PHO weigh in favor of
the hospital rather than the physicians. Entrepreneurial physicians rarely
find themselves advocating a PHO when IPAs or other horizontal integration strategies are feasible.

Disadvantages

The purpose of the PHO is to secure managed care contracts, but if the
PHO's sole activity is contract negotiations, then antitrust issues arise.

The Department of Justice (DOJ) sued two PHOs in October of 1995.
In consent decrees, it permitted the PHOs two options for legal operation: Competing physicians must share "substantial" risk via withholds
or capitation, or the PHO must use the messenger model to transmit fee

---

[4]Fred McCall-Perez. *Physician Equity Groups and Other Emerging Entities: Competitive
Organizational Choices for Physicians.* Healthcare Financial Management Association,
1994, p. 92.

information. By these actions, the DOJ articulated its definition of and tolerance level for price-fixing in healthcare networks.

Hospitals tend to dominate PHOs, and physician representation on governance structures is often limited or ineffective.

Disadvantages of PHOs include the insurer's perception of PHOs as competitors, the possibility that they may compete with community-based physician groups, and the fact that they may be seen as a threat by medical staffs.[5]

Future

The economic futures of hospitals and physicians are inextricably interwoven and both would be wise to seize the opportunity to pursue a new partnership that will facilitate a joint response to market challenges. Enhanced physician loyalty will likely result in increased patient volume for hospitals. Physicians can enjoy reduced practice operating costs, improved income, and increased market share. In addition, each could benefit from increased market share by working more closely together to provide managed care services through partnerships with employers.[6]

New PHO development these days is rare, primarily because most hospitals already have one. Very few have been successful in their ability to attract direct contracts from employers, a goal of many PHOs. The model is generally too weak to withstand market pressures that require coordinated care between a large number of physicians. PHOs are more likely to be successful in rural markets where the number of physicians is small.

MANAGEMENT SERVICES ORGANIZATIONS (MSOs)

Definition

A Management Services Organization (MSO) is a legal entity, owned by physicians, hospitals, or lay investors, that provides an array of practice management services.

Typically, an MSO is not licensed to practice medicine; it simply serves as a "services/asset leasing company that supports the back office of a

---

[5]Ibid.

[6]Gerald L. McManis and Jerry A. Stewart. "Hospital Physician Alliances: Building an Integrated Medical Delivery System." *Healthcare Executive*, March/April 1992, p. 21.

medical practice. . . . [I]n effect, the MSO is simply the expense side of the medical practice."[7] MSOs that engage in more comprehensive physician practice management are considered "aggressive mechanisms to encourage group practice development."[8]

Traditionally, MSOs have provided a variety of services to both medical practices and hospitals. An MSO can also be referred to as a Physician Services Network (PSN), a Management Services Bureau (MSB), or a Practice Asset Organization.

"In their [most] basic form, MSOs sell practice management services for a monthly fee,"[9] but the services provided by MSOs encompass a broad range and include, but are not limited to, operations management, marketing, contract negotiation, new assets acquisition, personnel management, leasing, providing support services to other organizations (i.e., hospitals), physician recruitment, MIS development, purchasing, and facilities development.[10]

The scope of services that can be provided illustrates the necessity of defining specifically the functions an MSO will perform, and underscores the fact that there is no one type of MSO. The term MSO is used generically to describe any of the large number of possible business combinations, from the low-tech MSO that provides only basic management consulting services to "full turnkey" MSOs that offer full-service office management.[11] In sum, once you've seen one MSO, you've seen one MSO. (See Exhibit 3-9.)

There are numerous types of MSOs, and the distinction between each type is based not solely on one factor but on a combination of them. These factors include: (1) the purpose of the MSO, (2) the functional models of the MSO, and (3) the ownership models of the MSO.[12]

---

[7]Gerald R. Peters, Esq. *Healthcare Integration: A Legal Manual for Constructing Integrated Organizations*. National Health Lawyers Association, 1995, p. 8.

[8]Douglas Goldstein. *From Physician Bonding to Alliances: Building New Physician-Hospital Relationships*. Capital Publications, Inc., 1992, p. 27.

[9]Kristie Perry. "Would an MSO Make Your Life Easier?" *Medical Economics*, April 10, 1995, p. 124.

[10]Douglas Goldstein. *From Physician Bonding to Alliances: Building New Physician-Hospital Relationships*, Capital Publications, Inc., 1992, p. 29; Gerald R. Peters, Esq., *Healthcare Integration: A Legal Manual for Constructing Integrated Organizations*, National Health Lawyers Association, 1995, p. 331.

[11]Gerald R. Peters, Esq. *Healthcare Integration: A Legal Manual for Constructing Integrated Organizations*. National Health Lawyers Association, 1995, pp. 300, 333.

[12]Ibid, p. 297.

EXHIBIT 3-9

Pyramid of MSO Goods and Services

Comprehensive MSO

- Full-service office management
- Facilities planning and management
- Purchase and maintain equipment and furnishings

- Financial services: budgeting, management information report, financial reports and forecasts, debt and staffing
- Medical records management

- Negotiate payor contracts for the provider group
- Operate the information system, phone system, etc.
- Utilization management/quality assurance

- Human resource management
- Manage all nonprofessional staff
- Consolidate/negotiate all insurance policies for group
- Accounts receivable and accounts payable management
- Centralized laundry service
- Operate and standardize payroll, workers compensation, and employee benefit accounts

- Conduct marketing and public relations functions
- Purchase all clinical supplies
- Conduct all vendor contract negotiations: contralised contract negotiations
- Obtain office supplies
- Administration of continuing professional education

Limited MSO

- Physician/provider recruitment assistance
- Management consulting services

History

MSOs have been around in some form or another for approximately 13 years.[13] First developed in California as a response to managed care, MSOs can also purchase tangible assets and employ physicians. As of late 1993, 8 percent of all community hospitals had developed an MSO and 33 percent of hospitals that had integrated arrangements with physicians had an MSO.[14] (Exhibits 3-10 and 3-11). Of the 5,229 acute care hospitals in the United States, 1,372 describe themselves as providing management services and 346 of them, or 6.6 percent, have developed MSOs. Eighty-two percent of these are less than four years old.[15]

Objectives of MSOs

The first and most foundational factor to be determined when developing an MSO as a part of a hospital network is the purpose the MSO will serve (see Exhibit 3-12). A list of the various purposes an MSO may serve is provided in the text below. The list is not exhaustive but provides a broad look at the range of purposes an MSO can serve within a hospital network.

Growth and Integration   Since many hospital networks seek to encourage the organization, consolidation, and/or development of medical practices, hospital networks often invest capital in these medical practices in the hopes of increasing their operational efficiencies for a variety of reasons.

When hospitals are the sponsoring organizations, the formation of an MSO is typically seen as a step toward integration.[16] In fact, 74 percent of hospital-sponsored MSOs cite vertical integration as a major objective of their formation. Affiliation with Primary Care Physicians (PCPs) is often a key element of hospital-physician integration efforts. Sixty-one percent of hospital-sponsored MSOs are composed of PCPs only. Another 25 percent are multispecialty, with a primary care focus. Primary care

---

[13]Kristie Perry. "Would an MSO Make Your Life Easier?" *Medical Economics*, April 10, 1995, p. 124.

[14]Michael A. Morrisey, Jeffrey Alexander, Lawton R. Burns, and Victoria Johnson. "Managed Care and Physician/Hospital Integration: Is Managed Care Driving Hospitals and Physicians Toward More Integration? New National Data Uncover the Trends." *Health Affairs*, 1996, 15(4), p. 66.

[15]*A National Initiative: The Survey of Hospital-Sponsored Management Services Organizations.* Medimetrix, 1997, pp. 2, 4.

[16]Gerald R. Peters, Esq. *Healthcare Integration: A Legal Manual for Constructing Integrated Organizations.* National Health Lawyers Association, 1995, p. 298.

EXHIBIT 3-10

Hospital/System Owned MSO

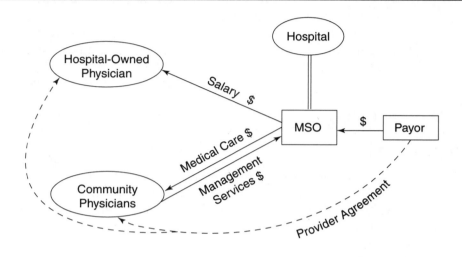

MSOs rate vertical integration as a more important formation objective than multispecialty MSOs.[17]

Hospitals also enhance their managed care effectiveness through the development of MSOs. Of the hospitals surveyed by Medimetrix in their recent survey on hospital-sponsored MSOs, 69 percent considered this one of their most important objectives.[18]

Asset Separation   Historically, physicians have distrusted hospitals and their administrative staffs. Therefore, when hospital networks want to involve themselves in physician practices, they often have difficulty gaining the physicians' trust and, ultimately, recruiting physicians. One way to alleviate this problem is, instead of attempting to integrate the physician practices directly into the hospital, to separate the MSO venture from the workings of the hospital as much as possible by making the MSO its own entity rather than a part of the hospital. Hospitals should also hire a director specifically for the MSO instead of having the MSO

---

[17]*A National Initiative: The Survey of Hospital-Sponsored Management Services Organizations.* Medimetrix, 1997, p. 4.

[18]Ibid, p. 9.

EXHIBIT 3-11

Joint Venture Hospital/Physician–Owned MSO

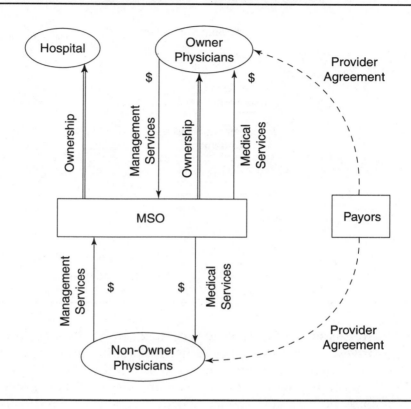

report to the board of directors of the hospital, and allow autonomy and physician input into the MSO's governance.

Practice Management Quality Sixty-nine percent of hospitals that own MSOs cited "increasing practice management sophistication" as one of their highest objectives in forming MSOs.[19]

Lay Investor Equity The purpose is to create an MSO with the intent to sell ownership in the MSO to outside investors. The distinguishing characteristic of MSOs formed with this objective is outside ownership.

---

[19]Ibid.

Exhibit 3-12

Physician Investor–Owned MSO

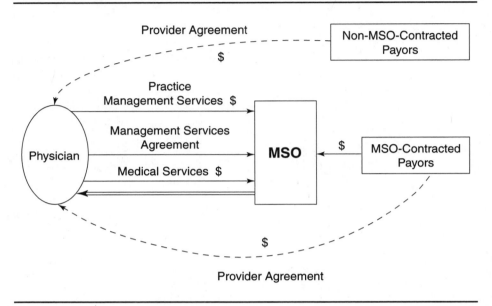

In this scenario, the MSO is created directly by a nonphysician outside investor, such as a hospital network (although it is possible that physicians may have some equity interest in the MSO). These types of MSOs are often publicly traded companies (i.e., PhyCor, MedPartners) that provide "turnkey" services to physicians who own their own practices.[20]

Precluding Potential Competition A hospital network can easily direct primary care business to its doors by affiliating in some way with an MSO, thereby precluding potential competition for the lives covered by the doctors in the MSO. Fifty-two percent of MSOs sponsored by hospitals listed this as one of their objectives in forming the MSO.[21]

Economies of Scale Only half of hospital-sponsored MSOs cited achieving economies of scale as a formation objective.[22]

---

[20]Gerald R. Peters, Esq. *Healthcare Integration: A Legal Manual for Constructing Integrated Organizations.* National Health Lawyers Association, 1995, p. 300.

[21]*A National Initiative: The Survey of Hospital-Sponsored Management Services Organizations.* Medimetrix, 1997, p. 9.

[22]Ibid.

Clinical Information Sharing   Forty-four percent of hospital-sponsored MSOs were formed with the objective of building clinical information sharing.[23]

Generating Revenue   Hospital networks are also interested in MSOs for their potential money-making abilities, but for the first three or four years the MSO will probably not quite break even. Twenty-three percent of such MSOs were formed with generating revenue (profit) as an objective.[24]

Functional Models of an MSO

As discussed previously, the functions that an MSO chooses to undertake are varied. According to most consultants, it is unlikely that you will find two MSOs organized to fill the same exact functions. To clearly illustrate the varied functions of MSOs, two functional models will be presented. These two models represent the extremes of the paradigm, so most MSOs fall somewhere in between these two models.

1. **Management Services Bureau or Low-Tech Model (MSB):** In this model, physicians remain separate and independent legal entities who contract for services from the bureau at fair market value. This model is representative of the least comprehensive of MSOs. Physicians pick and choose "cafeteria style" the benefits they would like to receive from the MSO and contract through the management services bureau. For example, the physician group may elect to receive only billing and collection services from the MSO. (See Exhibit 3-9.)

2. **Comprehensive or Turnkey Model MSO:** This type of MSO provides a comprehensive array of services including all of the nonclinical aspects of the practice's operations. Examples of services that would be provided include facilities planning and management, equipment and furnishings, financial services, marketing, utilization review, medical records, personnel management, negotiation of payor contracts, etc. (See Exhibit 3-9.)

Start-Up and Organizational Costs

An MSO's value is primarily in its contracts with members and payors.

---

[23]Ibid.
[24]Ibid.

Sources of Funds

1. **Hospital/Health System:** Eighty-four percent of hospital-sponsored MSOs responding to Medimetrix's 1997 Survey of Hospital-Sponsored Management Services Organizations were 100 percent hospital/health system owned.[25]

2. **Physician Equity Investments:** Fourteen percent of hospital-sponsored MSOs responding to the survey were jointly owned with physicians and 2 percent were 100 percent physician-owned. Despite the small percent of hospital-sponsored MSOs that are wholly or jointly owned by physicians, these MSOs are much more likely to break even financially.[26]

Start-Up Costs

1. The costs associated with organizing an MSO can range from $350,000 to over $3,000,000 if practices are acquired. The 1996 Survey of Emerging Healthcare Organizations cites the median total organizational capital requirements at $850,000, compared with $220,000 for PHOs.[27] Thirty percent of hospital-sponsored MSOs had capital start-up budgets between $300,000 and $999,999.[28] It is estimated that to launch a major physician management company and take the company public would cost $25 to $50 million.[29]

2. A group of physicians forming their own MSO can expect to spend $500,000 to $800,000; a group of 50 physicians spending $10,000 to 20,000 each would be able to fund an MSO, but at that funding level the MSO would only be performing back-office functions. An MSO that provides contracting services requires at least a $2 million initial cash investment.[30]

3. Organizational/development costs: median, $100,000; 75th percentile, $422,000. These figures are higher than the PHO (with a

---

[25]Ibid, p. 17.

[26]Ibid.

[27]*Capital Survey of Emerging Healthcare Organizations.* Ziegler Securities, MGMA, Integrated Healthcare Report, and IPA Associations of California, 1996, pp. 26, 28.

[28]*A National Initiative: The Survey of Hospital-Sponsored Management Services Organizations.* Medimetrix, 1997, p. 5.

[29]Ken Terry. The many Pluses of Investing in your own MSO. *Medical Economics*, April 10, 1995, p. 139.

[30]Ibid, pp. 136, 139.

median of $75,000 and a 75th percentile of $200,000).[31] (Median projected future MSO capital requirements are $2,500,000.[32])

Financial Status

1. *Financial Break-Even:* Eleven percent of the hospital-sponsored MSOs surveyed by Medimetrix had achieved financial break-even. Of these, 7 percent are physician-owned, 20 percent are under joint ownership, and the remaining 73 percent are hospital-owned.[33]

    MSOs with physician equity were more likely to break even, with 39 percent of MSOs with 100 percent physician equity having achieved break-even. This contrasts with only 16 percent of MSOs under joint physician/hospital ownership and 10 percent of those MSOs which are 100 percent hospital-owned.[34]

    Seventy-nine percent of the hospital-sponsored MSOs surveyed by Medimetrix that had achieved financial break-even did so within two to four years after start-up. The low percentage of those MSOs to have achieved break-even may be related to the age of the MSOs surveyed. Only 18 percent were started in 1993 or earlier and 62 percent were started in 1994 or 1995.[35]

2. *Operating Profit Challenges:* Hospital-sponsored MSOs listed the following "operating profit challenges":[36]

    - "Not enough participating provider volume": 52 percent
    - "Low physician productivity": 41 percent
    - "Added layer of staffing without cutting other costs": 30 percent
    - "Staff salaries/benefits higher than market average": 19 percent
    - Required use of hospital services at higher than market rates: 16 percent

    Also noted was a link between insufficient provider volume and a lack of demand for services in those hospitals surveyed.

---

[31]*Capital Survey of Emerging Healthcare Organizations.* Ziegler Securities, MGMA, Integrated Healthcare Report, and IPA Associations of California, 1996, pp. 26, 28.

[32]Ibid, p. 27.

[33]*A National Initiative: The Survey of Hospital-Sponsored Management Services Organizations.* Medimetrix, 1997, p. 27.

[34]Ibid, pp. 17, 27.

[35]Ibid, p. 7.

[36]Ibid, p. 28.

Organizational Structure

System-Owned. In this scenario, which is the most common (see Exhibit 3-10), the MSO is usually created, funded, and essentially governed by the hospital. Hospital-owned MSOs may be considered less attractive to physicians because affiliating with them often involves becoming a salaried employee of the hospital, an action that usually decreases practice autonomy.[37] Other physicians may find this model more attractive since a hospital can provide both increased capital for equipment and the increased security of a salaried staff position.

In turnkey arrangements like this, compensation for employed physicians is usually straight salary with no bonus. Alternatively, typical nonemployed physicians pay the MSO approximately 55 percent of their gross collections.[38] The MSO sometimes charges these physicians a monthly fee in addition to a percentage of collections as a protective measure against doctors slowing down their productivity.[39] It is important to note that in these types of arrangements physicians need protection from hospitals that take a percentage of billings but do a poor job of collections.[40]

There are several key elements to consider when establishing a hospital-owned MSO. First, you must ensure that charges are at fair market value in order to avoid violating Medicare fraud and abuse and Stark laws. Second, the hospital and affiliated physicians will most likely enter into separate managed care contracts, but any joint contracting must be coordinated to avoid violating federal and state antitrust laws. Third, it must be ensured that there is no violation of the IRS prohibition on inurement of benefit.

In addition, hospitals must make sure that they have strong physician leadership and direction. In order to do this, hospitals may want to try several ways to woo the necessary physicians—for example, create a physician advisory committee with representation from the entire physician community to aid in business development decisions. A hospital can also make sure that there is adequate physician representation on the MSO's board of directors. Finally, as mentioned earlier, a hospital can structure the MSO so that it operates at arm's length from the hospital.[41]

---

[37]Kristie Perry. "Would an MSO Make Your Life Easier?" *Medical Economics*, April 10, 1995, p. 126.

[38]Ibid.

[39]Ibid.

[40]Ibid.

[41]Scott C. Strausser. "MSOs: Why They Fail, and Corrections to Make." *Medical Network Strategy Report*, October 1997, vol 6; Numb 10, p. 6.

There are several legal constructions for hospital-owned MSOs, including the following.

Subsidiary Corporation (For-Profit or Not-for-Profit)   Many hospitals may place the MSO in a subsidiary organization in an effort to protect the hospital's tax-exempt status. It is important to note that this strategy is at risk if the IRS follows the money from the MSO to the source (i.e., the hospital) and finds that the funds benefited private individuals more than incidentally. Even if established as a not-for-profit corporation, the MSO is not likely to gain a tax-exempt status (unless it can be demonstrated that growth of the physician practice is beneficial to the community).

Business Corporation   This construction is useful if ownership will be shared at a later date.

Limited Liability Corporation   This construction carries a flow-through tax advantage.

Joint Venture MSO   Corporate structure may be chosen to shield participants from individual liability. (See Exhibit 3-11.)

- General partnership
- Nonprofit corporation
- For-profit business corporation
- Physician/hospital equity model MSO

Foundation Model MSOs   A not-for-profit foundation owned by a hospital system buys the practice and employs the physicians.

- Very popular in states with strict corporate practice of medicine laws (e.g., California)
- Easier to recruit primary care doctors
- Can grow very quickly

Physician Investor Owned.   In some cases, physicians may come together and form an MSO. There is no material difference between this type of MSO and a PPMC. See Exhibit 3-12 for an illustration of a physician investor–owned MSO.

Advantages of MSOs[42]

Strength of MSO	Advantage to Parent Company	Advantage to Physicians
Relationship Building: An MSO can serve as a transitioning vehicle toward tighter affiliation between hospitals and physicians.	✔	✔
Integration: Cultural acclimation and standardization of operational practices.	✔	✔
Flexibility: Services can be provided to physicians practicing in different styles (i.e., solo practitioners, IPAs, or group practices).	✔	✔
Adaptability: MSOs are not static; they can vary their purposes and structures as required by market conditions (e.g., by changing from a "back office" MSO to a full-service type).	✔	✔
Separation of Assets: The practice's assets may be transferred to the MSO, resulting in a decreased capital contribution for future partners.		✔
Equity Opportunity/Ownership Interests		✔
Reduced Hassles/Management Expertise: Successful MSOs allow physicians to focus more on clinical practice.		✔
Independence: Physicians retain clinical autonomy and practice identity.		✔
Governance: Physicians retain a strong voice in the governance of the MSO, having equal representation on the board.		✔
Efficiencies: Overhead reductions, discounts, streamlined operations.		✔
Contracting: Improved access to capitated managed care contracts.	✔	✔
Capital Infusion: Short-term capital infusion. An MSO with hospital participation can provide access to capital, which helps in meeting the expenses of consolidating practices, recruitment, and supplementing physician incomes.		✔

[42]Gerald R. Peters, Esq. *Healthcare Integration: A Legal Manual for Constructing Integrated Organizations*, National Health Lawyers Association, 1995; Douglas Goldstein, p. 303, *From Physician Bonding to Alliances: Building New Physician-Hospital Relationships*, Capital Publications, Inc., 1992, p. 29.

Advantages of MSOs

Strength of MSO	Advantage to Parent Company	Advantage to Physicians
Corporate Practice of Medicine: In states where such practice is prohibited, MSOs may provide a vehicle through which hospitals and physicians can integrate.	✔	✔
Licensing: Because an MSO does not itself provide healthcare services, it need not be a licensed healthcare provider (but it may be subject to other licenses).	✔	✔

Disadvantages of MSOs[43]

Weakness of MSO	Disadvantage to Parent Company	Disadvantage to Physician
Cannot Mandate Referrals	✔	
Integration Limitations	✔	✔
Power Struggles: Assuring appropriate physician representation in decision making.	✔	✔
Inurement of Benefit Vulnerability: As attempts are made to fund primary care practices from not-for-profit funding sources, this problem continues.	✔	✔
Incentives: Unified incentives of parent organization and physicians are not necessarily the byproduct of forming an MSO.	✔	✔
Clinical Practice: Impact is limited (i.e., CQI (continous quality improvement), utilization review, etc.).	✔	✔
Management Expertise: Expertise available through the parent organization may not be applicable to physician practice management.[44]		✔
Capital Intensive: Potentially large investment with ambiguous financial returns.	✔	✔
Managed Care Contracting: Less leverage than in more integrated approaches.	✔	✔
Legal Risk: Anti-kickback and Stark legislation make it more difficult for groups to own ancillary services, for example, under the MSO model.	✔	

---

[43]Gerald R. Peters, Esq. *Healthcare Integration: A Legal Manual for Constructing Integrated Organizations.* National Health Lawyers Association, 1995, p. 304.

[44]"Beware the Hospital-Directed MSO." *The Physicians Advisory, Medical Group Management Association,* 93(12), 1993, p. 5.

Legal and Regulatory Issues

The legal system was not established with integrated healthcare systems in mind. Therefore, setting up a hospital-based MSO requires diligent observation and balancing of regulations.

The Office of the Inspector General as well as IRS officials have expressed concern that some MSO arrangements violate anti-kickback laws and prohibitions on inurement. In addition, after passage of the Stark law revisions in 1995, many MSO arrangements became unacceptable because doctors who received services from a hospital-sponsored MSO could not refer patients to the hospital. Even if these potential problems are surmountable, it is necessary to develop a tax strategy to address the tax exemption risks posed by this type of MSO.

What follows are the legal and regulatory considerations one faces when dealing with a hospital-owned MSO, including antitrust issues, tax status issues, the corporate practice of medicine, and anti-kickback considerations.

Antitrust Issues. When dealing with antitrust issues specially pertaining to MSOs, there are several points that need to be watched carefully as possible antitrust trouble spots.

When a hospital and a medical group create an MSO, the two entities remain separate legal entities, which could qualify them under antitrust laws as competitors for outpatient care. Thus, any managed care contracting within the MSO that benefits both entities needs to comply with antitrust laws relating to price-fixing, market division, and concerted refusals to deal in order to avoid possible illegal horizontal or vertical collusions. If, however, an MSO becomes part of a true risk-sharing arrangement, the parties "may be able to negotiate joint capitation rates or withhold arrangements with minimal antitrust risk."[45]

If the MSO has been created as a division of the hospital or a hospital subsidiary, then the MSO must also comply with the antitrust laws applicable to a Physician Hospital Organization (PHO). Among the potential antitrust problems that should be discussed with legal counsel are:

- *Market Division:* What percentage of the market does the MSO have or is it likely to have?
- *Collateral Restraints for Competitors:* Does this arrangement lessen competition or tend to create a monopoly?

---

[45]*Hospital-Affiliated Integrated Delivery Systems: Formation, Operation, and Contracts Handbook*, American Academy of Hospital Attorneys of the AHA, 1995, p. 25.

- *Collusion:* Could the arrangement look like or actually be vertical or horizontal collusion?
- *Tying Arrangement:* Is a product or service sold only on the condition that another tying product also is purchased?
- *Provider Exclusion:* Does this arrangement remove the ability of another provider to compete in the market?
- *Boycott:* Does this arrangement look like an attempt to boycott another provider or hospital?

Fraud and Abuse—Stark II: "The Ethics in Patient Referrals Act". If a hospital is subsidizing an MSO with operational losses on a continuing basis, the government is apt to argue that the physicians affiliated with the MSO are receiving remuneration for referrals.

Methods to reduce risk are the same as those outlined in the anti-kickback laws discussion below. However, it should be noted that the main distinction between the anti-kickback and the Stark law is that the Stark law does not consider whether or not there was an intent to solicit referrals from physicians. Put simply, if a compensation arrangement exists that is not within the restrictions of the Stark law, the arrangement will be considered in violation.

- Does the MSO constitute a financial relationship through which a hospital pays remuneration to referring physicians?
- Valuation implications: assets, space rental, personal contract.
- Are the items provided (space, services, etc.) consistent with the reasonable needs and purposes of physicians?[46]

Anti-Kickback. Hospital subsidy of an MSO may be viewed as payment for referrals, and as such may be considered a violation of anti-kickback laws. Compliance with all safe harbor laws is imperative.

When determining whether a relationship is in compliance with safe harbor laws, two main issues should be addressed: (1) Is the arrangement a fair market value (FMV), transaction constituting an "arm's length transaction"? and (2) Does the MSO compensation account for the volume and value of referrals (or other business) between the parties?[47] The most

---

[46]Gerald R. Peters, Esq. *Healthcare Integration: A Legal Manual for Constructing Integrated Organizations.* National Health Lawyers Association, 1995, pp. 311–312.

[47]Gerald R. Peters, Esq. *Healthcare Integration: A Legal Manual for Constructing Integrated Organizations.* National Health Lawyers Association, 1995, p. 307.

important tool in discerning the legitimacy of these transactions is, of course, documentation.

Tax Status

MSOs may be organized as either for-profit or not-for-profit organizations, but are typically organized as for-profit entities.

In most instances, MSOs will not qualify for 501(c)(3) tax status, for two reasons: (1) it is unlikely to have a charitable purpose, and (2) it is typically organized to serve the private interests of the physicians involved.

> When MSOs subsidized by exempt organizations suffer operational losses while furnishing goods and services to physician practices, the exempt organization's exemption may be questioned. The IRS won't look kindly on an MSO learning curve defense. The hospital also may find its exemption challenged by the IRS if the MSO suffers operating losses while it puts a cap on percentage of physician practice revenues the MSO collects.[48]

Corporate Practice of Medicine

These restrictions vary on a state-by-state basis. In states with strong laws governing corporate practice of medicine, the MSO should not control physician compensation, referral decisions, physician fees, payor contracts, or anything that may constitute fee splitting. This doctrine is intended to preclude hospitals and other lay corporations from employing physicians to practice medicine or otherwise exercising undue influence over physicians.

In the event that a hospital subsidizes an MSO that is showing an operating loss, a strong argument will be presented that the hospital is in actuality subsidizing referrals. Regardless of other reasons for subsidizing the practices (i.e., physician retention, recruitment, etc.) the argument will be a strong one. The table below outlines some measures that hospital-subsidized MSOs can take to reduce the risk.

Conclusion

Successful MSO development and operations are subject to numerous general considerations. The following tenets are provided for MSOs although most are applicable to other physician integration projects.

---

[48]Excerpt from speech given by T. J. Sullivan, Special Assistant to the IRS's Assistant Commissioner for Exempt Organizations. *Healthcare Financial Ventures Report*, January 18, 1995.

Risk Reducers

Compensation	Increase compensation to the MSO over time. This will ensure that the MSO will break even financially over a three- to five-year period. Be realistic about your financial projections.
Contracts	A contract mandating that the physician practices merge with the hospital at some point in the future may reduce the legal risk of the MSO arrangement.
Reasonable Expenditures	Anticipated losses of the MSO should "remain equal to the reasonable expenditures necessary by the hospital to fulfill its own valid business purposes." If the MSO has unlimited downside risk, and the physicians do not share the risk, the terms might be subject to anti-kickback investigation.
Fair Market Value (FMV)	Physician compensation should be set at fair market value, with excess directed to the MSO until it is at a financial break-even point.
Differentiate	Costs to develop the MSO and the costs related to the ongoing concerns of the physician practice should be separated. The losses associated with development costs might be defensible.

Source: Gerald R. Peters. *Healthcare Integration: A Legal Manual for Constructing Integrated Organizations*. National Health Lawyers Association, 1995.

General Guidelines.   "The Four Legs of the Table"—Safeguarding Patients Through Practice Preservation

1. "Seat at the table."

   Providers need meaningful marketplace input and decision making authority—"Who gets to decide?"

2. "He with the most information wins!"

   Data equals power. Providers must have the ability to measure data on quality and outcomes measurement, utilization, and costs.

3. Sharing in diverse healthcare delivery system revenue sources.

   In order to maintain quality patient care it is necessary to have a diversity of revenue sources to offset professional fee component reduction in one or more areas.

4. Access to the market.

   Providers must develop relationships with market access mechanisms.

You Gotta Wanna!! Among the many challenges hospital-sponsored MSOs face, many are due to a lack of commitment from both the hospital and the physicians. Commitment-related challenges cited by MSOs recently surveyed[49] were:

- "Understaffed to manage MSO": 31 percent
- "Lack of capital": 30 percent
- "Lack of interest on part of physicians": 20 percent

Develop a Win-Win Design. Design the MSO *with* physicians, not *for* physicians. "You don't set up an MSO and then invite the doctors. You don't just copy what worked well in California, because the circumstances of physicians" are different across the country.[50] Hospitals' and physicians' goals for MSO involvement can only become compatible if physicians are involved in the planning stage. Fifty-three percent of hospital-sponsored MSOs cited "balancing physician interests with sponsor interests" as a challenge faced by the MSO.[51]

Get Physicians Involved. Physician involvement is important to the success of any form of physician affiliation program. This involvement should include both governance and equity. Those MSOs including physician equity were much more likely to achieve financial break-even.[52]

"A Little Form before Function." A couple of obvious but often overlooked or insufficiently addressed issues during the organization of the MSO should be mentioned. First, the role and functions of the MSO must be specifically designed at the onset of the project. Second, outline the divorce process before the contracts are signed.[53]

Information Equals Power He with the most information wins. Providers and consultants need to get informed and stay informed. Research is critical and must encompass the legal and regulatory issues, the healthcare environment, and all pertinent economic issues.

---

[49]*A National Initiative: The Survey of Hospital-Sponsored Management Services Organizations.* Medimetrix, 1997, p. 29.

[50]Kristie Perry. "Would an MSO Make Your Life Easier?" *Medical Economics*, April 10, 1995, p. 129.

[51]Ibid, p. 29.

[52]Ibid, p. 27.

[53]Kristie Perry. "Would an MSO Make Your Life Easier?" *Medical Economics*, April 10, 1995, p. 130.

Strong MIS is critical, especially if the MSO is to serve as a managed care contracting vehicle, which is a formation objective of the majority of hospital-sponsored MSOs. Yet 62 percent of hospital-sponsored MSOs are not electronically integrated with the sponsoring hospital. Forty-five percent of these MSOs said that they faced the challenge that there was "inadequate MIS to run MSO."[54]

Understand human relations issues

- Group dynamics
- Communication

Develop MSO alongside other physician integration models to attract physicians at each stage of the integration continuum.

Don't underestimate the start-up capital required to form an MSO and the value of including physician equity.

GROUP PRACTICE WITHOUT WALLS (GPWW) MODEL

Definition

A Group Practice without Walls (GPWW), also called a clinic without walls, is a network of physicians who have merged into one legal entity but maintain control over individual practice sites. A GPWW does not include the participation of hospitals or other nonphysicians, such as venture capitalists or managed care organizations. In forming of this type of organization, physicians aggregate their practice assets (tangible and intangible) into one entity, providing them with contracting leverage with managed care organizations. From a distance, a GPWW looks exactly like an MSO. It is not an MSO for two basic reasons: (1) only physicians may be owners of GPWWs, and (2) a GPWW acquires all assets, while an MSO acquires just tangibles. The issue of the type of assets that MSOs acquire has been a source of confusion since the emergence of MSOs. In the most common arrangement, an MSO will hold the tangible assets and an affiliated professional association of physicians will hold the intangible assets (e.g., goodwill). The GPWW is a simpler model than the MSO in that one legal entity owns all assets. Refer to Exhibit 3-13 for an organizational diagram of a GPWW.

---

[54]*A National Initiative: The Survey of Hospital-Sponsored Management Services Organizations.* Medimetrix, 1997, p. 29.

EXHIBIT 3-13

Group Practice Without Walls

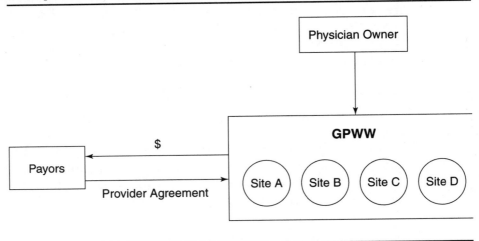

Organizational Structure

The structure of a GPWW is quite simple. The GPWW is owned exclusively by its member physicians, and the GPWW may provide general office support services for the practices. GPWWs also negotiate managed care contracts without the limitations of a messenger model, where the central company acts as an intermediary in the contract negotiations, thus shielding the individual providers from being in violation of the antitrust laws against conspiring to fix prices. The structure of GPWWs has raised concerns that they may be sham organizations constructed to facilitate self-referrals or payments for referrals.

Capital Requirements

A recent survey found that the median total organizational capital requirement for GPWWs was $185,000. However, the range of responses was large, with costs of $41,000 at the 25th percentile and $1,309,000 at the 75th percentile. The largest components of these capital requirements were information systems, with median costs of $118,000, and operating cash requirements, with $200,000. The median total future capital requirement for the GPWWs surveyed was $888,000.[55]

[55]*Capital Survey of Emerging Healthcare Organizations: Second Annual Report 1996, Based on 1995 Data*. Integrated Healthcare Report, Medical Group Management Association, and Ziegler Securities, 1996, pp. 22–23.

Functionality

There is wide variance in the functions performed by a GPWW. GPWWs are enticing to many physicians because most GPWWs have little impact on business operations at the site level. Thus, office staff, patients, and physicians do not generally notice a GPWW affiliation. Each practice and office in a GPWW becomes an individual profit center, with doctors retaining the right to see private patients, manage employees, maintain scheduling, and determine where to refer patients for the best care. However, some GPWWs do contract with outside companies or build an infrastructure for providing of management services such as human resource management and billing/collections.

The level of services a GPWW performs for the individual sites depends on how much authority the physicians delegate to the executive director.

Advantages

- Solo physicians retain some autonomy.
- Personal income of the physicians is affected by performance of the group as a whole.
- Offers a vehicle to attract capital for additional ancillary ventures.
- Low-risk approach to organizing individual physicians and creating a larger economic unit.
- Possibility of achieving economies of scale.

Disadvantages

- Links between individual practices and the company may not be strong.
- Implementation of utilization review and quality control are difficult due to geographic separation of offices.
- May be difficult to access capital without including nonphysicians.
- May not be attractive to managed care entities in highly competitive environments.

Future

GPWWs are not attractive EHOs to many physicians because all assets are lumped into one entity, generally without payment for the assets. With only physician-owners, GPWWs generally lack access to capital. Since capital seems to be driving much of the evolution of healthcare markets, due largely to information system requirements, a model that does not provide access to capital is not likely to enjoy long-term success. GPWWs are also often viewed as an intermediate model that is less desirable than more integrated models due to the range of legal issues relating to their structure and the costs associated with multiple practice locations.

FULLY INTEGRATED MEDICAL GROUPS (FIMGs)

Definition

A Fully Integrated Medical Group (FIMG) is a medical group practice organized as a single legal entity. Management is centralized and has sufficient authority to effectively manage both the medical and business operations of the group. This allows FIMGs to integrate clinical, financial, and operational aspects of the practice. An income distribution plan for physicians aligns the incentives of the physician and the group. FIMGs represent the most horizontally integrated of the EHO models. FIMGs fall into the category of organizations often called "physician equity groups," which can vary in their level of integration from that of traditional practices to that of FIMGs. The characteristics described above help to distinguish FIMGs from other physician equity groups, but it should be noted that there is a wide range of physician groups and the real differentiating factor between them and FIMGs is the level of integration—a subjective quality in itself.

History

Since FIMGs are more of a class of group practices than a distinct type of organization, it is difficult to establish a history of this type of EHO. FIMGs can be considered a result of the long evolution of group practice management.

Objectives of Model

FIMGs result from the continuous quest for management of group practice operations. Most FIMGs have in-house medical management and sophisticated information systems to support operations and contracting activities. Although the strong medical management of FIMGs should be attractive to managed care plans, if the practice is not large it may not realize full leverage from its quality management in negotiating contracts. FIMGs that can dominate a specialty niche within their market may be an exception. Once a management system is in place, FIMGs can expand through mergers or internal growth to improve leverage.

Start-Up and Organizational Costs

The costs of establishing a highly integrated group such as an FIMG can be substantial and can initially lower physician income without providing access to outside sources of capital.[56]

A recent survey of EHOs defined an Expanding Free-Standing Medical Group as "an existing medical group (3 or more physicians practicing within a common legal entity) which is expanding through hiring/recruiting, mergers/acquisitions of small/solo practices (sometimes referred to as the 'physician equity model')." For the purposes of gauging the capital requirements of FIMGs, this type of physician equity model may be comparable. According to the survey, the median amount of organizational capital needed for the Expanding Free-Standing Medical Group was $500,000. These costs range from $370,000 (at the 25th percentile) to $1,638,000 (at the 75th percentile). The areas of highest capital requirements were buildings, with a median expenditure of $2,400,000; major medical equipment and other equipment, with a median expenditure of $791,000; operating cash requirements, with a median expenditure of $350,000; and medical practice acquisitions, with a median expenditure of $293,000.

The median amount of future capital requirements reported for Expanding Free-Standing Medical Groups is $3,450,000. The total reported future costs range from $1,250,000 to $7,250,000 for respondents from the 25th and 75th percentiles respectively. The areas of highest capital projections were buildings, with a median expenditure of $8,000,000; major medical equipment and other equipment, with a median expenditure of $2,000,000; management information systems (MIS), with a median expenditure of $350,000; and fixtures, furnishings, and minor medical equipment, with a median expenditure of $250,000.[57]

Organizational Structure

An FIMG's central organization is often a corporation governed by a board of directors with the power to control clinical utilization, medical management, compensation, operating budgets, and other management of the group. Physicians own shares in the organization but no practice assets, tangible or intangible. (See Exhibit 3-14.)

---

[56]Gerald R. Peters. *Healthcare Integration: A Legal Manual for Constructing Integrated Organizations.* National Health Lawyers Association, 1995, p. 235.

[57]*Capital Survey of Emerging Healthcare Organizations, Second Annual Report 1996, Based on 1995 Data.* Integrated Healthcare Report, Medical Group Management Association, and Ziegler Securities, 1996, p. 25.

EXHIBIT 3-14

Fully Integrated Medical Group

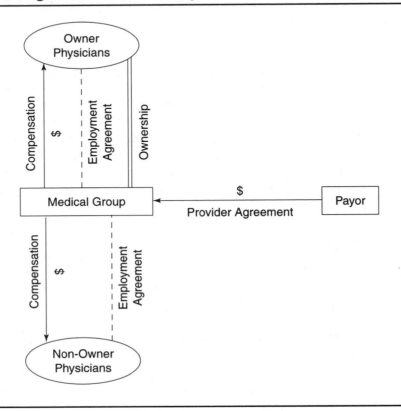

Functionality

To achieve the level of management and control over the operations on which an FIMG depends requires both authority and information. The first is assured through the organizational structure of FIMGs; the second depends on sophisticated management information systems (MIS). These systems allow multiple locations to operate consistently as a single entity. They also provide management with the information required to control utilization, manage medical quality, and efficiently oversee the financial operations of the group.

One of the key characteristics of FIMGs that allows them to align the interests of the physicians and the group is their compensation or income distribution plan. Appendix 14 shows a diagram for a sample income distribution plan. The compensation system must be designed to reward individual effort and act as an incentive for physicians to perform at their highest levels.

Advantages

In order to realize financial advantage from this high degree of integration, FIMGs must have contracting leverage in their markets. This may be difficult for a relatively small group, as its market leverage is small. However, relatively small, single-specialty or specialty-focused groups can command leverage through their strength with a specialty market niche. Such groups can contract on a "carve-out" basis, where they assume responsibility for specialty care within a managed care organization's capitated contracts. Carve-outs are more common for some specialties, including mental health, oncology, emergency medicine, cardiovascular medicine, neonatology, and orthopedics.

FIMGs can also benefit from having a single organization name, which allows for unified marketing efforts and improved name recognition in promoting all of the physicians and locations as being part of a single mission.

Disadvantages

The highly integrated nature of FIMG management can cause physicians to lose their sense of individual autonomy. Also, the costs of management systems can impinge on physician compensation and outweigh some of the advantages during start-up.

INTEGRATED DELIVERY SYSTEMS (IDSs)

Definition

Integrated Delivery Systems (IDSs) are the most ambitious of the vertically integrated healthcare organizations. These systems represent the ultimate integration goal of many hospitals and health systems, although in practice only a few systems are true IDSs. This is because ownership does not effectively realize integration until there are effective communication links about patient care among providers. The IDS structure is intended to accomplish not only managed care contracting and economies of scale, but also the management of the health of populations. To accomplish this health-management goal, integrated delivery systems assemble health providers across the continuum of care, from physician practices to hospitals and nursing homes. The inclusion of an insurance capability enables the organization to accept global capitation where it is responsible, on a prepaid basis, for all of the healthcare needs of a population. Ideally, the system itself is linked by an information system that can track patients across all delivery sites. (See Exhibit 3-15.)

Others have defined integrated delivery systems:

> By definition, IDSs are vertically integrated, frequently composed of insurers, hospitals, physician practices, and other entities that provide medical care for a defined population.[58] Moreover, by coordinating services so as to prevent enrollees from becoming patients, or to discharge patients in a timely way from a hospital to an appropriate subacute care setting, an IDS represents a new generation of managed care.[59, 60]

The American Hospital Association (AHA) has a new membership category that defines an IDS as a "provider-based organized delivery system providing a continuum of community-based healthcare services that consists of service components that are owned, leased, contract-managed, or religiously sponsored and include at least one licensed hospital."[61]

A complete definition of an IDS would include:

- Vertical integration: incorporates acute hospital care, physician services, other nonacute services such as home health care, skilled nursing care (nursing home), rehabilitation, and hospice, and an insurance capability (like a health plan) that can at least manage the financial risk of capitation, if not market itself directly to employers and other purchasers.

- Managed care contracting on a global scale, meaning for all levels of healthcare.

- Operations linked or combined to reduce overhead through group purchasing, centralized management, and other economies of scale, and to enable global capitation.

---

[58]Stephen M. Shortell, et al. "The Holographic Organization." *Healthcare Forum Journal*, Vol. 36, no. 2 (1993), pp. 20–26.

[59]J. Sokolov. "On the Brink of a Third Generation," *Healthcare Forum Journal*, Vol. 36, no. 2 (1993), pp. 29–33;Stephen M. Shortell, R. Gillies, and D. Anderson, "The New World of Managed Care: Creating Organized Delivery Systems," *Health Affairs*, Vol. 13, no. 5 (1994), pp. 46–64.

[60]David W. Young and Diana Barrett. "Managing Clinical Integration in Integrated Delivery Systems: A Framework for Action." *Hospital & Health Services Administration*, Vol. 42, no. 2 (Summer 1997), p. 256.

[61]Deanna Bellandi. "A Welcome to Systems: Finally, AHA Opens Its Door to Integrated Networks." *Modern Healthcare*, Vol. 27, no. 50 (Dec. 15, 1997), p. 2.

EXHIBIT 3-15

Integrated Delivery System

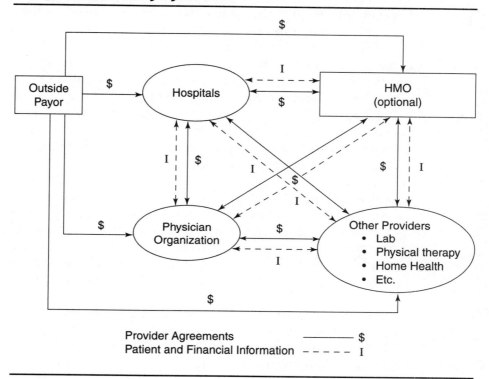

Provider Agreements —————— $
Patient and Financial Information – – – – – I

- Population-based health management that studies the health needs of the population before designing programmatic solutions.
- An intent to contain costs and improve care processes.

Objectives of the Model

The objective of the integrated delivery system model is to provide a whole universe of medical care for a large number of patients enrolled in managed care plans the IDS has contracts with. This does not mean that local competition is eliminated, because there may be other IDSs and many other providers in a market area. Since most people obtain access to healthcare through their membership in a group (employment, Medicare, Medicaid, etc.), an IDS can take responsibility for a group by attracting the healthcare purchaser, including managed care companies representing many purchasers.

Which strategy will make an IDS attractive to purchasers is the topic of continuing debate in the healthcare field. Common ideas include a responsiveness to the market and a culture that values creativity and learning. One assertion is that integrated delivery should be based on four principles: "marketplace focus, a single point of contact for purchasers, teaming with employers, and rationalization of assets."[62] Since purchasers and customers define value differently (consistency, low cost, improved health status, satisfied patients, etc.), IDSs must be careful to use strategies that accomplish many goals at once.

It is as important to consider information flow as it is to consider physical and human resources when designing an IDS. Integrated Delivery Systems essentially function in two worlds, one of tangible resources and one of intangible information.

Information systems are especially pertinent when IDSs want to measure the quality of their services and systems. *Outcomes* is the term used to describe the results that a health delivery system produces in terms of immunization rates, disease screening rates, and general health/functional status of the population the system serves. An information system that can track patients and their diagnoses, treatments, and results is necessary to quantify outcomes for purchasers and to initially manage costs and processes.[63]

Whether integrated healthcare will last or not depends on whether IDSs succeed in adding value in the marketplace. The majority of healthcare leaders believe value-added healthcare can be achieved by focusing on some combination of the following:

- Improving quality of care
- Emphasizing service
- Improving accessibility
- Reducing unit costs
- Improving operating efficiency
- Strengthening customer relationships
- Enhancing product offerings[64]

---

[62]Jim Morell and Ron Mills. "The Marketplace Helps Determine Integration Opportunities." *Healthcare Financial Management*, July 1996, p. 29.

[63]Douglas A. Conrad and Stephen M. Shortell. "Integrated Health Systems: Promise and Performance." *Integrated Delivery Systems: Creation, Management, and Governance.* Health Administration Press, 1997, p. 13.

[64]Elizabeth A. Fischer and Dean C. Coddington. "Integrated Health Care: Passing Fad or Lasting Legacy?" *Healthcare Financial Management*, Jan. 1998, p. 44.

When hospitals started receiving reimbursement via a prospective payment system based on Diagnostic Related Groups (DRGs) it became imperative to shorten hospital stays and use that inpatient time very efficiently. This need motivated the implementation of inpatient care pathways, which are fixed standards for the provision of care for specific diagnoses or procedures. Care pathways were initially developed to cover diagnoses and procedures that are high-cost, high-volume, and/or problem-prone, such as total hip replacement, stroke, or open-heart surgery. It quickly became apparent that extending the care pathway to the doctor's office and to post-hospital care (skilled nursing, home care, etc.) is also useful, but without global pricing, there isn't necessarily a financial incentive. The provision of healthcare is moving toward more standardization in patient care. This trend in care management can extend across different facilities and services to improve quality and to lower costs by integrating treatment. Integrated delivery systems enable providers to contract for the entire continuum of care, and thus make extended care pathways financially logical.

History

As providers consolidate and Managed Care Organizations seek to contract on a capitated basis for the provision of all of the care that patients require, hospitals and physicians, as the traditional providers of care, are destined to become more and more integrated into single organizations. Most existing IDSs began when hospitals acquired or affiliated with physicians through PHOs or MSOs for the purpose of managed care contracting.[65] The desire of these organizations to expand the range of services they provide has led to their merger, acquisition, or affiliation with other types of facilities such as long-term care, skilled nursing facilities, and ambulatory surgery centers as well as with ancillary providers including laboratories and diagnostics.

Organizational Structure—Anatomy

The organizational structure of an integrated delivery system typically includes four players:

- Hospital(s)
- Physician practices

---

[65]Paul R. DeMuro. *Managed Care & Integrated Delivery Systems: Strategies for Contracting, Compensation & Reimbursement.* Irwin Professional Publishing, 1995, pp. 13–14.

- Subacute services (home health, skilled nursing, etc.)
- Health plan (or ability to accept capitation)

The governance of an IDS is often structured by a central corporation that owns or controls the individual entities; this enables global contracting.

One of the hardest things in making an IDS work is getting the various players with their different cultures and attitudes to come together and acknowledge the same goals. Hospital executives find it difficult to internalize the fact that getting patients into the hospital is no longer the goal. Rather, proactive primary care services, including patient education and primary and secondary prevention of disease (immunization and early detection, for example), are used to keep patients healthy.

One method that encourages staff to cooperate is to link the personal compensation of the executives in charge of the various entities to the financial health of the whole organization. Other successful approaches are to rotate senior managers around the system to get a variety of points of view,[66] or to make some senior managers responsible for systemwide issues.[67]

Legal and contractual issues are important structural considerations. "Integration among the entities is taking place in a legal environment that was designed to promote fragmentation rather than affiliation. Indeed, consideration of legal matters, such as antitrust and any-willing-provider requirements, is key to avoiding conflicts with other institutions in the IDS's market, as well as among entities within the IDS itself."[68]

If the IDS is not-for-profit (a medical foundation or otherwise not investor-owned), it must be careful in acquiring physician practice assets: "It must acquire those assets for no more than fair market value, and the purchase price must be based on independent appraisals and arm's length negotiations between the parties. No part of the acquisition price should be for any possible referrals to the hospital component of the integrated delivery system."[69]

---

[66]Stephen M. Shortell, et al. "Creating Organized Delivery Systems: The Barriers and Facilitators." *Hospital & Health Services Administration*, Vol. 38, no. 4 (Winter 1993), p. 447.

[67]David W. Young and Diana Barrett. "Managing Clinical Integration in Integrated Delivery Systems: A Framework for Action." *Hospital & Health Services Administration*, Vol. 42, no. 2 (Summer 1997), p. 264.

[68]Ibid, p. 260.

[69]Paul R. DeMuro. *Managed Care & Integrated Delivery Systems: Strategies for Contracting, Compensation & Reiumbursement.* Irwin Professional Publishing, 1995, p. 107.

Information Systems

In any integrated system, it is important to have someone in the organization (e.g., the medical director) that understands how to present performance data to physicians and convince and motivate them to change their behavior in an appropriate manner. This person must have complete access to the data, both on the inpatient and outpatient sides, and must be able to communicate that data effectively. Supplying this individual with data and the staff to interpret it is an important step in fostering the development of effective utilization management. Numerous managed care industry software products are available that can be adapted for use within the program, either in collaboration with a payor partner or on a freestanding basis. As the program begins to fully evolve, linking compensation to performance and aligning the incentives of the entire system will ultimately produce a high-performance integrated delivery system. The transition from fee-for-service to capitation is difficult for any integrated delivery system; however, sophisticated MIS systems enhance an IDS's ability to manage risk and track utilization and outcomes.

Functionality

An IDS has several functional issues that bear discussion: capitation, transfer prices, regulations, risk sharing, and incentives.

Capitation. All of the advantages of vertical integration—such as centralized management, increased market share, economies of scale, etc.—have costs associated with them, but the ability to accept and manage capitation is the benefit that gives providers the greatest incentive to push for further development of IDSs. Capitation "creates strong incentives for vertical integration in two ways:

1. By focusing total cost responsibility on a single provider organization, capitation transforms the focal organization's incentive from one of minimizing only costs at its stage of production to minimizing total costs incurred along the continuum.

2. To the extent that capitation not only changes the method and locus of provider payment, but also signals the payer's desire to reduce the level of payment, providers along the continuum of care are stimulated to integrate as a means of coping with reduced payment."[70]

---

[70]Douglas A. Conrad and Stephen M. Shortell. "Integrated Health Systems: Promise and Performance." *Integrated Delivery Systems: Creation, Management, and Governance.* Health Administration Press, 1997, pp. 10–11.

Transfer Prices. A transfer price is an internal financial management tool whereby a department "sells" its products or services to another department. How an IDS handles transfer prices can have a huge effect on its success. The costs of centralized services can be allocated to various users based on historical usage patterns, or a transfer price can be established to encourage the use of the in-house service. Once the decision is made, users can make rational management decisions concerning unit budgets.[71]

Regulation. There are some IDS-specific regulations to consider pertaining to reimbursement and licensure:

> Integrated delivery systems may be limited in their ability to accept payments from health plans by applicable state law and may even be subject to licensure requirements. In such an event, the entities comprising the delivery system may have to contract with the payors and assign their revenues to the PHO, MSO, medical foundation, or other entity in the integrated delivery system. If such entities are not limited by state law in contracting for hospital, physicians, and ancillary services, there will be more inherent flexibility in the integrated delivery system.[72]

Risk Sharing. Risk sharing is one of the key functions of an IDS. It is important in circumventing the risk of antitrust allegations, because entities that share risk behave financially as one entity.

> A key characteristic of many IDSs is risk sharing among the partners. The risk-sharing arrangements can have a significant effect on the roles and responsibilities of each partner, and in turn on the success of clinical integration efforts. Indeed, one potential conflict resolution mechanism is a risk-sharing incentive compensation system (i.e., a motivation process) that promotes "goal congruence" among the various parties (physicians, managers, non-physician clinicians, etc.). Presumably, as risk sharing increases, the incentive of the involved parties to resolve their conflicts to their mutual benefit also increases. The result should benefit the IDS overall.[73]

---

[71]David W. Young and Diana Barrett. "Managing Clinical Integration in Integrated Delivery Systems: A Framework for Action." *Hospital & Health Services Administration*, Vol. 42, no. 2 (Summer 1997), p. 263.

[72]Paul R. DeMuro. *Managed Care & Integrated Delivery Systems: Strategies for Contracting, Compensation & Reiumbursement.* Irwin Professional Publishing, 1995, pp. 77–78.

[73]David W. Young and Diana Barrett. "Managing Clinical Integration in Integrated Delivery Systems: A Framework for Action." *Hospital & Health Services Administration*, Vol. 42, no. 2 (Summer 1997), p. 267.

Incentives. "Alignment of physician and system incentives is probably the most important single determinant of delivery system success, since costs are driven largely by the physician's pen."[74]

Incentive alignment is often achieved via reimbursement mechanisms and culture merging. In a simple example, fee-for-service reimbursement of primary care physicians encourages greater utilization of the primary care office. Inpatient utilization can be more appropriately managed when coupled with capitation of specialists and specialist risk sharing with hospitals.

Culture merging also induces people to work toward a common goal: profitability or efficiency of the IDS. The cultures of the once-independent parties of an IDS are merged together based on principles of organizational/industrial psychology. Experience dictates that the parties should proceed slowly and not invest too much, because culture merging is a long process that may never fulfill expectations.

Advantages

The ability to align incentives of all the providers in the organization is a tremendous challenge for, and also a potential advantage to, an IDS governance structure. Only when all parties are working toward the same goal can clinical, service, and financial benefits arise. The goal of an IDS that has signed global capitation contracts is to attract enrollees and keep them healthy, thereby keeping the total cost of their care low over time. This strategy retains business by treating patients well, maintains the base of enrollees, and allows the system to benefit from the preventive care it provides.

Disadvantages

There are several barriers to integrating health systems, including:

- Resource barriers
- Mental models and organizational culture incentives
- Management and governance systems
- The external market
- The legal and regulatory environment[75]

---

[74]David W. Young and Diana Barrett. "Managing Clinical Integration in Integrated Delivery Systems: A Framework for Action." *Hospital & Health Services Administration*, Vol. 42, no. 2 (Summer 1997), p. 268.

[75]Douglas A. Conrad and Stephen M. Shortell. "Integrated Health Systems: Promise and Performance." *Integrated Delivery Systems: Creation, Management, and Governance.* Health Administration Press, 1997, pp. 18–24.

Future

Physicians have to be very careful when relinquishing autonomy in vertical integration arrangements. Market environments are constantly changing and may turn what seem like necessary decisions into bad choices. Hospitals are finding that building a primary care clinic base is not as profitable as they may have thought. There are many potential legal and financial pitfalls, and environmental or regulatory changes can affect an IDS's performance quickly. The bigger they are, the harder they fall.

However, a motivated, flexible, and resilient IDS leadership team can serve its constituent members and the community well if it focuses on its core mission and alignment of incentives. If the organization has twin goals of serving the community and staying in business, efforts at each of these goals should serve the other.

The following factors will influence the future of the IDS structure.

1. *Regulatory Changes:* How will antitrust concerns be balanced with the development of systems large enough to accomplish the goals of an IDS, including the well-being of communities? Will legal authorities recognize IDSs' inherent advantages of more cooperation as being more significant than their disadvantages of less competition?

2. *Popularity and Success of Capitation:* Will capitation, as a reimbursement mechanism, succeed in the marketplace? Capitation can motivate high-quality and appropriate care, emphasize preventive care, and be priced reasonably for both providers and customers.

3. *Creative, Responsive Internal Incentive Structures:* Can the members of an IDS be motivated to work for the good of the whole? This issue pertains to all levels of the organization—individual, department, delivery site. It also relates to the perception of fairness; for example, physicians must feel their interests are legitimately represented in an IDS.

4

General Consulting Methods

INTRODUCTION

This material beginning here and running through Chapter 8 describes *who* is providing consulting services to build and maintain EHOs and describes the methods of developing and maintaining EHOs utilized by consultants, or *how* consultants meet client objectives.

Who? Accountants, academics, healthcare business executives, physicians, nurses, attorneys, and MBAs are successfully leading the development of EHOs as consultants. Each brings an important perspective and skill set to strategy and implementation. There are strong examples of how each type of person has built a successful EHO. The background/training of a good consultant is less important than his/her ability to demonstrate:

- Tenacity
- Good listening skills
- Knowledge of the industry
- A "Whatever it takes!" philosophy

How? The development of EHOs is not magical, but the work is difficult, time-consuming, frustrating, and yet rewarding. Remember that EHO models are just that—models, a framework for achieving the specific objectives of a particular client. *Process drives the development of successful EHOs.* These chapters describe some processes through which consultants lead clients to arrive at workable solutions. Consider the tools of these chapters to be like the trusty road atlas in your glove compartment—they tell you how to get there, no matter where you are going (within reason, of course).

"OUR PRODUCT IS OUR PROCESS"

Although healthcare consulting requires a large body of specialized knowledge, healthcare organizations are businesses subject to many of the same rules and market forces as businesses in other industries. Therefore, similar business consulting processes will underlie most healthcare consulting engagements. In the chapters that follow, many of these tools and processes will be used and modified to fit the context of specific types of engagements. This chapter discusses general underlying principles and processes (or "standard, accepted practices") that are useful in numerous types of consulting situations.

CONSULTING SKILLS

Two classes of skills are required in consulting: strategic and organizational.

- **Strategic:** Strategic thinking requires a sound understanding of general business principles as well as specialized knowledge of the market. This knowledge can be derived from both research and experience. The research can be either specific (to the engagement) or general (about the industry, market, etc., and gathered from public sources); experience may accrue from any number of sources, including education, work, training, etc. An accurate understanding of the depth of this experience is crucial to a consultant's decision to accept engagements relating to specialized topics. It is the intent of this book to provide a means of gaining some understanding of consulting for the new organizations in the healthcare industry by adding to the body of research literature available in this area.

- **Organizational:** However, what is most important for any consultant is to establish a process for conducting, planning, and organizing projects. The tools presented in this chapter, along with an understanding of a few sound principles, can serve as a basis for such a process.

THE SIX Ps: PROPER PRIOR PLANNING PREVENTS POOR PERFORMANCE

Proper planning of a project can be accomplished by classifying project elements both by topic and priority. This approach provides organization of the project via the following three tools:

1. Milestone chronology
2. Process outline
3. Timetable of events

Exhibit 4-1 illustrates the relationship between these planning tools.

EXHIBIT 4-1

Hierarchy of Organizational Tools

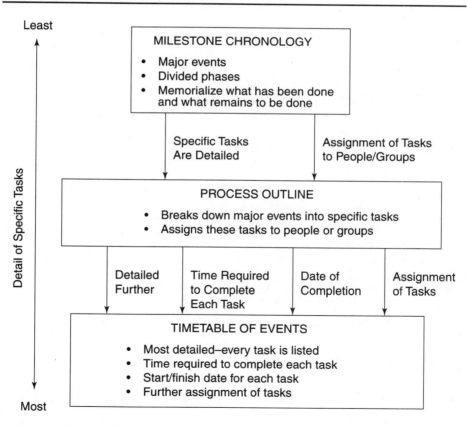

Establishing a Milestone Chronology

In most cases, the planning and implementation of a project involves many individuals accomplishing numerous specific tasks along the way, all in an attempt to make progress toward a common goal. Using milestones enhances the implementation process by motivating the participants to accomplish certain specific tasks. A milestone chronology presents a graphic portrayal of the progress the program has made to date and the remaining steps that need to be taken in order to complete the program. Success and motivation are enhanced as each individual goal, task, and milestone is completed. A sample milestone chronology for the physician integration process follows.

Milestone Chronology

Phase 1: Preliminary Feasibility Assessment
- Form project team.
- Identify prospects.
- Perform market assessment.

Phase 2: Review
- Survey prospects.
- Investigate desired services.
- Present integration models to prospects.

Phase 3: Consensus
- Select targets from prospects.
- Determine organizational structure.
- Develop package of services.
- Prepare operating budget.

Phase 4: Implementation
- Close on new entity.
- Staff new entity as needed.
- Convert to new systems and services (i.e., accounting, MIS, insurance, etc.).

Process Outline

A process outline expands on the milestone chronology by delineating specific tasks and assigning them to members of the project team. Below

Process Outline

Phase	Task	Assigned to
Phase 2	1. Discuss with project team and develop the approach to, and solicitation of, prospects.	Consultant
	2. Survey the prospects to: a. Verify and gauge their level of interest in affiliation/integration/association. b. Measure the group's compatibility as to practice modality and organizational philosophy. c. Determine the degree of participation at which the group would feel comfortable at this point. d. Determine the reasons and rationale for their participation. e. Discern the current areas of consensus and/or disagreement among group members. f. Discuss the level of each member's participation in, and ownership of, the process.	Consultant
	3. Request and gather *all* relevant practice information regarding the prospects.	Administrative
	4. Project team investigates the desired services of the organization and reports back to the prospects regarding compatible organizational structures for the new entity.	Consultant
	5. Project team provides the prospects with an overview of strengths and weaknesses of the different organizational structures from a legal, regulatory, cost, administrative, and control perspective.	Project Team/ Consultant

is a sample process outline for the second phase of the physician integration process.

Timetable of Events

The timetable of events is simply an extension of the process outline, with specific times stated for completion of tasks as well as estimated dates of completion. A timetable of events distills the process outline down into smaller, measurable, accomplishable tasks. A "task assigned to" column may also be helpful in tracking progress on individual tasks. Below is a sample of a timetable of events for the second phase of a physician integration project.

Timetable of Events

Event/Task Description	Estimated Time Required	Approximate Date of Completion	Task Assigned To
Conference call to review approach to physicians.	2 hours	2/1	Project Team/ Consultant
Send letter to prospective physician participants (prospects).	1.5 hours	2/3	Administrative
Follow up calls to prospects, schedule interviews.	1.5 hours	2/6	Consultant
Conduct initial interviews on-site, request initial documents.	3–5 days	2/13	Consultant
Conference call to provide update of prospects' interviews/surveys.	1 hour	2/17	Consultant
Collect and review data received.*	3 days	2/20–2/23	Consultant
Complete second phase of interviews (as needed).*	2 days	2/27–2/29	Project Team/ Consultant
Conference call to reevaluate original goals and objectives based on documentation analysis and prospects interviews.**	1.5 hours	2/29	Project Team/ Consultant
Conference call or general meeting to present advantages/disadvantages and options of services offered through the new entity.**	2 hours	3/6	Consultant
Determine level of integration, types of services offered, organizational structure, and governance of the new entity.**	4 days	3/10	Project Team/ Consultant

*Contingent upon level of physician cooperation.

**Includes preparation and analysis required to conduct meeting or conference call.

Timetable of Events—Continued

Event/Task Description	Estimated Time Required	Approximate Date of Completion	Task Assigned To
Develop projections of costs and revenues associated with the new entity.*	6 days	3/12–3/20	Consultant
Project team reports proposed structure and service offering of new entity to entire group.*	2.5 hours	3/21	Project Team
Project team develops preliminary list of legal and regulatory concerns to be discussed with legal counsel.	2 hours	3/25	Project Team

*Contingent upon level of physician cooperation.

**Includes preparation and analysis required to conduct meeting or conference call.

VISION, STRATEGIC INITIATIVES, AND TACTICAL PLANS

An effective way of organizing the strategic planning process is by using the hierarchy: vision, strategic initiatives, and tactical plans. It is important not to confuse the scope and definition of these terms. Refer to Exhibit 4-2.

1. *Vision Answers: "Why?" (Long-Term):* First, the client must define or confirm their vision. The vision statement answers the long-term question, "Why are we in business?"

2. *Strategic Initiatives Answer "What?" and "Who?" (Intermediate):* Second, the focus must be directed to strategic initiatives that address questions involving "What?" and "Who?" Strategic initiatives are generally objectives that, if met, would satisfy the vision of the organization.

3. *Tactical Plans Answer "How?", "When?", and "Where?" (Short-Term and Ever Changing):* Third, the details of the organization's strategy must be addressed by defining tactical plans. Tactical plans describe how, when, and where the strategic initiatives will be met.

EXHIBIT 4-2

Vision Statement

VISION STATEMENT
*Broadly Defined Statement of Purpose
That Distinguishes an Organization from Its Competitors*

Components Include
- Target customers and markets
- Indicate the principal services delivered by the organization
- Specify the geographical area within which the organization intends to concentrate
- Identify the organization's philosophy
- Specify the organization's desired public image

**STATEMENT OF
STRATEGIC INITIATIVES**

*Specific Element Required
to Achieve Vision $_1$*

**STATEMENT OF
STRATEGIC INITIATIVES**

*Specific Element Required
to Achieve Vision $_2$*

**STATEMENT OF
STRATEGIC INITIATIVES**

*Specific Element Required
to Achieve Vision $_3$*

**TACTICAL
PLAN**
*Specific Method
to Achieve
Statement of
Strategic Initiative*
1a

**TACTICAL
PLAN**
*Specific Method
to Achieve
Statement of
Strategic Initiative*
1b

**TACTICAL
PLAN**
*Specific Method
to Achieve
Statement of
Strategic Initiative*
2a

**TACTICAL
PLAN**
*Specific Method
to Achieve
Statement of
Strategic Initiative*
2b

**TACTICAL
PLAN**
*Specific Method
to Achieve
Statement of
Strategic Initiative*
3a

**TACTICAL
PLAN**
*Specific Method
to Achieve
Statement of
Strategic Initiative*
3b

THE PHASES OF THE CONSULTING ENGAGEMENT

The purpose of consulting work is the provision of opinion. The consulting process consists of four basic phases: proposal, research, analysis, and presentation.

The first phase, proposal, involves business development activities culminating in the delivery of a proposal for specific consulting work.

Business development is beyond the scope of this book, but there are numerous considerations pertaining to the development of a proposal and acceptance of an engagement that weigh heavily on the successful outcome of the project, and thus are of interest here. The "Consulting Engagement Pre-Engagement Acceptance Form" in Appendix 43 leads the consultant through many of the questions that must be addressed before accepting an engagement, including the self-assessment of expertise, resources (personnel and financial), conflicts of interest, and many other issues.

Once the consultant accepts an engagement, the next phase, research, involves compiling the necessary data. The specific research consists of gathering information from the subject entity, including financial, business, operational, staffing, and other information. The "Medical Practice Documents and Materials Request Form" and the "Medical Practice Workbook" in Appendices 11 and 13 outline most of this type of data. The other portion of this phase is the general research using materials that are available through published governmental and private sources and may include information on the market, local economic conditions, competitors, healthcare facilities, Managed Care Organizations (MCOs), benchmarking statistics, reimbursement trends, specialty or industry trends, supply of practitioners and facilities, and many other relevant topics.

The third phase of an engagement, analysis, involves summarizing and interpreting the information gathered in the research phase and comparing the specific research with the general research. This analysis can range from simple summaries to in-depth financial analysis within the same engagement. There are a number of standard tools for analysis that consultants should understand.

- *Summarization:* Includes tables, matrices, abstracts, etc., that are designed to allow for the distillation of a body of information into one or more of its essential characteristics. These tools provide readers with an overview or comparison of information.
- *Benchmarking:* Refers to the comparison of specific research data on the subject with industry norms. This may be as simple as a variance analysis on a single characteristic such as physician's compensation or as complex as an analysis involving numerous variables and incorporated within another, larger analysis.
- *Forecasting:* Generally involves trend analysis and produces a prediction of future values or performance. Financial pro formas, budgets, demand analysis, and space or staffing forecasts are all examples of this type of analysis.

- *Complex or Compound:* Describes multifaceted analysis that incorporates different types of tools to synthesize an overall conclusion. A large proportion of consulting analysis falls into this category.

The final phase of a consulting engagement, presentation, involves the reporting of results to clients or other parties. Though presentation is the final phase, presentation aspects such as progress reports, updates, interim reports, and other intermediate communications will occur throughout the engagement. These reports may be in a variety of formats including business correspondence, oral presentations, and written reports. Generally, final reports should be formal, written in a technical style, and include the results of all analysis as well as the recommendations of the consultant.

THE FOUR PHASES OF PHYSICIAN INTEGRATION

A generic sample of the different phases of the physician integration process is provided in Exhibit 4-3 as an illustration of the relationship between the phases of a typical consulting engagement and those of a physician integration project. Physician integration has been selected because it represents the majority of healthcare consulting activity today. The main difference is the involvement of the client and other parties, most notably during the consensus phase. Also, in a project of this type and scope, the presentation phase gives way to an implementation phase as the consultant remains involved in the organization of the new entity.

RECORD MANAGEMENT, MEMORIALIZING, AND ARCHIVING

The organization of any project requires diligence and planning in the keeping of project and business records. The first portion of this duty for the consultant involves memorializing events, discussions, correspondence, decisions, and records. The process includes the creation and retention of agendas and minutes for all meetings, results or summaries of all appropriate decisions, options, lists, and other documents. Memorializing information serves a number of functions, most notably legal concerns for both the client and consultant, and provides a complete history of events as well as evidence for facilitating dispute resolution.

The records-management and archiving process consists of four consecutive functions: identification, classification, storage, and retrieval. These steps provide a framework for the design and maintenance of a

EXHIBIT 4-3

Four Phases of Physician Integration

	PHASE 1	PHASE 2	PHASE 3	PHASE 4
	FEASIBILITY	REVIEW	CONSENSUS	IMPLEMENTATION
	Preliminary Feasibility Assessment	Data Gathering, Analysis and Review, Client Education	Develop Model	Implementation
	• Geographical proximity of prospective participants • Analysis of market and physicians • Type/mix of physicians • Practice life cycles • Compelling reasons to affiliate • Environmental influences	• Collect pertinent data from prospective participants • Managed care status—issues/concerns • Present integration model • Perform best-fit analysis	• Additional data gathering • Consensus building • Governance issues • Utilize synergies • Types of services offered • Development of legal documents	• Payroll vendors • Accounting & MIS • Legal • Integration of staff • Other vendors • Ongoing managed care contracting
	Objectives	Objectives	Objectives	Objectives
	Report preliminary findings & make "go/no-go" decision	Report finding	Finalize organizational structure and governance issues for new entity	Closing on new entity and commence implementation process

Approach:

1. Health System (HS) Driven	Health System (HS)	Health System (HS)	HS/Legal Counsel	HS Legal/Mgt. Team
2. Phys. Driven	Phys./HS	Phys./HS	Phys./HS/Legal	Phys./HS Legal/Mgt.
3. PPMC Driven	PPMC/HS	PPMC/HS	PPMC/Legal Counsel	Team
				PPMC/Legal Counsel

records-management system. There are numerous document-tracking systems and much software available for these purposes. Beyond the obvious reasons for careful design and upkeep of records-management systems (such as internal project management ability) there are numerous legal and ethical concerns requiring the diligent preservation of client business records.

THE ENGAGEMENT PROCESS

Each consulting engagement will include specific project tasks and steps; however, most engagements will include numerous standard procedures, as illustrated in the following list.

Engagement Checklist

1. Evaluate whether to accept the engagement.
   a. Identify all parties to prospective engagement, e.g., client, subject company/practice, company/practice owners, hospital affiliations. Use "Consulting Engagement Pre-Engagement Acceptance Form." (Refer to Appendix 43 for a copy of this form.)
   b. Conflict Search: Disclose any potential conflicts to client and obtain permission/agreement before proceeding.
   c. Capabilities, resources, skill sets assessment.
   d. Scheduling, timetable review.
2. Develop an estimate of required chargeable hours and fees.
   a. Fee Indicators: number of FTE providers, number of locations, gross revenues.
   b. Complexity of legal structure, availability and sufficiency of data.
   c. Purpose, scope, and format of report.
3. Prepare and submit to client a proposal letter and engagement agreement with Schedule of Professional Fees.
   a. Fee Basis: straight hourly, hourly with cap, flat fee.
   b. Set forth required retainer and expense requirements.
   c. Send two original agreements. Letter should include instructions for client to sign both originals and return both to consultant.
4. Submit a "Documents and Materials Request" and a "Medical Practice Worksheet" in the proposal package, where appropriate.
5. Obtain a signed engagement agreement and retainer from client.
   a. Consultant to sign both originals after they are returned from client with client's signature.

b. One original (with both signatures) should be returned for client's records; the other one will be kept in consultant's secured records.

6. Develop a detailed work program.

a. Assign tasks to appropriate staff based on skill sets, experience, and availability. Complete a preliminary budget.

b. Identify project milestones and estimated date of completion (EDC) schedule in conformity with client needs and expectations. Discuss with client; set up telephone conferences if necessary and appropriate.

7. Collect and analyze the data appropriate for the engagement methods to be used.

a. General Data: economic, demographic, industry, specialty, managed care environment, utilization demand, physician/population ratios.

b. Specific Data (obtained from subject company): financial statements, tax returns inventory list, staff listing, and other relevant data. Discuss with client as to appropriate means to obtain data: directly from subject company, from accountant(s), and attorney(s), etc.

8. File all documents in project binder(s) separated by numbered indexes. Prepare a table of contents detailing contents of binder(s) according to the numbering system. The first section is generally reserved for correspondence and the second for copies of client agreements (signed), copies of any invoices sent, and any work in progress (WIP) detail.

9. Follow up with client or subject company regarding documents still needed, if necessary.

10. If marking or writing on data and documents is necessary during the engagement process, make copies before writing! Never write on original client documents, as they may have to be returned to the client at the end of the engagement.

11. Consider obtaining a representation letter regarding accuracy and validity of data submitted to consultant by client, if appropriate and possible.

12. Staff members use the consulting and analysis methods selected under the supervision of an experienced consultant or supervisor.

a. Trend analysis and comparison to industry norms.

b. Perform ratio analysis of subject company and compare those ratios with industry or specialty ratios. Describe and analyze these comparisons in the narrative report.

13. Prepare narrative to document and communicate to reader of the report all work performed and conclusions reached, in a manner that will allow the reader to replicate consultant's work.

14. Prepare a final discussion draft of the report.
    a. Update industry and specific sources of documents used (located near the end of report).
    b. Attach copies of subject company financial data utilized in the appendix of the narrative report.

15. Perform a detailed review of the work papers and final discussion draft of the report.

16. Obtain an independent internal review of the work papers and report draft.

17. Resolve any professional disputes relative to methodologies employed.

18. "Tick and Tie" report: Correct any errors.

19. Discuss engagement findings and final report draft with client. Request that client disclose any errors of omission or commission that may have been discovered in client's review of the final discussion draft of the report.

20. Determine that all review points and open items have been cleared.

21. Prepare and bind the final report in multiple originals, according to client agreement.

22. Sign and apply embossed certification seal, if applicable, to the multiple original reports on both the transmittal letter and certification pages.

23. File all work papers, data sources, and other engagement-related documents for safekeeping.

24. Prepare and submit final billing for engagement to client.

25. Conduct a post-engagement review to evaluate the staff's performance and quality of final work product.

PROFESSIONAL FEES

It is important to discuss options for arranging professional fees and to understand how different types of engagements require different fee arrangements. Countless factors can affect the amount of time and resources an engagement requires and therefore have an impact on its profitability for the consultant. Fee options range from flat fees, where payment is fixed regardless of the amount of work performed, to hourly rates, where consultants are compensated based on their time spent on the project. Consultants must learn what factors can affect the amount of time spent on various engagement types and contract using the appropriate fee arrangements. Fee levels will depend on the consultant's internal costs as well as the value that their work and experience can command in the market. Six of the common types of professional fee arrangements in consulting are shown in the table below. For example, Fee Option 1 would include an hourly rate with a retainer, but no cap on professional fees. This is a common arrangement in law firms.

Fee Options Discussion Matrix

	Fee Option 1	Fee Option 2	Fee Option 3	Fee Option 4	Fee Option 5	Fee Option 6
Hourly Rate	✔	✔	✔	✔	✔	
Retainer	✔	✔	✔	✔		
No Cap	✔				✔	
10% Cap over Estimate		✔	✔	✔		
Estimate at Client Expense		✔				
Estimate at Limited Client Expense			✔			
Estimate at Consultant Expense				✔		
Flat Fee						✔

## Chapter 5

Overview of an EHO Start-Up Program Stressing Physician Advocacy

INTRODUCTION

This chapter presents the different advantages, disadvantages, and considerations related to the various models of integration current in the marketplace, the do's and don'ts of integration, the development and implementation of an integration program (hereinafter, "the program"), and other strategies designed to aid entrepreneurial physicians in their management choices.

The details of integration efforts are specific to the needs of each group and local market. However, the national, regional, and local trends leading to physician integration efforts can assist in guiding EHO start-up programs. The recent changing relationships between physicians have taken place in the context of a dramatic change in the attitudes of physicians nationwide. Progressive physicians have tired of what they perceive to be the developing attitude among some of their colleagues that physicians are the *victims* of change. Out of this impatience is emerging a growing recognition that physicians must remain at the center of the medical care delivery system decision-making process, and that physicians who are organized and empowered to make their own choices can develop solutions that are far more imaginative, relevant, responsive, and cost-effective than solutions imposed by government. Organized physicians can be instrumental in building integrated systems that can respond adequately to the realities of the fiscal environment and to the rules of the healthcare marketplace. Such physician-driven systems can engage in long-range financial planning, reward cost-saving and efficiencies, and organize themselves into delivery patterns that better serve people in need of medical services. The organization of these systems can allow for effective participation in MSOs and other innovative partnerships in the larger healthcare marketplace. Physician-sponsored organizations foster management strategies that are more flexible and responsive to the present volatile healthcare environment. The most important success factor with physicians is the level of their commitment as reflected in their involvement, both financially and in management. This commitment may be more difficult to obtain in situations where the new organization is sponsored by other parties. Meeting the challenge requires cooperation among key physicians in leadership and planning positions in the development of an effective system of care. The difficulty is to actively involve physicians in the planning process in such a way as to allow them meaningful participation in the development of the system while adhering to a strict project timetable. The task is challenging because of its political (in the broad sense) ramifications. All physicians who eventually participate in new systems must be committed to the goals established by the system even though they may not have participated in every step at every level of the planning process.

Because key physicians in leadership/planning positions will have the continuing responsibility to implement the new system once it is formed, they should maintain a primary leadership role throughout the planning process.

THE DO'S AND DON'TS OF PHYSICIAN INTEGRATION

Three general concepts should guide the program-planning process:

- The process of integration does not lend itself to ad hoc decision making.
- "The Six Ps": Proper prior planning prevents poor performance.
- A little form before function goes a long way.

The following sections address some things that can be done to make the architecture of integration in healthcare delivery work.

Consultants and Physician Leaders Must Articulate a Vision That Can Be Explained and, More Importantly, Felt

Part of this feeling needs to be a sense that someone has thought things through, that they have broken through complexity to create simplicity. "Thinking the goal through is important. Partners need to be clear on the reasons for, and benefits of, integration. The more time they can spend on articulating that, and the clearer the vision is, the more likely they are to design a system that will get them there."[1]

Train Managers and Physicians in the Principles of Systems Thinking

Building an integrated system is not simply a matter of constructing a new set of boxes on a clean sheet of paper, each nicely connected and labeled in appropriate legalese. Markets and patients are not boxes; they are complex systems. Although the basic concept of systems thinking is intuitive and widely accepted, its principles are rarely applied in healthcare. The dynamic nature of systems requires structural fluidity. Integrated organizations will need to be elastic and evolve if they are to withstand buffeting from the marketplace.

The Organization Needs to See Whole Processes

Identifying key processes and mapping them out on paper allows for a clearer understanding of critical interconnections. The very act of drawing a dynamic organizational picture forces new thinking. The boxes and lines that many planners draft today are shadows of the real promise and the necessary architecture of tomorrows integrated organizations. The most important questions to ask in this dynamic picture are:

- Does everything on the chart create value for the customer?
- As an organization, what must we own versus what must we influence?
- What is the mechanism for engendering alignment of interests across participants in the resulting organization?

---

[1]Allen Fine and James G. Wiehl. *Integrated Health Care Delivery Systems Manual.* Thompson Publishing Group, July 1995, p. 7.

The organizational structure of the new healthcare entity must be loosely aligned from a structural standpoint. However, the values of all participants must be strongly aligned.

Customers Should Participate in the Design Process so that Their Needs Are Addressed

Healthcare planners often repeat the sins of the past when they attempt to create new integrated organizations. One of the mistakes planners often make in their quality improvement efforts is assuming that they know what the customer wants or needs. Although there is common agreement that quality is defined from the customer's perspective, planners often assume this perspective rather than actively seek it out. Employers and patients must be included at the design phase.

New Healthcare Organizations Need to Reconnect with the Over-60 Population

The most powerful voting bloc in America is senior citizens, and they fill many physicians offices every day. Senior citizens and their representatives, most notably the American Association of Retired Persons (AARP), are among the most influential groups in Washington, D.C.

The influence of seniors today is considerable, as politician after politician promises to cut spending, yet will not touch the entitlement programs for the elderly. By 2015, no politician or businessperson will make a move without considering the impact on those who are 60 years of age or older. Healthcare providers should put that leverage to work today in building integrated organizations that will have the support of this powerful customer base.

Today's Healthcare Organizations Require Value-Added Information Systems

Historically, computer-based information systems operating in healthcare were creatures of finance and as such were not *value-added*—that is, did not contain any information that would allow an organization to respond more effectively and profitably to customer needs.

New systems can integrate financial and clinical data and perform sophisticated analysis, providing managers with the information needed to effectively manage capitation and other challenges to the profitability and outcomes of healthcare providers. Beyond these important functions, MIS facilitates effective communication between and coordination of multiple organizations or divisions and geographically separated locations. This ability is essential to the effective management and operation of today's new integrated organizations.

Building New Organizations Requires Getting Everyone On Board

Integration must cast a wide net. Part of the challenge of getting providers involved is getting them to step off the shore. Realistically, the only way they are likely to see beyond their functional and specialty areas is to let them participate in redesigning the delivery of care. There are three questions that all participants in integration must address:

- What does the customer want?
- How can we best organize to meet the customer's needs?
- How do we need to change the work we do every day?

Teamwork is critical to success. Therefore, everyone's expertise should be utilized in addressing questions in their area to share in creating the overall solution.

Set Milestones to Establish Visible Indicators of Progress

It is also important to communicate goals in an understandable fashion. Participants will ask questions along the way. What will we look like once we are integrated? How will the roles of participants change? Milestones allow the organization to have a visible destination in mind and to develop a sense of progress toward meeting the ultimate goal.

Balance Different Perspectives

Integration requires a balanced approach that is broad enough to be comprehensive yet anchored to the realities of implementation. The old notion of not seeing the forest for the trees conveys part of this message. The other part of the message is the danger of not seeing the trees for the forest. Big plans and small details must be kept in balance.

Build an Image of Consistency

The hallmark of a truly integrated organization is consistency of operations. Effective integration makes this consistency possible. Consistency is therefore a critical goal for healthcare organizations seeking integration.

Develop New Kinds of Leaders

Leaders must build a new mindset that molds different perspectives into something solid and powerful, a coherent vision that puts patients, physicians, facilities, nurses, quality, and cost in one box.

The Emerging Healthcare Organizations (EHOs) that are being built for tomorrow should not be regarded as fences around today. Instead, they must become springboards to higher quality and lower costs. We must look beyond the acquisitions, alliances, mergers, start-ups, foundations, and Management Services Organizations (MSOs) toward enterprises that can make good on the real promise of integration: seamless care of the highest quality, delivered in a way that gives patients the greatest value.

"In the integration process the test of every decision should be, 'Does this decision hold the promise of higher quality and lower cost for our patients?' The answer to that question ultimately determines whether we end up as architects of or merely tenants in the healthcare delivery system of the future."[2]

CONCEPTUAL FRAMEWORK

Objectivity

Input to the integration process should be based on factual observations, both within and external to the practice environments; on actual strengths and weaknesses of the prospective participants as compared with those of their peer groups; on the planning issues which will drive the process; and on the expressed interests and desires of those with a stake in the system.

Sound Methodology

The planning, development, and implementation of the program that is part of an evolving integrated system is a process that does not lend itself to ad hoc decision making. It requires discipline and thoroughness. Consultants should employ a process, in an almost scientific way, that has been tested and refined in similar engagements. These processes should not be learned along the way. Any deviation from a predetermined process must be considered thoroughly before being implemented. The maxim in consulting is that, in the end, *the product is the process*.

---

[2]Ibid, p. 10.

Balanced Involvement

It is important to structure the approach to the program so that it neither leads to an entity created solely by one party nor abdicates the consultant's responsibility to advise the organization in the future. The goal is to blend these two extremes by interactively involving each participant— physicians, consultant, and legal staff—as an integral part of the team.

Commitment to Results

When implementing an integration program, physicians will want to create an entity capable of satisfying the demands of tomorrow's marketplace.

Independence

In the evolving healthcare environment, physicians need to speak with a strong, independent voice and to act from a position of organized strength. All recommendations should lead toward this objective. The goals must be to enhance independence and ensure meaningful participation in the new organization.

FACTORS DRIVING THE APPROACH

Facilitation

This means working to establish objectives, analyze issues, consider options, set priorities, assess benefits and disadvantages, develop recommendations, and build a meaningful, participatory consensus on informed dialog and compromise. Encouraging the development of sustainable leadership—people, including empowered physicians, who can take control of the new organization once the engagement is over—is one of the most important attributes of a successful approach.

Program Management

Many great ideas do not make it to reality because of poor project management and documentation. The key to project management is open communication channels and focusing on small victories in the project process. This means providing consultation and guidance to committees when necessary, setting milestone chronologies and realistic timetables, scheduling and coordinating meetings, creating agendas, making assignments, resolving issues, and reporting on progress.

Legal and Business Acumen

This means possessing the skills to competently and efficiently complete the technical legal work required and to provide the business experience to move the process to a practical, flexible result. To limit legal risk and effectively manage projects, consultants must provide superior document-management services, a skill not emphasized by many firms. All agreements and arrangements discussed and finalized must be organized in a readily retrievable system.

INTEGRATION PROGRAM PLANNING

The efficiency and success of the program will depend upon the planning that takes place well before the program process commences. Several standard tools aid in the planning process, including:

- Milestone chronology
- Process outline
- Timetable of events

These tools are used in sequential order. While the scope of the planning process remains the same, the specific tasks become more detailed. Refer to Chapter 4 for a full description of these tools.

Determining the Appropriate Integration/Affiliation Model

Determining the appropriate physician integration/affiliation model is paramount to the overall success of the program, and this process underlies much of the integration/affiliation process. The entire process can be broken down into four phases: feasibility, review, consensus, and implementation, as illustrated in Exhibit 5-1.

Phases of the Physician Integration Process. Within the program, each individual market and integration project will have unique characteristics. Depending upon the level of integration desired and the specific integration model selected, the individual tasks and milestones may vary slightly. However the phases of the project and, usually, the tasks within each are the same for all physician integration projects. Refer to Exhibit 5-1 for an illustration of the project phases and participants. The physician integration process has been divided into the following four phases.

EXHIBIT 5-1

Four Phases of Physician Integration

	PHASE 1	PHASE 2	PHASE 3	PHASE 4
	FEASIBILITY	REVIEW	CONSENSUS	IMPLEMENTATION
	Preliminary Feasibility Assessment	Data Gathering, Analysis and Review, Client Education	Develop Model	Implementation
	• Geographical proximity of prospective participants • Analysis of market and physicians • Type/mix of physicians • Practice life cycles • Compelling reasons to affiliate • Environmental influences	• Collect pertinent data from prospective participants • Managed care status—issues/concerns • Present integration model • Perform best-fit analysis	• Additional data gathering • Consensus building • Governance issues • Utilize synergies • Types of services offered • Development of legal documents	• Payroll vendors • Accounting & MIS • Legal • Integration of staff • Other vendors • Ongoing managed care contracting
	Objectives	Objectives	Objectives	Objectives
	Report preliminary findings & make "go/no-go" decision	Report finding	Finalize organizational structure and governance issues for new entity	Closing on new entity and commence implementation process

Approach:

1. Health System (HS) Driven	Health System (HS)	Health System (HS)	HS/Legal Counsel	HS Legal/Mgt. Team
2. Phys. Driven	Phys./HS	Phys./HS	Phys./HS/Legal	Phys./HS Legal/Mgt.
3. PPMC Driven	PPMC/HS	PPMC/HS	PPMC/Legal Counsel	Team
				PPMC/Legal Counsel

1. *Feasibility:* The first phase of any project involves assessing its feasibility. The basis of this assessment will be the specific and general research gathered during this phase. A decision to go on with the project or not must be made here before the parties involved commit the resources required for further analysis.

2. *Review:* The second phase, review, is designed to permit a more detailed analysis of the data gathered in the first phase. During this phase, research will be ongoing and more information will be gathered from the prospective participants. A review of the integration models and a best-fit analysis occur at this time and the phase culminates in a report synthesizing its findings.

3. *Consensus:* In the consensus phase, participants work to develop details of the integration model selected. Among the organizational issues to be addressed are governance, services, and potential synergies among the participants. Legal documents are developed and the organizational structure and governance are finalized at the end of this phase.

4. *Implementation:* The final phase is concerned with planning implementation of the new organization. It is during this phase that operational integration is designed for areas such as accounting, management information systems (MIS), staff, managed care contracting, and vendors. The phase ends with closure on the new entity and the commencement of the implementation process.

The rectangular portion of Exhibit 5-1 illustrates the required steps of an integration project. The four phases are not mutually exclusive and in many instances may be in process simultaneously. For example, certain legal documents may be in the process of being prepared in the third phase as data collection is still being completed.

The arrow portion of the exhibit illustrates the parties involved at each phase of the physician integration process. The "approach" (rows of the arrow) indicates which method is being employed in the program. For purposes of the exhibit, "HS" means the organization's project team responsible for the project. The role of each party (i.e., the sponsoring organization, physicians, legal counsel, and management team) will vary at each phase of the process. For example, a majority of the feasibility phase will most likely be handled by either the project team or the program-development committee.

During the implementation period (the fourth phase), the management team will have an increasing role as the new entity becomes operational and many transitional issues arise. The management team should include the executive director of the new entity, member(s) of the project team, and outside advisors (e.g., accountants, consultants, vendors) as deemed necessary by the project team.

Some of the key factors to consider when determining the appropriate physician integration/affiliation model are listed below.

Managed Care Penetration   An analysis of the Managed Care Organizations (MCOs) and managed care penetration in the market in which the new organization will compete should be completed during the first two phases of the physician integration/affiliation process. As a general rule of thumb, the more penetrated a market is (as measured by a percentage of the entire population enrolled in managed care plans), the more integrated an integration/affiliation model should be in order to effectively compete.

Level of Consolidation   The level of consolidation, like managed care penetration, is a general market characteristic. Research and interviews should be conducted during the feasibility and review phases of the project (phases one and two, respectively) in order to narrow the potential physician integration/affiliation models down to those that will be considered. Analysis of the level of consolidation should cover both hospital/health system consolidation and physician practice consolidation. In markets where there has been a limited degree of integration (i.e., independent hospitals, solo practitioners, and small medical groups), physicians are likely to prefer less integrated models, such as Independent Practitioner Associations (IPAs), Physician Hospital Organizations (PHOs), and Group Practices without Walls (GPWWs). See the discussion of these models below.

Autonomy/Leverage   The degree of practice autonomy a physician is willing to abdicate in return for practice leverage is a critical factor when determining the type of physician integration/affiliation model to pursue. (See Exhibit 5-2.)

For example, a solo practitioner has a high degree of autonomy but has limited leverage in a managed care environment. At the other end of the continuum, a single physician in an Integrated Delivery System (IDS) would have little autonomy but a much larger degree of leverage in the market. Physicians lose autonomy as groups and governance structures form with standard operating procedures, clinical protocols, and case management systems, limiting individual decision making. There is a direct relationship between the level of integration and leverage. As the degree of integration increases, a physician's leverage in the marketplace increases.

EXHIBIT 5-2

Autonomy/Leverage Diagram

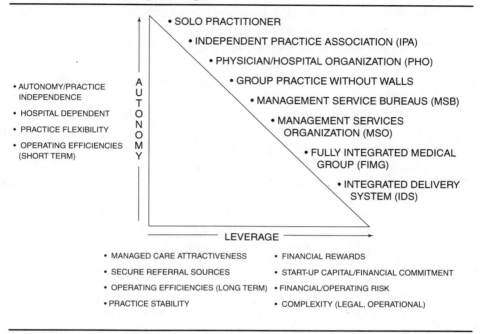

- AUTONOMY/PRACTICE
  INDEPENDENCE
- HOSPITAL DEPENDENT
- PRACTICE FLEXIBILITY
- OPERATING EFFICIENCIES
  (SHORT TERM)

AUTONOMY

- SOLO PRACTITIONER
- INDEPENDENT PRACTICE ASSOCIATION (IPA)
- PHYSICIAN/HOSPITAL ORGANIZATION (PHO)
- GROUP PRACTICE WITHOUT WALLS
- MANAGEMENT SERVICE BUREAUS (MSB)
- MANAGEMENT SERVICES
  ORGANIZATION (MSO)
- FULLY INTEGRATED MEDICAL
  GROUP (FIMG)
- INTEGRATED DELIVERY
  SYSTEM (IDS)

LEVERAGE

- MANAGED CARE ATTRACTIVENESS
- SECURE REFERRAL SOURCES
- OPERATING EFFICIENCIES (LONG TERM)
- PRACTICE STABILITY

- FINANCIAL REWARDS
- START-UP CAPITAL/FINANCIAL COMMITMENT
- FINANCIAL/OPERATING RISK
- COMPLEXITY (LEGAL, OPERATIONAL)

Consensus Building   During the second phase of the integration process, review, the consultant must ensure that all physicians are fully informed of the differences between the potential integration/affiliation models. As the process moves into phase three, consensus, it is better to encourage a higher level of integration. It is well documented that loosely affiliated organizations (e.g., IPAs, PHOs) have not been as successful as more integrated models (e.g., MSOs, Fully Integrated Medical Groups [FIMGs]), in large part because there is no "glue"—financial contributions and shared economic risk—holding the organization together. For example, a physician who pays $500 to join an IPA has a very limited investment in the organization and shares no economic risk with the other physician participants. Developing a consensus among physicians requires a person or team that is highly skilled as an intermediary, negotiator, and facilitator.

Potential Physician Integration/Affiliation Models.   A brief discussion of the benefits and disadvantages of potential physician integration/affiliation models (described in depth in Chapter 3) follows. Each of the models may be tailored to fit the appropriate context.

Independent Practice Association (IPA) Model   An IPA is usually established by physicians who intend to maintain their independent practices but seek to offer their services to Health Maintenance Organizations (HMOs) or other risk-sharing MCOs on a collective basis. The IPA negotiates and often enters into payor contracts as a single entity on behalf of its physician owners.

Physicians often prefer an IPA because it is easy (and relatively inexpensive) to implement, and it does not require them to transfer their practices to a new organization. Instead, the IPA allows them to retain control over their private practices. The IPA is sometimes viewed as a first step in medical practice integration, a means by which independent physicians can learn to work together in a managed care environment. It is uncertain whether an IPA actually fulfills this goal. Physicians tend to become comfortable in the IPA arrangement and resist taking the difficult next step toward partial or full integration. In markets where physicians refuse to integrate operationally, an IPA might be better than nothing.

The inherent weakness of an IPA is that physicians remain in separate competitive practices. They do not have the unity of economic interests that would encourage them to implement operational integration. Overall, the IPA physician works in the best interests of his or her private practice, not in the best interests of the IPA. In addition, the IPA often is unable to exert the clinical discipline necessary to change physician behavior related to utilization of services, as required by payors in many markets.

Physician Hospital Organization (PHO) Model   A Physician Hospital Organization (PHO) is a legal entity formed by a hospital and a group of physicians that combines both parties into a single organization for the purpose of gaining greater negotiating leverage in obtaining managed care contracts. A PHO creates a more cohesive medical staff, and can provide economic and service incentives to payors through formal agreements that contractually obligate physicians and the hospital to carry out medical management protocols.

One of the strengths of a PHO for physicians is the retention of autonomy because of minimal changes in practice locations and ownership. A PHO can provide the vehicle to initially organize a medical staff dominated by solo partnerships and small groups. It is therefore often a first step for physicians or hospitals seeking eventual greater integration.

PHOs achieve only a low degree of physician integration with the hospital. PHOs find it difficult to obtain authority to contractually obligate individual physician members, and so can only minimally influence utilization of services and usually can't effectively manage higher-risk contracting. Another disadvantage of PHOs is that assertive management can be difficult to achieve due to the split on governing boards between physicians and hospital administrators.

Group Practice without Walls (GPWW) Model   A GPWW is a legal entity owned exclusively by physicians. It owns all the assets of all of its affiliated physicians. While a GPWW may provide management services, its primary business objective is managed care contracting.

GPWWs are an integration model that, for a number of reasons, has fallen out of favor as a viable organizational form. It is an intermediate step between an IPA and an MSO, without many of the benefits of either. In many markets, physicians either do not require this level of integration or must integrate further in order to compete.

The strengths of GPWWs lie in their providing solo physicians with the ability to retain some autonomy while integrating some functions. They can be a vehicle to attract capital for additional ancillary ventures or further integration. GPWWs are a low-risk approach to organizing individual physicians and creating a larger economic unit, but they should be considered with caution as their few advantages are often outweighed by the lack of cohesion and leverage.

GPWW weaknesses include the fact that links to the central company often are not strong. Implementation of utilization review and quality control is difficult due to the geographic separation of offices. Lastly, GPWWs may not be as attractive to managed care entities in highly competitive environments as more integrated organizations that are more capable of controlling quality and costs.

Management Services Bureau (MSB) Model (Less Comprehensive)   An MSB contracts with physicians to provide management services. The physician practices remain separate, independent legal entities with input into the MSB through its advisory board. MSBs are often an initial step for hospitals seeking to form a relationship with physicians and potentially strengthen that relationship through further integration over time.

A clear, objective system for review of MSB performance should be established as part of the development process. It is important to have quantifiable criteria against which to measure the cost/benefit of the program to both the physicians and the sponsor.

An aggressive internal and external communication and marketing effort is an important part of the planning, development, and ongoing management of the MSB program. The success of the program depends on strong support and involvement from both the hospital and the physician participants. A strong, consistent public relations effort will be integral to the long-term success of the program.

Management Services Organization (MSO) Model   The MSO typically establishes a separate legal entity that equally shares responsibility between physicians and the hospital for establishing and operating the entity. The governing board of the MSO has equal representation from physicians and hospital management. The organization has a separate operational staff, managed by a senior executive.

All members of the medical staff do not necessarily participate in the MSO ownership, although most physicians can participate in one of the benefit programs sponsored by the MSO if they support the hospital. Because these strategies highlight many legal concerns and involve significant capital investment, the MSO model tends to carry great risk. Sharing the risks and control of the MSO with physicians is an integral part of the MSO model. Implementation of the MSO typically requires a minimum of six months, due to the need to create a separate legal entity. Lead time may need to be longer if physician investments are delayed or if recruitment of senior management staff is difficult.

MSOs have become popular integration vehicles, although in practice they are quite varied in their composition and the range of services they provide. MSOs are flexible because they can provide services to individual practitioners, an IPA, or group practices. This adaptability allows MSOs to evolve in several directions depending on market conditions.

On the other hand, MSOs do not effectively link the incentives of physicians and those of the company. All transactions between physicians and the company must be at arm's length. In highly competitive markets, MSOs are less able to compete for managed care contracts than fully integrated groups (see below). MSOs have relatively little shared risk.

Fully Integrated Medical Group (FIMG)(Equity) Model   FIMGs represent the most integrated type of physician organization and as such have the greatest contracting and market leverage. Information systems, management, and other administrative functions may be centralized so that the organization can efficiently act as a single entity. The primary disadvantage of an FIMG is that physicians lose their sense of individual autonomy. If the compensation system is not designed to reward individual effort, physicians may also lose the incentive to perform at their highest levels. In addition, the costs of developing the FIMG can reduce physician income unless outside sources of capital are available.

Integrated Delivery System (IDS) Model   An IDS is a group of legally affiliated organizations in which hospitals and physicians combine their assets, efforts, risks, and rewards, and through which they deliver comprehensive healthcare services to the community. The legally affiliated entities perform all strategic planning and payor contracting for the various interests. Typically, one organization operates the medical practices and is often called a "foundation." An Integrated Healthcare Organization (IHO) is similar to an IDS, except that an IHO is formed through the merger of the hospital and the medical practices into a single legal entity. After structural integration into an IDS or IHO, the parties typically focus on unified governance, the use of consolidated management and clinical systems, and the implementation of consolidated budgets for the entire system. The economic interests of the parties are unified, and participants do not maintain separate economic businesses that compete with each other.

An IHO is a single organization that operates an entire healthcare delivery system. Sometimes it will comprise a hospital division and a physician division. An IHO is the simplest and possibly the most effective of all the models because it encourages all providers to unify their economic interests and act as a single enterprise. The economic fate of the organization is the fate of all providers. The IHO can be a for-profit business corporation that is owned by shareholders. In states that have a corporate practice of medicine law, shareholders of an IHO must be physicians.

DESIGNATED MARKET ASSESSMENT

Implementation of the program involves many tasks and the accumulation of large amounts of data gathered from various sources. An effective approach to this is to begin by collecting a broad scope of information (e.g., general market data) and then progress to an increasingly narrow scope of data (e.g., specific medical practices).

Assessment of the designated market is beneficial for many reasons, if done properly and on a timely basis. The first step of the implementation process will help create a road map for the program by identifying major market forces that may impact the program or related development and implementation efforts. It also provides participants with an overview of the major market competitive forces. Refer to the Appendices for bibliographies of research sources.

The following sections describe key issues that may have significant impact on the program.

Assessment of Area Hospitals and Healthcare Facilities   A general review should be conducted of the hospitals and other healthcare facilities within the service area of the designated market. There are a number of excellent general reference sources in this area, notably The AHA Guide by the American Hospital Association. This guide provides summary information regarding facilities, services provided, number of beds, annual admissions, census data, outpatient visits, newborn data, expense/payroll, and personnel.

Further analysis of the area hospitals should include identification of hospital system relationships, alliances, networks, current or anticipated mergers and acquisitions of hospitals and/or practices in the area, and the potential impact of these interrelationships on the program.

Consultants should consider and analyze practice acquisition/ physician integration activity involving competing hospitals and local providers during the planning stages of the program. The pace of implementation, the selection of particular integration models, and the level of aggressiveness taken are a few of the many variables that may fluctuate depending on the current market forces.

Major Employers/Alliances/Coalitions   Planners can create a list of all of the major employers in the area from sources including the local chamber of commerce, the business or economic development council for the area, the secretary of state's office, etc. This list should include information on each employer's location, number of employees, and current method of providing healthcare benefits to employees. In many cases, compiling this list will involve direct inquiry to the employers, which can be combined with a friendly "public relations call." It will also be helpful to identify any existing or anticipated alliances between employers and insurance plans or other coalitions in the area.

This information will be useful in the initial planning stages of the integration process, and will constitute the basis for the managed care contracting plans that will be discussed later.

Managed Care Organizations (MCOs), Preferred Provider Organizations (PPOs), Health Maintenance Organizations (HMOs), and Other Plans   Qualitative and quantitative information on PPOs, HMOs, and other MCOs is available from a number of public and private sources. State and federal governments, research and investment firms, and numerous associations all collect varying amounts of data on managed care and MCOs. The "Competitive Edge" series, published by Interstudy, provides information on managed care penetration, costs, and competition for metropolitan areas nationwide.

Planners should identify all insurers in the area and answer the following questions.

- What percentage of the population in the community does each health insurance company cover?
- What percentage of patients served are covered under each policy?
- What are the limitations in payment or processing of insurance coverage?
- What are the patterns of coverage under various managed care programs?

Medicaid/Medicare Mix   Medicare and Medicaid payments often constitute a large percentage of reimbursement for providers. In addition to assessing the MCOs in the market, it is necessary to gauge the influence of Medicare and Medicaid relative to the program. Planners should determine the percentage of the hospital's and the physician's patients that are covered by Medicare and Medicaid, then assess the financial impact of these patients on program providers. The relationship between providers and Medicare and Medicaid in terms of speed of reimbursement, procedures for reimbursement, and resolution of problems may also be pertinent to this assessment.

Demographic and Economic Overview   A demographic and economic overview should be developed for the service area. At a minimum, the overview should focus on three external factors: geographic area, social and demographic characteristics, and the economic environment.

All analysis will depend on the *geographic service area* that is defined for the subject community. The estimated area should be compared with data obtained from patient lists. Areas defined by postal zip codes can provide a sufficient geographic breakdown for analysis. This comparison will identify inconsistencies between perceived and actual service areas.

Potential service areas for the next five years should be identified for the planned organization. Planners should also identify differences in the actual and potential service areas and assess the implications that an increased or decreased service area will have for the new organization. They should define urban and rural, geographic and physical travel and traffic patterns and evaluate how these patterns affect the providers both currently and in the future.

Information on social and demographic charactertistics may be obtained from census reports, the most recent copies of which are available from the Regional Census Center of the Bureau of the Census or the State Data Center. Using this information, planners should describe as accurately and thoroughly as possible the current and near-future trends within the community. The analysis should include the following topics:

- Age distribution
- Growth or decline of population as measured by migration statistics
- Sex ratio (percentage of women to men) in the total population and workforce
- Female labor force participation
- Minority population, including handicapped individuals
- Mortality and morbidity statistics
- Family statistics, including percentage of married, divorced, widowed and never married
- Education levels

Based on this information, providers can be evaluated with respect to how well they have catered to the primary patient population. Services in demand but not currently offered, as well as other populations that the organization can target, may be identified.

Other sources of data to consider include:

- Most current census data
- Department of Motor Vehicles registration data
- Voter registration data
- Enrollment statistics from local schools
- Patient mailing lists
- Medical and administrative records

To what extent do certain barriers inhibit people from obtaining healthcare services? Consider each item below in terms of population subgroups, including minorities, women, handicapped patients, employed population, elderly, AIDS patients, and others with infectious diseases.

- Transportation difficulties, including travel time, convenience, and ability to obtain transport. What are the types and causes of the problems?

- Cultural and religious barriers.
- Financial problems. For example, is the care provided too expensive? Are patients unable to afford services?
- An excess or inadequate number of providers. Specifically, what are the oversupplied and undersupplied specialties?
- Emotional and mental states of patients receiving care. Are factors of work stress, domestic affairs, and social pressures afflicting patients?
- Information barriers. Analysts should consider the patients' ability to effectively choose a provider by assessing the number of competing media advertisements; the clearness of information in newspapers, telephone advertisements, and pamphlets; and any other communication barriers that inhibit people from obtaining health services. Do people have a difficult time deciding which medical group to choose because there is an overabundance or deficiency in the number of competing advertisements?

An overall written assessment of the local *economic environment* will identify issues and factors, both current and anticipated, that could have an impact on the program. Useful sources of information on these issues include the local chamber of commerce, city/county/state departments of economic development, the secretary of state's office, etc. Below are some of the economic factors to consider when assessing the economic environment.

1. List the major employers in the community.
   a. Who are they, and how many does each employ?
   b. Which insurance programs does each employer offer its employees? What types of coverage are available (dental, psychiatric, preventative care, hospitalization)?
   c. What are the patterns of industrial growth or decline in the community (i.e., expansion or closing of existing and new industries)? Locate each industry and identify its characteristics and growth or decline potential.
   d. What future changes in transportation are anticipated in the community?
2. Consider the present and future implications of the following factors:
   a. Unemployment and employment rates
   b. Number, type, and location of employers in the community
   c. Type of industry and employers (service, industrial)
   d. Construction and renovation of commercial and residential buildings

  e. Retail sales in area

  f. Stability of banking and financial industry

Managed Care Market Assessment   The managed care market assessment is a description of the dynamics driving the local healthcare market. Specifically, it should identify opportunities for the new organization.

The managed care market assessment can be accomplished in a number of ways. Telephone surveys or personal interviews can take many forms, including informal conversations and formally scheduled meetings. Written surveys are another tool that can not only ascertain the needs of potential clients but may, through the questions raised, also educate them about the implications of moving to a new kind of plan. Sources to contact may include, but not be limited to: (1) board members, (2) key physician contacts, (3) benefits managers, (4) the chamber of commerce, and (5) brokers. The market assessment includes the following activities.

- Conduct interviews with local employers, business and purchaser coalitions, brokers, managed care organizations, unions, and payors.
- Assess the attractiveness of the proposed network of physicians or hospitals to sponsors of existing or potential managed care plans.
- Enumerate the specific opportunities for physicians to contract directly with the region's self-funded employers for a full range of services or specific healthcare packages.
- Determine what types of provider payment arrangements, plan design and patient steering mechanisms, education programs, utilization review systems, provider selection criteria, and marketing strategies are in use.

Once the managed care assessment is complete and the business plan established, the program team must evaluate the results and decide which partners to work with. Questions to ask include:

- What partnership alternatives are available?
- How flexible are the various interested parties?
- What is the attitude of the parties' management toward creative solutions to challenges?
- How competent is the management of potential partners?
- How well do the parties communicate, externally and internally?

OTHER FACTORS AFFECTING THE PROGRAM

In addition to the direct market forces of competitors and the relationships and alliances among providers and hospitals, other factors may affect the program in various ways, either providing opportunities or creating obstacles. Examples of these elements may include the following.

- Internal agreements with medical equipment and supply vendors should be reviewed, as integration may provide an opportunity to renegotiate these agreements or initiate quantity discounts that were not previously possible. Researching other local vendors may allow for more favorable negotiations.

- Identifying healthcare purchasing groups may also provide opportunity to lower costs through higher-volume purchasing of equipment and supplies.

- At this point planners should conduct an analysis of management information systems (MIS) that are in place and identify community and competitors' data networks. Current systems should be reviewed for usability and expandability for expected future information needs. Will the current MIS provide the needed cost and utilization data for anticipated managed care contracts?

ASSESSMENT OF POTENTIAL AFFILIATE PHYSICIAN PROVIDERS IN THE AREA

Participants in new EHO projects may be existing physician groups or providers who have decided that they must change the way they practice and compete in their market in order to be successful in the face of increasing economic and competitive pressures. However, identifying enough providers with similar goals to form an effective organization often requires recruiting efforts. These may range from informal efforts to well-designed, extensive recruiting programs. Regardless of their scope, the efficacy of these programs depends upon the quality of their planning and design. Ideally, such a program involves the incremental evaluation of potential affiliates or acquisitions using a selection process. Such a process first involves identifying potential "suspects" from research on existing practices. Next these suspects are evaluated and those suitable for further consideration become "prospects." Prospects are contacted and further evaluated in order to further refine the list to "targets." Targets are then presented with further details of potential affiliation, and through this process, selected practices becomes "deals" and may be acquired or affiliated. A full description of this physician integration/ affiliation and practice-acquisition program is presented in Chapter 6.

DETERMINATION OF CONSENSUS ON INTEGRATION MODEL TO USE

The role of the program team is to meet the goals of the program while providing a consensus that is beneficial to all stakeholders in the program. Achieving a consensus among the stakeholders involves selecting the appropriate integration model.

Selecting the appropriate level of integration or the model that may best fit the objectives of the program, the market, and stakeholders involves educating the program team on the various integration models (as discussed previously in detail). Although it may not be necessary to consider every possible integration model for the program, the program team should thoroughly discuss and present at least three or four models. The team must then select the model that best fits the group in terms of the degree of autonomy desired and the willingness to share economic risk.

REGULATORY ISSUES

Once an integration model has been selected, an exhaustive review of all pertinent regulatory issues must be conducted. This stage should also involve the counsel of an experienced healthcare attorney. The regulatory environment in which the integration, consolidation, and acquisition of healthcare entities resides is immensely complex. The following are examples of issues that are significant to the typical healthcare entity transaction. For further information, refer to Chapter 2 and to the specific legal considerations described for each EHO model in Chapter 3.

Fraud and Abuse   "Fraud and abuse" refers to a wide variety of laws, including those dealing with the Medicare and Medicaid programs, the Stark laws (described below), and numerous other federal and state laws. Generally, fraud deals with the misrepresentation of material facts. Abuse, in the context of the Medicare and Medicaid programs, is defined as the provision of excessive, inappropriate, harmful, or poor-quality healthcare. Fraud and abuse enforcement and penalties by various government agencies have intensified in recent years. In practice, the two main categories of these laws deal with inappropriate billing practices and kickback schemes, or paying for referrals.

In their simplest form, the anti-kickback statutes prohibit anyone from "knowingly and willfully" offering or paying any remuneration to induce an individual to furnish or arrange to furnish any item or service for which payment is to be made under the Medicare or Medicaid program, and prohibit anyone from soliciting or receiving such remuneration. A narrow set of safe harbors—specific situations in which entities are deemed exempt from prosecution—have been adopted.

Self-Referral Prohibitions (Stark I & II) As part of the Omnibus Budget Reconciliation Act of 1989 (OBRA '89), Stark I prohibits a physician from referring a Medicare patient to a laboratory if he/she or a member or his/her immediate family has any financial interest in the facility. Stark II (enacted through OBRA '93) expands the self-referral ban to Medicaid patients and other "designated services." These designated services include physical and occupational therapy; radiology (including MRI, CT, and ultrasound); radiation therapy and supplies; durable medical equipment and supplies; parenteral and enteral nutrients, equipment, and supplies; prosthetics, orthotics, and prosthetic devices and supplies; inpatient and outpatient hospital services; and home health services and outpatient prescription drugs.

Antitrust As will be discussed later in the section entitled "Antitrust Compliance," various activities and agreements may be deemed monopolistic or anticompetitive and thus in violation of federal and state antitrust statutes.

Corporate Practice of Medicine State licensing statutes generally preclude ownership of a professional practice by anyone except individuals who have a license to practice medicine.

Medicare Reimbursement Constraints Medicare will only reimburse for activities "incident to" physician services and requires strict adherence to rules regarding Medicare provider numbers and Medicare benefits.

State Licensure While all states have differing definitions for specific types of healthcare organizations, all states require licensure for most of the entities. Approximately forty states still have certificate-of-need laws in effect, where proposed facilities must be approved by the state as warranted by demand or other criteria.

"Any Willing Provider" Laws "Any willing provider" laws require healthcare payors such as HMOs, PPOs, and insurance companies to contract with any healthcare provider willing to meet the payor's established

terms of participation. The laws have also been at issue regarding consumer freedom to use non-network providers and regarding providers dropped from preferred- or exclusive-provider panels.

Tax Exemption/Tax Status   The IRS determines tax-exempt status with a two-pronged test (community benefit standard and private inurement prohibition). Some factors relevant to the IRS's treatment of healthcare entities include nonemployee physician incentives, provision of charity care, hospital involvement in joint ventures such as PHOs, and the control structure of the Integrated Delivery System (IDS).

The regulatory enforcement agencies have recently become more interested and active in the healthcare industry. Federal resources devoted to healthcare fraud have increased; Medicare/Medicaid carriers and intermediaries have intensified their scrutiny; the Office of the Inspector General (OIG) of the Department of Health and Human Services has created a hotline used by competitors, former employees, and others; anti-kickback statutes are being interpreted more aggressively; the IRS has become active in policing healthcare and cooperating with the OIG; and new state and federal laws have been enacted aimed at curbing physician referrals based on financial interests. Extensive knowledge and thoughtful planning are essential to addressing the regulations facing those forming any healthcare entity. Planners should obtain legal counsel for any transaction or change in entity status.

Antitrust Compliance   The federal antitrust laws are designed to encourage free and fair competition by preventing anticompetitive or collusive agreements by groups of competitors and monopolistic practices by a single competitor. Failure to abide by the antitrust laws can lead to serious financial and/or criminal liability for individuals or the organizations of which they are a part.

The program should seek to ensure full compliance with the antitrust laws by the organization itself and by its members/participating providers. To this end, each participant within the program should adopt an antitrust compliance program. The program should be memorialized with formal policies intended to insure that all the members/participating providers comply with the antitrust laws in their performance of, or participation in, any program activities, as well as in any of their personal dealings that could affect the program.

A collection of federal and state laws establish the requirements of the antitrust laws. The various federal statutes are as follows.

- *Section 1 of the Sherman Act* prohibits any contract, combination, or conspiracy which unreasonably restrains trade. The reach of this prohibition is extremely broad. Agreements that restrain trade can be formal or informal, written or oral, and can be proven with either direct or circumstantial evidence. Among the actions that would raise significant concerns under Section 1 are agreements to fix prices or to use the same pricing mechanisms, allocation of patients or territories between competitors, or agreements to boycott or refuse to deal with some third party.

- *Section 2 of the Sherman Act* prohibits actual or attempted monopolization. Monopolization, for purposes of this statute, is commonly defined as willfully acquiring or maintaining monopoly powers—the power to control prices or exclude competitors. Monopoly power may exist whenever a single source provides a sizable majority of the goods or services available to the public. Market power that stops short of monopoly power may be sufficient to support a claim of attempted monopolization.

- *The Clayton Act* specifically prohibits certain types of business arrangements. Few of these arrangements are likely to pertain to the program's activities, although Section 7 of the Clayton Act limits the types of mergers, acquisitions, or joint ventures in which an entity can engage.

- *The Federal Trade Commission Act* prohibits unfair methods of competition and unfair or deceptive acts or practices. While this act prohibits many of the same types of activities as do the Sherman and Clayton Acts, its reach may be even broader.

- *The Revised Justice/FTC Enforcement Guidelines for the Healthcare Industry* set forth statements of antitrust enforcement policies, analytical principles, and safety zones relating to various joint activities in the healthcare area, including providers' collective provision of non-fee-related and fee-related information to purchasers of healthcare services.

CENTRALIZED SERVICES

The program team will need to address whatever malpractice and vicarious liability issues may arise during the implementation of the program. The scope of services offered to affiliates will vary depending on the following factors:

- Specialty of affiliate
- Financial, technical, and staff resources of both the affiliate's practice and the program team

- Current situation of affiliate's practice (i.e., practice life cycle, managed care influence, employee relatives, etc.)
- Nature of the program (forming a GPWW versus developing an MSO or FIMG)

Prior to selecting what services will be offered to the affiliates, it is necessary to assess what services are currently being provided to the practices and the sources of service (i.e., provided internally by practice employees or provided externally by third-party vendors). The program team should prepare a summary of practice services. This work should be a synthesis of all the affiliate's practices in the aggregate, which will help the program team identify services that are not being provided and to what extent services are provided internally. Refer to Appendix 27 for a sample "Summary of Practice Services Worksheet."

A range of current and prospective services should be made available to physicians who are interested in the program. There will be several possible ways in which to deliver services to the affiliate's practices. Each of the services should be presented in a format that will compare the relative advantages and disadvantages of the available options. A program team may wish to present the options available for billing and collections and claims resolution services. The options available for these services are:

1. *Maintain the "Status Quo":* The individual practices continue to have billing and collections and claims resolution services delivered or tasks performed in the present manner, regardless of whether the source is internal or external.

2. *Internally Centralize the Services:* Have the new entity provide billing and collections and claims resolution services internally to all the affiliate's practices.

3. *Externally Centralize the Services:* Contract with a third-party vendor to provide centralized billing and collections and claims resolution services to all the affiliate's practices. The program team should use careful consideration when developing the service offerings, as legal, political, and personal issues will likely arise. Below is a partial list of services that affiliates may offer or desire.

   a. Management consulting services
   b. Billing and collections, claims resolution
   c. Utilization management/review, quality assurance
   d. Physician/provider/staff recruitment
   e. Centralized laundry services
   f. Administration of CME

g. Accounts receivable/accounts payable management

h. Group purchasing of:

- Clinical supplies

- Office supplies

- Pharmaceuticals

- Group insurance (health, malpractice, office)

i. Vendor contract negotiation/management

j. Centralized payroll, worker's compensation, employee benefit accounts

k. Human resource/personnel management

l. Managed care contracting services

m. Marketing/public relations

n. Financial services: budgeting, accounting, financial reports, tax returns/consulting

o. Facilities planning and management

p. Management information systems

q. Medical records management

Management Information Systems Management information systems (MIS) can be an obstacle to integration. Information systems are the key to the integrated organizations of the future. For example, hospitals produce large amounts of critical and informative data. Yet hospitals, on average, invest about half of what businesses in other industries spend on information systems. The design of an information system is just as important as the amount of the investment. A well-designed MIS collects information once, at its source.

MIS is essential in the ongoing evaluation of the performance of physicians in the program. Integrated contracting systems that are not well managed from a quality and utilization standpoint should be of great concern. In order for the program to be successful, the planning team must develop and implement tools for utilization and quality evaluation.

Managing the program to meet the customer's needs will be the bottom line. In any integrated system, it is important to have someone in the organization (e.g., the medical director) who understands how to present performance data so as to motivate physicians to achieve the program's goals. This person must have complete access to the data, both inpatient and outpatient, and must be able to communicate that data effectively. There are numerous managed care industry software products that are available and that can be adapted for the program, either in collaboration with a payor partner or on a freestanding basis. As the program begins to fully evolve, linking compensation to the incentives of the entire system will yield a more profitable integrated system. The transition from fee-for-service to capitation is difficult for any integrated system. However, sophisticated MIS systems enhance the ability to manage risk and track utilization and outcomes.

The objectives of a management information system include:

- Providing an efficient healthcare claims and financial settlement transactions process.
- Providing an efficient, unobtrusive system for meeting the program's shared healthcare data needs.
- Providing the community with information on the cost, appropriateness, and effectiveness of healthcare services so that people can make responsible healthcare choices.

The functions of a management information system include:

- Linking healthcare providers electronically to payors and purchasers in order to verify eligibility, speed claims and payments, and reduce paperwork.
- Supporting patient surveys and special studies.
- Storing and aggregating information from providers and patients so that a physician has on-line access to a patient's history of previous illnesses and care by other providers, including diagnoses, procedures, and medications. The patient will also have access to their information.
- Addressing the quality and cost-effectiveness of the program by a process of data review, education, and dissemination of information.

"Right-Size" the Organization   To successfully operate as a business in the 1990s, an organization must be staffed so as to produce a product or service in a cost-effective and efficient manner. Right-sizing the organization should include all employees and affiliates of the program, respective of the integration model chosen. The organization should develop and maintain an appropriate mix of providers as the entity evolves. This mix of providers should exist at both the MD level (i.e., primary care, specialists) and the non-MD level (i.e., allied health personnel/paraprofessionals, therapists, and technicians), allowing for a broader range of services available to patients from both a clinical and a location perspective (i.e., inpatient, outpatient, home-based).

Support staff and management personnel of the organization must include people possessing the appropriate skills and experiences to run the organization efficiently. The required skills will vary depending on the type of integration model developed within the program. For example, hiring people who have medical practice management experience is very pertinent to an MSO. When staffing the new organization, the program team should be careful to avoid pitfalls such as using only employees from the affiliates' practices. While no one enjoys laying off existing employees, overstaffing a new organization with people possessing an abundance of the same skills (e.g., billing and claims resolution, secretarial, hospital management) or inadequate skills (e.g., no managed care background, limited computer experience) can be detrimental to the success of the program.

All staffing issues are potentially volatile for the organization and the consultants involved, so the program team should approach them only through a carefully thought-out and documented plan that has been approved by the organization's governance and investors.

Right-sizing an organization is a difficult yet extremely important component of the program. When developing a new organization it is important to find the appropriate balance between hiring an adequate number of qualified personnel and maintaining a lean budget during the start-up phase.

Transfer/Closure of Pension Plans   Qualified retirement plans, as defined by the Employment Retirement Income Security Act of 1974 (ERISA), should be reviewed to verify that they are qualified in form and operation and are in compliance with Internal Revenue Code (IRC) guidelines. Failure to comply with the qualification requirements of ERISA either in the form of the document or in the plan's operation can result in disqualification of the plan, which can create numerous problems (i.e., denial of past deductions, loss of trust's tax-exempt status, current taxation to participants, additional expenses in amending returns, recalculations and reallocations, and excise taxes and/or penalties).

The analysis of pension plans must focus on the relationships created in the integration process from both a structural standpoint (i.e., C-corporation, S-corporation, limited liability company, limited partnership) and an employer/employee standpoint (employee or independent contractor). The program lead should consult professional tax advisors regarding three areas that may have an impact on qualified pension plans: Affiliated Service Groups (IRC §414 (m)), Employee Leasing (IRC §414 (n)), and Shared Employees (IRC §414 (o)).

Managed Care Contracting   Prior to marketing the new organization's services to managed care organizations, it is imperative to identify the needs and concerns of purchasers of healthcare services. This process should include meeting with employers, payors, managed care organizations, business coalitions, unions, and brokers. It is important to incorporate the concerns and expectations of these parties into the marketing plan of the program, and to discuss the implications of these findings with all physicians in the program.

It is not enough to form an alliance among physicians and, potentially, hospitals in order to attract purchasers and payors. The program must be able to demonstrate that it possesses characteristics that will sufficiently interest these parties in considering the issues and then reaching an agreement with the organization for the provision of medical care.

In conclusion, the new organization should be able to demonstrate:

- Commitment to reducing cost
- Evidence that tangible steps are being taken to reduce administrative expenses
- Commitment to quality through clinical outcomes and customer service
- Documentation of outcomes and demonstration of superior results as compared with competing facilities
- Physicians' commitment to the program
- Physicians' ability to participate in policy design and governance
- Organized physician panel and adequate supply of primary care physicians
- Ability to meet patients' medical care needs
- Ability to assume risk and accept risk-based payments
- Reliable, accurate, and comprehensive management information systems to track cost per covered life and support integration of services that are provided in different settings
- Ability to agree on standards for the use of high-cost, high-risk services and to monitor, report, and control these services
- Willingness to share information with purchasers
- Willingness to address purchaser concerns
- Physicians' willingness to change their practice styles to reflect changes necessary under capitation

Physician Integration/ Affiliation and Practice Acquisition Programs: A Development Plan and Agenda

This chapter describes the development of a physician integration/ affiliation and practice acquisition program. The program presented is a systematic process designed to complement and further the corporate strategic efforts of hospitals, health systems, and established Emerging Healthcare Organizations (EHOs) seeking to integrate more fully with physician practices. The program outlines the development and maintenance of a strong base of physicians affiliated with, or integrated into, the existing provider system.

PROGRAM BACKGROUND

Such a program can enhance a current focus within the primary service area, particularly in delivering a measurably higher quality of care and superior levels of service at lower prices. To accomplish these goals, the program aims to provide a range of flexible options for physician affiliation/integration, recognizing that physician integration should be an incremental process. This process may include the acquisition of selected physician practices that are deemed appropriate to meet program needs and that complement physician practices that the organization may have acquired in the past. A further objective of this program is to continue developing and maintaining a detailed database of those physicians within the organization's service area. In this way, the program enhances the impact of all of the organization's existing facilities.

Organizations implementing such a program will accrue direct and indirect benefit over an extended period in the following ways.

- Continuity in how the program is developed, saving time and money
- Consistency in how the acquisitions are handled, protecting the organizations with fair and legal transitions
- Predictability of how providers will respond to an approach
- Benchmarking norms that can be modified to fit any market, allowing for regional implementation

Prior to implementing such a program, organizations should establish goals and milestones that are consistent with their strategic plans, and evaluate personnel and financial resources available to implement the program.

This type of program development is designed to avoid ad hoc decision making. Therefore, it is essential that multiple integration models be considered and a consensus built that will result in the most appropriate integration scenario. A cookie-cutter approach in the design and application of physician integration programs should not be used; rather, extensive market analysis and consensus building should determine the appropriate integration model to implement.

The analysis phase of the program should involve investigation into the area's hospitals, employers, business coalitions, and payors. The organization should conduct utilization demand review to determine the supply and demand for services and identify any surplus of services offered in the relevant market.

As provider candidates move through the recruiting and selection process, careful scrutiny should be given to regulatory issues (antitrust, fraud and abuse, Stark I and II, etc.) and postacquisition considerations (income distribution plans, centralized services offered, management information systems [MIS], etc.).

There are several alternative approaches to this type of integration program. These approaches, or perspectives, include an organization-driven approach that stresses the needs of the established organization, a physician-driven approach that seeks to serve the needs of the potential physician affiliates and those of the organization through the creation of a third organization, and a Physician Practice Management Company (PPMC)–driven approach where the organization would seek a PPMC with which to partner in forming a separate management company under joint ownership. This chapter will focus on the physician-driven approach, where the organization and the physicians create and jointly own the profit center. This approach provides physicians with a sense of ownership and balances leverage and autonomy concerns.

Once planners have determined that an organization has a strategic need for a physician integration/affiliation and practice acquisition program, the strategies and tools presented in this chapter will allow them to properly plan and successfully implement the program. The next step in determining the feasibility of implementing this type of program is to evaluate existing resources (personnel and financial) and determine what is needed within these areas in order to begin the program.

Strategic Statement of Objectives for the Program

It is critical for an organization contemplating a physician integration program—or, for that matter, any project of this scope—to codify their goals through a formal, written strategic statement of objectives for the program. Such a statement gives high-level direction to those charged with forming the program and provides a framework for assessing its progress and success.

Specific Research on the Organization Sponsoring the Program

In any consulting engagement, and especially in one of this scope, it is necessary to research the client organization as early in the engagement as possible. As stated earlier, this type of work does not support a cookie-cutter or prefabricated approach to consulting. In order to customize the program to suit the particular needs of the client and the market, the consultant must understand the history, operations, scope, and business philosophy of the client. Most of this information can be provided by the client and should be requested at the onset of the engagement. Tools such as the development of a milestone chronology for the organization are valuable in gaining an understanding of the client's needs. Summaries or charts describing the scope, number, and location of the organization's operations within the geographic market are also very useful.

Analysis of Growth Trends/Position in Market

Analyzing the growth of the organization and its relative position in the market can provide insight into the strategic goals being furthered by the proposed integration program. These goals may include expanding market share, acquiring low-cost healthcare providers, integrating providers into local market delivery systems, participating in area provider networks, creating affiliated EHOs, pursuing merger and consolidation opportunities with competitors, and expanding the range of services provided.

Management complacency and inertia are the two greatest threats to success and survival in the current healthcare environment. Competition in today's marketplace requires organizations to strengthen their operations and develop adaptive strategies for a climate of change and challenges. The continued restructuring of our country's healthcare system will create abundant opportunities for well-managed companies that can properly adjust to the changing environment. The successful healthcare companies of the future will understand the marketplace's demand for value in terms of quality and price.

The business of healthcare is becoming more and more competitive. Large, publicly traded companies dominate their markets by acquiring providers and merging with or acquiring other management companies.

To determine how the organization measures up to its competition, the consultant should construct a brief description and consolidated competitive overview/analysis of the major competitors. This analysis should include information on the competition's strategic philosophy, geographic range, size, strength, amount of direct competition, and other pertinent factors.

Required Organizational Resources

As stated above, in order to successfully implement a physician integration/affiliation and practice acquisition program, the organization must determine the resources (personnel and financial) that are both required and available and decide how to allocate these resources appropriately.

Personnel Resources. The program planners should draw up a current organizational chart, allocate staff to administer the program, and form a program-development committee. A troubleshooting committee may also be formed to triage problems or concerns that may arise. When assessing personnel resources, it is important to determine whether the people within the client organization have:

- Substantial knowledge of managed care
- Working knowledge of the regulatory environment
- Experience working in a medical practice setting and/or experience working exclusively with physicians
- Skills in MIS

- Negotiation and intermediary skills
- Leadership abilities
- Knowledge of financial issues and cost-accounting skills

While it is important to have people within the organization who possess these necessary skills, the organization must also determine if these people have the time available to allocate to the program.

Financial Resources.   A properly planned and implemented physician integration program requires adequate financial resource—that is, capitalization. Capitalization is needed to fund start-up, to subsidize operations, and for investment for future needs.

A study prepared by Ziegler Securities, Medical Group Management Association (MGMA), and Integrated Healthcare Report surveyed 537 EHOs, and captured information on how much debt, equity, and capital these organizations have, and also projected how much more will be needed. The results indicate that the higher the degree of consolidation, the more capital is required to fund an integration program. For example, median organizational development costs (professional fees) ranged from $25,000 (or about $380 per physician) for an Independent Practice Association (IPA) to $250,000 (or about $4,700 per physician) for a foundation model (tax-exempt model which acquires the assets of medical practices). Future capital requirements for consulting, legal, and accounting also illustrate this trend.

Adequate capitalization is required to fulfill future needs, which may include facility expansion, MIS upgrades, or physician practice acquisitions. The survey identified median "total future capital requirements" of the different integration models. Again, the more integrated and consolidated the model, the more capital is needed to meet future needs. According to the survey, IPAs have median total future capital requirements of $200,000 (approximately $3,000 per physician), Physician Hospital Organizations (PHOs) $613,000 (about $6,000 per physician), Management Services Organizations (MSOs) $2,500,000 (about $45,000 per physician), and a foundation model $15,900,000 ($300,000 per physician).[1]

The program may include the acquisition of physician practices. To arrive at an estimate of the capital required to fund the acquisition costs for practices under the program, it is useful to examine a survey spon-

---

[1] *Capital Survey of Emerging Healthcare Organizations: Second Annual Report 1996, Based on 1995 Data.* Integrated Healthcare Report, Medical Group Management Association, and Ziegler Securities, 1996, pp. 20, 21, 22, 23, 27, 29, 31.

Hospitals' Overall Per-Physician Acquisition Costs for Primary Care Physician Practices

Practice Specialty		Overall Per-Physician Acquisition Cost				
		Midwest/ Great Lakes	Northeast	Southeast	West/ Southwest	Total Sample
Family Practice	Mean	$130,547	$123,792	$164,743	$126,000	$134,883
	Median	$120,000	$112,500	$125,000	$125,000	$120,000
	Standard Deviation	$73,364	$80,699	$112,002	$86,190	$79,000
Internal Medicine	Mean	$101,875	$116,519	$202,889	$96,636	$130,549
	Median	$85,000	$130,000	$159,000	$103,000	$125,000
	Standard Deviation	$59,855	$54,558	$129,368	$53,246	$91,546
Pediatrics	Mean	$90,000	$80,909	$103,800	$111,000	$94,000
	Median	$76,500	$80,000	$115,000	$90,000	$90,000
	Standard Deviation	$59,719	$37,420	$34,649	$88,723	$59,420

sored by the Healthcare Financial Management Association (HFMA) detailing acquisition costs of primary care physicians' practices acquired by hospitals.[2] The survey, performed in early 1995, is based on 630 respondents, 38 percent of which were 100- to 299-bed hospitals and 35 percent of which were hospitals with less than 100 beds.

It should be noted that each acquisition must be structured according to its own merits, and may not involve the purchase of both tangible and intangible assets. For the purpose of analysis, tangible assets are defined as furniture; fixtures and equipment; office and medical supplies; tangible aspects of records, books, and files; and, in some cases, leasehold improvements. Intangible assets are defined as a trained and assembled workforce in place, enterprise/start-up expense, entrance factors, leasehold interest, and other permissible intangible asset components. In the case of each acquisition, a fair market value appraisal must be prepared by a qualified outside valuation expert. The organization will not acquire any assets that may be reasonably deemed by counsel not to be in compliance with any applicable law or regulation.

---

[2]John E. Hill and Jennifer Wild. "Survey Provides Data on Practice Acquisition Activity." *Healthcare Financial Management*, September 1995, p. 54.

The above HFMA survey indicates that in most cases the acquisition costs included tangible assets and some forms of intangible assets, such as noncompete agreements, charts, or unspecified goodwill.

In addition to the acquisition costs discussed above, it is reasonable to anticipate that the cost of outside professional services, including legal, consulting, and accounting services, should be in the range of 12 to 18 percent of total acquisition expenditures.

The purpose of this section is not only to stress the importance of adequate capitalization for the program, but also to demonstrate the magnitude of financial resources required. Organizations must properly assess both the financial resources required and those available, and budget the financial resources accordingly.

PROGRAM PLANNING AND DESCRIPTION

Program Structure

Once both the personnel and financial resources available to the program have been assessed, the organization must develop a corporatewide structure that will utilize resources in an efficient manner yet allow any affiliated entities to retain a minimum level of autonomy. An illustration of a sample program structure follows.

Physician integration programs consist of numerous projects (e.g., practice acquisition, MSO development), potentially at different sites (i.e., affiliated entities) across the organization. The organization should develop a program-development committee that will perform the following tasks:

- Manage the entire program, including but not limited to preparing budgets, structuring specific acquisition strategies, and organizing new product-development strategies
- Serve in an advisory capacity to any project team within the program, as discussed below
- Participate on selected project teams as deemed necessary by the program-development committee

Structuring the program in this manner can help to ensure that the organization's goals and visions are adhered to, while allowing access to the expertise and experience of the organization's personnel. Due to the wide disparity of projects within the program and, potentially, at each of many sites, many different individuals will be participating on project teams. Exhibit 6-1 is an example of how the project teams might be set up at a hypothetical site.

- *Project Team 1:* Suppose Project 1, at Site A, is the acquisition of a group of four orthopedic surgeons. Project Team 1 may consist of the local organization administrator, a member (or members) of the organization's program-development committee, legal counsel, and an independent outside party (e.g., consultant or accountant) responsi-

EXHIBIT 6-1

Program Structure

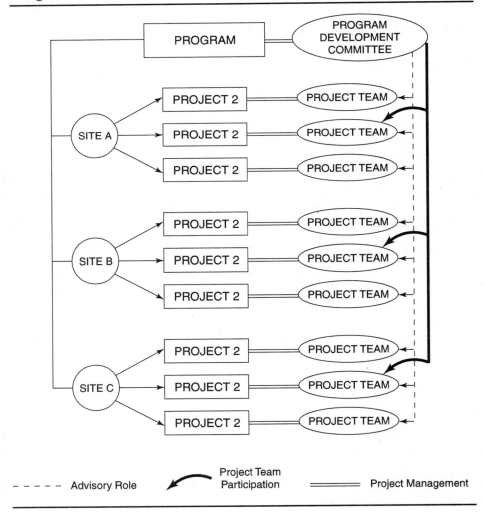

ble for the due diligence and/or valuation work that is required. Depending on the personnel resources available at the affiliated entity, the program-development committee may need to participate in a more active fashion.

- *Project Team 2:* By contrast, if Project 2 at Site A was the recruitment of a single radiologist, Project Team 2 may simply consist of a member of the local organization's administrative team (e.g., CEO, CFO, COO), the president of the medical staff, and the physician liaison. Project Team 2 would not have any representative from the program-development committee; rather, the committee would be available to serve in an advisory capacity on an as-needed basis.

- *Project Team 3:* Suppose Project 3 at Site A is the development of a physician integration model (e.g., Group Practice without Walls [GPWW], MSO, Fully Integrated Medical Group [FIMG]) which involves 20 to 40 physicians. Project Team 3 may include the local organization's administrator, three to five physicians representing the physician participants, and a member or members of the program-development committee.

Careful consideration should be given when developing the project teams, as many of the physician integration/affiliation/acquisition projects may have certain internal political ramifications for the local organizations' employees. In many cases it may be necessary to retain an independent outside party to assist in various tasks of certain projects.

Alternative Ways to Achieve the Objectives of the Program

Of the available corporate approaches to achieving the objectives of the program, three are considered and evaluated here. This chapter will describe in detail Approach 2 (Physician-Driven Approach) with Approach 1 (Organization-Driven Approach) incorporated to some extent where applicable. Approach 3 (PPMC-Driven Approach) is briefly described but not explored in depth.

Approach 1: Organization-Driven Approach   A separate entity/profit center owned 100 percent by the organization. Organized as illustrated in Exhibit 6-2.

- Established by the organization, either as an unincorporated division or a wholly owned subsidiary set up as a separate incorporated entity.
- In either event, the organization retains full ownership.

EXHIBIT 6-2

Organization-Driven Approach

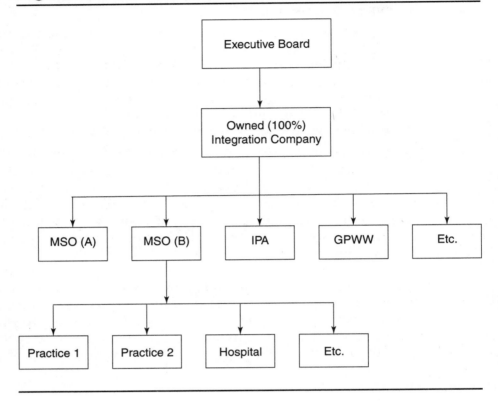

- The organization's governance controls all program activity.
- Separate profit centers are maintained for the organization.

Approach 2: Physician-Driven Approach   A separate company/profit center, with ownership divided among affiliated physicians and the organization. Organized as illustrated in Exhibit 6-3.

- Established by the organization in conjunction with the physician shareholders.
- The affiliated physicians and the organization's governance control all program activity.
- The affiliated physicians and the organization both have ownership in the established company.
- Benefits are realized by owners.

EXHIBIT 6-3

Physician-Driven Approach

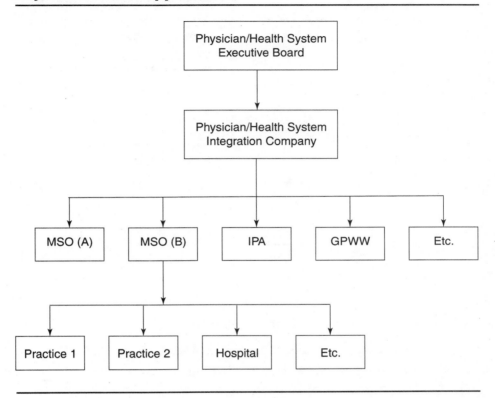

Approach 3: PPMC-Driven Approach An affiliation/partnership to be formed between the organization and a selected PPMC, resulting in the establishment of a new entity owned jointly by the PPMC and the organization. (This approach is only one possible option for this type of project, and is not detailed in this chapter.) Organized as in Exhibit 6-4.

- PPMC and the organization's governance control all program activity.
- PPMC and the organization have ownership of company.
- Benefits are realized by owners.

Phases of the Physician Integration Process

With physician integration projects, every different market and project will have its own unique characteristics. Depending upon the level of integration desired and the specific integration model selected, the

EXHIBIT 6-4

Physician Practice Management Company (PPMC)–Driven Approach

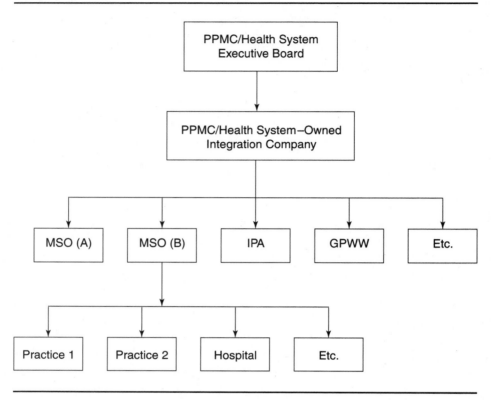

individual tasks and milestones may vary slightly. A generic sample of the different phases of the physician integration process appears in Exhibit 6-5.

The box portion of Exhibit 6-5 illustrates the required steps of an integration project. The arrow portion of the exhibit shows the parties involved at each phase of the physician integration process. The "approach" (rows within the arrow) indicates which method the organization is using in the program. For the purposes of the exhibit, "HS" means the project team responsible for the project.

Challenges and Problems

When organizations use staff or consultants who do not have extensive experience in the financial analysis and structuring of practice acquisi-

EXHIBIT 6-5

Four Phases of Physician Integration

	PHASE 1	PHASE 2	PHASE 3	PHASE 4
	FEASIBILITY	REVIEW	CONSENSUS	IMPLEMENTATION
	Preliminary Feasibility Assessment	Data Gathering, Analysis and Review, Client Education	Develop Model	Implementation
	• Geographical proximity of prospective participants • Analysis of market and physicians • Type/mix of physicians • Practice life cycles • Compelling reasons to affiliate • Environmental influences	• Collect pertinent data from prospective participants • Managed care status–issues/concerns • Present integration model • Perform best-fit analysis	• Additional data gathering • Consensus building • Governance issues • Utilize synergies • Types of services offered • Development of legal documents	• Payroll vendors • Accounting & MIS • Legal • Integration of staff • Other vendors • Ongoing managed care contracting
	Objectives	Objectives	Objectives	Objectives
	Report preliminary findings & make "go/no-go" decision	Report finding	Finalize organizational structure and governance issues for new entity	Closing on new entity and commence implementation process

Approach:

1. Health System (HS) Driven	Health System (HS)	Health System (HS)	HS/Legal Counsel	HS Legal/Mgt. Team
2. Phys. Driven	Phys./HS	Phys./HS	Phys./HS/Legal	Phys./HS Legal/Mgt.
3. PPMC Driven	PPMC/HS	PPMC/HS	PPMC/Legal Counsel	Team
				PPMC/Legal Counsel

tions, and who do not possess a thorough understanding of the rapidly changing regulatory and legal issues involved, the following problems often occur.

- The organization may pay an inflated purchase price and, often, concede too high a salary. This can cause resentment and alienation among the medical staff, be a potential violation of private inurement and reasonable compensation prohibitions, and effect a loss of much-needed capital.

- If the acquisition is completed after somewhat turbulent or even amicable negotiations, conflict or animosity toward the administrative team may be carried forward post-transaction. Utilizing the services of a qualified consultant who is attuned and sensitive to the dynamics of the physicians can shield the organization and its administration from many of these problems.

- Few consultants have the necessary expertise to assist their client through complex issues. Due to the booming business of physician integration, many healthcare consulting companies have started to offer this service; however, few have the necessary expertise to navigate their client through the complex and highly regulated environment of practice acquisition.

Acquisition Issues

When an organization considers the question of acquiring physician practices, these are issues it should resolve:

- Why do we want to acquire these practices? What are our short-term, intermediate, and long-term objectives?

- What criteria should we use in determining the practices to acquire? Should our process be based on competitive/turf issues, loyalty, production, quality care, excellent utilization, or political considerations?

- Does the organization have the internal resources to adequately manage the practices it acquires? (Often, home health agencies, skilled nursing facilities, physician groups, and other business ventures of different types from the acquiring organization are neglected post-transaction in terms of financial and administrative oversight.)

- What happens after the practice is purchased? For example, will the organization be ready to commit the resources to ensure an information system that will facilitate optimal reimbursements from managed care contracts?

- What will be the impact of the Stark laws, the Thornton letter, and other regulatory issues on the organization's acquisition strategy?
- What savings can we expect from enhanced bargaining power with managed care plans? Can savings occur through economies of scale and joint purchasing among the groups?

Relationship Issues

In order to make a mutually beneficial and satisfying arrangement between the organization and acquired or affiliated physicians, these issues should be addressed.

- Which asset components of the practice can be purchased and what can be paid for these assets to minimize the organization's exposure with the IRS, OIG, and other regulatory concerns?
- Does the physician compensation plan encourage the physicians to practice quality and efficient medicine within the constraints of capitated payment systems while not reducing productivity? Which methodology is best for this particular group: straight salary, salary plus percentage of receipts, cost accounting, points system, or a hybrid of these?
- Does the group's complement of managed care plans coincide with the organization's, thus reducing friction when group bargaining is pursued?
- Is the group managed effectively? Can savings occur through responsible management?

Process Flow Model

A sample of a process flow model for physician integration and practice acquisition activity appears in Exhibit 6-6. The process flow model, including each of the stages within the model, will be described later.

Project Planning

The efficiency and success of each of the projects within the program will depend upon the planning that takes place well before the project process commences. Several tools have been developed, to aid in the planning process, including:

- Milestone chronology
- Process outline
- Timetable of events

EXHIBIT 6-6

Practice Acquisition/Valuation Process Flow Model

SUSPECTS
Possible candidates for acquisition submitted by field staff or developed from comprehensive database.

Preliminary screening as to location, site, services

PROSPECTS
Possible candidates for acquisition selected for further review.

Secondary screening through selection matrix.

TARGETS
Selected candidates for acquisition.

- Intensive due diligence
- Analysis of data
- Valuation

DEALS

- Regulatory review
- Remove contingencies
- CLOSING

AFFILIATES

These tools are used in sequential order. While the scope of the planning process remains the same, the specific tasks become more detailed as the process moves forward.

Establishing a Program Milestone Chronology. The planning and implementation of the program, in most cases, involves many individuals accomplishing numerous specific tasks along the way, all in an attempt to make progress toward a common goal. Using milestones offers advantages to the implementation process by motivating the participants to accomplish certain groups of specific tasks. A milestone chronology is a graphic portrayal of the progress the project has made to date and the remaining steps that need to be taken in order to complete the project. Success and motivation are enhanced as each individual goal/task/ milestone is completed. A sample Milestone Chronology follows.

Phase 1: Preliminary Feasibility Assessment
- Form project team
- Identify "prospects"
- Perform market assessment

Phase 2: Review
- Survey prospects
- Investigate desired services
- Present integration models to prospects

Phase 3: Consensus
- Select targets from prospects
- Determine organizational structure
- Develop package of services
- Prepare operating budget

Phase 4: Implementation
- Close on new entity
- Staff new entity as needed
- Convert to new systems and services (i.e., accounting, MIS, insurance, etc.)

Process Outline. A process outline is a list of selected definable tasks required throughout the implementation of the program, with a column in which to assign these tasks to specific people. A process outline expands on the milestone chronology by delineating specific tasks and assigning them to members of the project team.

Process Outline

Phase	Task	Assigned To:
Phase 1	1. Identify key, influential people (physicians, hospital administrator, chairman of the board, organization's corporate executive, etc.) who share a common goal of an affiliation/integration effort, to form a project team. 2. Provide a copy of the process outline for the integrated organization ("entity") to each project team member. 3. Establish a preliminary working name for the entity. 4. Review and discuss the list of prospective physician participants ("prospects"). 5. Discuss with project team the range of affiliation/integration/association models and alternative organizational structures that may be presented to the prospects.	

Phase 2	6. Discuss with project team and develop the approach to, and solicitation of, prospects.
	7. Survey the prospects to:
	  a. Verify and gauge their level of interest in affiliation/integration/association.
	  b. Measure the group's compatibility as to practice modality and organizational philosophy.
	  c. Determine the degree of participation at which the group would feel comfortable at this point.
	  d. Determine the reasons and rationale for their participation.
	  e. Discern the current areas of consensus and/or disagreement among group members.
	  f. Discuss the extent of each member's participation in, and ownership of, the process.
	8. Request and gather all relevant practice information regarding the prospects.
	9. Project team investigates the desired services of the organization and reports back to the prospects regarding compatible organizational structures for the entity.
	10. Project team provides the prospects with an overview of strengths and weaknesses of the different organizational structures from a legal, regulatory, cost, administrative, and control perspectives.	

Phase 3	11. Targets are selected from prospects, based on all gathered practice information. 12. Project team investigates the chosen services, develops costs and cost savings alternatives, and reports back to the targets. 13. The project team, with feedback from the member physicians, develops a more defined package of services to be provided. 14. An implementation plan is developed whereby time frames for the action items, operating budget, and personnel decisions will be determined.	

Process Outline—Continued

Phase	Task	Assigned To:
Phase 3	15. The project team, with input from all members, will select the preliminary services to be combined or provided by the entity. These services may include, but not be limited to: a. Integrated billing and claims resolution b. Managed care contracting c. Integrated information/accounting system d. Management consulting e. Malpractice insurance f. Utilization review/quality assurance g. Group health insurance h. Marketing/public relations i. Pension plans j. Administer Continuing Medical Education (CME) k. Payroll and personnel functions l. Supply ordering m. Quality improvement n. Practice development o. Physician and allied/paraprofessional recruitment 16. The project team reports back to the entire organization of physician participants and requests final approval as to the services to be offered and the organizational structure of the entity. 17. The project team develops an operating budget for the organization with consideration given to all costs associated with the provision of the defined services. Develop a consensus regarding the allocation of the costs to the individual participants. 18. Propose a schedule of required capitalization, with appropriate pro forma cash flow projections, to ensure adequate funding and viability of planned development. 19. The project team recommends a policy regarding the inclusion of additional members and expansion of affiliations/associateship opportunities to the entire organization of physician participants. 20. The project team reports back to the entire organization of physician participants for final approval of the implementation plan, operating budget, allocation of costs, investment schedule, and other related topics. The team then requests approval of the entire group to proceed with implementation. 21. The project team, with the assistance of legal counsel, proceeds with the formation of the new legal entity.	
Phase 4	22. Commence implementation of plan. 23. Arrange periodic meetings to evaluate progress of plan.	

Timetable of Events. The timetable of events is simply an extension of the process outline with specific times stated for completion of specific tasks, as well as estimated dates of completion. A timetable of events breaks down the process outline further into smaller, measurable, accomplishable tasks. A "Task Assigned To" column may also be helpful in tracking progress on individual tasks. A sample timetable of events for Phase 2 is illustrated in the following table.

Timetable of Events

Event/Task Description	Estimated Time Required	Approximate Date of Completion	Task Assigned To
Conference call to review approach to physicians.			
Send letter to prospective physician participants ("prospects").			
Make follow-up calls to prospects, schedule interviews.			
Conduct initial interviews on-site, request initial documents.			
Conference call to provide update of prospects' interviews/surveys.			
Collect and review data received.*			
Complete second phase of interviews (as needed).**			
Conference call to reevaluate original goals and objectives based on documentation analysis and prospects' interviews.**			
Conference call or general meeting to present advantages/disadvantages and options of services offered through the new entity.**			
Determine level of integration, types of services offered, organizational structure, and governance of the new entity.**			
Develop projections of costs and revenues associated with the new entity.*			
Project team reports proposed structure and service offering of new entity to entire group.*			
Project team develops preliminary list of legal and regulatory concerns to discuss with legal counsel.			

*Contingent upon level of physician cooperation.
**Includes preparation and analysis required to conduct meeting or conference call.

INTEGRATION/AFFILIATION MODELS

Determining the Appropriate Integration/Affiliation Model

The process of determining the appropriate physician integration/ affiliation model is very similar to the process described in the previous chapter on EHO start-up consulting, with a different set of selection considerations depending on the hospital's, health system's, or EHO's strategic goals in acquiring or affiliating with physicians. This selection process is paramount to the overall success of the program.

Integration projects are a strategic plan designed to enhance an organization's competitive advantage in the marketplace. The advantages sought depend on the organization seeking to acquire or affiliate with practices and may include the following.

For Hospitals and Health Systems
- Strengthening of relations with the physician community
- Vertical integration to allow for managed care contracting for a greater range of services

For Existing EHOs and Physician Sponsored Organizations (PSOs)
- Horizontal integration to increase market share
- Expansion of specialty coverage to improve ability to accept capitated contracts
- Building of critical mass to obtain financing for management information systems (MIS), building services, etc.
- Achievement of economies of scale through group purchasing, shared equipment and facilities, and improved centralized management

Recognize that for each project within the program, different models will provide a better fit depending on several key factors. Some of the key factors to consider when determining the appropriate physician integration/affiliation model are listed below. These factors are the same as those that need to be analyzed when planning an EHO start-up project but, again, must be evaluated based on the strategic goals of the organization. This type of research should be completed during the first two phases of the physician integration/affiliation process.

Managed Care Penetration. The analysis of the managed care penetration in the market in which the specific project competes is generally very descriptive of the level of competition for enrolled lives and managed care contracts. When assessing this statistic, it is important to understand that the greater the percentage of the population that is covered under a managed care plan, the higher the degree of integration that should be considered in an EHO model in order for it to be able to effectively negotiate for managed care contracts in the market. Managed Care Organizations (MCOs) are further discussed later in this chapter. A "Managed Care Organization/Insurance Worksheet" is provided in Appendix 6.

Level of Consolidation. The level of consolidation is another general market characteristic that should be researched during the first two phases of the project in order to narrow down the potential physician integration/affiliation models under consideration. The level of consolidation should include both hospital/health-system consolidation and physician practice consolidation. Physicians have historically tended to resist the loss of autonomy involved in integration. In less consolidated or integrated markets, organizations may initially need to consider a less integrated model.

Autonomy/Leverage. For physicians forming an EHO or considering integrating with a hospital, health system, or existing EHO, the degree of practice autonomy they are willing to abdicate in return for practice leverage is a critical factor. Assessment of this factor will help determine the appropriate physician integration/affiliation model to use in each market and project. Interviews are one method of obtaining direct feedback from physicians as to their willingness to relinquish some measure of practice autonomy in return for leverage in the market. Exhibit 6-7 illustrates a continuum of the physician integration/affiliation models in relation to the degree of autonomy and leverage inherent in each model.

Consensus Building. The third phase of the physician integration process, consensus, can only be effectively completed if the prospective participants have been well educated about the variations among each of the potential integration/affiliation models. In the consensus phase it is important to get the prospects to take the biggest bite they can swallow out of the integration apple. Less integrated organizations such as IPAs and PHOs haven't been as successful, financially or otherwise, as more integrated models such as MSOs and FIMGs in large part because they involve smaller financial contributions and less shared economic risk. Shared economic risk aligns the goals of the various participants and is a powerful means of maintaining organizational consensus.

Potential Physician Integration/Affiliation Models

Following is a brief discussion of potential physician integration/affiliation (or EHO) models that describes the selection considerations

EXHIBIT 6-7

Evolution and Continuum of Physician Integration

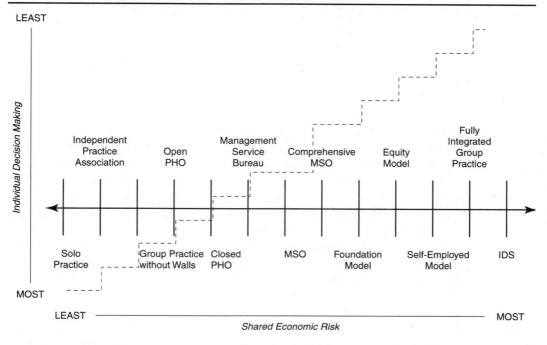

for hospitals, health systems, and EHOs seeking to form a new organization of integrated physician practices. This portion of the chapter is not pertinent to existing EHOs seeking to use the acquisition/affiliation program as a guide to recruiting physicians into the existing organization. Each of the models may be modified to fit the context of the specific project being developed.

Independent Practice Association (IPA) Model. Independent Practice Associations (IPAs) were described in Chapter 3 as a means of enhancing managed care contracting for physician practices without structurally integrating their practices. However, the model is somewhat malleable, and various levels of operational integration can occur in an IPA. These services include contract and price negotiation billing and collections, utilization management, quality assurance, general marketing, bookkeeping, tax services, and other business services relating to the IPA.

IPAs, as loosely integrated organizations, are more appropriate for less integrated or more rural markets where they may fit in with the competitive level of the market. Their benefits may be marginal, but they can act as a stepping-stone to further integration with other providers through internal organizational evolution. Hospitals, health systems, or existing EHOs may affiliate in various ways with IPAs to improve their own contracting ability or as a preliminary stage in eventual greater integration. Established IPAs may also be considered potential affiliation prospects and should be identified in the research phase of the program. However, it should be noted that the IPA may stand to benefit most from such an arrangement.

Physician Hospital Organization (PHO) Model. A Physician Hospital Organization (PHO) is a legal entity formed by a hospital and a group of physicians and as such is not a vehicle for other established EHOs to integrate with physician practices. This is not to say that some types of EHOs may not negotiate with hospitals to form PHOs.

The main goal with this type of organization is, once again, to gain greater managed care contract negotiation leverage, but here the EHO model is vertically integrated. PHOs have been a popular means for hospitals to integrate with physicians. Often, however, in retrospect, they have not been as popular with the physicians involved due to their lack of control within the organization and only moderate contracting benefit. Some PHOs offer various practice-management services, but generally these have not been effectively managed. Hospital management is very different from physician practice management, and hospital-provided management services have a poor track record. As an indicator of this lack of management ability, hospital acquisitions of physician practices have consistently resulted in losses of large sums of money for hospitals across the country. Since 1994, hospitals have acquired the practices of 5,000 primary care physicians per year on average.[3] A recent survey of 17 hospitals by Coopers & Lybrand found that hospitals were incurring average annual losses of $97,000 per acquired physician.[4] Another survey developed a model to forecast profits per physician during the first year after acquisition. Whereas medical groups and PPMCs' profits per physician were both forecast to be just over $20,000, hospitals were forecast to lose over $11,000 per physician.[5] The reasons for this include payment of inflated acquisition prices, poor production due to compensation of physicians on an employed basis, and poor man-

---

[3]"Hospitals That Gobbled Up Physician Practices Feel Ill." *Wall Street Journal*, June 17, 1997, p. B-4.

[4]Ibid.

[5]William O. Cleverly, et al. *The 1997–98 Physician Practice Acquisition Resource Book.* The Center for Healthcare Industry Performance Studies, 1997, p. 4.

agement by inexperienced hospitals. Many PHOs, however, leave the management of practices to the physicians. This arrangement results in less control over the practices and means that hospitals have little ability to control physician utilization of resources and thus to achieve true integration.

PHO strengths include the fact that physicians retain autonomy because of minimal changes in practice locations and ownership. Also, PHOs lower political risks due to the acceptance of IPAs and shared control. Lastly, PHOs provide the vehicle to initially organize a medical staff dominated by solo partnerships and small groups.

On the other hand, PHOs offer minimal ability to influence utilization behavior, and make it difficult to obtain authority to contractually obligate individual physician members.

Group Practice without Walls (GPWW) Model. Group Practices without Walls (GPWWs) are an intermediate model between IPAs and MSOs on the autonomy/leverage continuum. The practices are treated as individual profit centers with doctors retaining some autonomy, including the right to see private patients, manage employees, maintain scheduling, and determine where to refer patients for the best care. The central administrative office provides purchasing, personnel, billing, collections, negotiation of managed care contracts, and other administrative services. The degree of integration of this alliance model depends on how much control physicians may wish to transfer to central management and the relationship that is established with the central company.

As an intermediary model, GPWWs may be an appropriate organizational form in some developing markets, although weak links between physicians and the central company and lack of control over geographically separated practices can reduce contracting effectiveness as markets become more competitive.

Management Services Bureau (MSB) Model (Less Comprehensive). A Management Services Bureau (MSB) is an effective means of forming an initial alliance among or between hospitals and physicians who are not presently willing to relinquish any control over ownership of their practices. The MSB is an organized, focused effort to attract primary care physicians to a hospital and to strengthen the alliance over time, with the long-term goal of creating a more structured, mutually bonding relationship. The MSB is a less comprehensive version of an MSO. In the MSB version of the MSO, the physicians remain separate, independent legal entities that contract for services from the bureau at fair market value. The physician groups have significant input into the bureau via an advisory board.

Program services might include:

- Practice assessments
- Billing and collections support
- Group purchasing agreements
- Practice marketing support
- Third-party payor contract analysis, negotiation, and management
- Physician referral services
- MIS development
- Office staff recruitment and personnel management
- Financing
- Facilities development
- Medicare RBRVS payment review

As a result of the flexible, independent nature of the MSB, it does not closely tie the physicians to the hospital. The model is less effective than MSOs, IPAs, PHOs, or GPWWs at competing for managed care contracts in highly competitive markets. Since there is little shared risk, there is less shared incentive for overall success and pursuit of common goals. All transactions and exchanges between physicians and the hospital must be at arm's length.

Whether the specific MSB service is provided via outsourcing, subcontracting, or by the hospital directly, it is assumed that the charge to the physician will cover the direct cost of providing the service to the physician. In addition to the direct, recoverable costs, there are some non-recoverable costs to consider. The projected dollar amount for each category represents costs in addition to the hospital's administrative staff time invested in the process.

Management Services Organization (MSO) Model (More Comprehensive). A Management Services Organization (MSO) is a legal entity that provides administrative and practice management services to a physician entity (MD group) that is owned by participating physicians and that contracts with the MSO for services. "MSO" generally refers to the organization that provides administrative, management, and support services to individual physicians and/or group practices. An MSO does not provide clinical services, and physicians retain their own provider numbers. As a separate legal organization, an affiliated MSO provides an additional layer between the affiliating organization and physicians and can provide hospitals a means of organizing physicians outside of the traditional medical staff structure, and perhaps in outlying regions served by smaller hospitals. An MSO may become a significant mechanism for providing assistance to private-practice physicians wishing to organize into group practices having one or more sites in the defined primary, secondary, and outlying service areas.

Significant capital may be required to create an MSO, including legal and consulting fees. The capital necessary for the MD group would be relatively small in the case of association of an existing group practice; however, the amount of capital needed increases when a number of individual practices merge, including costs incurred for practice assessments and valuations of the practices being acquired. The operating expenses vary in proportion to the size of the group practice under management.

MSOs avoid licensing requirements because they are not engaged in the practice of medicine. They are flexible because they can provide services to individual practitioners, an IPA, or group practices, and adaptable because over time they can evolve in several directions depending on market conditions.

On the other hand, MSOs don't closely link the incentives for physicians with those of the company. They're less able than more integrated organizations to compete for managed care contracts in highly competitive markets, they offer little shared risk, and all transactions between physicians and the company must be at arm's length.

Fully Integrated Medical Group (FIMG) (Equity) Model. A Fully Integrated Medical Group (FIMG) is a medical group practice with centralized governance and management that exercises strong authority over its business and clinical operations. FIMGs have fully unified administrative, business, and clinical systems, and distribute income among physicians through a single compensation system that rewards behavior that furthers the group. Physicians in FIMGs can suffer the disadvantage of the loss of their individual autonomy.

The organizational costs for FIMGs can be high as MIS, operational systems, and new management personnel and staff are added. These development costs can reduce physician income unless outside sources of capital are available. Also, if the compensation system is not designed to reward individual effort, physicians may also lose the incentive to perform at their highest levels.

Integrated Delivery System (IDS) Model. An Integrated Health System (IHS) or Integrated Delivery System (IDS) is a group of legally affiliated organizations in which hospitals and physicians combine their assets, efforts, risks, and rewards, and through which they deliver comprehensive healthcare services to the community. The economic interests of the participants are unified, as they do not maintain separate businesses in competition with each other.

If hospitals seek to establish an entity model IHO with physicians (where physicians share ownership with the hospital), the hospital holding company may lease or otherwise transfer its assets to the IHO, while a physician group may transfer all of its assets (mostly, the physician practices) to the IHO. The IHO would operate all hospital and physician services, and would distribute profits from those operations to the physician organization and hospital holding company in proportion to the capital interests of each party.

This model seeks to align the incentives of both the hospital and physicians. Unlike the PHO, integration is effective for all operations, not just managed care contracts negotiated by the PHO. The hospital holding company could be established as a partnership that distributes income to its hospitals without requiring them to surrender their respective missions, or, as a corporation's physicians become increasingly important in the healthcare delivery system, it might become simlarly important that they have an equal stake in the IHO with hospitals.[6]

IMPLEMENTATION OF PROGRAM

Designated Market Assessment

As with a start-up EHO, the geographic market in which the program sponsor operates and draws its patients must be thoroughly researched. Many of these research topics were discussed in Chapter 5. A number of additional research topics follow that are specifically pertinent to an affiliation/acquisition program.

Major Employers. The market assessment should include an analysis of the major employers and their current insurance plans. Refer to the "Major Employer Worksheet" found in Appendix 5 for a guide to this analysis.

Utilization Demand Review. Utilization demand review (UDR) is an essential component of a designated market assessment. There are a number of methodologies and sources of data that can be used to prepare a comprehensive market assessment. The nature of the project within

---

[6]Gerald R. Peters. *Healthcare Integration: A Legal Manual for Constructing Integrated Organizations.* National Health Lawyers Association, 1995, p. 399.

the program will dictate the appropriate methodologies and data sources to employ. UDR can be segregated into numerous classes. A common method of analyzing utilization rates is to disaggregate inpatient services from outpatient and physician services.

Inpatient Services. Analysis of inpatient services is a useful method of determining whether a facility has a surplus or an insufficient supply of a given service relative to the demand in the market. Two methods of analyzing inpatient utilization rates are Major Diagnostic Category (MDC) and Diagnosis Related Groups (DRG).

Major Diagnostic Category (MDC). Medicare Part A recognizes 23 Major Diagnostic Categories of inpatient services. Utilization demand review by MDC is a common method hospitals use to track services by specialty. MDC data may be analyzed and measured using a range of criteria (patient days, discharges/admissions, gross receipts). An MDC utilization demand report, "Analysis of Cases by Medical Specialty of Provider and MDC," illustrates the percentage of total cases attributable to both MDC and medical specialty. Hospitals and health systems can compare their MDC utilization rates to national averages based on facility size, ownership, or geographic location. Refer to "Analysis of Cases by Medical Specialty of Provider and Major Diagnostic Category (MDC)" in Appendix 1.

Diagnosis Related Groups (DRGs). Diagnosis Related Groups (DRGs) were implemented by the government on October 1, 1983, as a method for the Medicare Hospital Prospective Payment System to classify cases for payment. Presently, there are 477 DRGs and the number continues to increase. Utilization demand review using DRGs is similar to that using MDCs, although there are substantially more categories. A sample DRG utilization demand report, "Analysis of DRG Demand by MDC Summary Report," may be found in Appendix 2.

Outpatient/Physician Services. Outpatient services are among the fastest growing sector of the healthcare industry. Utilization demand review for outpatient services should be included during the implementation phase of the program. When conducting due diligence and data analysis during any component project within the program, outpatient/ physician services should be analyzed.

Current Procedural Terminology (CPT). Current Procedural Terminology (CPT) is a system of codes and descriptions published annually by the American Medical Association since 1966. The CPT coding system is required by the Medicare and Medicaid programs and is accepted by virtually all commercial insurance carriers. Two of the most common methods of utilization demand analysis for outpatient/physician services are by (1) CPT code and (2) cost & production.

Economic Environment. Refer to the "Economic Environment Worksheet," found in Appendix 7, for a brief list of economic factors to consider when assessing the economic environment. Used in conjunction with the "Employer Worksheet" found in Appendix 5, it can be a useful tool in analyzing the economic environment in which the organization will operate and compete.

Assessment of Physician Providers in the Area

There are many ways to approach the assessment of physician providers in a given market. The goal is to identify the physician providers within the primary service area in a manner that will facilitate ease of classification and evaluation through the later use of established selection criteria. One proven method begins with a broad "suspects" stage, progresses through intermediate stages that funnel the database of prospective physician providers or groups through a selection-narrowing process, and culminates in the final "affiliates" stage.

Suspects Stage. The suspects stage, which is very broad in scope, is the process by which planners identify physician practices and collect information to create prospects for the program. The suspects stage begins with determination of the minimum preliminary criteria the project team requires for a practice to become a prospect (e.g., group of three or more physicians, specific geographic market, primary care, physician-owned, etc.). The next step is creation of a database identifying all candidate practices within each chosen market. Information needed to convert the suspects into prospects (e.g., size of group, location, site, specialties, services, ownership, etc.) can be obtained through public means including directories, electronic databases, publications, etc., or from the individual practices themselves. This information is then organized in a format (datasheets, tables, etc.) in which the program administrator can screen the suspects and determine if they qualify for the prospects stage.

Prospects Stage. Although the consideration of physicians and practices is a subjective endeavor, it is useful to develop a methodology that enhances the objective aspects of the process of considering and selecting specific physicians and practices to approach for participation in the project. Selection criteria may include:

- Location and proximity of practice to the organization
- Loyalty factor and admissions relationship with area hospitals
- Physician reputation and qualifications
- Physician quality improvement and utilization review factors
- Pattern of referrals to physician specialists
- Managed care payor relationships and plan participation
- Practice life cycle
- Receptiveness of physician to program
- Practice patient volume and financial viability

In addition to the above criteria, other considerations (for the purposes of this report, "political considerations") should be taken into account, including the relationship of the targeted physicians and practices to competing institutions, which other hospitals are competing for the targeted physicians and practices, internal medical staff concerns, and, in the case of group practices, the group cohesiveness factor (i.e., will the group act as a unit or will individual physicians be willing to split off to affiliate with the organization?).

A selection matrix rating system may be developed to permit the comparison of physicians or practices under consideration for the project. A sample of the selection matrix rating system worksheet follows, and is provided in the Appendices as a worksheet. Again, this methodology is simply a tool to enhance the objective assessment of what is, in many respects, a subjective process that will require the judgment and expertise of the project team and their advisors on-site.

After considering and selecting specific practices, planners may prepare financial analysis and post-transaction projections on a case-by-case basis. In those cases where practice assets will be acquired, outside qualified valuation experts may prepare valuation reports to determine the fair market value of the assets. These reports should be prepared in accordance with the Uniform Standards of Professional Appraisal Practice (USPAP) under U.S. Title XI, and should meet the recognized standards of the appraisal profession.

Some of the individual tasks related to the prospects phase are as follows.

1. Develop a selection matrix utilizing appropriate selection criteria.
2. Use the selection matrix to conduct secondary screening of prospects and refine the database to include only prospects.
3. Initiate contact with each prospect via mail.

4. Use the customized questionnaire to determine prospect physician's potential interest in affiliation/integration.

5. Distribute initial requests for production of documents, questionnaires, surveys, etc.

6. Evaluate prospects and identify potential leaders and project team members.

7. Add physicians to project team (refer to the following detailed discussion under "Project Team Selection and Formation").

8. Steering committee decides which model and/or level of integration will be implemented.

9. Develop the approach that will be taken with all prospects.

10. Delegate tasks. (Who will approach whom?)

Selection Rating System Matrix

| Rating | Rating Points | | | | |
| | (1 = Least Favorable, 5 = Most Favorable) | | | | |
Criteria	1	2	3	4	5
Location and proximity of practice to the organization					
Loyalty factor and admissions relationship with area hospitals					
Physician population qualifications (e.g., board certification)					
Physician quality assurance and utilization review factors					
Pattern of referral to physician specialists					
Managed care payor relationships and plan participation					
Practice life cycle					
Receptiveness of physician to program					
Practice patient volume and financial viability					
RATING SUBTOTALS					
TOTAL SCORE					

Project Team Selection and Formation

The purpose of forming a project team is to gather a group of individuals who are willing to work together to achieve the stated mission and goals of the project. When selecting individuals to participate as project team members it is important to look for the following essential characteristics.

- Belief in the "dogma" behind the project
- Willingness to put forth the time required (i.e., evenings, weekends, and hours during the workday)
- Leadership skills
- Strong reputation within the community
- Ability to remain flexible and consider many options and alternatives
- Effective communication skills

The project team should be structured in a manner that gives representation to all stakeholders. It is important to ensure that there is an appropriate mix of primary care physicians, specialists, and nonphysician providers. There should also be representatives of both parties in a joint venture engagement (organization and physician representatives) to ensure that the process develops in a mutually beneficial manner. It may also be useful to include an independent, third-party representative to serve as a facilitator or intermediary and provide past experience to the project.

Determination of, and Consensus on, Integration Model to Be Utilized

Once the project team has been educated regarding the pros and cons of the different integration models, the team must focus on those models which roughly meet their integration goals. This subset of the EHO models should then be presented to the program-development committee. A model must then be selected based on numerous factors including available funds and financing, the ability of the sponsoring organization to provide specific practice management and other services, the level of competition and integration in the local market, and others. However the central considerations are the degree of autonomy desired and the willingness of the participants to share economic risk.

Approach to Prospective Physician Providers

In preparing to approach those physicians and practices it has identified as targets of opportunity, the project team may choose to articulate several strategic points that it will stress in order to distinguish its own integration/affiliation efforts from competitors' and encourage physicians to consider the program. These points include a personal approach to physician relationships, the financial stability and long-term viability of the program and organization, an opportunity and invitation to participate in a provider system that will help steer the way through the vagaries of healthcare reform, the organization's willingness to maintain flexibility in its relationship with physicians in order to meet the individual physician's or practice's needs, the excellent match of existing and planned services to physician requirements, and the organization's ability to successfully manage acquired practices.

Targets Stage

Next the project team conducts an in-depth survey of the practices that qualify as prospects, given the criteria in the selection rating system matrix, in order to:

- Verify and gauge their level of interest in affiliation/integration/ association.
- Measure the group's compatibility as to practice modality and philosophy.
- Determine the degree of participation at which the group would feel comfortable at this point.
- Determine their reasons and rationale for participating.
- Discern the current areas of consensus and/or disagreement among group members.
- Discuss the level of each member's participation in, and ownership of, the integration/affiliation process.

The prospects that meet all of the qualifications become target practices. The project team then performs due diligence and analysis of data. Valuation of practices and/or assets may be necessary, given the integration model selected. Some of the tools of the targets stage include valuation calculations, follow-up requests for production of documents, site visits, interviews, and confidentiality/standstill agreements.

Deals Stage

The deals stage of the program is the point where professional advisors memorialize the planning process, consensus-building process, and negotiated details. Depending on the individual project within the program, the deals stage could be limited to development of an employment agreement and, if appropriate, an asset purchase agreement. In a project where a new entity will be formed, the closing checklist may be similar to the following.

Closing Checklist

1. Formation of new entity
   - Organization documents
     - Articles of organization/incorporation
     - Operating agreement/bylaws
       a. List of members/shareholders
       b. Articles of organization/incorporation
       c. Allocations, distributions
       d. Form of service agreement
     - Good standing certificate issued by appropriate secretary of state
     - Initial consent of members/shareholders
     - Initial consent of board of managers/directors
   - Third-party agreements
     - Management services agreement between new entity and each member/shareholder
     - Provider services agreements between new entity and each member/shareholder and physician/provider
     - Shareholder agreements among Incorporated Practice A
     - Shareholder agreements among Incorporated Practice B
     - Physician employment agreements between new entity and employed physicians
     - Independent contractor agreements between new entity and independent contractors
     - Antitrust compliance policy executed by all entities and providers
2. Acquisition of assets
   - Medical Practice XYZ
     - Asset purchase agreement by and between new entity and Medical Practice XYZ
       a. Schedule 1: Assets
       b. Schedule 2: Purchase price
       c. Schedule 3: Insurance
       d. Schedule 4: Litigation
       e. Schedule 5: Intangible property

f. Schedule 6: Contracts and other agreements

    g. Schedule 7: Personnel

    h. Exhibit A: Bill of sale

- Bill of sale
  - Assignment and assumption agreement
  - Assignment of lease
  - Equipment lease
  - Uniform commercial code search results
  - Authorizing resolutions of Practice A
  - Certified articles of incorporation of Practice A
  - Good standing certificate of Practice A
  - Authorizing resolutions of new entity
  - Termination of pension plan
  - UCC termination statements
  - Appraisal

Regulatory Issues

The deals stage must include an exhaustive review of all pertinent regulatory matters. Many of the complex regulatory issues relating to the integration, consolidation, and acquisition of healthcare entities were discussed in Chapters 2 and 5. However, the following issues may be especially pertinent to healthcare entity transactions and bear further discussion.

Fraud and Abuse. There are numerous fraud and abuse laws that are relevant to acquisitions, affiliations, mergers, and other business alliances between healthcare organizations and physicians. The following points are of note.

Hospital Incentives to Physicians The Office of the Inspector General (OIG) of the U.S. Department of Health and Human Services has issued a Special Fraud Alert regarding the offering of financial incentives in the recruiting and retention of physicians by hospitals and other healthcare facilities. Just as these organizations cannot pay for referrals from physicians, a number of other incentives are considered suspect as disguised or indirect payment for referrals. These include below-cost or free office space, equipment, or billing services; low-interest loans; significantly discounted group insurance rates; income guarantees; and others. The IRS also addressed the issue of hospital recruiting incentives to physicians in its closing agreement with Hermann Hospital, October 14, 1994. In this case, the issue was that physician incentives constituted inurement of private benefit from a tax-exempt entity; thus, the entity's tax-exempt status was endangered. The physician recruitment incentives deemed allowable by the IRS mirror those detailed in the OIG's Special Fraud Alert but in this case the hospital had to demonstrate that there was a community need for the physician before any recruiting would be allowed.

The Thornton Letter   Thornton stated, in this interpretation of the Stark laws, that any amounts paid to MDs in excess of the fair market value of practice's hard assets are suspect and could be considered improper inducement for referrals.

The Thornton letter does not affect practice acquisitions by fully integrated and capitated organizations, and does not affect practice sales from physician to physician that are permitted under safe harbor rules issued by OIG in 1991.

Self-Referral Prohibitions (Stark I & II)   The Stark I and Stark II laws prohibit physicians from referring Medicare patients to a laboratory or other "designated services" if the physician or a member of his/her immediate family have any financial interest in the referred facility. These designated services include physical and occupational therapy; radiology (including MRI, CT, and ultrasound); radiation therapy and supplies; durable medical equipment and supplies; parenteral and enteral nutrients, equipment, and supplies; prosthetics, orthotics, and prosthetic devices and supplies; inpatient and outpatient hospital services; home health services; and outpatient prescription drugs.

Corporate Practice of Medicine   Various state licensing statutes prohibit the practice of medicine by entities or individuals other than licensed professionals. These can forbid ownership of medical practices by healthcare organizations.

State Licensure   All states require licensure for most healthcare entities and the majority of states have Certificate of Need (CON) laws in effect where new facilities must be approved by the state based on a determination of need within the state or community.

ERISA Issues   There is a complicated framework of issues pertaining to the inclusion of physicians and employees within the hospital's pension and benefit plans.

Antitrust Compliance The federal antitrust laws are especially pertinent to acquisition and affiliation projects that increase the market share of any organization. Anticompetitive or collusive agreements between groups of competitors and monopolistic practices by a single entity are examples of potential violations of these laws. It is essential to have an experienced healthcare attorney review any acquisition or affiliation project plan to determine if any potential antitrust issues may be involved.

Affiliates Stage/Post-Acquisition Considerations

The affiliates stage is the final stage in the process flow model. In this stage, the physicians/practices have been acquired or have affiliated. Even though the acquisition/affiliation has already taken place, there are still many issues to resolve. These issues are much the same as those that new EHOs face at this stage and that were discussed in Chapter 5. They may include some or all of the following: income distribution and compensation plans, use of centralized services, management information systems (MIS), "right-sizing" the organization, transfer/closure of pension plans, and managed care contracting.

Income Distribution Plan and Incentive Packages. When implementing the program, the project team should take care in structuring the income distribution plan and incentive/benefits package. For those physicians whose practices are acquired, the compensation plan offered will provide a competitive base salary, with an incentive-based productivity component for overall compensation.

Axioms of Compensation
- People do what they have incentive to do.
- Doctors are bright people.
- Make sure the behaviors you motivate are those you want.

Key attributes for the design of a good compensation plan include:

- Simplicity (ability to be understood by all parties)
- Fairness/equivalent unfairness
- Recognition of biases
- Compensation in accordance with the way dollars flow into the corporation
- Reward for productive and profitable behavior

Managed Care/Prepaid Income. The distribution of fee-for-service revenue is relatively simple because physician productivity can be directly tied to revenue. Capitation dollars are not as easy to distribute. There are four basic options one must consider in designing a distribution plan for capitation dollars (see table). All four have strengths and weaknesses. For example, option D will have the greatest impact on costs, but is difficult to implement or get PCPs and specialists to agree upon rates for. Option A is easy to implement because of the way physicians are used to being paid, but it has little to no effect on costs.

CAPITATION INCOME DISTRIBUTION PLAN OPTIONS

Specialist

		Fee-for-Service	Capitation
Primary Care	**Fee-for-Service**	A	B
	Capitation	C	D

Incentives   It is essential that the compensation and income distribution plans have an incentive component that correlates compensation to production, thereby fostering a risk-sharing arrangement that will motivate all parties to achieve common, mutually beneficial goals. It is also important that the incentives reward the desired behavior.

Cost Accounting   Actual practice costs must be identified in order to determine funds available for distribution to the physicians. Management information systems (MIS) play an important role in this function. To compensate physicians by the number of patients seen or number of procedures performed would be self-defeating in a capitated environment, because the physician incentives would be contrary to the organization's incentives. In this instance, a cost-accounting methodology could be a viable alternative. This would entail allocating to each individual physician all revenues received and all expenses incurred in relation to the services provided. Under this arrangement the physician would receive a guaranteed amount of historical earnings and make more money for performing at the same level of productivity as in prior periods. While this methodology can be difficult to institute and requires strong management skills and an integrated information system, it strengthens the partnership between the organization and the individual physician, allows for the transition to the managed care environment by providing the ability to measure performance under current agreements, and bolsters the organization's bargaining power in negotiating future managed care agreements.

Common Types of Plans   Common plan types include the following.

- Straight salary
- Straight productivity
- Salary plus incentives
- Incentive/benefits package: A compensation and income distribution plan should also give consideration to an incentive/benefits package that a larger organization may offer but that is not economically feasible for a sole proprietorship, for example:
  - Insurance: health and professional liability
  - Pension plan
  - CME allowance
  - Deferred compensation
  - Vacation, leave time

Critical Success Factors   The plan must be developed in collaboration with management and physicians. Also, money is a touchy subject; diplomacy on the part of all parties is necessary.

Potential Pitfalls   Straight productivity is incompatible with capitation. High productivity will enhance earnings for a practice with traditional fee-for-service patients; the exact opposite is true with capitated patients. Other potential pitfalls include the self-referral prohibitions (Stark I and II) discussed earlier. Parts of some productivity compensation plans are illegal for Medicaid and Medicare patients.

Considerations for Compensation Plans   Please refer to the "Analysis of Compensation Package" in Appendix 15, which illustrates a comprehensive analysis of a compensation package that may be offered to an affiliate. Considerations for plans include:

- Base salary
- Insurance: health and professional liability
- Pension plan
- Incentive compensation
- CME allowance
- Deferred compensation
- Purchase price of practice
- Tangible assets
- Intangible assets
- Covenant not to compete
- Vacation, leave time
- Indemnification
- Termination clause

The program-development committee and project team should draw upon their past experience in acquiring and managing practices, as well as in the administration of its current quality-improvement program, in addressing whatever malpractice and vicarious liability issues may arise during the program's implementation.

Centralized Services.   The scope of services offered to affiliates will vary depending on the specialty and current situation (practice life cycle, employees, managed care influences) of the affiliate, the resources of the practice and project team (financial, technical, and staffing), and the nature of the integration model used.

Once again, the first step in this process is to assess what services the practice currently receives and whether they are provided internally or outsourced. A range of current and prospective services should be made available to physicians who wish to affiliate with or enhance their current affiliation with the organization, but whose practices are not acquired. A list of services or tasks to be provided will allow for comparison of the relative advantages and disadvantages of the available options. A "Summary of Practice Services Worksheet" is found in Appendix 27. Most of these services or tasks can be delivered to the affiliates by maintaining the arrangement of the practices, internally centralizing the services, or centralizing the services through outsourcing.

Billing/Collections and Claims Resolution Services

	Description	Advantages	Disadvantages
Option 1	Maintain the Status Quo	1. No staff disruption 2. No implementation required	1. Fragmented data sources 2. Not managed care–friendly to customers with billing inquiries
Option 2	Internally centralize the services.	1. Centralized site improving customer satisfaction 2. Control over types of reports generated 3. Consolidated data enabling easier managed care contracting	1. Capital-intensive and time-consuming to implement 2. Staff disruption/potential reductions
Option 3	Externally centralize the services.	1. Less initial capital required than Option 2 2. Consolidated data enabling easier managed care contracting 3. Quick and easy implementation	1. Less control/flexibility of reports generated 2. Staff disruption/potential reductions

Centralizing service offerings can cause a variety of legal, political, and personal issues to arise and should be undertaken in a careful, planned manner.

The range of services affiliates may be offered will depend on the organization's capabilities and experience. Refer to Chapter 5 for a list of potential services to be offered.

A range of other important issues are involved in the implementation phase, including those relating to MIS, right-sizing the organization, the transfer or closure of pension plans, and managed care contracting. These issues were discussed in detail in conjunction with EHO start-up projects in Chapter 5.

CONCLUSIONS AND RECOMMENDATIONS

Prior to implementing the program, the organization should examine it in the context of the ongoing sea change in the healthcare industry. Increasing consumer demands and an ever-changing reimbursement structure are forcing all providers in the healthcare industry to operate within the bounds of the highly competitive financial and economic realities that have existed in corporate America for decades.

Currently, the healthcare industry is going through the first phase of a major reorganization that can best be characterized as consolidation. Market forces are beginning to squeeze the excess supply of facilities and providers out of the system. As the consolidation continues, organizations should recognize the need to develop an integrated system that can present itself as the low-cost, high-quality provider of a continuum of services in its market.

As the organization develops and adapts its goals, objectives, and vision, it should build the program with enough flexibility to make it transferable to future affiliation projects and, potentially, other markets. The degree of flexibility must be balanced with a detailed, specific agenda that will ensure that defined objectives are accomplished. The program is a considered response to the challenge of physician integration not being an activity that lends itself to ad hoc decision making; it sets in motion a process of predetermined approaches agreed to by all of the stakeholders to enhance the effectiveness of their respective physician integration activities.

Management Status Assessment and Operational Review

This chapter presents a case study of a final report assessing the management performance and services provided by an Emerging Healthcare Organization (EHO). Compiling such a report requires the collection, review, and analysis of both general and specific data obtained through written requests to, and personal interviews with, management and physicians affiliated with the EHO. The EHO model in this case study is a Management Services Organization (MSO) that can be considered a representative provider of many of the types of EHO services.

The purpose of an independent, third-party assessment is to determine the effectiveness of an organization's management and operations and to provide recommendations for improvement. Various elements can serve as the focus of the assessment or may be omitted depending on the specific needs of the organization. However, as operations and management are largely interdependent, the limitations of any analysis should be identified to the client and in the report.

THE PROCESS

The process begins with the development of a consensus with the client on the purpose, scope, approach, methodology, and format of the report. Once the engagement has been defined, the research and data gathering phase starts with the collection of specific data from the client. This provides the consultant with background information on the organization, its staff, and operations. The consultant then collects general research on the local market, competition, and other factors influencing the organization's business operations. Next, preliminary site visits and interviews with management, staff, and providers are conducted. At this point, depending on the scope of the engagement, a preliminary written or verbal report may be made to the client, in part to determine if and how any further data will be obtained. A second set of interviews and data requests may then be made. The consultant then works to complete an analysis of the information gathered and determine recommendations. The preparation and presentation of the final report concludes the engagement. The final report may, however, offer continued services from the consultant relating to further planning or implementation efforts.

MANAGEMENT STATUS ASSESSMENT

The evaluation should utilize a variety of approaches designed to assess different aspects of management including the following.

Strength of Management   Organizations rely on staff with the requisite skills and experience to achieve their mission and strategic goals as well as to effectively manage day-to-day operations.

Governance Structure   An organization's governance determines the framework in which management operates within the organization. The bylaws or operating agreement and other operational charters (i.e., management services agreement, provider services agreement, employment agreements, etc.) as well as the organizational chart should provide such a framework for effective management.

Leadership   Although to a large extent an intangible quality, leadership can nevertheless be readily perceived in managers. Interviews with management and staff can identify leaders and voids in leadership which affect the organization's movement toward its mission. Many times healthcare organizations lack strong leadership among providers (e.g., physicians) despite strong administrative leadership. Leadership must also be present in the organization's provider community if there is to be provider support and unity with the organization's goals.

Communication   An organization's internal and external communications should be analyzed including barriers to communication and the direction and form of communication among staff, levels of management, and departments. The analysis should include utilization of physical and electronic means of communication.

Human Resources Management Human resources are central to the successful operation of any business and should be included in any comprehensive management status assessment. Among the elements of an organization's human resources management which may be assessed are staff orientation and training, recruiting, performance evaluation, compensation, benefits, policies, and motivational techniques.

Strategic Planning Planning methods and means of implementation should be evaluated to determine the efficacy of current strategic planning practices. Appropriate provider involvement includes input from physician and provider leadership without undue succession of control of the planning process to those unfamiliar with business negotiations and strategy. Research methods used to gather supporting data should be reviewed and should include thorough competitor analysis, market demographics, reimbursement trends, and regulatory issues. Although beyond the scope of many management assessments, a brief comment on the appropriateness of overall strategy should be made by describing the market in which the subject organization operates, potential affiliations, and managed care contracting opportunities.

OPERATIONAL REVIEW

Management Services EHOs provide a varying range and level of centralized services. Services provided by the organization should be appropriate for the needs of the market and organization type, current and future provider needs, the experience of the staff, and achieving efficiencies or adding value through centralization. The qualitative and quantifiable benefit of centralizing these services is the central issue in such an evaluation.

Management Information Systems (MIS) The ability to centralize computing resources is potentially one of the main advantages of provider consolidation. It is also one of the frequently mismanaged and inefficient aspects of EHO operations. The goal of MIS should be to improve the quality and quantity of information available to management for decision making as well as to streamline financial and clinical operations. These facets of MIS may be analyzed separately, but modern MIS should integrate these functions. MIS is expensive and cost benefit analysis may be possible concerning improved efficiency of operations based on comparison with historical or benchmark costs.

Financial Management   Assessing an organization's financial management will require the analysis of its financial records but should not be limited to this approach. Financial planning, budgeting, analysis, and reporting may all be viewed as higher level functions that require interaction with management and should be evaluated through interviews with management in conjunction with analysis of these financial reports. The day-to-day functions of financial management such as cash flow, accounts receivable, accounting, billing, and collections must also be reviewed. Managed care contracts place additional requirements on financial management. Capitation requires cost accounting to provide meaningful information to managers negotiating contracts and allocating and controlling costs. Income distribution and transfer payments can also be complex and require sophisticated financial management to effectively distribute earnings.

Thus, the process of conducting a management status assessment and operational review is to gather data on every aspect of an organization through interviews, site visits, and document requests and then to evaluate the effectiveness of its operations and to assess its future plans. The result of this analysis should be a formal report that summarizes the state of the organization as well as the consultant's analysis and recommendations for improvement. The report should serve as both an organizational review and a strategic planning document to allow management to review both their planning methods and their plans.

The MSO in this case study currently provides management services for the primary care physicians employed by the health system. The MSO, with assistance from the health system, provides comprehensive services to a group of employed physicians. At the time of the assessment, the MSO provided turnkey management services to one independent practice. The MSO has shown steady growth since incorporating as a for-profit corporation several years ago.

The health system has recruited a diverse team of individuals with practice-management experience who have been instrumental in developing the infrastructure of the MSO over the past six years. The MSO is generally regarded as having done a good job of providing business office operations for medical practices, but has yet to develop a long-range strategic plan to aggressively market its members and services to the community and payors.

The MSO's success hinges on management's commitment to developing a strategic plan that will allow the MSO to become a recognized leader in practice-management services and be a part of a system that can be successfully marketed to the community.

CASE STUDY: PURPOSE, SCOPE, APPROACH, METHODOLOGY, AND FORMAT OF MSO REPORT

Purpose To provide the MSO's board of directors and the parent health system with an independent, third-party report on the MSO's management and operational performance.

Scope To assess the MSO's management performance and the services it currently provides to the medical practices, as well as to provide comments relative to services that the MSO does not presently provide, but that it should provide given the environmental context.

Approach and Methodology The approach of this report has been to collect, review, and analyze both general and specific data; interview physicians receiving management services from the MSO; interview the entire MSO management team; and interview the representative of the governance of the health system and the MSO.

Format of Report The management status assessment and operational review is structured according to operational or management area. The report is divided into five major areas:

1. Operations management
2. Financial management
3. Strategic planning
4. Human resources management
5. External and internal environments

At the end of the discussion of each major operational or management area, conclusions and recommendations are presented, including strengths, weaknesses, and recommendations. The report concludes with a brief narrative summary of the present status of the MSO.

BACKGROUND

The subject organization is an MSO that provides practice-management services to medical practices in an outer suburban area. The MSO was incorporated as a for-profit corporation by its parent health system, which remains the sole shareholder. The MSO currently employs over 50 full-time equivalents at its five practice locations and central business office. The MSO originally served primarily as a billing service organization. The number of physicians receiving management services from the MSO has increased to its current level of 15. The MSO has facilities in five separate cities in a two-county area.

The first section of the case study describes the subject entity's operations including Management Information Systems (MIS), medical records management, and communications. These are important areas of operations for EHOs, but are only a subset of the operational issues affecting the provision of services to member providers. Any or all operational or service areas may be included in an operational review including Quality Assurance (QA), Utilization Management (UM), marketing, purchasing, facilities management, vendor relations, and others. The determination of which operational areas to review should be made jointly with the client based on the analyzed or perceived cost, scope, and efficiency of each service provided or lack of information available. For those operational areas in which little or no information is available prior to the review concerning efficiency or provider satisfaction, the review may include a needs analysis and the development of the criteria appropriate to evaluate the service's or operation's effectiveness.

MANAGEMENT INFORMATION SYSTEMS (MIS)

Information should first be collected on the organization's MIS uses, needs, and potential applications as well as its current staff expertise, hardware, software, and network connectivity. The organization's operations, services provided, budget, and management needs will be the primary determinants of its MIS requirements. This information will provide a framework in which the organization's current MIS may be reviewed and recommendations developed for the evolution of the organization's MIS structure. MIS is not an end in itself, but rather a means to more efficient operations and better management decisions. As such it should be evaluated using a cost/benefits analysis approach.

One of the initial and often persistent obstacles to realizing the benefits of MIS in EHOs is the costs and commitment required to achieve appropriate levels of connectivity and systems integration to provide organization-wide services and data collection. The organization's locations, systems, and current network connectivity (e.g., LAN, WAN, etc.) should be analyzed and possible recommendations developed based on current and future needs. Such a location map may need to be developed for each of the organization's software applications in order to determine where and how input data is collected and then shared with other applications. This will identify inefficiencies and other limitations and allow for recommendations to correct these problems.

MEDICAL RECORDS MANAGEMENT

Medical records document clinical information which serves as the basis for patient billing. As such they represent the key customer information source for the business of medicine. The storage, filing, maintenance, and general management of medical records is a labor intensive area of practice administration and is the subject of numerous books and educational materials and has created great interest in the current development of computerized patient records (CPR). In addition to the administrative, legal, and other issues involved, multiple practice sites and centralized billing and storage can complicate the effective management of medical records for EHOs. Medical records management should be evaluated with the goal of having established consistent procedures which allow for timely access to records at any practice site, eliminating unnecessary duplication of data entry, and conforming with patient privacy and other legal constraints.

COMMUNICATIONS

Communications is a broad area underlying much of operations and may be subdivided into systems and organizational dynamics which may be defined as the means of communication and the governance and human issues affecting it. Business communications systems continue to improve or at least diversify and there are many options to support communication in various media. Current use of communications systems should be reviewed and recommendations made for use of additional means of communication if needed. Electronic mail and faxing capabilities are relatively inexpensive and have streamlined modern business communications. The assessment of the EHO's organizational dynamics affecting communications should include their speed and accuracy, formal and informal channels, accessibility of key managers, and regularity through scheduled meetings, distributions of news documents, and so forth.

OPERATIONS MANAGEMENT

Management Information Systems

An Overview   The MSO's management information system (MIS) is fragmented between functions that are provided internally by the MSO and functions that are provided externally by the health system. The MSO utilizes a central business office for all the member practices and practice locations. The internal MIS performs practice-management functions, while externally provided functions include accounting, financial reporting, and payroll.

Review of Functions and Applications   The MSO uses a popular, commercial practice-management software system for appointment scheduling, patient registration, electronic claims submission, charge entry, and report generation. The MSO receives financial services from its parent health system. The health system controls the information systems used for the MSO's accounting, accounts receivable/collection, accounts payable/general ledger, payroll, and inventory management. Later in the report, financial management reporting is addressed for the MSO; however, assessing the health system's information systems was beyond the scope of this engagement.

The MSO does not currently use e-mail or have access to the Internet. Each physician has a direct-inward-dial number that allows patients to contact the physician's office assistant directly when scheduling an appointment.

Staff Training and Technical Support   Initial staff orientation includes basic exposure to the medical manager system software. No other formal training session is offered internally; however, individuals who work extensively with the software may attend seminars specific to it. The MSO has an extensive, formal agreement for technical application support services, at a significant cost. Users can access the technical support via telephone, or assistance can be provided on-site.

Future Systems   The health-system-affiliated Physician Hospital Organization (PHO) does not currently use the same medical management system, but plans to use another product for managed care contracting and tracking purposes in the future. This may cause difficulty in integrating these organizations or in joint contracting.

(continued)

Medical Records Management

Format and Standards   The MSO maintains medical records at all its practice locations. At one facility the medical records are kept in a central file room that is easily accessible from all areas of the offices; at another a large room is utilized; at a third facility the MSO shares medical records storage with the parent health system's urgent-care facility, with those medical records separated from the MSO's. The other facilities were not physically inspected, but through the interview process it was determined that adequate space is reserved in each of these locations for medical records storage.

Review of Forms   The health system provides transcription services. Notes are dictated over the phone and transcribed at the hospital, then printed out at the office where the patient's medical record resides. There is a two-day turnaround time for transcripts. The employed physicians like the system, and, although some had not dictated medical records before, the physicians now feel that it is an efficient method of completing the medical records documentation and that transcription saves significant administrative time.

File System   Presently, the medical records are color-coded and alphabetized. The MSO will maintain an alphabetized and color-coded system, but will begin using noncolored charts to recognize a significant labor savings in the cost per chart.

Availability of Records   The MSO office assistants in charge of medical records management are the only employees allowed to pull or shelve the medical records. The records are signed out and remain on the unit until the responsible physician reviews and approves transcription and labs. If the medical records are not returned within 24 hours, the office assistants remind the physician to complete and return the medical records as soon as possible. Copies of the medical records for patients seen at the fifth facility, which lacks a storage area, are brought from the closest facility by the nurse on duty. If a patient is seen at a facility other than their primary location, a copy of the medical record is faxed to the appropriate location, to a machine located in a private area that is not accessible to the public.

Retention, Storage, and Destruction   As mentioned above, all locations have adequate storage for active medical records. The medical records are purged on an annual basis, and the inactive medical records are boxed alphabetically, by year. The inactive medical records of minors are kept separate from those of adults. Each year a private data-destruction company destroys the medical records of adults that have been inactive for more than ten years, while the inactive pediatric medical records are kept until the patient is 21 years of age.

Legal and Ethical Policies   The MSO's policy manual explicitly outlines the policies and procedures related to maintenance of medical records, confidentiality of medical records, and release of information from medical records.

Communication Systems

Current System Evaluation   The MSO currently uses technology that allows for functions such as voice mail, appointment scheduling from remote locations, and conference calls. The MSO did not have e-mail capabilities or access to the Internet as of the date of the report. The MSO employees are adequately trained and utilize the communication systems and processes that are in place within the MSO.

Review of Specific Areas   Each physician has direct inward dialing, which allows the patient to call and speak with the particular physician's receptionist or office assistant, who relays appointments and messages directly to the physician rather than going through a second receptionist/secretary. Presently, there is no demand for a centralized number for appointment scheduling; however, most managed care organizations will require or desire a centralized telephone number. The patient accounts department handles telephone billing inquiries.

Operations Management: Conclusions and Recommendations

For the purposes of this report, and as outlined above, management information systems, medical records management, and communication systems are classified as *operations management.*

Strengths

- The medical management system provides adequate functionality for practice-management applications (i.e., accounts receivable management, appointment scheduling, billing and claims processing, and limited managed care processing) for the present healthcare environment.

(*continued*)

- Internal and external technical support for information systems is available.
- Adequate storage space for medical records is presently available.
- Formal policies for the availability, completion, maintenance, retention, and destruction of medical records are in place and are adhered to.
- A centralized number for billing inquiries is available to patients.
- Direct inward dialing to each physician enables convenient appointment scheduling for the patient.

Weaknesses

- Financial information systems applications are provided and controlled outside of the MSO.
- There are no e-mail or Internet capabilities.
- There is no centralized telephone number for nurse triage or promotional purposes. The medical management application is a text-based product utilizing primarily second- and third-generation languages rather than fourth-generation languages or relational databases, and it is not a Windows-based application. These factors indicate a system that is based on older software which may not be as easily upgraded to include modern functions and capabilities.
- Financial data and productivity data are gathered and stored in separate applications and are controlled by different entities, limiting the decision-support capabilities.

Recommendations

- Develop an information system that is able to generate outcomes measurement.
- Develop an information system/application that can provide contract management, benefits management, member services, utilization management, claims management, and case management functions for managed care contracting.
- Integrate financial systems and productivity systems to develop a decision support mechanism that will measure costs per procedure (CPT, RVU, etc.) and have other cost-accounting capabilities.
- Enhance communications systems for internal use (i.e., e-mail and Internet access) and for external use (i.e., centralized numbers to schedule appointments). Having a centralized number for appointment scheduling is potentially more cost-efficient and will be de-

manded by third-party payors. As the MSO attempts to expand services to more independent practices and more actively pursues managed care contracting, centralized internal and external communication systems will become imperative.

Historically, healthcare financial management focused on accounting and reporting functions mandated by the federal government for reimbursement purposes (i.e., hospital cost reports). Managed care and other industry forces have led to increasing financial pressures, larger organizations, and the need for more sophisticated financial management including forecasting and strategic planning. Physician organizations have moved from cash accounting to accrual basis accounting and many are now implementing cost accounting systems to manage capitation.

Financial management encompasses all of the financially related functions of an organization including accounting, short- and long-term cash and asset management, financing, financial analysis, forecasting, and strategic financial planning. In the following section of the case study, a subset of these functions is reviewed. Many EHOs divide the functions of financial management with a hospital or other sponsoring organization or system. This can often lead to limited, "corrupted" financial information and management functions. Such divisions result in poor financial management of the EHO and ultimately, poor planning. The following is a description of the issues involved in the accounts receivable, cash management, and financial planning and budgeting functions which are then reviewed in the case study.

Accounts Receivable (A/R)   Billing for medical services is a complex area involving the transcription of medical records, assignment of standardized codes to procedures, and completion of numerous forms from government and other third-party payors. All activities in the billing process are subject to legal scrutiny by fraud and abuse laws, confidentiality, etc. Trained, experienced, and certified staff are preferred and internal compliance programs dealing with adherence to the Medicare fraud and abuse laws are becoming necessary for large organizations. Coding, billing, credit, and collections are common centralized services for EHOs. Collections can become more difficult when transferred to a larger organization from the practice level where there is a relationship with patients and staff may be more attentive to accounts. Effective policies should therefore be in place and the department must be adequately staffed. Patient billing and collections are further complicated for EHOs because of multiple practice locations requiring the coordination of staff at the practice sites and the central business office. The complexities involved in EHO A/R also require detailed, thorough policies and procedures.

Cash Management   A policy for the management of cash payments accepted at the practice sites should be in place and include internal checks and balances with staff monitoring the process other than the cashiers who accept the payments.

Historically, medical practices used cash-basis financial statements. EHO's financial statements must be prepared on an accrual basis to allow expenses to be tracked in a meaningful manner. The actual method allows for accurate comparisons of the organization's financial results to be made over time.

Financial Planning and Budgeting   Financial planning includes budgeting as well as financial projections and strategic financial planning. Budgeting is generally based on historical costs and provides a means of monitoring EHO administrative expenses and direct physician expenses. Expected revenues and capital needs also should be incorporated into the process using provider input. Financial reporting is a crucial function for effective management. EHOs should be able to produce budgets and financial statements for all of their individual practice locations or various businesses. Benchmarking of financial information against industry sources and other practices is a valuable management and budgeting technique.

Traditional accounting and reporting methods do not provide sufficient information for the management of capitation and tight profit margins. Managed care contracts require providers to adopt new management techniques and increased financial vigilance over expenses. The negotiation of contracts requires information on historical expenses and profits. Cost accounting systems are therefore highly desirable management tools.

FINANCIAL MANAGEMENT

The MSO does not provide financial management services; the health system provides them to the MSO. Analysis of the financial management services is limited to those areas that are directly related to the management of the MSO and to issues identified during the interview process.

An Overview of Financial Management

Management of Accounts Receivable. The MSO recently assumed accounts receivable management services from the health system. Following is a list of general comments regarding certain accounts receivables management areas, in lieu of an assessment of the MSO's performance for a short period.

Staff Resources The MSO's central business office staff provides accounts receivable management services. The business office staff is managed by the manager of business office, who reports to the executive director. The staff responsible for accounts receivable management services and all billing functions consists of three full-time individuals. The present staff are all former employees of the health system's billing service who had previously worked the accounts for the MSO.

Credit and Collections All patients' accounts staff are planning to commit five hours per week to collections efforts. The MSO's training manual specifically outlines the collection process for self-pay patient billing and third-party billing. After issuing an initial bill and subsequent statement, staff follows up the patient account with either a letter or a phone call, depending on the amount due. The collection process is as follows.

- *Third-Party Billing:* The process for third-party collections begins with a phone call to the third-party payor, which occurs on approximately the 26th day, and the insurance portion of the patient account is entered into the insurance collection module. On the 40th day, the patient account becomes the responsibility of the patient/guarantor. On the 41st day, a patient bill is sent to the patient/guarantor, with a follow-up statement sent on the 68th day. On the 82nd day, the patient is put into the collection module and a phone call is placed to the patient/guarantor. On the 84th day, a blue reminder letter is sent, stating the outstanding balance and payment options. On the 94th day, a yellow collection letter is sent, stating that no payment has been received and that without a payment or contact to structure a payment plan, the account will be turned over to an outside collection agency within 14 days. On the 103rd day, the patient account is written off to the outside collection agency.

(*continued*)

- *Self-Pay Patient Billing:* Initial collection on a self-pay patient account is made on the date of service. Self-pay patient account balances not collected at the time of service are billed the second day after service is rendered, with a follow-up statement generated on the 28th day. If no payment or contact has been made by the self-pay patient by the 42nd day, a phone call is made (on accounts greater than $200) to the patient reminding them of the balance due to the practice. That call is followed, on the 44th day, by a blue reminder letter stating the outstanding balance and payment options. On the 54th day, a yellow collection letter is sent, stating that no payment has been received and that without payment or a call to structure a payment plan, the account will be turned over to an outside collection agency within 14 days. On the 73rd day, upon manager approval, the patient account is written off to the outside collection agency.

- *Cash-Basis Policy:* The MSO has instituted a "cash-basis" policy to minimize the risk for bad debt and increase the collection rate. Patient accounts that have been either sent to an outside collection agency or written off due to bankruptcy or wage-earner status are designated as cash basis accounts. Patients who have had their account put on a cash basis are notified by letter that future office visits will require a $50 payment (credit card, money order, cash) at the time of service. Personal checks are generally not accepted from a patient who has been designated as cash basis. The exceptions in the training manual are as follows.

  - HMO patients: Collect only the copay.

  - Medicare patients: Should not be on a cash basis; if found, notify supervisor.

  - Workmen's Compensation: If Workmen's Compensation is verified and the visit is an approved visit.

  - Medical emergencies.

  - Checks may be accepted at the office manager's discretion.

  The MSO's training manual has several useful sample letters and formal policies that serve as a valuable resource for handling the cash basis policy.

Internal Control of Receivables   The MSO's training manual and policy manual outline several policies, methods, and opportunities to ensure that receivables are collected. The cover sheets attached to patient charts contain the patient's due balance to enable the cashier/receptionist to easily request any past-due amounts. The MSO's policy manual contains policies regarding write-offs, delinquent accounts, collection placement, bankruptcy, wage-earner claims, accounts receivable in litigation, and handling of accounts receivable monies.

Patient Billing   As previously mentioned, patient billing became the responsibility of the MSO recently, so only a brief overview of the process is provided here. Currently there are three full-time individuals, working in the patient accounts department at the MSO's resource center, who provide posting, billing, and collecting services for the MSO's practices. The three employees are cross-trained in all aspects of the accounts receivable process (i.e., posting, billing, adjustments, and collections). The only activities that are not centralized are the posting of copays and charge entry; these tasks are performed by the cashiers/receptionists at each of the practice locations. It is the practice of the MSO offices to post charges and related payments within 24 hours of the patient visit. The patient accounts department at the MSO's resource center generates the patient's bill on the Monday, Wednesday, or Friday immediately following posting of the charges. Presently, the MSO submits electronically all possible insurance that has electronic claims submission capabilities. At the time of this report, the MSO was in the process of evaluating the cost/benefit of electronic filing. Electronic filing of claims occurs every Monday, Wednesday, and Friday. Secondary billing is done either manually or electronically, depending on the capabilities of the secondary payor, and is completed after the primary source is billed. Rebills were only performed to correct errors by the health system's billing service; however, the MSO is currently investigating the medical management application's codes to allow for accurate rebills.

Policies and Procedures   The health system's billing system established many policies and procedures regarding accounts receivable management. Since the MSO took over the management of billing and collections and accounts receivable management, many policies and procedures have been revised both to fit the practice setting and to meet the goals of the MSO. A new policies and procedures manual is being developed specifically for the patient accounts department staff. The policies and procedures updates will also be revised in conjunction with the MSO's certification process.

(continued)

Cash Management

Internal Control Functions   The office assistants (cashier/receptionist) collect cash for copays and services at the time of the visit. The office assistant posts the copayment, balances the drawer daily against the cash analysis report, and deposits the cash at the bank as necessary (three to five times per week). The balancing of the cash drawer is not physically audited by another employee other than the person collecting and depositing the funds; however, the office manager keeps and reviews a daily cash log.

Cash versus Accrual Accounting   The MSO's annual financial statements are prepared on an accrual basis. As compared with cash-basis financial statements, accrual statements provide a more consistent and accurate measure of a company's financial activity, provide more comparable financial results between periods, result in less fluctuation in financial results, and are the most accepted, understood, and commonly utilized form of financial statement preparation. The ability to track all expenses including incurred but not reported (IBNR) expenses requires that financial statements be prepared on an accrual basis.

Financial Planning and Budgeting

Financial Planning   Financial planning for the MSO presently consists of the budgeting process. Financial planning is not part of the MSO's strategic planning process.

Budgeting Process   The MSO is on a fiscal year that begins on May 1 and ends on April 30. The MSO's budgeting process begins in January and involves the health system, the MSO's management, and the employed physicians, all with input to specific areas of the process. The health system initiates the budgeting process by providing expense worksheets to the MSO's management. The health system participants are primarily members of the corporate finance staff. The health system determines the budget for interest, depreciation, rent, and benefits assumptions. The members of the MSO's management who participate in the budgeting process are the CEO, executive director, directors, and, to some extent, the office managers. The MSO's management develops the budget for administrative expenses and direct physician expenses. The directors and office managers develop budgets based on historical data and anticipated changes in expenses, then submit the preliminary budgets to the employees' supervisor (in most cases, the executive director) for revisions or approval. The MSO's managers prepare the budget for capital needs and present it to corporate finance for approval. The managers work with the employed physicians to develop the projected revenues for the coming fiscal year.

Financial Reporting   The health system is the employer of all of the employed physicians and incurs the expenses on their statement of revenues and expenses related to salaries, physician's benefits, and recruiting. In return for incurring these expenses, the health system receives a credit equal to 40 percent of the MSO's net collections. Although the present format of allocating these expenses to the health system is technically correct, the validity and usefulness of the MSO's statements are limited at best. At the time of the assessment, the MSO had no cost-accounting system in place. Cost-accounting systems are one of the most desired and valuable tools to evaluate capitated contracts and to track performances of individuals or groups of physicians. For the MSO to provide value-added services (to existing and future practices) and to compete in the marketplace, meaningful financial statements and cost-accounting statements are of paramount importance. The current MSO's financial statements do not provide a true economic picture of the owned practices or the performance of the MSO. The MSO does not have any financial analysts or accounting personnel who create the reports medical practices need in today's reimbursement environment. There is no consolidated financial statement that provides a tool for assessing the individual physician practices.

Managed Care   The MSO has one part-time employee serving as its managed care specialist. The managed care specialist is responsible for preparing physician/provider applications, providing plan descriptions and directories to the practices, preparing and distributing managed care contract grids, consulting with the health system hospital's managed care contract specialist, maintaining a relationship with the managed care plan's representatives, and maintaining all managed care files. The present managed care contracting efforts consist primarily of managing the provider application process and serving as the repository and conduit of managed care contracting information. The MSO has not done any contract analysis or extensive marketing with the area's managed care plans. The MSO has received authorization to

(continued)

hire an individual who is experienced in managed care contracting to review, analyze, and negotiate contracts on the MSO's behalf. The MSO has a designated reimbursement specialist who is responsible for coding and pricing. The reimbursement specialist performs random chart audits to ensure proper coding and educates the physicians in proper coding and pricing procedures to maximize reimbursement.

Financial Management: Conclusions and Recommendations

Within this report, and as outlined above, management of accounts receivable, cash management, cash versus accrual accounting, financial planning, budgeting processes, financial reporting, and managed care contracting have been classified as *financial management*.

Strengths

- The business office manager has several years of experience in posting, billing, and collection activities.
- Clear policies and procedures are in place to increase collections at the time of the patient visit.
- Unaudited financial statements are prepared on an accrual basis.
- The budgeting process involves physician participation on the revenue side.
- A "bottom up" approach is used for budget development on the expense side.
- Financial reports are broken down by location.
- A part-time position has been created to serve in the role of managed care coordinator, whose primary responsibility is to assist physicians in the credentialing and plan participation process.
- The MSO provides selected benchmarking (i.e., primarily productivity-based numbers) of industry comparisons.

Weaknesses

- The MSO has only recently assumed the responsibility for billing, collections, and accounts receivable management services. These are core services that are generally provided by an MSO rather than by a hospital. The MSO needs to develop an efficient system of providing these services, one that will be attractive to potential medical practices that may seek services from the MSO.

- Policies and procedures are not fully developed. The MSO is in the process of further developing or refining the policies and procedures that were in place with the health system's billing services.

- The MSO has no internal person to handle financial statement preparation and reporting. The MSO is unable to present a true economic picture of organizational performance or individual practice performance.

- There is no control over the types of accounting/financial reports generated or the allocation of certain expenses (i.e., rent, interest, depreciation, amortization). The MSO should have a level of autonomy that allows for control over the allocation of significant expenses.

- No cost accounting system is in place. The MSO is unable to evaluate a capitated contract or provide meaningful physician efficiency measures based on the cost per unit of service (i.e., Current Procedural Terminology [CPT] code) without an established cost-accounting system.

- There is an internal control issue regarding the handling of cash payments. The same MSO employee receives, posts, and deposits the cash payments made at each facility, which creates a risk of fraud.

- The MSO currently has no individual experienced in or providing managed care contract review, negotiation, and development services.

Recommendations

- Develop a capital budget within the strategic planning process to incrementally build alliances between the employed and independent physicians.

- Hire an individual to provide financial reporting and accounting services specific to physician needs and to expand the range of services.

- Prepare financial statements to give a true economic picture of the practices and develop benchmarking of financial indicators to industry norms.

- Develop more autonomy regarding the appropriate allocation of expenses such as rent, interest, depreciation, and amortization.

(continued)

- Develop a cost-accounting system that can be used for existing practices and marketed as a service to independent practices.
- Further develop the MSO policies and procedures for financial management areas.
- Separate duties to improve internal cash controls. Have a separate individual (other than the office assistant/cashier who collects the cash) balance the monies and prepare the bank deposits.
- Hire an individual or firm to provide managed care contracting expertise to enhance the existing practices and expand the range of services.

Strategic planning is central to the effective development and management of business. It is the necessary counterpart to operations management or administration which allows an organization to foresee changes in its business and adapt its operations to changing market conditions and opportunities. It is often overlooked or given less emphasis than the organization's daily administration and is therefore an important area for review and recommendations.

Clientele   EHOs serve providers and may consider them as clients for recruiting and service planning purposes. However, as the effective managers of these providers in strategic planning, the organization should define the patients as its ultimate clients. Current patients and patient volume should be identified. The overall market should be defined in order to estimate the potential client base within the primary and secondary markets. The more demographic and marketing information the organization can gather on its clients and potential clients, the better able it will be in keeping or getting them.

Access to the Market   Healthcare client relationships are constrained by payors and other providers in a variety of ways. Managed care organizations have implemented controls that regulate which providers their enrollees can see and which services will receive coverage. Local managed care organizations and the number of enrollees in their different plan types should be identified. Providers make decisions based on a number of criteria to which providers or facilities they will refer their patients. Knowing who refers patients to your practices and to whom your providers are referring is important information in assessing the strength of these relationships and their future prospects. The role of marketing in accessing new patients and maintaining a patient base should be evaluated.

Services   Identify the organization's current services and potential additional service offerings. The level of competition for these services should be researched including how the organization's services and level of service differ from the competition. The organization should know what level of service (e.g., cost, quality, convenience, access, etc.) they represent. The profit margins of the organization's various services will influence the prospect of remaining profitable in these areas.

Competitors   Research should be done on the organization's service competitors, their methods of competition, and their market shares. The competitors should be evaluated in terms of their size, strengths, experience, strategies, service offerings, and other relevant business characteristics. The objective of this analysis is to determine if and how the organization can better compete on a service-by-service basis.

SWOT Analysis   One tool used to assist in strategic planning is a SWOT analysis. SWOT is the acronym for strengths, weaknesses, opportunities, and threats. It is an analysis of the organization's relation with its competitors and market in terms of its internal abilities and external competition.

Market Evolution   Strategic plans are developed for short- and long-term purposes and therefore their success depends, to a varying degree, on the organization's ability to foresee changes in its markets. A number of factors may be used to determine the local market's current development stage including the level of consolidation, integration, managed care penetration, incursion of national healthcare organizations, and other indicators of increasing competition. Predictions of future market conditions may then be based on national trends for similar markets.

Integration   The organization's own level of integration should be assessed for competitiveness in the current and future market. Loosely integrated EHOs will not have favorable contracting strength compared to more integrated organizations in an advanced market where providers are competing based on cost and quality of services.

Planning Process   Strategic planning can benefit from the application of form and processes designed to provide structure to the planning efforts. A hierarchy of types of plans ranging from the development of an organizational mission statement, to statements of strategic initiatives identifying the strategies needed to support the mission, and down to the tactical plans designed to implement the strategic initiatives is a useful planning technique. It forces planners to break the process into manageable tasks which have been derived from the overall mission and goals of the organization. The information gathering and research process should also be reviewed as current, thorough, and accurate information is necessary for meaningful decision making.

A healthy strategic planning process should involve key management and representative provider leadership and should result in regular formal meetings and reports which are used as the basis for the implementation of organizational change in response to market forces and trends.

STRATEGIC PLANNING

Strategic Planning for the Overall Organization

Current Planning Processes Strategic planning for the health system is an ongoing, formal process handled at the board/system level. The MSO does not have a formal strategic planning process. The CEO of the MSO is involved in the health system's strategic planning process. The MSO's managers attend seminars and continuing education classes, which provides exposure to professional development and supports strategic planning initiatives.

The Strategic Plan The MSO currently has no strategic plan in place.

Managed Care Issues There is no strategic plan or strategic planning process in which to incorporate managed care issues or strategies.

Strategic Planning: Conclusions and Recommendations

For the purposes of this case study report, and as outlined above, the current planning processes, the strategic plan, and managed care issues have been classified as *strategic planning*.

Strengths
- Experienced leadership is involved in the health system's strategic planning process.

Weaknesses
- The strategic planning process does not involve the MSO's management.

- The MSO's board has limited physician participation.
- The strategic planning process does not formally involve the employed physicians.
- Independent, non-MSO-affiliated physicians are involved in and provide input to management on an ad hoc basis, which can be disruptive and redirects the focus of the organization.
- The MSO has no strategic planning process or a formal, written strategic plan.
- Marketing efforts of the MSO and the employed physicians are controlled by the health system.

Recommendations

- Involve the MSO's management in the strategic planning process.
- Involve the employed physicians and managed physicians in the strategic planning process.
- Limit ad hoc end runs from non-MSO-affiliated physicians.
- Develop a vision or mission statement for the MSO that is supported by all stakeholders.
- Develop a statement of strategic initiatives and tactical plans to achieve the strategic initiatives.
- Focus strategic planning efforts on the needs of the market and prepare for the incursion of managed care.
- Hire an independent party to facilitate the strategic planning process and assist in developing a consensus.
- Prepare a formal written strategic plan and update it periodically.
- Implement the strategic plan.

In the following section of the case study, different facets of the organization's human resources (HR) management are examined. The goal is a functional analysis of the staff's skills, interaction, communication, policies and procedures, and overall effectiveness. To accomplish this, in the case study, HR functions are divided into four areas: physicians, executive director and medical director management, employee management, and organizational dynamics.

Physicians may be viewed as the clients of the EHO. Among the HR services which may be provided to physicians, depending on their employment status or relationship with the EHO, are recruiting, orientation, compensation, benefits, Continuing Medical Education (CME), credentialing, malpractice insurance, performance evaluation, grievances, analysis and reporting of practice information, and retirement. Many of these functions are generally provided to EHO staff. What is unique about the HR needs of physicians is that they are essentially the organization's clients and are its primary revenue producers. Thus, some of the HR services provided are more closely related to customer service than internal HR. Interviews with physicians can readily uncover their level of satisfaction with the services provided.

Supervisory reporting, disciplinary procedures, and position descriptions are examples of other elements of EHO staff HR management which should be evaluated in addition to those functions listed above that concern both staff and physicians.

Management and staff skills and staffing levels must be appropriate for the size of the organization, the number of providers and facilities to which services are provided, and the type and scope of services offered.

Interviews with physicians, HR staff, and management are the primary tool for gathering information on the strength of HR management and the physician's and staff's satisfaction with the organization's HR. HR is highly dependent on the use of policies and procedures and copies of these documents should be obtained and reviewed in conjunction with the information gained through interviews.

HUMAN RESOURCES MANAGEMENT

Physicians

Responsibility   The CEO of the MSO has ultimate responsibility for the employed physicians in the employed physicians group. The reporting relationship between the physicians and the CEO is clearly understood. The physicians also work closely with the executive director and report to him/her on day-to-day operations. The CEO and executive director both have an open-door policy with the physicians and are easily accessible for the physicians' needs.

Recruitment   Physician recruitment is a service provided by the health system and had been the responsibility of the vice president of ambulatory services for the health system. Until recently, a director of physician services recruitment managed physician recruitment under the direction of the MSO's CEO. Corporate restructuring has shifted the director of physician services recruitment to another area within the health system; however, physician recruitment is still a responsibility of the CEO of the MSO. There have been discussions about hiring a middle-management person to provide physician recruiting services to the MSO.

Orientation   Physician orientation is provided by the director of patient services and the office manager of the facility where the physician will be working. The director meets with each new physician and provides general information regarding policies and procedures and expectations. Each new physician is provided literature on physician efficiency at the start of his or her employment. The meeting with the director and office manager includes a tour of the facility and also specifically addresses the following issues:

- Parking
- Security system and issuance of keys
- Patient flow of office
- Business cards and stationary
- Medical records policies
- Prescription pads
- Office phone numbers and in-service training on operation of phone
- Office hours
- Ancillary ordering (lab, x-ray, physical therapy, etc.)
- Review of forms
- Managed care forms
- Dictation procedure

After completing orientation with the director and office manager, the new physician meets with the MSO's business office manager and the MSO's reimbursement specialist to review:

- Pricing
- Coding and coding book
- Encounter forms (hospital and office) in terms of flow and completion
- Billing procedure
- Insurance plans

(continued)

- Payment policy
- Professional courtesy policy
- Problem correction forms

Compensation   The physician compensation arrangements within the employed physician group utilize a base salary, with one exception where compensation is based on a percentage of collections. The range of these base salaries is large but well within the national averages.

Monitoring Performance   The MSO has a quarterly review process for each employed physician. The executive director (and, as appropriate, the medical director) conducts the quarterly review process based on feedback received from the director of patient services and office manager(s). The quarterly practice reviews focus on the following operational, financial, and patient satisfaction indicators.

- *Schedule Summary:* Each physician is evaluated on scheduling practices. Scheduling is monitored by the waiting time to see an established patient, waiting times for new patients, the ability to stay on schedule, the time requirements for new or established patients, and the ability to accommodate urgent patient visits.

- *Review of Provider:* Each physician is reviewed on specific issues of their practice. This section of the review process is used to specifically address areas where improvement can be made or to recognize areas of strength. A wide range of issues is covered, including but not limited to timeliness of appointments, teamwork, accuracy of coding, patient satisfaction results, methods to build/expand practice, communication skills, and attendance.

- *Practice Capacity:* Each physician's practice is assessed in terms of production/revenue capacity, volume/patient encounter capacity, and number of new patients seen on a monthly and daily basis. Capacity levels are compared to MGMA industry norms. If outliers exist, additional research and analysis are completed to identify the causes of any discrepancies. The capacity statistics are presented as a benchmark against the employed physicians' capacities and national trends by specialty and years in practice. The quarterly review process serves as an opportunity to address methods of improving capacity levels and to provide suggestions to develop the practice.

- *Patient Satisfaction Surveys:* Patient satisfaction survey results, prepared by an outside firm, are presented to each physician. The survey results compare each individual physician to the employed physicians as well as to other, nonemployed physicians who are participating in the survey at locations throughout the region.

- *Recommendations:* The quarterly review process provides an opportunity for the physician and management to determine appropriate methods for improving performance areas discussed in the review process. The recommendations portion of the quarterly reviews provides an excellent opportunity to designate specific areas that need improvement and to discuss ways in which management may assist the physicians in becoming more productive and efficient.

Interpersonal Relationships The majority of employed physicians began their professional careers with the health system or the MSO. The current employed physicians participate in physician recruiting by being involved in the interviewing/hiring process and providing feedback prior to the hiring decision. During the site-visit/interview process there were no expressions of ill will toward physician colleagues. The physicians who have been around for more than one year expressed a growing movement toward a group mentality. If there are disagreements or issues between physicians, the physicians initially discuss them between themselves, and if they cannot reach a resolution or agreement they seek the advice of the medical director.

Leadership Development During the interview process certain aspects of physician leadership were apparent. The medical director of the employed physicians group is inherently a leadership position. The present medical director has been in practice for ten years and has been employed by the health system for several years. The medical director's experience as a practicing physician, as well as his tenure with the MSO, gains him respect from physician colleagues. The medical director is very interested in becoming a leader in the medical community and regularly requests additional involvement in management issues. Presently, the MSO offers no formal leadership seminars to physicians. Among the other employed physicians, none has emerged to become a leader in the physician community.

(*continued*)

Retirement   The health system has not lost any of the employed physicians to retirement. With the majority of physicians in an early stage of their practice life cycle, physician retirement is not expected to be an issue in the provision of management services by the MSO in the next five years.

Executive Director and Medical Director Management

Recruitment and Orientation   The health system places advertisements and collects applications. The president/CEO is responsible for recruiting and selecting the executive director, and also provides the orientation regarding expectations, policies, and procedures. The CEO appoints the medical director, and the CEO, executive director, human resources department, directors, and office managers, as appropriate, provide orientation to new physician hires.

Compensation   The executive director receives a salary and benefits (health, life, disability, pension plan) and is eligible for bonuses based on organizational performance. The executive director does not have an employment agreement with the MSO.

The medical director receives a salary and benefits. There is a formal agreement, with an initial term of three years. The contract automatically terminates if revised terms are not agreed upon between 120 and 90 days prior to the last day of the initial term. The medical director also receives a monthly salary for practice development services.

Performance Evaluation   The CEO of the MSO conducts the executive director's annual evaluation in August of each year. Evaluation criteria include budget goals, predetermined operational goals, growth of practices, and bonus criteria. During the evaluation process, goals and objectives and bonus criteria are set for the next year.

The CEO and executive director of the MSO conduct the medical director's annual evaluation in August of each year. The evaluation is based on general leadership and performance criteria.

Technical Competency, Skills, and Relations   The CEO of the MSO provided the following evaluation of the executive director and the medical director:

> The executive director is a very competent manager who has a strong sense of priority and completes projects in a diligent and effective man-

ner. She is an extraordinarily hard worker (i.e., regularly working over 40 hours), involving peers and subordinates in all critical decision making. The executive director also demands and expects top performance from the staff. The executive director is tenacious in follow-up and highly organized in scheduling and routines, which is comforting to the physicians she serves. The executive director is not comfortable in the "gray area," preferring instead to have issues clearly defined.

The executive director reports to the CEO, with whom she has a good working relationship. They appear to have their respective responsibilities clearly defined, with the executive director being responsible for the majority of operations and the CEO focusing on strategic planning, political situations, and physician and corporate relationships.

The medical director is also the founder and medical director of the employed physician group. The medical director brought his practice into the group and became an employee. He is fulfilling a vision and dream he and the health system share. The medical director is a board-certified internist who is the moral and spiritual leader of the employed physicians group. The medical director meets with the group numerous times per month to communicate with and encourage physician colleagues. The other physicians look to the medical director for leadership, and it would appear that they have a great deal of trust and confidence in his abilities. In turn, the physicians' trust level with administration seems to be very healthy.

The medical director's principal weakness is limited knowledge, formal training, and experience in business. This limitation, although surmountable, presently limits his ability to see the big picture (i.e., bottom line of the group as a whole) and to understand the implications of certain actions. The medical director does have a very good working relationship with the CEO and executive director and is willing to discuss and try alternative strategies to accomplish the vision of the MSO and the health system. These three key executives appear to have full trust in one another, which is a major asset in moving this organization forward.

Problem-Solving Ability   The executive director plays a vital role as an intermediary between the CEO of the MSO and the physicians who receive services. The executive director has very strong verbal communication skills and keeps the president informed as to the status of day-to-day activities.

The medical director's role as communicator between the MSO's management and the medical staff is very strong. He serves as a liaison between his physician colleagues and the MSO's management.

(continued)

Employee Management

Staff Recruitment and Application Processes   Staff recruitment and the application process are services that the health system's human resources department provides to the MSO. As new positions develop or job openings become available, the appropriate MSO manager (i.e., office manager or director) completes a position request form and obtains the approval of MSO management. The completed position request form then goes to the health system's human resources department. The job opening is then posted on the health system's job line (which is used both internally and externally) and a newspaper advertisement may be placed. The applications are forwarded to the office manager (or, if applicable, a director) for review, and interviews are scheduled. The office manager conducts the interviews and completes the necessary interview form. When a candidate is selected, a job offer is made contingent upon references, criminal checks, and drug screenings. The office manager verifies references and the health system's human resources department completes a verified form which includes the criminal check and scheduling of a drug screening, which takes place after the job offer and before employment starts. A director or other individual one level higher than the interviewer signs the completed application. The health system's benefit manager conducts the pre-employment drug screening and clears the employee to start. The new employee is scheduled to meet with the health system's human resources department for payroll and benefits administration. The department initiates the employee file and forwards it to the MSO's resource center for permanent storage. The employee health department of the health system maintains the paperwork for the pre-employment physical.

The human resources management functions provided by the health system consist primarily of the job application process. The MSO's management is responsible for screening the applicants and conducting interviews. As the MSO expands to offer management services to additional medical practices, the MSO will need to have an internal human resources function to handle hiring and employee benefits issues more efficiently.

Job Descriptions and Analysis   At the time of this report, the MSO's management was in the process of developing job descriptions for the MSO's administration and the patient account staff. Currently, the MSO has job descriptions that clearly label the job title, supervisor of the position, qualifications for the position, the major goal of the position, and the key results areas. The key results areas identify the specific tasks and skills expected, the commitment to a team approach, and the customer service expectations for the position. The job descriptions are used during the evaluation process, with the key results areas serving as the evaluation criteria.

Orientation and New Staff Training   The MSO has a formal orientation process that each new employee goes through. The initial half-day orientation includes a meeting with the executive director, who provides a brief introduction. The major agenda items for the half-day orientation are:

- Description and history of the MSO
- The MSO's relationship with the parent health system
- Purpose of the orientation
- Opportunities and responsibilities
- Investment the MSO will make in the new employees
- Expectations the MSO has of the new employees
- Confidentiality issues
- Customer service policies
- Structure for success
- Benefits review and discussion of the employee assistance program as it relates to both home and work
- OSHA requirements
- New employee orientation

On a monthly basis, the MSO provides a half-day customer service training seminar for all new employees. The seminar, conducted by the director of quality and customer service, teaches skills to improve customer service and presents guidelines and expectations for an employee of the MSO. The seminar includes a video, an interactive lecture session, and a quiz at the end of the seminar.

Compensation: Wages   The MSO's compensation levels are comparable to those of other practice settings in the greater market area. The salaries for nurses have been an issue, as the nurses in the hospitals are presently paid much more than those at the MSO. In some instances

(continued)

the lower nurse salaries have been given as the reason for nurses leaving the MSO. Several of the physicians interviewed cited nurse turnover as an important issue. The local market also suffers from a shortage of medical assistants due to the absence of a local training facility and the fact that medical assistants are paid higher hourly wages in nearby urban facilities.

Compensation: Benefits   The MSO has a separate benefits package from those of the other health system entities. The summary of benefits (for full-time employees) is as follows:

- *Life Insurance:* One times salary (to $50,000) subject to 90-day probationary period. Additional life insurance is available for purchase for employee, spouse, or child.
- *Short-Term Disability:* Available for purchase.
- *Long-Term Disability:* Provides 60 percent of benefits after five months of disability. Eligible after one year of employment.
- *Tuition Reimbursement:* Eighty percent reimbursement for college tuition up to $2,000 per annum, subject to 90-day probationary period.
- *Flex Spending Account:* Pre-tax money for health, dental, and child-care expenses, subject to 90-day probationary period.
- *Dental Insurance:* Premiums for single ($18.75/mo.) and family ($45.01/mo.), subject to 90-day probationary period.
- *Health Insurance:* Employee pays a premium inversely related to the amount of the deductible, subject to 90-day probationary period.
- *401(k):* Tax-deferred plan, employee contributions, no firm matching or profit-sharing plan.
- *Other Benefits Available to All the Health System's Employees:* Child care, free checking, free flu and Hepatitis B vaccinations, financial planning education, professional services discounts, employee assistance program, and mileage reimbursement.

Employee Facilities   The three main facilities were physically inspected during the site visit period. The first facility is located in a commercial area, with the MSO occupying a portion of the large single-story building it shares with other health system affiliates. This is the location for the MSO's management (excluding the CEO, who is located at the health system's hospital), the business office staff, and the centralized information system. The MSO has adequate space available to expand physically as needed. This location has a shared dining room, with vending machines and restaurant, available to employees. There is a reception and waiting area for visitors, as well as separate lavatories for employees' use. The facility is approximately fifteen years old, but was recently remodeled.

The second facility was constructed three years ago and is located in a residential/commercial area. It consists of 15,000 square feet, of which 3,000 square feet is used for laboratory and diagnostic services by the health system's analytics department. This facility is the primary practice location of one pediatrician, two internists, one family practitioner, and one obstetrician/gynecologist. There is a proposal to incorporate an immediate-care unit into the facility that will eliminate the current employee break room. The layout of the facility allows for centralized medical records, one centralized procedure room, and separate "pods" in each corner of the building that allow for practices to be separated by primary care discipline (i.e., family practice, internal medicine, pediatrics, and obstetrics/gynecology). The layout is very efficient for the staff and considerate of the patients' particular needs. The waiting room is very large and has a separate corner for children to play in, patient/visitor lavatories, and very modern and pleasant furnishings.

Construction of the third facility, a two-story building, was completed in 1996. The MSO pays rent for the entire 18,000 square feet of the second floor of the third facility, even though it only occupies 50 percent of the space. The MSO should only be charged rent for the space its practices and employees physically occupy. The first floor of the two-story building is occupied by a health system urgent-care facility and laboratory and diagnostic services. This facility is the primary practice location of one pediatrician, one internist, two family practitioners, and one obstetrician/gynecologist. Approximately 50 percent of the MSO's portion of the facility is presently vacant. The original design was structured to have completely separate areas for each of the primary care disciplines. Currently, five physicians utilize half of the available space. The facility has a large medical records room on the second floor that is shared with the health system's urgent-care facility, located on the first floor. The medical records for the MSO and the immediate-care facility are kept in separate locations within the same storage room. The facility has a large break room with employee

(continued)

bathrooms, vending machines, and kitchen appliances. The facility has adequate exam rooms and a waiting/reception area, and contains very modern and pleasant furnishings.

In addition to the three main facilities, the MSO has three satellite facilities that are used for direct patient-care activities. The first satellite facility consists of a suite in a business office building that is located in a nearby suburban city and is used on a part-time basis to serve patients in that area. A portion of the suite is subleased to an allied health professional. This satellite facility has a reception area, a small business office, and two exam rooms. The second satellite facility is located in a small city approximately ten miles from the MSO's central business offices and is used as the full-time practice location for one physician. This satellite practice has a reception area, nurse's station, two exam rooms, staff lounge, physician office, and bathroom. The third satellite facility is located in another suburban city and is now occupied by a single physician. This third satellite facility will be staffed with two or three physicians at either the present location or a new location. The facility has approximately 2,000 square feet and contains a reception area, four exam rooms, two physician offices, a business office, and a small lab area.

Job Security Individual job performance is the primary indicator of job security for the MSO's employees. Employees who perform to expectations, exhibit strong customer services skills, and are strong team players have advancement opportunities within the MSO. Historically, the MSO has not laid off any employees who exhibited the skills and attitude that coincide with the mission of the MSO. The majority of turnover experienced by the MSO can be attributed to employees not clearly understanding the expectations or practice setting, employee changes in careers or family status, inability of the MSO to meet salary demands, inability of the employee to work as a team member, or nonperformance issues. As a new, growing organization, the MSO has been in an expansion mode and has not experienced any downsizing to date.

Grievances The MSO has an employee grievance policy that addresses the grievance process. The policy clearly states the purpose and scope of the employee grievance procedure. The procedure requires the employee with a grievance to take the following steps.

- The employee discusses the issue with the employee's manager; the manager responds within ten days.

- If a resolution or answer has not been provided, the employee may request a conference with the appropriate director.
- If a resolution or answer has not been provided, the issue may become a formal grievance subject to the following steps.
  1. The employee may submit a written request for a conference to the executive director. Response is due in ten days.
  2. If the issue is not resolved by Step 1, the employee may request a conference with the president/CEO of the MSO. Response from the president/CEO is due in fifteen days.
  3. If not resolved by Step 2, the employee may request a conference with human resources and the president/CEO of the MSO or his designee. Response from the president/CEO is due in 30 days.

Equal Employment Opportunity (EEO)   The health system provides human resource services, and formal EEO policies are the responsibility of the health system's human resources department.

Personnel Policies   The MSO has a policy manual that describes a variety of personnel policies and procedures. The MSO is in the process of further developing the manual to be in accordance with certification standards.

Supervisory Role   The supervisory roles and reporting requirements are clearly illustrated and communicated to new employees on the first day of employment. All individuals interviewed said they had a clear understanding of whom they reported to in a variety of situations.

Employee Relationships   The staff is structured around a team approach that requires extensive interaction among all personnel. The medical office settings are structured such that each physician has a nurse (RN, LPN, or MA) who assists with direct patient-care activities and an office assistant who schedules appointments, answers patient questions, and provides general administrative functions. This approach requires that the three individuals work very closely together and develop strong working relationships. Individuals who have difficulty working in small groups tend not to fit into the MSO's medical practice setting. The MSO organizes and encourages social functions and activities to promote employee relations and allow employees the opportunity to interact outside the workplace.

(continued)

Performance Review   New employees are reviewed after their initial 90-day probationary period. The annual review occurs on an employee's anniversary date each year. All of the MSO's employees are reviewed by their immediate supervisor (i.e., director, office manager) with input from the employee's team members, physicians, and director. The evaluation is based upon the key results areas that are incorporated into each job description. During the review process, the staff employees have the possibility of being elevated one level on a ten-step scale, which equates to a cost-of-living increase for good performance. It is very uncommon for an employee to increase more than one step in the annual review process. If an employee is promoted but is still on the ten-step scale system he or she may be categorized on a higher-level ten-step scale. The MSO's management (i.e., managers, directors, executive director) are evaluated in August each year, with any raises based on predetermined bonus criteria.

Corrective Action   The MSO's policy manual has a clearly defined corrective action policy. The first step taken if an employee fails to perform adequately or follow rules or policies is to have a formal "talk and listen" session. The purpose of the verbal counseling/warning is to identify and acknowledge the problem, develop any supervisory assistance plan to correct the problem, and prevent a recurrence of the issue.

The next step beyond the verbal warning involves a formal corrective action procedure.

Step 1: Written Warning—If two verbal counselings or warnings have been issued within six months, a written warning, at the discretion of the manager, may be issued to the employee.

Step 2: Second Written Warning with Possibility of Suspension—An employee receiving a second written warning within six months may be suspended without pay for a period not to exceed five work days. The employee is notified that the next corrective action may include discharge.

Step 3: Dismissal—Dismissal is the final step in the corrective action process. The dismissal policy is discussed below.

Dismissal Policy   The MSO has established a dismissal policy that applies to all employees in all facilities managed by the MSO. The policy clearly and explicitly outlines the guidelines regarding employee dismissals, listing acts or actions subject to immediate dismissal and acts and actions that may result in dismissal following the corrective action procedure discussed above. The policy also outlines the necessary documentation required and parties to inform in the event of a dismissal.

Employee Recourse   The employee recourse action is explicitly outlined in terms of the process and time requirements for appeals to be filed.

Organizational Dynamics

Motivation: Recognition and Achievement   The MSO has instituted an employee recognition and bonus program that rewards teams and individual employees for customer service and exemplary performance. Monthly awards are given in the form of gift certificates and annual bonuses. The employees are evaluated based on managers' observations, merit evaluations, and patient surveys.

In addition to this program, birthday cards are sent to the employees and accomplishments are acknowledged during the annual evaluation process. Individual and organizational goals and challenges are identified during the annual evaluation process.

Motivation: Autonomy   Management-level positions are more conducive to autonomy and therefore a greater degree of autonomy is afforded to these positions. The staff-level positions tend to be more structured due to the nature of the tasks performed. The MSO's employees have freedom to accomplish tasks within the parameters of the organization's policies and procedures; however, creativity and more effective or efficient methods of accomplishing tasks and responsibilities are encouraged.

Leadership   In various situations the office managers, lead positions, and directors all exhibit leadership skills. There are informal leaders who provide guidance and assistance at the various locations and within the different departments.

Communication and Small-Group Interaction   The MSO's personnel communicate both verbally and in writing on a day-to-day basis. In addition to the day-to-day communication, the MSO has the following monthly meetings.

(continued)

- Full staff
- Office managers
- Medical staff (i.e., RNs, LPNs and MDs)
- Office assistants
- Medical records staff
- Cashiers
- Leadership development for management staff
- Quarterly full group physician meetings

Employees are appropriately informed of the daily activities and changes occurring in the organization. Small-group interaction is encouraged and task forces are formed on a regular basis, as deemed necessary.

Problem Solving   Problem solving is generally led by the office managers or director; however, staff input is needed in many instances. For example, staff members may assist management by troubleshooting or gathering information on special projects to identify causes of problems.

Innovation and Change   The MSO's management communicates potential changes to the medical staff and employees prior to instituting significant revisions in policy. As mentioned above, certain positions are better adapted than others to innovative behavior and planning. The MSO's management encourages innovation and change if the outcomes, quality of service, and policies are maintained or exceeded. Staff meetings are used, in part, to identify problems or gather suggestions to resolve certain issues.

Human Resources Management: Conclusions and Recommendations

For the purposes of this report, and as outlined above, human resource management encompasses physician issues, executive director and medical director management, employee management, and organizational dynamics.

Strengths
- The MSO has an established physician performance evaluation process.

- Physicians view themselves as being an integrated group practice.
- The MSO is not paying the health system for human resource services.
- Staff-level employees have clearly defined job descriptions.
- The MSO facilities are modern, class-A facilities.
- Infrastructure and management emphasize a team approach.
- Strong practice-management background and extensive experience of the MSO's management team.
- Clearly defined human resources policies and procedures.
- Extensive, formal orientation and customer service training programs.
- Established employee review process with clearly defined expectations and key results areas.
- Strong communication between management and staff through monthly meetings and open-door policies.

Weaknesses

- Physician employment agreements are not based on productivity.
- The majority of the human resource functions are supposed to be provided by the health system but have been limited to job posting/advertisements. This has limited the expertise related to specific medical practice issues and the potential marketability of the MSO to independent practices.
- Communication between executive director and CEO needs to be enhanced in certain areas.
- Lack of managed care expertise in the MSO.
- Limited physician leadership.
- Limited benefit package (i.e., no profit sharing) compared to other health system entities.
- Decentralized human resource files. Some files are maintained by the health system and others are maintained and stored by the MSO.

Recommendations

- Consider spinning off the physicians employed by the health system into a Friendly PC. A Friendly PC is a professional corporation

(*continued*)

owned by physicians who are friendly to nonphysicians who are capitalizing and indirectly controlling the practice. It is a means of avoiding direct ownership prohibited by state corporate practice of medicine laws.

- Develop a relationship with an established physician leader.
- Develop an internal human resources component to provide benefits management and recruiting services and expand the MSO's range of services.
- Develop internally or contract externally to acquire managed care expertise to conduct contract management and product-development services.
- Review the nursing wages and employee benefits packages to ensure that they are competitive. Conduct a cost/benefit analysis of the cost of training new employees.
- Involve the executive director in the MSO's management in aspects of managed care contracting and the health system's PHO activities as they relate to the MSO and the market.

The next section of the case study concerns the analysis of both specific and general research gathered on the organization and its environment. Such an analysis can encompass numerous organizational issues as well as market and industry trends affecting the business. This information provides the basis for evaluation of the effectiveness of the organizational structure, the strength of the organization's business strategy in the local market, and its awareness of and reaction to industry factors affecting its operations.

External Environment

The local market's demographics, socio-economics, managed care penetration, provider community, and healthcare facilities should be included in this analysis. This data can be used to identify competitors, the level of competition, the supply of facilities and providers, market share, demand for health services, potential EHO members, contracting opportunities with managed care organizations, managed care plan types and enrollees, and any other factors influencing the organization's business. Limited benchmarking information for EHOs is just becoming available and may be used to assess the organization's performance on a variety of financial and other indicators. Local market information should be evaluated in light of pertinent industry trends, information on national reimbursement, and regulatory issues and developments. The case study has summarized and evaluated research specific to the organization in relation to its major operational components.

Internal Environment

In addition to HR management, the organization's internal environment including legal, governance, and staff structure should also be reviewed in the context of its operational and strategic goals.

Legal Issues   In reviewing the legal and regulatory issues pertinent to an EHO, the following areas should be considered. Many of the legal issues will require further investigation by legal or tax counsel, however a preliminary review should be made by the consultant. The regulatory aspects that should be considered are antitrust compliance and fraud and abuse risk. General legal considerations include the review of the corporate structure (i.e., C-corp, S-corp, LLC, limited partnership, etc.) to determine if there is the proper balance between tax advantages and liability protection, formal executed agreements between the parties in the EHO should be in place and should be reviewed for appropriate termination and compensation provisions as well as any covenants, and the existence of corporate records such as minutes from meetings and appropriate filings with the IRS and state and local government.

Governance   The governance of the EHO should be structured to allow various stakeholders input into the decision-making process yet malleable enough to enable the organization to make the necessary changes or decisions in a timely manner. The governance structure should have provisions to terminate agreements, personnel, and a formal exit strategy and valuation formula for participant's equity in place from the outset of the organization's existence. Decision-making on day-to-day operations needs to be delegated to a level that allows for efficient operations, however, high level strategic decision making should reside at an executive level.

Staff Structure   The composition and structure of the staff is one of the most vital assets of an EHO. The review process should include an evaluation of staffing levels, leadership of managers, appropriate levels of competency, and the allocation of resources between departments.

EXTERNAL AND INTERNAL ENVIRONMENTS

Evaluation of the External Environment

Service Community: Geographic Area   The MSO's central business offices are located in the outer suburbs of a major metropolitan area. Terrain, climate, and other geographic factors are not extreme or unique and so are not relevant to this analysis.

Service Community: Demographic, Economic, and Social Characteristics The Metropolitan Statistical Area (MSA) in which the MSO is located has a stable population and a typical age distribution. Income and housing data are likewise close to the average for this part of the country and so do not warrant particular discussion.

     The area's employment distribution is 20.3 percent in the professional sector, 28 percent in manufacturing, 20.3 percent in trade, 6.5 percent in construction, and 7 percent in finance and real estate, with the remaining 17.9 percent divided among several other industry sectors. The MSO's parent health system is one of the four largest employers in the area. The workforce is highly diverse: 31 percent of employed persons' occupations are in technical areas, sales, and administrative support; 23.1 percent are managerial or professional specialists; 21.1 percent are factory workers and laborers; 11.9 percent are precision craftsmen and repairmen; 11 percent are in service occupations; and 1.8 percent are in farming, forestry, or fishing. However, the area has an unemployment rate of 7.1 percent.

     The metropolitan area has numerous cultural and recreational institutions and facilities.

Current Status of the Provider Community   The provider community in the greater market area remains very independent. The majority of physicians are in practices that contain less than four physicians. The provider community is represented by a wide array of ethnic backgrounds, cultures, and medical training. The independent nature of the provider community has, in part, limited the success of previous physician integration efforts. As the incursion of capitated contracts and larger discounts becomes more prevalent in the market, it will become increasingly difficult for the physicians to remain independent.

Hospital Resources and Affiliations   The MSO is a for-profit corporation whose sole shareholder is the health system. As of the time of this review the health system or its hospital provides certain management services to the MSO and its practices. The health system provides human resource functions, financial management (i.e., payroll, accounts payable, and financial reporting), and marketing and transcription services to the MSO practices. In addition to providing these services, the health system is the employer of the MSO's employed physicians. As discussed above, the strategic planning process is presently a centralized process conducted at the system level.

The MSO is also affiliated with the health system's Physician Hospital Organization (PHO). The PHO is a joint venture between the health system hospital and medical group. The employed physicians have gained access to some managed care plans through the PHO.

Interprovider Relationships   The employed physicians obtain the majority of their referrals through word of mouth and patient referrals. Some physician referrals come from within the employed physicians group; however, there have been a limited number of referrals to the employed physicians from the independent physician community. Many independent primary care physicians (PCPs) in the community have been critical of the health system employing physicians, which has created tension and a limited working relationship between the employed physicians and the independent PCPs that have privileges at the health system hospital. Many community activities have been suggested to the employed physicians to enhance their reputation and increase their exposure to community residents. The majority of the employed physicians do not reside in the local area, but live in suburban areas closer to the nearby urban city.

Third-Party Payors
The MSO has not established any formal relationships with third-party payors. The extent of the interaction with the third-party payors has been to get the employed physicians credentialed in the various managed care plans. An employers' healthcare coalition has not been established yet in the greater area.

(continued)

Organizational Assessment

Current Assessment Process   The present management status assessment and operational review is the first independent review that the MSO has had performed for the entire organization. There is no formal organizational assessment process in place. The MSO does have an internal, individual assessment process that takes place during the annual evaluation.

Profile of Medical, Support, and Administrative Staff   At the time of the assessment site work, the MSO managed the practices of 12 physicians and had an agreement to manage the practice of one additional physician in the near future. The 12 physicians presently under the MSO's management include four family practitioners, four internists, two pediatricians, and two obstetricians/gynecologists. The 12-physician medical staff is composed of six female and six male physicians. Eight of the 12 physicians joined the employed physicians group directly out of residency training, while the other four had been in private practice prior to their affiliation with the health system. The eight physicians who came directly from residency programs are in the process of building their practices and have yet to reach full capacity.

Organizational Hierarchy and Structure   The MSO's board of directors presently consists of the following six members.

- Chairman: President of the health system, chairman/president of the MSO
- Secretary: Chief operating officer of the health system
- Treasurer: Chief financial officer of the health system
- President: Vice president of ambulatory services of the health system, chief executive officer of the MSO
- One MSO-employed physician and one other physician

The MSO's administrative team consists of the following positions.

- CEO
- Executive director
- Director of patient services
- Director of quality and customer services
- Manager of business office

Four practice managers are responsible for the MSO's six locations.

Governance   The MSO is governed by the health system as the sole shareholder of the MSO. The board, which is appointed by the sole shareholder, serves as the governing body and approves and/or develops such items as the budget and the strategic plan. The overall performance of the MSO is the responsibility of the CEO of the MSO, while the day-to-day activities of the MSO are the responsibility of the executive director of the MSO. The daily operations of the practice sites are the responsibility of either the director in charge of the particular location or the office manager of the site.

Procedures   The MSO's bylaws address certain written procedures of the governing board. The bylaws clearly state the powers of the sole shareholder; the duties of all the officers of the board; the election, term, and removal of board members and officers; the definition of a quorum, notice, and attendance at meetings; the corporation's policies on conflicts of interest; and a description of fiscal matters.

Monitoring and Assessing Performance   There are regular board meetings at which members review and explain all aspects of the MSO's activities. In addition, both the CEO and the executive director receive a personal financial review that takes the MSO's performance into account.

Financial Management Responsibility   Financial management services are provided by and are the responsibility of the health system and therefore are not evaluated in this report.

Environmental Surveillance   Presently no formal environmental surveillance takes place on a regular basis.

Evaluation of the Legal Environment

The MSO as a Legal Entity: Legal Structure   The MSO is structured as a for-profit corporation. The health system is the sole shareholder of the MSO, and hence holds all authority, rights, and privileges that accompany majority ownership. The current organizational structure has worked well given the MSO's present relationships with the majority of the affiliated physicians (i.e., they are employees of the MSO).

(*continued*)

The MSO as a Legal Entity: Organizational Documentation and Agreements
The bylaws and agreements of the MSO address many of its voting, control, and procedural issues. The bylaws adequately address the relevant issues given that the MSO is owned and governed by the sole shareholder. The physician employment agreements explicitly outline the requirements of both parties; however, in most cases the employment agreements do not specifically indicate the criteria used to determine the amount or method of determining bonuses.

Laws and Regulations   The MSO's legal counsel regularly reviews its transactions and business practices to ensure that it is in compliance with applicable laws and regulations.

Medical Malpractice   All of the employed physicians have active malpractice policies that provide $1,000,000 of coverage per incident and $3,000,000 in the annual aggregate. All physicians are required, by the terms of their employment agreements, to obtain supplemental (or "tail") coverage. In the case of two of the physicians who became employees several years ago, the health system is required to pay for the tail coverage; the remaining ten physicians are required to purchase the tail coverage at their own expense. The MSO is not aware of any outstanding claims, suits, or contingent liabilities involving the MSO's or the health system's physicians.

External and Internal Environments: Conclusions and Recommendations

Strengths

- The MSO has strong name recognition and reputation through its relationship with the health system.
- Underdeveloped market in terms of managed care incursion creates strong opportunities.
- Growing population base.
- Affiliation of MSO with various health system entities.
- Strong leadership ability on the MSO board.

Weaknesses

- Formal relationships with third-party payors have not been developed, but are in the early development process.
- Sole shareholder possesses total control of governance.

- Need additional physician participation in governance.
- Potential conflict of interest for management between various health system entities (i.e., the MSO and the PHO).
- Confusion among various roles and incentives of physician-related ventures (i.e., the MSO, medical office buildings, ancillaries, and immediate care).

Recommendations

- Establish relationships between the MSO and managed care organizations and large employers through one-on-one interactions and through the development of an employers' health coalition.
- Review the bylaws and ownership structure of the MSO as well as the health system's role as sole shareholder. Ownership in the MSO should be offered to physicians through a pedestal acquisition (where a well-known or respected group is first approached to encourage others to follow) or other tactical plan.
- Seek additional physician involvement in the governance of the MSO.
- Determine the role of the MSO in relation to the other physician initiatives the health system is involved in, and structure management and governance to avoid conflicts of interest.
- Formally develop the MSO's statement of strategic initiatives and develop tactical plans to support the initiatives. Implement these plans.

SUMMARY

This report presents the health system's management with an independent, third-party assessment of the MSO's management and operational performance. The preceding sections have set forth our conclusions and recommendations pertaining to the five major operational and management areas. Following is our overall assessment of the MSO as an entire entity.

The infrastructure of the MSO adequately meets the needs of a hospital-owned physician organization. The management of the MSO is experienced in practice management and has developed a strong support staff to enable the physicians to focus on the practice of medicine. The policies and procedures address most of the day-to-day operational issues for the MSO. The tasks and operational areas for which the MSO has control and responsibility are handled well. However, the MSO has not yet developed a fully articulated mission and does not yet have a strategic plan or a strategic planning process in place. The MSO has no stated goals, and therefore it is impossible to assess its performance in relation to its objectives. System management must develop a consensus for a mission, vision, or strategic direction which the MSO will take in the future, and then measure all future projects and strategic initiatives against that vision and its related tactical plans. In order to expand management services to independent practices, the MSO would need to control these services and offer additional ones. Currently, many of the MSO's important operational aspects (e.g., finance, information systems, human resources) are controlled at the system level, which limits the MSO's ability to effectively market its services to independent practices. Communication and information systems are areas that could be improved and enhanced. The financial reporting of the MSO does not provide cost-accounting data, nor do the financial statements show a true economic picture of the MSO and the employed physicians' practices.

At the direction of the CEO, the analysis did not include financial benchmarking or comparisons to industry norms. Future efforts should include financial analysis of the employed physicians' practices and a marketing plan for physician strategies. Such a plan should be presented to the health system's management in order to initiate a strategic planning process that can help identify a long-range vision for the MSO.

In summary, the areas that the MSO is responsible for are handled well, and the management does a good job of delivering practice-management services. The MSO could be enhanced by developing a consensus as to a vision, developing strategic initiatives to achieve the vision, and formulating tactical plans to accomplish the strategic initiatives. The MSO has most of the resources necessary to bring its organization to the next level of the evolutionary process, and those resources and skill sets that are not currently in place could be brought into the organization on a full-time or contractual basis. The key to the MSO's future success is for the leadership to devote the resources necessary for strategic planning and implementation (e.g., management time, financial resources) and to continue to develop and provide a range of marketable healthcare products to a range of purchasers in the community.

## Chapter 8

Due Diligence Engagement: Evaluating the Potential for Success of an Investment in a Primary Care Physician Practice-Management Company

The following chapter presents a case study of the final report from a consulting due diligence engagement done for a large healthcare corporation considering investing in a private, primary care model Physician Practice Management Company (PPMC). The engagement was based upon the PPMC's business report and other information.

OVERVIEW OF THE PROPOSED VENTURE

ABC Healthcare Corporation (ABC) is currently evaluating the potential for return on investment in a private Physician Practice Management Company. The PPMC is a venture capital–financed company formed to develop and manage new primary care physician practices and networks in underserved second- and third-tier cities and rural markets.

As ABC investigates various options to address the issue of a primary care physician shortage in their local markets, it is exploring a relationship with the PPMC for the "right fit." Concurrently, the PPMC is searching for additional working capital and investor groups to fund its projected business plan and growth. These mutual needs and interests have resulted in a proposed investment in the PPMC by ABC. The details and magnitude of this proposed investment have yet to be determined, and are not discussed in this report.

It is of note, however, that the PPMC's business plan reaches significantly farther in geographic scope than necessary to meet ABC's initial local needs. The current status of this project is that the PPMC may provide a solution to ABC's shortage of primary care physicians in its local market area, as well as an opportunity for growth and investment in the rapidly growing practice-management field on a broader scale.

Scope of This Engagement

The purpose of this consulting engagement is to perform certain due diligence procedures pertaining to the prospective association of ABC with the PPMC.

> *Due Diligence:* Such a measure of prudence, activity, or assiduity, as is properly to be expected from, and ordinarily exercised by, a reasonable and prudent man under the particular circumstances; not measured by any absolute standard, but depending on the relative facts of the special case.[1]

The scope of the engagement included gathering data from the parties involved; review and analysis of the PPMC's business plan, including practice models, financial statements, and projections; and a comparison of the information gathered with current market standards. The engagement included performing due diligence/financial analysis and providing findings and conclusions as requested by ABC as to the accuracy, integrity, and validity of the PPMC's business plan based on the written plan provided by the PPMC and verbal information communicated by ABC.

Executive Summary

The PPMC has delineated its business plan and projections by defining prominent environmental, market, and competitive issues that could have significant impact on its future. It has assembled a management team and targeted selected markets for the initial practice office openings based on factors that it projects will contribute to quick growth for the practices once they are open and in operation. As supported by the

---

[1]Henry C. Black, M.A. *Blacks Law Dictionary,* fifth edition. West Publishing, St. Paul, Minn., 1979, p. 411.

articles within the business plan and by industry trends, the PPMC is attempting to position itself for entry into one of the most prominent niches of healthcare integration—that is, the expanding networks of primary care physicians that are developing in order to promote the survival of small practices in the future capitated environment of medicine.

There are several factors that may cause deviations from the business plan, such as timing delays and deviations from projected levels of productivity and profitability. The physician recruitment component of the overall business plan as it relates to the practice model adopted by the PPMC is clearly a significant cause for concern, as the results of the PPMC's physician recruitment efforts will have an impact on all other aspects of the business plan.

At first glance, the physician recruitment strategy outlined in the business plan appears to be structured to appeal to physicians based on the PPMC's current trends and on the desires of physicians looking for new practice opportunities. However, the conceptual arrangement and manpower plans of the PPMC's practice models appear to contradict the intended message to physicians regarding the physician-friendly nature of the practice opportunities. With the growing shift toward gatekeeper-model delivery systems in some markets, and with the resulting demand for primary care physicians, their physician recruitment in the current market and beyond will be difficult at best. A number of facets of the PPMC's plan may result in a lengthy and strenuous process to recruit and retain high-quality physicians with the necessary credentials.

The plan's physician recruitment strategy has an impact on the following.

- The timing of opening of new practice offices as stated in the plan.
- The budgeted costs associated with opening the new practice sites.
- The practice's ability to participate in certain managed care plans based on stringent and lengthy credentialing requirements and processes.
- Other underestimated projected costs associated with physician relocation expenses and other start-up costs.
- In some of the prospective locations, revenue projections that may be overly optimistic from the timing standpoint (i.e., from start-up to "full practice" productivity).

Based on their curriculum vitae, the assembled leadership team members appear to possess many strong characteristics; however, the time required for the PPMC to reach the desired level of success may be longer than anticipated, and profit levels may be lower than anticipated.

BACKGROUND OF THE PPMC

Ownership and Corporate Structure

The PPMC is a corporation with stock distributed among four investment shareholders.

The PPMC is headed by a board of directors representing the four investors, a president and executive vice president, and vice presidents for finance, network development, marketing and client relations, and physician recruitment. The vice president for physician recruitment supervises two other recruiters.

There are plans to add a chief financial officer and a vice president of managed care within the next year. Other personnel to be added within three years include physicians in administrative capacities overseeing quality care issues, as well as personnel for physicians relations programs, continuing medical education, oversight of managed care patient management initiatives, and other clinically oriented programs.

Services Provided

The stated purpose of the company is to develop and manage primary care physician practices in selected markets. The individual tasks necessary to achieve this overall objective are numerous and complex. The current management team appears to be capable of implementing the required steps, exhibiting organizational, market identification, financial, practice management, and managed care expertise. However, the physician recruitment and MIS departments may lack depth of knowledge and experience in relation to the magnitude of the goals they must achieve in order for the business plan to succeed.

Current State of Affairs

Since its inception as a corporation, the PPMC has not realized a profitable level of operation. Additional funding is required for continued operation and growth. The growth projected in the PPMC's business plan hinges on the actual opening of the planned practice sites. The timely opening of these practice sites depends, to a great degree, on the success of the physician recruitment program. The continued viability of each practice ultimately depends on the PPMC's ability not only to attract but to retain, motivate, and manage quality physicians. Again, this emphasizes the importance of continuing physician recruitment activity.

Business Plan for Growth of the Firm

The "cluster strategy" as outlined in the business plan appears to be strategically sound and economically prudent because of the aspects of physician coverage, operating efficiencies, and managed care contracting benefits that derive from the proximity of practices to one another. The target markets appear to be appropriately defined, and the cluster strategy seems to be a reasonably viable approach to these markets. Significant demographic research and the planned effective use of physician extenders (paraprofessional providers) also lend strength to the outlook for success. Use of outside specialty (e.g., managed care) consultants, contacts with managed care companies, and ongoing efforts to work in conjunction with hospitals and hospital-management companies are all elements of the business plan that should enhance the opportunity for success of the PPMC, as well as attract additional investors and potential physician recruits.

While acknowledging that all of the planning, forethought, and preliminary steps that have been taken may be vital to the PPMC's ultimate success, it is critical to remember that the recruitment program may still be the fragile link to reality. The regional undersupply of primary care physicians to meet the gatekeeper needs of the growing managed care environment is one of the greatest challenges facing the PPMC's plan. The success of the PPMC's growth plan depends on its ability to rise to the challenge of recruiting, retaining, motivating, and managing quality primary care physicians at their designated practice sites. Geographic location has historically been a major hurdle in physician recruitment. Most physicians look for opportunities in major cities or suburbs of metropolitan areas. The PPMC's plan will work against this tendency and its recruitment team may experience difficulty generating interest, response, and commitment from physicians for the smaller, more remote clinic locations.

THE CLIMATE OF PRIMARY CARE MEDICINE TODAY

Current Trends

Just as cost-containment measures, increased regulatory oversight, and other market forces are driving a massive movement toward managed healthcare, so is primary care playing an increasingly important role in those markets dominated by traditional HMOs. The recognized primary care specialties include family medicine/general practice, general internal medicine, and general pediatrics.[2] Primary care physicians are not homogeneous. For example, some emphasize well-patient care, some engage in urgent care, some serve in the role of gatekeeper, while others specialize in geriatrics. Less than 40 percent of all U.S. physicians are primary care physicians.[3] Provider organizations have discovered the value of using nonphysician providers, including nurse practitioners and physician assistants, in lieu of primary care physicians. A recent study found that 60 to 80 percent of primary care services can be provided by a nonphysician who possesses specialized training in primary care, with the same or better results.[4]

Between 1982 and 1995, the number of people enrolled in HMOs increased from ten to fifty million. The trends predict that HMO enrollment will surmount 100 million by the turn of the decade. As further illustration of the movement of healthcare delivery to primary care settings, between 1971 and 1990 the number of hospital beds in the United States decreased from 1.7 to 1.2 million, while the average hospital occupancy rate decreased to under 66 percent and average length of stay dropped from 8.1 days to 7.2 days. Managed care, capitation, and the introduction of Diagnostic Related Groups (DRGs) and the Resource Based Relative Value Scale (RBRVS) have reshaped our country's values regarding the delivery of healthcare.[5]

Between 1940 and 1993, the average physician did not experience a decrease in net income. Since 1993, the decline of average physician incomes has spared only primary care physicians (PCPs).[6] Of ten medical fields surveyed in one study, family practice, internal medicine, and psychiatry were the only groups with net income gains in 1993.[7] The decreases in net income may be attributable more to increased administrative expenses than to decreases in revenue.[8] While median gross practice revenue increased 14.8 percent for family practice physicians in 1993, median gross practice revenue decreased 12.4 percent for surgical

---

[2]Richard A. Cooper. "Seeking a Balanced Physician Workforce for the 21st Century." *Journal of the American Medical Association,* 272:9 (September 7, 1994), p. 680.

[3]Ibid.

[4]Philip R. Alper. "Primary Care in Transition." *The Journal of the American Medical Association,* 272:19 (November 16, 1994), p. 1523.

[5]William Winkenwerder, Jr. "The Impact of Health Care Reform on Group Practice." *Physician Executive,* 20:10 (October, 1994), p. 7.

[6]Joel Goldberg. "Doctor's Earnings Take a Nosedive." *Medical Economics,* 71:17 (September 12, 1994), p. 123.

[7]Ibid.

[8]Ibid.

specialties. The effect of capitation's incentive for providers to minimize care is demonstrated by the fact that gross revenues realized by primary care practices in 1993 increased, while at the same time the number of patient visits in these practices declined.

Running an office-based primary care practice that derives its patient base entirely from third-party payors (indemnity insurance plans, HMOs, PPOs, etc.) has proven risky. Since the physician is dependent upon the third-party payor for referrals, his or her financial success is correlated to referral decisions and marketing efforts of the payor over which he or she has no control.[9] Furthermore, withholds and risk pools have increasingly put primary care physicians at financial risk through increased liability.[10] Stop-loss insurance has become common among risk-sharing providers as a means of protecting physicians against exorbitant liability. As managed care companies penetrate markets, practice management concurrently becomes more complicated. Each time a new managed care contract is signed, office operations, management information systems, and billing procedures become more complex and expensive. As practice operations require more and more resources, overhead costs increase and reimbursement decreases.[11] The pressure to reduce costs and provide a return to the shareholders has forced managed care companies to reduce physician panel size and increase the volume of patients seen by physicians. The right of the insurance company to remove a physician from a provider panel has been successfully defended in court.[12]

Under the gatekeeper model there is an undersupply of PCPs; thus, managed care has benefited primary care physicians by allowing them to potentially sell their practices for above market value. Unfortunately, once managed care has penetrated a market and all of the desired practices have been purchased, the value of the remaining practices generally declines.[13]

Referral Patterns

In many managed care and integrated delivery systems where the system is not fully capitated, primary care physicians serve as the care coordi-

---

[9]Philip R. Alper. "Primary Care in Transition." *The Journal of the American Medical Association,* 272:19 (November 16, 1994), p. 1523.

[10]Ibid.

[11]Jim Montague. "Striking Back: Managed Care Plans Are Dumping Physicians, but the Doctors are Fighting Back." *Hospitals and Health Networks,* 68:20 (October 20, 1994), p. 38.

[12]Ibid.

[13]Ibid.

nators (or gatekeepers) in the referral process for many healthcare services. In these systems, it is thought that the use of primary care physicians as gatekeepers to coordinate care is the best way to maintain wellness and educate patients about prevention and care.[14] Specialty physicians and hospitals depend on primary care physician referrals for much of their patient volume. Currently, physicians receive almost 45 percent of their new patients from referring physicians, with this percentage being much higher in certain specialties. It has also been discovered that a new patient who is physician-referred generates twice the revenue per year of an established patient, and up to three times more revenue annually than a patient who is self-referred.[15]

Resource Based Relative Value Scale (RBRVS)

The Omnibus Budget Reconciliation Act of 1989 (OBRA 89) established a Medicare fee schedule for physician services based on estimates of resource costs incurred in an efficient medical practice. Under the RBRVS fee schedule, physicians in primary care specialties are, on average, expected to fare relatively well compared with those in surgical specialties. However, the portion of Medicare dollars attributable to primary care has shown only a minimal increase in recent years. Consequently, between 1991 and 1993, primary care revenues did not keep pace with rising practice costs, and the fee structure has become highly skewed toward procedural services. For example, during this same period of time, general internists experienced a 6 percent decline in Medicare payments under RBRVS.[16] If the RBRVS fee schedule were adjusted, it is believed that many in organized medicine would prefer a unified cross-specialty fee schedule. Since the Health Care Financing Administration (HCFA) began phasing in RBRVS in 1992, other government agencies and some private payors have begun phasing in this payment methodology.[17] For the most part, third parties are adopting the fee schedule in a budget-neutral fashion (i.e., fees are adjusted up or down, but the payor pays the same amount overall). In a recent survey of 333 payors, one-third had already

---

[14]David Azevedo. "New Strategies for Clamping Down on Referrals." *Medical Economics,* 72:7 (April 10, 1995), p. 61.

[15]Rajshekhar Javalgi, W. Benoy Joseph, William R. Gombeski, Jr., and Judith A. Lester. "How Physicians Make Referrals." *Journal of Health Care Marketing,* 13:2 (Summer, 1993), p. 6.

[16]Philip R. Alper. "Primary Care in Transition." *The Journal of the American Medical Association,* 272:19 (November 16, 1994), p. 1523.

[17]David Azevedo. "How Many Third Parties Will Buy into RBRVS?" *Medical Economics,* 71:14 (July 25, 1994), p. 88.

[18]Ibid.

adopted the RBRVS fee schedule.[18] The declining reimbursement levels under RBRVS are pushing Medicare payors toward managed care.[19] The shift of practice patterns resulting from the use of RBRVS has dramatically lowered the amount of utilization for surgical procedures.[20] RBRVS ranks each medical service by physical and mental effort, technical skill, and practice expense.

Capitation/Reverse Capitation Trends

Using per-member per-month payments to providers, capitation shifts the insurance risk from the carrier back to the provider.[21] Although subspecialists manage 60 to 70 percent of U.S. healthcare dollars, historically these physicians have rarely participated in risk sharing.[22] Because of their ability to control referrals, utilization of resources, and length of stay, primary care physicians are often targeted for participation in capitated insurance programs.[23]

The decrease of hospital inpatient visits is a result of capitation's incentive to decrease utilization of resources.[24] As most health plans and group practices shift their primary care physicians to capitated payment mechanisms, several plans in California are contracting with primary care physicians on a fee-for-service basis and with subspecialists on a capitated basis.[25] This payment structure, called *reverse capitation,* can be used to recruit primary care physicians in markets where they are in low supply. Due to their relative oversupply and loss of influence, subspecialty physicians are less able than primary care physicians to resist capitation. Payors adopting reverse capitation strategies target subspecialty physicians for cost cutting and reward primary care physicians for controlling referrals to specialists, who are perceived as costly providers in the system.[26]

---

[19]Ibid.

[20]Ibid.

[21]Greg Borzo. "Market Induces a New Approach to Capitation: Prepayment for Specialists, Fee for Service for Generalists." *American Medical News,* 38:13 (April 13, 1995), p. 3.

[22]Ibid.

[23]Philip R. Alper. "Primary Care in Transition." *The Journal of the American Medical Association,* 272:19 (November 16, 1994), p. 1523.

[24]Ibid.

[25]Greg Borzo. "Market Induces a New Approach to Capitation: Prepayment for Specialists, Fee for Service for Generalists." *American Medical News,* 38:13 (April 3, 1995), p. 3.

[26]Ibid.

Reverse capitation is most successful in markets with a surplus of physicians and a high penetration of managed care. Since capitation of subspecialty physicians is uncommon, setting realistic capitation rates has evolved to be reverse capitation's major drawback. To compensate for the financial difficulties inflicted by subspecialty capitation, many physicians are forming single-specialty networks and groups that have the capacity to bear risk.[27] As reverse capitation matures and gains acceptance, some experts predict that it will migrate throughout the United States.[28]

The PPMC plans to be heavily involved in managed care, which may result in a significant percentage of capitated revenue. As a result, the PPMC, in its pro forma, appears to have taken capitation into account when estimating practice revenue. The PPMC presumably expects to receive a level of contractual allowances that is higher than industry norms. While the PPMC plans to enter the managed care market, it remains uncertain whether a two-physician-per-practice model is the most efficient and effective delivery model for primary healthcare services in a capitated environment.

PRIMARY CARE CLINIC MODELS SELECTED

Description of the Models

The PPMC's business plan calls for "an ideal mix of between ten and 21 practice clusters with either 21 physicians in ten clusters or ten physicians in each of the 21 clusters." The ultimate goal is to employ 210 physicians within the next five years, with a minimum of two physicians per practice office. The unique attribute of this arrangement, as expressed in the PPMC's business plan, is "the application of the principles of contract management to primary care physician practice start-up and development." The plan goes on to say that "the PPMC is one of the first companies to focus on second- and third-tier towns and cities in rural areas." Its plan is to establish multiple practices in relatively small geographic areas.

---

[27]Ken Terry. "Look Who's Guarding the Gate to Specialty Care." *Medical Economics*, 71:16 (August 22, 1994), p. 124.

[28]Greg Borzo. "Market Induces a New Approach to Capitation: Prepayment for Specialists, Fee for Service for Generalists." *American Medical News*, 38:13 (April 3, 1995), p. 3.

The size and model of practice adopted has both time and finance implications for the PPMC's plans. For the purposes of this engagement, a "small practice" is defined as two physicians and a "large practice" means eight or more physicians. According to the 1994 Physician Market Place Statistics published by the American Medical Association (AMA), physicians in small practices work an average of 48 weeks per year and provide services in the office an average of 29.9 hours per week. Physicians in large practices work fewer weeks (an average of 46.3 weeks per year) and provide fewer hours of services in the office (an average of 26.5 hours per week). Physicians in large practices spend an average of 10.7 hours per week completing hospital rounds and an average of 7.1 hours per week in outpatient clinics and emergency rooms. Physicians in small practices spend less time on hospital rounds (an average of 2.5 hours per week) and log fewer hours (an average of 4 hours per week) in outpatient clinics and emergency rooms than do physicians in large practices. In aggregate, physicians participating in large and small practices spend approximately 55 hours per week fulfilling their patient-care responsibilities.

Comparison of Practice Models to Industry Trends

The cluster concept is designed both to be successful and to attract prospective managed care company clients. It will, however, add difficulty to the challenge of recruitment. While the PPMC's promotional literature and business plan portray its practices as being set up in a physician-friendly manner, the reality is that they will function as small private practices with evening and weekend hours of operation, tight (i.e., one in two) call/coverage rotations, and, in some cases, a need for the family practitioner to perform obstetrical services (i.e., deliveries) on an as-needed basis. While at one time this scenario was not considered extraordinarily discouraging to candidate physicians, these practice circumstances often make the primary care physician recruiting process difficult at best. The working environment of this scenario may inhibit the PPMC's ability to distinguish itself from the rest of the masses of physician recruiters in a crowded market, who may be diligent and skilled at the task of recruiting and who may offer highly competitive packages in competing for the same pool of available, high-quality, eligible primary care physicians.

The PPMC plans, however, to offer physicians a larger-than-average compensation package ($130,000 per year versus the industry norm of $118,750 for primary care physicians). Moreover, physicians targeted for recruitment will be offered the security of being directly employed by the PPMC, with a guaranteed salary and regularly scheduled working hours. The PPMC will also no doubt emphasize that its employed physicians will not be burdened with administrative and financial concerns. Employed physicians (currently over 36 percent of all physicians) work, on average, seven hours per week and two weeks per year less than self-employed physicians.

Summary

The practice model and strategy the PPMC has selected, coupled with prudent practice-management skills and quality personnel, could conceivably succeed. The challenge will be in obtaining commitments from physicians who typically resist smaller communities, who prefer call/coverage rotations of one in five or greater, and who strongly resist involvement in obstetrical procedures because of the liability exposure and long, unscheduled hours.

GEOGRAPHIC TARGET MARKETS SELECTED

Practice Locations

In the next six months, the PPMC plans to open five initial clusters of practices (of three, four, one, one, and six practices, with two physicians at each location except for one solo practice) in five different large area markets around the country.

Analysis of Locations

These initial clinic locations do not include ABC's local market, and the PPMC's business plan does not address other markets beyond the initial five clusters.

The first two markets, with three and six practices, are in urban areas and are attractive locations to many physicians. Response to recruitment efforts for these two locations should prove strong, but the cost of living and the level of competition for physicians in these areas are high.

The third cluster, with four practices, represents smaller communities and, as the PPMC's management states, will involve obstetrical procedures in some instances. In addition, the cities are geographically dispersed, preventing increased call/coverage rotations among the PPMC's physicians.

The fourth cluster, with one practice, may appear initially to be attractive to physician candidates; however, physicians typically balk at the quality-of-life issues inherent to the largely rural region. The fact that the PPMC plans to recruit urgent-care physicians in this market should allow them to generate more responses than the standard family practice models would generate.

The fifth and last cluster, with one OB/GYN physician, is in a small city. While there has apparently been a positive reception to this start-up, the survival of the practice will depend on call/coverage and available backup. Recruitment of another physician here may be critical to retaining the existing physician for the long term.

Summary

To date, the PPMC's selection of locations seems to be consistent with its business plan. It is important to remember that the larger metropolitan areas will remain more appealing to a larger number of physician candidates, and smaller communities and rural areas will require more effort and recruitment cost to allow for successful staffing of the practices. In either case, competition for the prime physician candidates will be stiff, and it will take more than just the promise of a nice location to obtain commitments from physician prospects.

BUSINESS PLAN: FINANCIAL PROJECTIONS AND ANALYSIS

Sources of Comparison Data

Several sources of published data are available for comparison of the financial aspects of the PPMC's projected medical practices with the historical performance of existing practices on a nationwide scale.

Socioeconomic Characteristics of Medical Practice. American Medical Association, 1995.

Physician Characteristics and Distribution in the U.S. American Medical Association, 1994.

Physician Marketplace Statistics. American Medical Association, 1994.

Cost Survey: 1994 Report Based on 1993 Data. Medical Group Management Association.

Physician Compensation and Production Survey: 1994 Report Based on 1993 Data. Medical Group Management Association.

In comparing the PPMC's projections with industry averages and norms, the following steps were performed:

1. Analysis and categorization of revenue and expense projections provided by the PPMC.

2. Comparison of the appropriate industry data, from the above sources, that coincides with each of the PPMC's categories, combining categories where necessary and appropriate.

3. Calculation and expression of variances of the PPMC's projections from the industry averages and norms in terms of both dollar amounts and percentage of variation.

Comparison of Pro Forma with Industry Norms

See Exhibit 8-1, pages 243–245.

Comparison of 1995 Projections with MGMA Norms

See Exhibit 8-2, pages 246–247.

Comparison of Pro Forma Ratios with Industry Norms (FSSB)

See Exhibit 8-3, pages 248–265.

Ratio Analysis

Key financial ratios were derived from the data obtained from both the PPMC's FY 1994 financial statements and the pro forma financial statements prepared by the PPMC's staff. These ratios were compared to industry norms obtained from survey data in *Financial Studies of the Small Business* (FSSB).

Comparison of Subject Actual Financial Statements (1994) to 1994–95 FSSB. During 1994, the current ratio (7.6) and quick ratio (7.2) for the PPMC were higher than those published in FSSB, which had values of 1.3 for both ratios (see Exhibit 8-3, page 18 of 18). This discrepancy could be due to the PPMC's heavy inflow of cash from investors for the purchase of the PPMC's equity (par value) and additional paid-in capital that it received in preparation for its operations as a start-up business entity. The FSSB studies consist of a survey of a number of established physician practices; therefore, it is reasonable to expect some variance of those figures from the PPMC's actual 1994 figures. The same is true of the large variance between the PPMC's short-term debt to total debt ratio (0.05) and the FSSB figure (46.6). The PPMC's actual 1994 balance sheet shows only $70,010 in short-term liabilities, while long-term liabilities amount to $1,357,380 (see Exhibit 8-3, page 6 of 18). The bulk of these

EXHIBIT 8-1

(Page 1 of 3) PPMC Comparison of Production and Costs: Subject Pro Forma with Industry Norms

Item #		(A) Subject Projected Year 1	(B) Subject Per MD FTE		(C) Norms Per MD FTE		(D) Variance Per MD FTE	(E) Percent Variance Per MD FTE
	REVENUE ITEMS:							
1	Visits per physician per workweek	136.6	136.6		133.5		3.1	2.3%
2	Visits per physician per workday	27.3	27.3	(1)	26.7	(2)	0.6	2.2%
3	Office visits—new patients (fee)	$59	$59		$60		($1)	-1.7%
4	Office visits—new patients (% of visits)	54.6%	54.6%	(3)	10.4%	(4)	44.2%	80.9%
5	Office visits—established patients (fee)	$38	$38		$40		($2)	-4.5%
6	Office visits—established patients (% of visits)	41.8%	41.8%	(5)	67.6%	(6)	-25.8%	-61.7%
7	Hospital visits—established patients (fee)	$76	$76		$52		$24	32.2%
8	Hospital visits—established patients (% of visits)	3.6%	3.6%	(7)	10.3%	(8)	-6.7%	-185.1%
	EXPENSE ITEMS:							
9	Physicians (per FTE)	$130,000	$130,000		$118,750	(9)	$11,250	8.7%
10	Registered nurse (per FTE)	$27,040	$27,040		$30,160	(10)	($3,120)	-11.5%
11	Licensed practitioner nurse (per FTE)	$16,640	$16,640		$22,963	(11)	($6,323)	-38.0%
12	General administrative personnel (per FTE)	$14,560	$14,560		$21,154	(12)	($6,594)	-45.3%
13	Payroll taxes (%)	11.0%	11.0%		8.9%		2.1%	19.1%
14	Physician benefit expense (13)	$12,000	$6,000		$13,266	(14)	($1,266)	-21.1%
15	Nonprovider benefit expense (15)	$13,500	$6,750		$11,209	(16)	$2,291	17.0%
16	Other benefits (per physician) (17)	$5,000	$5,000		$1,636		$3,364	67.3%
17	Medical/surgical supplies (% of revenue)	4.0%	4.0%		3.6%		0.4%	10.0%
18	Laboratory expenses (% of revenue) (18)	1.4%	1.4%		3.3%		-1.9%	-132.9%
19	Outside medical services (% of revenue)	1.8%	1.8%		0.9%		0.9%	48.6%
20	Telephone/telecommunications	$4,440	$2,220		$3,368		($1,148)	-51.7%
21	Practice advertising	$1,800	$900		$1,000		($100)	-11.1%
22	Computer supplies	$1,000	$500	(19)	$2,455		($1,955)	-391.0%
23	Administrative expenses (20)	$8,398	$4,199		$8,178		($3,979)	-94.8%
24	Office rental	$45,000	$22,500		$23,624		($1,124)	-5.0%
25	Other nonprovider expenses (21)	$3,000	$1,500		$3,837		($2,337)	-155.8%

Exhibit 8-1

(Page 2 of 3)

	(A)	(B)	(C)		(D)	(E)
		Norms				Percent
					Variance	Variance
	Projected Year 1	Per MD FTE	Per MD FTE		Per MD FTE	Per MD FTE
INCOME STATEMENT ITEMS:						
Revenues:						
26 Office visits—new patients	$324,454	$162,227	$39,782	(22)	$122,445	75.5%
27 Office visits—established patients	$267,976	$133,988	$171,000	(23)	($37,012)	–27.6%
28 Hospital care visits	$39,825	$19,913	$33,674	(24)	($13,762)	–69.1%
29 Ancillary services component	$94,760	$47,380	$6,037	(25)	$41,343	87.3%
30 Gross revenue	$856,903	$428,452	$426,677		$1,775	0.4%
31 Number of FTE physicians	2					

Exhibit 8-1

(Page 3 of 3)

Notes:

1. First year average (ranging from 3 in month 1 to 40 in month 12).
2. Based on AMA norms (133.5 total visits per week/5 days per week).
3. First year average (ranging from 95% in month 1 to 20% in month 12).
4. Based on AMA norms (13.9 new patients per week/133.5 visits per week).
5. First year average (ranging from 5% in month 1 to 75% in month 12).
6. Based on AMA norms (90.3 new patients per week/133.5 visits per week).
7. First year average (ranging from 0% in month 1 to 5% in month 12).
8. Based on AMA norms (13.7 hospital visits per week/133.5 visits per week).
9. Based on 2–5 years experience and working 2,080 hours a year.
10. Based on 2–5 years experience and working 2,080 hours a year.
11. Based on 2–5 years experience and working 2,080 hours a year.
12. Based on MGMA norms (support staff payroll taxes $7,376/total support staff salaries $83,166).
13. Consists of benefit costs per physician ($500 per physician per month).
14. MGMA norm includes insurance: health, life, etc. ($5,564) and retirement/profit sharing/etc. ($7,702).
15. Based on costs of $250 per FTE per month (1.42 FTE registered nurse, 1.58 FTE licensed practical nurse, and 1.5 FTE administrative personnel).
16. MGMA norm includes insurance ($5,508), retirement and profit sharing ($4,313), and other benefits ($1,388).
17. Consists of employment incentives (moving/hiring per physician, first year only).
18. Consists of chemical reagents.
19. Based on MGMA norms (information services equipment/rental/maintenance).
20. Consists of postage, office supplies, and printing and stationery.
21. Consists of practice development and miscellaneous.
22. Based on AMA norms (13.9 new patients per week, * 47.7 weeks worked per year, * $60 average fee).[1]
23. Based on AMA norms (90.3 established patients per week, * 47.7 weeks worked per year, * $40 average fee).[1]
24. Based on AMA norms (13.7 hospital visits per week, * 47.7 weeks worked per year, * $52 average fee).[1]
25. Based on AMA norms (gross revenue from other activity).

[1] * = multiplication

Exhibit 8-2

(Page 1 of 2) PPMC Comparison of 1995 Projections with MGMA Norms

Item #		(A) Subject Projected FYE 10/31/95	(B) Subject Projected Per M.D. FTE	(C) Subject Common Size	(D) MGMA Per M.D. FTE		(E) MGMA Common Size	(F) Dollar Variance (Physician FTE)	(G) Percent of Dollar Variance	(H) Percent of Common Size Variance
	REVENUES:									
1	Gross charges	$856,903	$428,452	140.35%	$426,677		121.67%	$1,775	0.4%	18.7%
2	Adjustments & write-offs	($246,360)	($123,180)	-40.35%	($78,878)		-22.49%	($44,302)	36.0%	-17.9%
3	Other revenue	$0	$0	0.00%	$6,715		1.91%	($6,715)	0.0%	-1.9%
4	Total net medical revenue	$610,543	$305,272	100.00%	$350,682		100.0%	($45,411)	-14.9%	0.0%
	PHYSICIAN (PROVIDER) EXPENSES:									
5	Direct compensation	$260,004	$130,002	42.59%	$118,750		24.1%	$11,252	8.7%	18.5%
6	Payroll taxes	$28,601	$14,300	4.68%	$5,607		2.2%	$8,693	60.8%	2.5%
7	Physician benefit expense (1)	$19,135	$9,567	3.13%	$13,266		0.4%	($3,699)	-38.7%	2.7%
8	Dues, membership & licenses (3)	$6,000	$3,000	0.98%	$1,849	(2)	0.6%	$1,151	38.4%	0.4%
9	Other benefits (4)	$10,000	$5,000	1.64%	$1,636		1.2%	$3,364	67.3%	0.5%
10	Total physician expenses	$323,739	$161,870	53.02%	$141,108		43.9%	$20,762	12.8%	9.1%
	NONPHYSICIAN (PROVIDER) EXPENSES:									
11	Nonprovider salaries	$86,494	$43,247	14.17%	$83,166		24.1%	($39,919)	-92.3%	-9.9%
12	Nonprovider benefit expense (5)	$13,500	$6,750	2.21%	$11,209	(6)	5.3%	($4,459)	-66.1%	-3.1%
13	Telephone/telecommunications (6)	$4,432	$2,216	0.73%	$3,368		1.8%	($1,152)	-52.0%	-1.1%
14	Laboratory expenses (8)	$11,958	$5,979	1.96%	$13,063	(9)	3.3%	($7,084)	-118.5%	-1.3%
15	Medical supplies	$34,276	$17,138	5.61%	$12,846		3.4%	$4,292	25.0%	2.3%
16	Radiology/imaging expenses	$0	$0	0.00%	$4,477		1.2%	($4,477)	0.0%	-1.2%
17	Physical therapy expenses	$0	$0	0.00%	*		*	$0	0.0%	0.0%
18	Building/occupancy expenses	$45,000	$22,500	7.37%	$23,624		6.8%	($1,124)	-5.0%	0.6%
19	Furniture/equipment expenses (10)	$600	$300	0.10%	$4,513	(11)	1.4%	($4,213)	-1404.3%	-1.3%
20	Administrative supplies/expenses (12)	$10,823	$5,412	1.77%	$8,178		2.1%	($2,767)	-51.1%	-0.3%
21	Insurance expenses (13)	$14,808	$7,404	2.43%	$8,582	(15)	2.0%	($1,178)	-15.9%	0.4%
22	Outside prof fees (14)	$15,681	$7,841	2.57%	$5,229		0.8%	$2,612	33.3%	1.8%
23	Promotion/marketing expense	$1,800	$900	0.29%	$1,486		0.4%	($586)	-65.1%	-0.1%
24	Depreciation	$8,952	$4,476	1.47%	$3,449		0.5%	$1,027	22.9%	0.9%
25	Health business property taxes	$0	$0	0.00%	$1,229		0.3%	($1,229)	0.0%	-0.3%
26	Other nonprovider expenses (16)	$2,988	$1,494	0.49%	$3,837		1.1%	($2,343)	-156.8%	-0.6%
27	Total nonprovider expenses	$251,312	$125,656	41.16%	$195,260		53.3%	($69,604)	-55.4%	-12.1%
28	Number of FTE physicians	2								

Exhibit 8-2

(Page 2 of 2)

Notes:

1. Consists of provider portion of benefit costs.
2. MGMA norm includes insurance: health, life, etc. ($5,564) and retirement/profit sharing/etc. ($7,702).
3. Consists of licenses/professional dues/medical education
4. Consists of employment incentives.
5. Consists of nonprovider portion of benefit costs.
6. MGMA norm includes insurance ($5,508), retirement and profit sharing ($4,313), and other benefits ($1,388).
7. Consists of telephone and answering/paging services.
8. Consists of chemical reagents.
9. MGMA norm includes total laboratory expenses.
10. Consists of reception area costs.
11. MGMA norm includes total furniture/equipment expense.
12. Consists of general office supplies, postage, administrative purchased services, and printing and stationery.
13. Consists of professional liability coverage and insurance-hazard.
14. Consists of outside clinical services.
15. MGMA norm includes other medical/ancillary services.
16. Consists of other expenses and practice development.

Exhibit 8-3

(Page 1 of 18) PPMC Ratio Analysis: Comparison of Subject Pro Forma with 1994–95 FSSB, Year 1

BALANCE SHEET	Subject $	Subject Common Size
ASSETS		
Current assets:		
Cash	($166,045)	−209.21%
Investments	$0	0.00%
Accounts receivable	$245,730	309.61%
Less: allowance for accounts receivable	($70,647)	−89.01%
Net accounts receivable	$175,083	220.60%
Inventory	$5,285	6.66%
Other current assets	$4,996	6.29%
Total current assets	$19,319	24.34%
Fixed assets:		
Land	$0	0.00%
Buildings	$0	0.00%
Building/leasehold improvements	$0	0.00%
Medical equipment	$55,000	69.30%
Office furniture/equipment	$4,000	5.04%
Data processing equipment	$10,000	12.60%
Less: accumulated depreciation	($8,952)	−11.28%
Total net fixed assets	$60,048	75.66%
Other assets	$0	0.00%
TOTAL ASSETS	$79,367	100.00%
LIABILITIES & OWNERS' EQUITY		
Current liabilities:		
Short-term lease payable	$0	0.00%
Accounts payable	$8,421	10.61%
Other payables	$0	0.00%
Accrued liabilities	$0	0.00%
Total current liabilities	$8,421	10.61%
Long-term leases payable	$37,833	47.67%
Total liabilities	$46,254	58.28%
OWNER/STOCKHOLDER EQUITY		
Common stock	$0	0.00%
Retained earnings	$33,113	41.72%
Dividends payable	$0	0.00%
Total owners' equity	$33,113	41.72%
TOTAL LIABILITIES & EQUITY	$79,367	100.00%

Exhibit 8-3

(Page 2 of 18) PPMC Ratio Analysis: Comparison of Subject Pro Forma with 1994–95 FSSB, Year 2

BALANCE SHEET	Subject $	Subject Common Size
ASSETS		
Current assets:		
Cash	($52,147)	–20.74%
Investments	$0	0.00%
Accounts receivable	$283,639	112.83%
Less: allowance for accounts receivable	($55,310)	–22.00%
Net accounts receivable	$228,329	90.83%
Inventory	$8,517	3.39%
Other current assets	$4,996	1.99%
Total current assets	$189,695	75.46%
Fixed assets:		
Land	$0	0.00%
Buildings	$0	0.00%
Building/leasehold improvements	$0	0.00%
Medical equipment	$65,000	25.86%
Office furniture/equipment	$6,000	2.39%
Data processing equipment	$11,000	4.38%
Less: accumulated depreciation	($20,319)	–8.08%
Total net fixed assets	$61,681	24.54%
Other assets	$0	0.00%
TOTAL ASSETS	$251,376	100.00%
LIABILITIES & OWNERS' EQUITY		
Current liabilities:		
Short-term lease payable	$0	0.00%
Accounts payable	$10,000	3.98%
Other payables	$0	0.00%
Accrued liabilities	$0	0.00%
Total current liabilities	$10,000	3.98%
Long-term leases payable	$12,166	4.84%
Total liabilities	$22,166	8.82%
OWNER/STOCKHOLDER EQUITY		
Common stock	$0	0.00%
Retained earnings	$229,210	91.18%
Dividends payable	$0	0.00%
Total owners' equity	$229,210	91.18%
TOTAL LIABILITIES & EQUITY	$251,376	100.00%

Exhibit 8-3

(Page 3 of 18) PPMC Ratio Analysis: Comparison of Subject Pro Forma with 1994–95 FSSB, Year 3

BALANCE SHEET	Subject $	Subject Common Size
ASSETS		
Current assets:		
Cash	$165,335	33.73%
Investments	$0	0.00%
Accounts receivable	$307,853	62.80%
Less: allowance for accounts receivable	($60,031)	–12.25%
Net accounts receivable	$247,822	50.56%
Inventory	$10,220	2.08%
Other current assets	$4,996	1.02%
Total current assets	$428,373	87.39%
Fixed assets:		
Land	$0	0.00%
Buildings	$0	0.00%
Building/leasehold improvements	$0	0.00%
Medical equipment	$75,000	15.30%
Office furniture/equipment	$8,200	1.67%
Data processing equipment	$12,100	2.47%
Less: accumulated depreciation	($33,492)	–6.83%
Total net fixed assets	$61,808	12.61%
Other assets	$0	0.00%
TOTAL ASSETS	$490,181	100.00%
LIABILITIES & OWNERS' EQUITY		
Current liabilities:		
Short-term lease payable	$0	0.00%
Accounts payable	$11,882	2.42%
Other payables	$0	0.00%
Accrued liabilities	$0	0.00%
Total current liabilities	$11,882	2.42%
Long-term leases payable	$0	0.00%
Total liabilities	$11,882	2.42%
OWNER/STOCKHOLDER EQUITY		
Common stock	$0	0.00%
Retained earnings	$478,299	97.58%
Dividends payable	$0	0.00%
Total owners' equity	$478,299	97.58%
TOTAL LIABILITIES & EQUITY	$490,181	100.00%

Exhibit 8-3

(Page 4 of 18) PPMC Ratio Analysis: Comparison of Subject Pro Forma with 1994–95 FSSB, Year 4

BALANCE SHEET	Subject $	Subject Common Size
ASSETS		
Current assets:		
Cash	$419,154	60.53%
Investments	$0	0.00%
Accounts receivable	$320,167	46.23%
Less: allowance for accounts receivable	($62,433)	–9.02%
Net accounts receivable	$257,734	37.22%
Inventory	$10,629	1.53%
Other current assets	$4,996	0.72%
Total current assets	$692,513	100.00%
Fixed assets:		
Land	$0	0.00%
Buildings	$0	0.00%
Building/leasehold improvements	$0	0.00%
Medical equipment	$85,000	12.27%
Office furniture/equipment	$10,620	1.53%
Data processing equipment	$13,310	1.92%
Less: accumulated depreciation	($48,553)	–7.01%
Total net fixed assets	$60,377	8.72%
Other assets	$0	0.00%
TOTAL ASSETS	$752,890	108.72%
LIABILITIES & OWNERS' EQUITY		
Current liabilities:		
Short-term lease payable	$0	0.00%
Accounts payable	$12,339	1.78%
Other payables	$0	0.00%
Accrued liabilities	$0	0.00%
Total current liabilities	$12,339	1.78%
Long-term leases payable	$0	0.00%
Total liabilities	$12,339	1.78%
OWNER/STOCKHOLDER EQUITY		
Common stock	$0	0.00%
Retained earnings	$740,551	106.94%
Dividends payable	$0	0.00%
Total owners' equity	$740,551	106.94%
TOTAL LIABILITIES & EQUITY	$752,890	108.72%

Exhibit 8-3

(Page 5 of 18) PPMC Ratio Analysis: Comparison of Subject Pro Forma with 1994–95 FSSB, Year 5

BALANCE SHEET	Subject $	Subject Common Size
ASSETS		
Current assets:		
Cash	$687,986	66.83%
Investments	$0	0.00%
Accounts receivable	$332,974	32.35%
Less: allowance for accounts receivable	($64,930)	–6.31%
Net accounts receivable	$268,044	26.04%
Inventory	$11,054	1.07%
Other current assets	$4,996	0.49%
Total current assets	$972,080	94.43%
Fixed assets:		
Land	$0	0.00%
Buildings	$0	0.00%
Building/leasehold improvements	$0	0.00%
Medical equipment	$95,000	9.23%
Office furniture/equipment	$13,282	1.29%
Data processing equipment	$14,641	1.42%
Less: accumulated depreciation	($65,590)	–6.37%
Total net fixed assets	$57,333	5.57%
Other assets	$0	0.00%
TOTAL ASSETS	$1,029,413	100.00%
LIABILITIES & OWNERS' EQUITY		
Current liabilities:		
Short-term lease payable	$0	0.00%
Accounts payable	$12,815	1.24%
Other payables	$0	0.00%
Accrued liabilities	$0	0.00%
Total current liabilities	$12,815	1.24%
Long-term leases payable	$0	0.00%
Total liabilities	$12,815	1.24%
OWNER/STOCKHOLDER EQUITY		
Common stock	$0	0.00%
Retained earnings	$1,016,598	98.76%
Dividends payable	$0	0.00%
Total owners' equity	$1,016,598	98.76%
TOTAL LIABILITIES & EQUITY	$1,029,413	100.00%

Exhibit 8-3

(Page 6 of 18) PPMC Ratio Analysis: Comparison of Subject Actual Financial Statements (1994) with 1994–95— Actual 1994

BALANCE SHEET	Subject $	Subject Common Size
ASSETS		
Current assets:		
Cash	$503,252	86.61%
Investments	$0	0.00%
Accounts receivable	$0	0.00%
Less: allowance for accounts receivable	$0	0.00%
Net accounts receivable	$0	0.00%
Inventory	$0	0.00%
Other current assets	$31,045	5.34%
Total current assets	$534,297	91.95%
Fixed assets:		
Medical equipment	$0	0.00%
Office furniture/equipment	$39,597	6.81%
Data processing equipment	$6,295	1.08%
Less: accumulated depreciation	($4,389)	–0.76%
Total net fixed assets	$41,503	7.14%
Other assets (Security Deposits)	$5,285	0.91%
TOTAL ASSETS	$581,085	100.00%
LIABILITIES & OWNERS' EQUITY		
Current liabilities:		
Accounts payable	$48,707	8.38%
Current maturities of capital lease	$4,435	0.76%
Accrued liabilities	$16,868	2.90%
Total current liabilities	$70,010	12.05%
Long-term liabilities:		
Deferred operating lease payments	$5,860	1.01%
Redeemable preferred stock	$1,351,520	232.59%
Total long-term liabilities	$1,357,380	233.59%
Total liabilities	$1,427,390	245.64%
OWNER/STOCKHOLDER EQUITY		
Common stock	$759	0.13%
Additional paid-in capital	$103,137	17.75%
Retained deficit	($950,201)	–163.52%
Total owners' equity	($846,305)	–145.64%
TOTAL LIABILITIES & EQUITY	$581,085	100.00%

Exhibit 8-3

(Page 7 of 18) PPMC Ratio Analysis: Comparison of Subject Pro Forma with 1994–95 FSSB, Year 1

STATEMENT OF INCOME & EXPENSES	Subject $	Subject Common Size
REVENUES		
Office visits—new patients	$324,454	37.86%
Office visits—established patients	$267,976	31.27%
Hospital care visits	$39,825	4.65%
Ancillary services component	$94,760	11.06%
Procedure fees	$129,888	15.16%
Total revenues	$856,903	100.00%
DEDUCTIONS FROM REVENUES		
Bad debts/courtesy allowances	$32,134	3.75%
Contractual adjustments	$214,226	25.00%
Total deductions from revenues	$246,360	28.75%
TOTAL NET REVENUES	$610,543	71.25%
EXPENDITURES		
Total human resources expenses	$420,112	49.03%
Clinical supplies & services	$61,916	7.23%
Business development	$2,796	0.33%
G & A (without depreciation)	$83,655	9.76%
Depreciation	$8,952	1.04%
Total operating expenses	$577,431	67.39%
INCOME FROM OPERATIONS	$33,112	3.86%
Interest income	$0	0.00%
Interest expense	$0	0.00%
Pretax income	$33,112	3.86%
Income tax	$0	0.00%
NET INCOME AFTER TAXES	$33,112	3.86%

Source: Pro Forma Financial Statements (5 years), prepared by the PPMC.

long-term liabilities consist of redeemable preferred stock, which is presumably venture capital. Since the PPMC did not have any practice revenue during 1994, a comparison of performance ratios is not applicable for the year 1994.

Comparison of Subject Projected Financial Statements (Year 1) with 1994–95 FSSB. During year 1, as the PPMC projected, the amount of cash on the balance sheet is a negative value (see Exhibit 8-

Exhibit 8-3

(Page 8 of 18) PPMC Ratio Analysis: Comparison of Subject Pro Forma with 1994–95 FSSB, Year 2

STATEMENT OF INCOME & EXPENSES	Subject $	Subject Common Size
REVENUES		
Office visits—new patients	$233,357	16.91%
Office visits—established patients	$671,616	48.65%
Hospital care visits	$75,149	5.44%
Ancillary services component	$168,833	12.23%
Procedure fees	$231,422	16.77%
Total revenues	$1,380,377	100.00%
DEDUCTIONS FROM REVENUES		
Bad debts/courtesy allowances	$51,764	3.75%
Contractual adjustments	$345,094	25.00%
Total deductions from revenues	$396,858	28.75%
TOTAL NET REVENUES	$983,519	71.25%
EXPENDITURES		
Total human resources expenses	$501,047	36.30%
Clinical supplies & services	$103,619	7.51%
Business development	$2,656	0.19%
G & A (without depreciation)	$96,203	6.97%
Depreciation	$11,367	0.82%
Total operating expenses	$714,892	51.79%
INCOME FROM OPERATIONS	$268,627	19.46%
Interest income	$0	0.00%
Interest expense	$0	0.00%
Pretax income	$268,627	19.46%
Income tax	$72,529	5.25%
NET INCOME AFTER TAXES	$196,098	14.21%

Source: Pro Forma Financial Statements (5 years), prepared by the PPMC.

3, page 1 of 18). This is likely due to the use of cash for generating revenue when the PPMC commenced operations. However, this negative value appears to be offset by a comparable amount of net accounts receivable, apparently brought about by the addition of inventories. Therefore, the net effect of operations was to decrease the amount of current assets relative to current liabilities, thereby decreasing the current ratio (see Exhibit 8-3, page 13 of 18). The quick ratio increased, mainly because of the increase in accounts receivable and inventory,

Exhibit 8-3

(Page 9 of 18) PPMC Ratio Analysis: Comparison of Subject Pro Forma with 1994–95 FSSB, Year 3

STATEMENT OF INCOME & EXPENSES	Subject $	Subject Common Size
REVENUES		
Office visits—new patients	$242,691	15.12%
Office visits—established patients	$806,481	50.24%
Hospital care visits	$78,155	4.87%
Ancillary services component	$201,587	12.56%
Procedure fees	$276,319	17.21%
Total revenues	$1,605,233	100.00%
DEDUCTIONS FROM REVENUES		
Bad debts/courtesy allowances	$60,196	3.75%
Contractual adjustments	$401,308	25.00%
Total deductions from revenues	$461,504	28.75%
TOTAL NET REVENUES	$1,143,729	71.25%
EXPENDITURES		
Total human resources expenses	$551,839	34.38%
Clinical supplies & services	$124,343	7.75%
Business development	$2,523	0.16%
G & A (without depreciation)	$110,633	6.89%
Depreciation	$13,173	0.82%
Total operating expenses	$802,511	49.99%
INCOME FROM OPERATIONS	$341,218	21.26%
Interest income	$0	0.00%
Interest expense	$0	0.00%
Pretax income	$341,218	21.26%
Income tax	$92,129	5.74%
NET INCOME AFTER TAXES	$249,089	15.52%

Source: Pro Forma Financial Statements (5 years), prepared by the PPMC.

which are items that had zero values during 1994. The performance ratios for the PPMC also improved because of the generation of revenues (see Exhibit 8-3, page 1 of 18). The PPMC's sales-to-receivables and sales-to-net-worth ratios are higher than the comparable FSSB values. Its sales-to-total-assets ratio is lower than the comparable FSSB value, which could be due to the PPMC being in its start-up stage. This ratio may improve when the company's operations move toward a higher level of efficiency in utilizing its assets.

Exhibit 8-3

(Page 10 of 18) PPMC Ratio Analysis: Comparison of Subject Pro Forma with 1994–95 FSSB, Year 4

STATEMENT OF INCOME & EXPENSES	Subject $	Subject Common Size
REVENUES		
Office visits—new patients	$252,399	15.12%
Office visits—established patients	$838,740	50.24%
Hospital care visits	$81,281	4.87%
Ancillary services component	$209,650	12.56%
Procedure fees	$287,372	17.21%
Total revenues	$1,669,442	100.00%
DEDUCTIONS FROM REVENUES		
Bad debts/courtesy allowances	$62,604	3.75%
Contractual adjustments	$417,361	25.00%
Total deductions from revenues	$479,965	28.75%
TOTAL NET REVENUES	$1,189,477	71.25%
EXPENDITURES		
Total human resources expenses	$568,394	34.05%
Clinical supplies & services	$129,317	7.75%
Business development	$2,397	0.14%
G & A (without depreciation)	$115,058	6.89%
Depreciation	$15,061	0.90%
Total operating expenses	$830,227	49.73%
INCOME FROM OPERATIONS	$359,250	21.52%
Interest income	$0	0.00%
Interest expense	$0	0.00%
Pretax income	$359,250	21.52%
Income tax	$96,998	5.81%
NET INCOME AFTER TAXES	$262,252	15.71%

Source: Pro Forma Financial Statements (5 years), prepared by the PPMC.

Comparison of Subject Projected Financial Statements (Year 2 to Year 5) with 1994–95 FSSB.   During years 2 through 5, as the PPMC projected, the financial performance of the company continued to improve (see Exhibit 8-3, pages 14 through 17). In particular, the sales-to-receivables and sales-to-total-assets ratios are higher than the comparable FSSB ratios. The PPMC's pretax-profit-to-total-assets and the pretax-profit-to-net-worth ratios are, however, lower than FSSB figures. This variance may be because the PPMC, as a corporation, has a

Exhibit 8-3

(Page 11 of 18) PPMC Ratio Analysis: Comparison of Subject Pro Forma with 1994–95 FSSB, Year 5

STATEMENT OF INCOME & EXPENSES	Subject $	Subject Common Size
REVENUES		
Office visits—new patients	$262,495	15.12%
Office visits—established patients	$872,290	50.24%
Hospital care visits	$84,532	4.87%
Ancillary services component	$218,036	12.56%
Procedure fees	$298,867	17.21%
Total revenues	$1,736,220	100.00%
DEDUCTIONS FROM REVENUES		
Bad debts/courtesy allowances	$65,108	3.75%
Contractual adjustments	$434,055	25.00%
Total deductions from revenues	$499,163	28.75%
TOTAL NET REVENUES	$1,237,057	71.25%
EXPENDITURES		
Total human resources expenses	$585,446	33.72%
Clinical supplies & services	$134,490	7.75%
Business development	$2,277	0.13%
G & A (without depreciation)	$119,660	6.89%
Depreciation	$17,037	0.98%
Total operating expenses	$858,910	49.47%
INCOME FROM OPERATIONS	$378,147	21.78%
Interest income	$0	0.00%
Interest expense	$0	0.00%
Pretax income	$378,147	21.78%
Income tax	$102,100	5.88%
NET INCOME AFTER TAXES	$276,047	15.90%

Source: Pro Forma Financial Statements (5 years), prepared by the PPMC.

Exhibit 8-3

(Page 12 of 18) PPMC Ratio Analysis: Comparison of Subject Actual Financial Statements (1994) with 1994–95 FSSB, Actual 1994

STATEMENT OF INCOME & EXPENSES	Subject $
REVENUES	
Office visits—new patients	$0
Office visits—established patients	$0
Hospital care visits	$0
Ancillary services component	$0
Procedure fees	$0
Total revenues	$0
DEDUCTIONS FROM REVENUES	
Bad debts/courtesy allowances	$0
Contractual adjustments	$0
Total deductions from revenues	$0
TOTAL NET REVENUES	$0
EXPENDITURES	
Salaries & benefits	$403,689
Business development	$159,636
Professional & consulting fees	$88,491
Rent	$52,239
General & administrative expenses	$49,056
Utilities	$15,300
Insurance	$5,459
Depreciation	$3,452
Other	$564
Total operating expenses	$777,886
INCOME FROM OPERATIONS	($777,886)
Interest income	$25,511
Interest expense	$0
Pretax income	($752,375)
Income tax	$0
NET INCOME AFTER TAXES	($752,375)

Source: Financial Statements as of December 31, 1994.

Exhibit 8-3

(Page 13 of 18) PPMC Ratio Analysis: Comparison of Subject Pro Forma with 1994–95 FSSB, Year 1

	Subject Pro Forma	Median FSSB (a)	Variance
RATIOS			
Current	2.3	0.9	1.4
Quick	9.5	0.9	8.6
Current assets/total assets	0.2	48.1	–47.9
Short-term debt/total debt	0.2	100.0	–99.8
Short-term debt/net worth	0.3	3.4	–3.1
Total debt/net worth	1.4	6.7	–5.3
Short-term debt/total assets	0.1	28.3	–28.2
Long-term debt/total assets	0.5	0.0	0.5
Total debt/total assets	0.6	53.2	–52.6
Sales/receivables (b)	3.5	0.0	3.5
Average collection period	0.3	0.0	0.3
Sales/total assets (c)	7.7	11.9	–4.2
Sales/net worth (d)	18.4	10.7	7.7
Pretax profit/total assets	0.4	22.8	–22.4
Pretax profit/net worth	1.0	7.4	–6.4

a: From FSSB: professional services: physicians (total asset size $10,000–$100,000).

b, c & d: Sales is interpreted for the subject as net revenues; receivables is interpreted as net accounts receivable.

higher level of investment in tangible assets, while the physician practices in the FSSB survey are typically solo physician practices that do not have large amounts of tangible or fixed assets. Therefore, the large amount of total assets and net worth of the PPMC tended to lower both of those ratios.

Discussion of Revenue Projections

Analysis of the PPMC's pro forma revenue projections reveals notable variances from industry norms, as follows:

- By the end of year 1 (month 8, to be exact), visits per physician per workday are projected by the PPMC to reach 40 (see Exhibit 8-1, column B, row 2).

  - Projections for month 1 are three visits per physician workday.

Exhibit 8-3

(Page 14 of 18) PPMC Ratio Analysis: Comparison of Subject Pro Forma with 1994–95 FSSB, Year 2

	Subject Pro Forma	Median FSSB (a)	Variance
RATIOS			
Current	19.0	2.0	17.0
Quick	23.1	1.0	22.1
Current assets/total assets	0.8	63.4	−62.6
Short-term debt/total debt	0.5	90.2	−89.7
Short-term debt/net worth	0.0	14.9	−14.9
Total debt/net worth	0.1	38.8	−38.7
Short-term debt/total assets	0.0	21.6	−21.6
Long-term debt/total assets	0.0	3.6	−3.6
Total debt/total assets	0.1	51.9	−51.8
Sales/receivables (b)	4.3	2.4	1.9
Average collection period	0.2	46.0	−45.8
Sales/total assets (c)	3.9	3.2	0.7
Sales/net worth (d)	4.3	4.9	−0.6
Pretax profit/total assets	1.1	11.4	−10.3
Pretax profit/net worth	1.2	12.4	−11.2

a: From FSSB: professional services: physicians (total asset size $250,000–$500,000).

b, c & d: Sales is interpreted for the subject as net revenues; receivables is interpreted as net accounts receivable.

- This projection is very high compared with the AMA norm of 26.7 visits per workday.
- The PPMC's estimated office visit fees appear to be in line with industry norms (see Exhibit 8-1, column B, rows 3 and 5).
- The PPMC's projected year 1 average of percent of office visits for new patients is high when measured against industry norms (see Exhibit 8-1, column B, row 4).
  - This is to be expected given that the practice will just have begun operations.
  - The percent of new patients is projected to decline as year 1 continues (decrease to 20 percent in month 12 from 95 percent in month 1).
  - The high estimate of percent of new patients, in conjunction with high projection of visits per physician per workday, leads to what appears to be overestimated revenues from new patient office vis-

Exhibit 8-3

(Page 15 of 18) PPMC Ratio Analysis: Comparison of Subject Pro Forma with 1994–95 FSSB, Year 3

	Subject Pro Forma	Median FSSB (a)	Variance
RATIOS			
Current	36.1	2.0	34.1
Quick	39.8	1.0	38.8
Current assets/total assets	0.9	63.4	−62.5
Short-term debt/total debt	1.0	90.2	−89.2
Short-term debt/net worth	0.0	14.9	−14.9
Total debt/net worth	0.0	38.8	−38.8
Short-term debt/total assets	0.0	21.6	−21.6
Long-term debt/total assets	0.0	3.6	−3.6
Total debt/total assets	0.0	51.9	−51.9
Sales/receivables (b)	4.6	2.4	2.2
Average collection period	0.2	46.0	−45.8
Sales/total assets (c)	2.3	3.2	−0.9
Sales/net worth (d)	2.4	4.9	−2.5
Pretax profit/total assets	0.7	11.4	−10.7
Pretax profit/net worth	0.7	12.4	−11.7

a: From FSSB: professional services: physicians (total asset size $250,000–$500,000).

b, c & d: Sales is interpreted for the subject as net revenues; receivables is interpreted as net accounts receivable.

its ($162,227 per physician FTE), as compared with the industry norm of $39,782 per physician FTE.

- The PPMC's projected average percent of office visits by established patients for year 1 is low when measured against industry averages (see Exhibit 8-1, columns B and C, row 6).
  - Again, this is typical for a new practice.
  - The PPMC's estimate increases as year 1 continues; actually, by month 10, the percentage is projected to be higher than the industry norm of 67.6 percent (75 percent in month 12, from 5 percent in month 1).
  - Due to the low estimated number of established patient visits in year 1, the PPMC projects revenues from established patient visits per FTE to be $133,988, as compared with the industry norm of $171,000 (see Exhibit 8-1, row 27).

Exhibit 8-3

(Page 16 of 18) PPMC Ratio Analysis: Comparison of Subject Pro Forma with 1994–95 FSSB, Year 4

	Subject Pro Forma	Median FSSB (a)	Variance
RATIOS			
Current	56.1	1.3	54.8
Quick	59.9	1.3	58.6
Current assets/total assets	0.9	68.7	−67.8
Short-term debt/total debt	1.0	46.6	−45.6
Short-term debt/net worth	0.0	7.1	−7.1
Total debt/net worth	0.0	56.7	−56.7
Short-term debt/total assets	0.0	14.4	−14.4
Long-term debt/total assets	0.0	11.2	−11.2
Total debt/total assets	0.0	52.4	−52.4
Sales/receivables (b)	4.6	2.1	2.5
Average collection period	0.2	39.0	−38.8
Sales/total assets (c)	1.6	2.5	−0.9
Sales/net worth (d)	1.6	3.1	−1.5
Pretax profit/total assets	0.5	14.6	−14.1
Pretax profit/net worth	0.5	35.6	−35.1

a: From FSSB: professional services: physicians (total asset size $500,000–$1,000,000).

b, c & d: Sales is interpreted for the subject as net revenues; receivables is interpreted as net accounts receivable.

- The PPMC's estimated hospital visit fee is very high ($76 per visit) (see Exhibit 8-1, column B, row 7) when compared with industry norms ($52 per visit).
- Projected average hospital visits (as a percentage of total visits) for year 1 is low as compared with industry norms, but is predicted to increase as year 1 continues and as the patient base increases (see Exhibit 8-1, column B, row 8).
  - Forecasted year 1 hospital visits increase to 5 percent by month 8, from 0 percent in month 1.
  - AMA norm is 10.3 percent.
  - Due to low projected percent of hospital visits, revenue generated from hospital care visits (per physician FTE) appears to be below industry norms ($19,913 vs. AMA norm of $33,674).

Exhibit 8-3

(Page 17 of 18) PPMC Ratio Analysis: Comparison of Subject Pro Forma with 1994–95 FSSB, Year 5

	Subject Pro Forma	Median FSSB (a)	Variance
RATIOS			
Current	75.9	1.3	74.6
Quick	79.7	1.3	78.4
Current assets/total assets	0.9	68.7	−67.8
Short-term debt/total debt	1.0	46.6	−45.6
Short-term debt/net worth	0.0	7.1	−7.1
Total debt/net worth	0.0	56.7	−56.7
Short-term debt/total assets	0.0	14.4	−14.4
Long-term debt/total assets	0.0	11.2	−11.2
Total debt/total assets	0.0	52.4	−52.4
Sales/receivables (b)	4.6	2.1	2.5
Average collection period	0.2	39.0	−38.8
Sales/total assets (c)	1.2	2.5	−1.3
Sales/net worth (d)	1.2	3.1	−1.9
Pretax profit/total assets	0.4	14.6	−14.2
Pretax profit/net worth	0.4	35.6	−35.2

a: From FSSB: professional services: physicians (total asset size $500,000–$1,000,000).

b, c & d: Sales is interpreted for the subject as net revenues; receivables is interpreted as net accounts receivable.

- Neither the PPMC's business plan nor its pro forma includes the PPMC's ancillary services component (see Exhibit 8-1, column B, row 29).
  - The PPMC's projected ancillary services revenue is very high as compared with industry averages.
- Gross charges for year 1, as estimated by the PPMC's pro forma, appear to be in line with industry norms (see Exhibit 8-2, column B, row 1).
  - This estimate may be high, considering the practice will be in its first year of operation.
- The PPMC's estimated adjustments and write-offs for year 1 are significantly higher than industry norms (see Exhibit 8-2, column A, row 2).

Exhibit 8-3

(Page 18 of 18) PPMC Ratio Analysis: Comparison of Subject Actual Financial Statements (1994) with 1994–95 FSSB, Actual 1994

	Subject Pro Forma	Median FSSB (a)	Variance
RATIOS			
Current	7.6	1.3	6.3
Quick	7.2	1.3	5.9
Current assets/total assets	0.9	68.7	−67.8
Short-term debt/total debt	0.0	46.6	−46.6
Short-term debt/net worth	−0.1	7.1	−7.2
Total debt/net worth	−1.7	56.7	−58.4
Short-term debt/total assets	0.1	14.4	−14.3
Long-term debt/total assets	2.3	11.2	−8.9
Total debt/total assets	2.5	52.4	−49.9
Sales/receivables (b)	0.0	2.1	−2.1
Average collection period	0.0	39.0	−39.0
Sales/total assets (c)	0.0	2.5	−2.5
Sales/net worth (d)	0.0	3.1	−3.1
Pretax profit/total assets	−1.3	14.6	−15.9
Pretax profit/net worth	0.9	35.6	−34.7

a: From FSSB: professional services: physicians (total asset size $500,000–$1,000,000).

b, c & d: Sales is interpreted for the subject as net revenues; receivables is interpreted as net accounts receivable.

- The estimate of $246,360 contractual adjustments may be due to the PPMC's planned heavy involvement in managed care contracts.
- These forecasted adjustments and write-offs may lead to net revenue that is lower than industry norm.

Discussion of Expense Projections

- As set forth in its pro forma, the PPMC plans to compensate its physicians at a slightly higher rate ($130,000) than the industry norm for family practice physicians ($118,750) (see Exhibit 8-1, column B, row 9).
  - The PPMC's planned compensation package may be needed to aid in physician recruitment efforts.

- Projected registered nurse compensation is slightly lower than industry norms ($27,040 versus $30,160) (see Exhibit 8-1, column B, row 10).
- The PPMC's projected compensation for both licensed practitioner nurses and general administrative personnel is significantly lower than industry norms (on an average, 41.4 percent lower).
- The PPMC's estimated nonprovider salaries for year 1 appear to be much lower on a per-physician FTE basis than industry norms (see Exhibit 8-2, column B, row 11).
  - As patient base increases, there may be a need for additional non-provider FTEs.
  - The PPMC's estimate for nonproviders may be linked to its below-industry norm of individual positions (RN, LPN, general administrative personnel).
  - It should be noted that the PPMC predicts in its pro forma that salaries will increase as Year 1 continues (total support staff salaries and FATES are twice as high for month 12 as for month 1).
- As projected by the PPMC's pro forma, both physician benefit expense and nonprovider benefit expense, per physician FTE, are significantly below industry norms in year 1 (see Exhibit 8-1, column B, row 15).
  - The PPMC predicts physician benefit expense to be even lower after year 1 due to the fact that the $5,000 in moving and hiring expenses is incurred in only the first year of each physician's employment.
- The PPMC's projected laboratory and radiology expenses are also significantly below industry norms (see Exhibit 8-2, column A, rows 14 and 16), which may be due in part to the minimal lab and x-ray functions that the PPMC expects to perform and its expected high use of outside clinical services (Exhibit 8-1, column A, row 19).
- The PPMC's estimated furniture and equipment expense is very low as compared with industry norms (see Exhibit 8-2, column A, row 19).
  - The industry norm figure includes the practice's total furniture and equipment expense.
  - The PPMC's projected expense figure includes only the reception room furnishings.
  - The PPMC may have to rely upon the equipment and furniture provided by acquired practices.
- Expenses associated with creating a computer network linking the corporate office with each of the physician practices are usually very

high. However, the PPMC projects expenses of only $1,000 (Exhibit 8-1, item 22) of computer supplies in year 1.

BUSINESS PLAN: GROWTH AND PHYSICIAN RECRUITMENT STRATEGIES

Discussion of Growth Strategy and Timetable in a Competitive Environment

The concepts of being one of the first companies to apply contract management to primary care physician practice start-up and development and being one of the first companies to focus on second- and third-tier towns and cities in rural areas are posited by the PPMC as being innovative and aligned with the direction of the healthcare industry's future. The PPMC has distinguished its business plan from the approaches of other firms that they have identified as competitors, such as Coastal Healthcare Group, Inc., Pacific Physician Services, Inc., Summit Health, Ltd., and Health Spring. The bases of the PPMC's differentiation include geographic and population market factors, size of practice model (i.e., their two-physician model), and corporate structural and philosophical differences. However, firms such as Champion Health Care, Coram, First Physician Care, MedPartners, John Deere Healthcare, and other market players are actively pursuing somewhat similar strategies of practice development and are also structured to compete within the managed care environment.

The cluster concept, the structure of the clinic models, and the recognition on the PPMC's part that an emphasis on recruitment is crucial are all elements that contribute to the potential for success of this venture. The ability to implement its plan within the projected time frame may prove to be the PPMC's main challenge.

The PPMC's initial plan called for 17 practices to be opened, as follows.

January 1995	1 practice
May 1995	2 practices
June 1995	3 practices
July 1995	2 practices
August 1995	1 practice
September 1995	3 practices
Late Summer 1995	5 practices

This plan was revised to reflect nine projected practice openings, as follows.

January 1, 1995	1 practice
May 1, 1995	1 practice
June 1, 1995	1 practice
July 1, 1995	2 practices
August 1, 1995	1 practice
September 1, 1995	2 practices
October 1, 1995	1 practice

The PPMC's management has disclosed that to date there are no offices under contract other than one rural physician office. This is the only physician who has signed a binding agreement with the PPMC to date.

Based on the PPMC's projected practice site openings and the current status of signed physicians and contracted office space, it appears that the PPMC may experience difficulty in keeping pace with its goals and meeting the timetable as set forth in the revised projected practice opening schedule.

Discussion of Recruitment Strategy

As stated above, the PPMC's goal was to have nine practices and 18 physicians in operation by the end of 1995. To date, one physician has signed a physician agreement committing to employment with the PPMC. The overall goal is to have 210 physicians employed and practicing within the next five years. This translates to an average of 42 physician placements per year, or four placements per month.

In order to make four placements per month, the average recruiter must conduct 16 physician interview site visits (a one-to-four interview-to-placement ratio) per month. Even from an optimistic stand, assuming that the vice president of physician recruiting is able to lower the recruitment team's interview-to-placement ratio to one-to-three, 12 physician interview site visits per month would be required. This situation has not been addressed in the PPMC's business plan and is a primary cause of concern for its ability to achieve the stated goals within the projected time frame.

Some other key issues to address include:

- Who will conduct the physician site visit interviews?
- How much will this process cost?
- Are the stated goals achievable with the current manpower?

Physician interviews/site visits should consist of physicians residing out of town traveling with their spouse to the practice office location for a one- or two-day visit, and physicians residing in close proximity to the practice office location meeting with the PPMC personnel locally.

Typical physician interview/site visit expenses might be as follows.

	Cost	Approximate Out-of-Town Recruitment Expenses per MD	Approximate Local Recruitment Expenses per MD
Two round-trip airline tickets	@ $600 each	$1,200	$0
Rental car for two days	@ $70/day	$140	$0
Hotel for two nights	@ $100/night	$200	$0
Meals for two days	@ $50/person/day	$200	$100
Parking	@ $12.50/day	$25	$0
Totals		$1,765	$100

Assuming that 50 percent of the physician interview site visits will involve out-of-town physicians and 50 percent will involve local physicians, the out-of-town physician interview expenses of $1,765 multiplied by six physician interview site visits per month (50 percent of 12 visits) would come to $10,590 per month, and the local physician interview expenses of $100 multiplied by six physician interviews would come to $600 per month. This would indicate a total of $11,190 in estimated incremental monthly recruitment expenses. This is a conservative estimate and does not include any second visits or circumstances where the physician might bring additional family members on the site visit.

Another potential problem involves the actual on-site interviewing and entertaining of the out-of-town physicians and their spouses. Since the PPMC's model utilizes small clinics and start-up scenarios, the recruitment team may find it necessary to meet the physician and spouse personally at the interview site. As a result of these circumstances, two difficulties may impact the PPMC's business plan.

First, the PPMC recruiter could generate direct expenses, as follows.

One round-trip airline ticket	$500
Rental car for two days	$140
Hotel for two nights	$200
Meals for two days	$100
Total	**$940**

Assuming that this type of trip is necessary only 50 percent of the time for 50 percent of the candidates (i.e., three interviews per month), it will amount to an additional expense of $2,820 per month. When added to the physician-related expenses of $11,190 per month, this equals $14,010 per month (i.e., $168,120 per year) in potential additional expenses related to the physician recruitment process that have not been incorporated into the PPMC's financial projections.

Second, these trips requiring the PPMC's recruiter(s) to meet with the physician on-site would result in the recruiter spending time (i.e., days) away from the office, thus detracting from his or her ability to continue arranging new physician interviews.

The business plan makes no provision for an advertising budget for the physician recruitment process. To identify and attract primary care physician candidates requires a mix of purchased database information, direct mail advertising, medical journal classified advertising, or some of the more cost-effective tools in the new physician telephone "opportunity line" market. Primary care physicians in today's marketplace are deluged with messages in most of these advertising media regarding practice opportunities of every conceivable type. For an aggressive physician recruitment plan such as the PPMC's, a monthly advertising budget of $4,000 would be appropriate for planning purposes. This budget could be allocated among the different media at the discretion of the PPMC's physician recruitment department. Adding this amount to the $14,010 of potential monthly interviewing expenses would yield a total of $18,010 per month of expenses related to the physician recruitment effort ($216,120 per year) that the PPMC has not taken into consideration in its financial projections. Extrapolating this incremental expense to the entire five-year period that the PPMC has selected for its projections would indicate that the PPMC may incur $1,080,600 in incremental expenses related to physician recruitment efforts that it has not considered in its financial projections. The timing and cycles of physician recruitment could also have an impact on the ability of the PPMC's recruiters to staff the practices with qualified candidates. Physicians completing their residency training in June 1995 have, for the most part, already secured their positions.

One aspect of the PPMC's business plan that bears attention is its lack of an ideal physician candidate profile. As the PPMC's management has stated, their preference is to focus on physicians who have been in private or other practice settings involving long hours and tedious administrative duties. The PPMC assumes that physicians coming from such practice settings will be attracted to the two-physician model that utilizes the PPMC's corporate practice management system, because this model creates an environment where the physician can focus on practicing medicine and defer the administrative duties to the PPMC's corporate personnel. Judging by the career decisions these types of physicians have made to date, there is no reasonable basis for concluding that, by virtue of being recruited by the PPMC, the physicians will demonstrate a willingness to work evening and weekend hours and to carry the patient-encounter load set forth optimistically in the PPMC's business plan. Of the small percentage of 1995 primary care physician residents who may still be available, it is possible that few will realistically possess the qualities that the PPMC desires and requires. Similarly, experienced physicians have historically planned their practice relocations for the summer months, to coincide with school summer vacations and with contract terms that typically end in June. By May, most physicians who will be relocating have already made commitments to practice opportunities and are planning their relocations. This is not to imply that physician recruitment is impossible during the summer months; however, it may well be more difficult at this time of year.

Discussion of In-House Physician Recruitment Staff

The PPMC's physician recruitment staff consists of the following members.

- *Vice President for Physician Recruiting:* The vice president for physician recruiting has over seven years of physician staffing and physician recruitment experience. However, this experience is in the recruitment of radiologists, which is significantly different from and less challenging than the recruitment of primary care physicians. In today's marketplace, supply and demand issues are critical. The supply of radiologists looking for positions is relatively high. The demand by organizations looking for radiologists is relatively low. The most difficult element, therefore, is finding opportunities for radiologists. The balance of the equation is relatively uncomplicated compared to the process of recruiting primary care physicians.

  The supply and demand in today's marketplace for primary care physicians are completely reversed. The supply of primary care physicians available for practice is relatively small, while a large percentage of healthcare facilities in the nation are recruiting (i.e., have a demand) for primary care physicians. The reality is that family practitioners, as well as other primary care physicians, typically know that they are in high demand, and often exercise their ability to be very selective in their decision-making process. In today's marketplace it is significantly more difficult to obtain a commitment (i.e., signature on a contract) from a family practitioner than it is from a radiologist.

Given the projected continued high demand for primary care physicians, it is not likely that this situation will change in the near future, and it will have a direct impact on the efforts of the PPMC's physician recruiters.

- *Other Recruiters:* One of the other recruiters has had no physician recruitment experience prior to working for the PPMC. However, this recruiter seems to have sales experience in medical-related areas. The third recruiter's resume shows less than one year of experience assisting in the recruitment of nurses, and no physician recruitment experience.

In summary, the PPMC's physician recruitment team possesses a basic skill set. It is unlikely, however, that this collective skill set, operating within the current dynamic and challenging marketplace of primary care physician recruitment and within the confines of the PPMC's practice model, will be adequate for recruiting 210 primary care physicians within the next five years. The PPMC's managers have expressed their intention to assist in the physician recruitment process; however, their ability to realistically contribute significant amounts of time to the process is unknown. In addition, if the PPMC's overall physician recruitment efforts are to succeed, the financial results will reflect a minimum of approximately $225,000 and perhaps as much as $600,000 in additional unscheduled recruiting expense.

SUMMARY OF FINDINGS AND CONCLUSIONS

Models and Markets

The PPMC's model of small practices functioning with two physicians or two physicians and one extender, arranged in clusters within specified second- and third-tier geographic markets, is a plan with many potential inherent efficiencies. The targeting of second- and third-tier cities, combined with the application of contract management skills to primary care physician practice start-ups and development, may prove to be the key elements of the PPMC's business plan. This strategy can be advantageous from a market entrance perspective, as the targeted market niche is not yet crowded. These factors, however, may prove to be a hindrance to the physician recruitment component of the business plan.

Financial Aspects

As illustrated in Exhibits 8-1 and 8-2, certain line items within the revenue and expense projections in the PPMC's pro forma vary from industry norms during years 1 and 2, and these variances may be significant and material. Considering all five years of the projections, pro forma productivity and revenue projections are generally in accordance with industry averages, while the pro forma expenses are somewhat understated when compared with industry norms.

As shown in Exhibit 8-3, the PPMC's actual practice financial performance up to the present time has not been in accord with the performance indicated by its pro forma, primarily because the PPMC is in its start-up phase. The five-year financial projections, and comparison of these projections to industry norms, suggested that the PPMC expects financial performance to improve.

Growth and Physician Recruitment Aspects

The PPMC's growth plan is based on the cluster concept and depends on the success and effectiveness of the physician recruitment program. The physician manpower requirements of the proposed practice offices, combined with the demands related to the start-up nature of the practices, will require a commitment of significant amounts of time and expense for the physician recruitment component of the business plan. The PPMC's plan has not adequately addressed or budgeted for the growth issues.

The result of a successfully executed physician recruitment plan (i.e., 210 physicians signed within five years) would support a successful practice development plan for the PPMC. However, none of the financial projections, have adequately addressed the potential for an additional $216,120 of recruitment-associated expenses per year (an estimated $1,080,600 over five years, as set forth on page 270), which may result in significant profitability and cash flow variances from the projections.

Another significant aspect of a successful recruitment plan involves actual site visit interviews with physicians on-site at practice offices that may not be constructed or in operation at the time of the interview. While the PPMC may plan to build the offices and then recruit the physicians, it remains more difficult to obtain a physician commitment (i.e., signed contract) for a practice that is not yet established or is in a start-up mode. Selling the *concept* of a practice is inherently more difficult than selling a physician candidate on joining an already-established practice where there is an obvious, evident, ongoing need for the physician's services; this problem would be exacerbated by the lack of actual facilities and work space at the time of the physician's on-site visit.

The PPMC's corporate overhead, as well as the unaccounted-for incremental recruitment expenses, will continue even if the PPMC does not reach its goal of 210 physicians within the five-year time frame.

Therefore, an unsuccessful physician recruitment effort could mean significant protraction of the time necessary to achieve the revenue projections of the PPMC's plan, and could result in significant diminution of both revenues and earnings.

Risk versus Return

The essence of risk is that the actual future rate of return of an asset is unknown at the time the asset is bought. Investors require a premium for bearing that risk. In other words, the more risk an investor accepts, the higher the expected return on the investment.

As uncertainty increases, so does risk. Few other industries in the United States today face more uncertainty than the healthcare industry. Regulatory compliance issues are on the rise. The difficulty of making decisions increases because of the government's past record of retroactive enforcement of healthcare-related rulings. Topics related to regulation, cost-containment, and industry and payment "reform" dominate the industry, and both the general and trade press create the perception of even greater uncertainty and risk for providers and prospective investors.

Within the context of the general risk environment of the healthcare industry, the risks specific to an investment in the PPMC should also be considered relative to alternative investment opportunities.

It can be useful to consider the value of the PPMC's investment opportunity within the context of the principle of substitution, which states that the cost of an equally desirable substitute, or one of equal utility, tends to set the ceiling of value of a commodity. There are several "substitutes," or alternative investment opportunities, that are available to ABC that could meet its primary care physician practice development needs, including:

- Investment in or joint venture with a company similar to the PPMC with a proven track record. While the current geographical or market niche of these existing, established PPMCs may not be in strict alignment with the PPMC's business plan, they may be in accordance with, or be revised to be in accordance with, ABC's specific primary care physician needs in its local marketplace.
- Establishment of ABC's own practice development subsidiary, either:
  a. In-house with the existing management staff.
  b. Outsourced to a professional consulting firm.
- Acquisition of existing primary care physician practices.
- Development of strategic alliances with existing primary care physician panels and/or networks.

ABC should consider each of these alternative as to the risk versus return relative to the prospective investment in the PPMC.

Summary Statement of Findings and Conclusions

1. Physician recruitment expenses appear to be understated by approximately $1.1 to $3 million over the first five years of the PPMC's existence.

2. The PPMC has revised its timetable of practice development and this revision does not appear to be realistic because of a lack of signed commitments from physician candidates and executed office leases.

3. Actual historical performance data for the initial practice in operation is not in accordance with the pro forma.

4. The PPMC's two-MD model may not prove to be an effective or efficient delivery system for PCP services in a capitated environment.

5. Alternative investment opportunities may present less risk while still achieving ABC's PCP development goals.

CONTINGENT AND LIMITING CONDITIONS

The information and documents considered in this consulting engagement and report are a compilation of data furnished by others, including the officers, directors, shareholders, and staff of the PPMC and their agents, who have warranted that all information provided is accurate and complete to the best of their knowledge and belief. Therefore, in accordance with the terms of the engagement, this information has been accepted without further verification as correctly reflecting the current status and future plans for the subject company, and the consultant assumes no responsibility for its accuracy.

Any actual performance of the subject company may be at a higher or a lower level than projected in this preliminary report, depending upon the circumstances of the actual operation. Such circumstances could include, but not be limited to, changes in the economy; leveraging; cost of capital; the parties' individual abilities, knowledge, motivation, and synergies or lack thereof; negotiating skills; quality of counsel; and other individual or interrelated factors. Some assumed events inevitably will not occur, and unanticipated events and circumstances may occur, causing actual performance in the areas forecasted/projected to vary from the forecast/projection. These variations may be material. Therefore, this report does not express any form of assurance on the likelihood of achieving the forecasted/projected result or on the reasonableness of the assumptions, representations, and conclusions presented. Any such forecast/projection is a part of this report and is not intended to be used separately. The client is advised to obtain the advice of an attorney and a certified public accountant prior to making any investment in the subject company.

This report assumes that no litigious, regulatory compliance, environmental hazard, or similar problems exist. Should there be an investigation regarding such matters, items that could materially affect the consultant's stated opinions may be discovered. Therefore, no representations or warranties are expressed or implied regarding such conditions and no consideration has been given within this report to the possible effects of any such conditions. This report assumes that there are no restrictions or other qualifications that could materially affect the ability of the clients to conduct the business of the subject company, including, but not limited to, its transferability. This report is further subject to any other contingencies, assumptions, and limiting conditions as may be set out elsewhere herein.

Appendixes

DIRECTORY OF APPENDIXES

General Research

Appendix 1: Analysis of Cases by Medical Specialty of Provider and Major Diagnostic Category (MDC)   280

Appendix 2: Analysis of DRG Demand by MDC Summary Report   284

Appendix 3: Area Hospital Assessment Worksheet   286

Appendix 4: Employment Survey   288

Appendix 5: Major Employer Worksheet   290

Appendix 6: Managed Care Organization/Insurance Worksheet   292

Appendix 7: Economic Environment Worksheet   296

Appendix 8: Medical Practice Selection Matrix   298

Specific Research

Appendix 9: Due Diligence Checklist   300

Appendix 10: Equipment Inventory Worksheet   309

Appendix 11: Sample Medical Practice Documents and Materials Request Form   318

Appendix 12: Medical Practice Worksheet   320

Appendix 13: Medical Practice Workbook   331

Appendix 14: Sample Income Distribution Plan   354

Formation of EHO

Appendix 15: Analysis of Compensation Package   355

Appendix 16: Exit Strategies Worksheet   360

Appendix 17: Governance Checklist   363

Appendix 18: Operational Compliance Worksheet   367

Appendix 19: Capital Contribution Worksheet   370

Appendix 20: Physician Contact/Interview Summary   373
Appendix 21: Voting Checklist   375
Appendix 22: Exit Strategies   382
Appendix 23: Database Fields Sample   384

Centralization of Services

Appendix 24: Employee Insurance/Resource Worksheet   386
Appendix 25: Insurance Benefits Assessment   388
Appendix 26: Employer and Employee Insurance Expenses   389
Appendix 27: Summary of Practice Services Worksheet   391

Operational Review

Appendix 28: Sample Management Status Assessment and Operational Review: Practice Contracts Summary   393
Appendix 29: Sample Management Status Assessment and Operational Review: Synopsis/Timeline of Recommendations   395
Appendix 30: Sample Management Status Assessment and Operational Review: Summary of Issues and Concerns   397
Appendix 31: Sample Management Status Assessment and Operational Review: Format for Specific Recommendations   399
Appendix 32: Sample Management Status Assessment and Operational Review: Medical Practice Site Visit Summary   401

Management Information System

Appendix 33: Information System Vendor Key Business Selection Criteria   403
Appendix 34: Medical Management Software: Annual Maintenance Cost Comparison   404
Appendix 35: Medical Management Software: Pricing Comparison   406
Appendix 36: Practice Management Information Systems Request for Information   408

Healthcare Executive Search

Appendix 37: Healthcare Executive Search Overview of Conducting a Search for Healthcare Executives   424

Miscellaneous

Appendix 38: Confidentiality and Stand Still Agreement   442
Appendix 39: Letter of Intent A: Employment with Practice Acquisition   445
Appendix 40: Letter of Intent B: Option A = Employment and Option B = Affiliation   449

Appendix 41: Letter of Intent C: Employment—No Practice Acquisition   453

Appendix 42: Letter of Intent D: Affiliation Arrangement   457

Appendix 43: Consulting Engagement Pre-Engagement
Acceptance Form   460

Analysis of Cases by Medical Specialty of Provider and Major Diagnostic Category (MDC)

The Analysis of Cases by Medical Specialty of Provider and Major Diagnostic Category (MDC) is a method of tracking the volume of inpatient services. Many hospital MIS systems will provide this data in a relatively simple report. The Analysis of Cases by Medical Specialty of Provider and Major Diagnostic Category (MDC) may be very useful as an objective measure to track the most utilized hospital services.

Analysis of Cases by Medical Specialty of Provider & Major Diagnostic Category (MDC)

Period: _____

Client Input Table 1

Specialty	Major Diagnostic Category (MDC)							
	1	2	3	4	5	6	7	8
Addictionology								
Cardiology								
Endocrinology								
Family Practice								
Gastroenterology								
General Surgery								
Geriatrics								
Internal Medicine								
Nephrology								
Neurology								
Neurosurgery								
Oncology								
Ophthalmology								
Orthopedics								
Otorhinolaryngology								
Pediatrics								
Plastic Surgery								
Psychiatry								
Pulmonology								
Rheumatology								
Urology								
Total Cases								
% of Total Cases								

Source: Analysis and summary of hospital computer printout.

Specialty	Major Diagnostic Category (MDC)								
	9	10	11	12	13	14	15	16	17
Addictionology									
Cardiology									
Endocrinology									
Family Practice									
Gastroenterology									
General Surgery									
Geriatrics									
Internal Medicine									
Nephrology									
Neurology									
Neurosurgery									
Oncology									
Ophthalmology									
Orthopedics									
Otorhinolaryngology									
Pediatrics									
Plastic Surgery									
Psychiatry									
Pulmonology									
Rheumatology									
Urology									
Total Cases									
% of Total Cases									

Source: Analysis and summary of hospital computer printout.

Specialty	Major Diagnostic Category (MDC)									
	18	19	20	21	22	23	24	25	Total	% Total Cases
Addictionology										
Cardiology										
Endocrinology										
Family Practice										
Gastroenterology										
General Surgery										
Geriatrics										
Internal Medicine										
Nephrology										
Neurology										
Neurosurgery										
Oncology										
Ophthalmology										
Orthopedics										
Otorhinolaryngology										
Pediatrics										
Plastic Surgery										
Psychiatry										
Pulmonology										
Rheumatology										
Urology										
Total Cases										
% of Total Cases										

Source: Analysis and summary of hospital computer printout.

Analysis of DRG Demand by MDC Summary Report

The Analysis of DRG Demand by MDC Summary Report is another method of analyzing inpatient services volume. The sample report that follows shows a two-year trend by MDC; however, more comprehensive studies can be done by analyzing every DRG over a longer time period. The purpose of the Analysis of DRG Demand by MDC Summary Report is to track the utilization and demand of certain inpatient services.

SAMPLE HOSPITAL

Analysis of DRG Demand by MDC Summary Report—"TOTAL SERVICE AREA"

		Total Patient Days		Total Cases	
MDC	Major Diagnostic Category (MDC)	Year 1	Year 2	Year 1	Year 2
	All MDC categories				
1	Diseases and Disorders of the Nervous System				
2	Diseases and Disorders of the Eye				
3	Diseases and Disorders of the Ear, Nose, Mouth & Throat				
4	Diseases and Disorders of the Respiratory System				
5	Diseases and Disorders of the Circulatory System				
6	Diseases and Disorders of the Digestive System				
7	Diseases and Disorders of the Hepatobiliary System & Pancreas				
8	Diseases and Disorders of the Musculoskeletal System & Connective Tissue				
9	Diseases and Disorders of the Skin, Subcutaneous Tissue & Breast				
10	Endocrine, Nutritional & Metabolic Diseases and Disorders				
11	Diseases and Disorders of the Kidney & Urinary Tract				
12	Diseases and Disorders of the Male Reproductive System				
13	Diseases and Disorders of the Female Reproductive System				
14	Pregnancy, Childbirth & Puerperium				
15	Newborns & Other Neonates w/Conditions Originating in the Perinatal Period				
16	Diseases and Disorders of the Blood & Blood-Forming Organs and Immunological Disorders				
17	Diseases and Disorders of the Myeloproliferative & Poorly Differentiated Neoplasms				
18	Infectious and Parasitic Diseases				
19	Mental Diseases & Disorders				
20	Alcohol/Drug Use & Alcohol/Drug Induce Organic Mental Disorders				
21	Injuries, Poisonings, & Toxic Effects of Drugs				
22	Burns				
23	Factor Influ Health Status & Other Contacts with Health Services				
24	Multiple Significant Trauma				
25	Human Immunodeficiency Virus Infections				

Area Hospital Assessment Worksheet

The Area Hospital Assessment Worksheet is a useful early-stage tool to illustrate the competitors in the local market. When implementing the program, each affiliated entity should complete an Area Hospital Assessment Worksheet. A comprehensive assessment of the market competitors will help identify projects that may be demanded and successful in the community.

Area Hospital Assessment Worksheet

List all hospitals and competing facilities in the service area.

	Facility	Location	Number of Beds	Number of Admissions	Census	Number of Outpatient Visits
1.						
2.						
3.						
4.						
5.						
6.						
7.						
8.						
9.						
10.						
11.						
12.						

For each facility, the following questions and issues may be considered:

1. Are they actively pursuing physician integration/practice activity?
2. If yes, then to what extent? And, what have they accomplished so far?
3. Which providers have already affiliated with this particular facility?

Employment Survey

The Employment Survey should be used to expand the Major Employment Worksheet. The purpose of the Employment Survey is to conduct an economic analysis of the markets in which the program will be implemented to determine the feasibility of potential projects. The Employment Survey provides a brief, preliminary list of questions that should be addressed when assessing the market.

EMPLOYMENT SURVEY

Consider the present and future implications of the following factors.

1. Unemployment and employment rates:

_____

_____

_____

_____

2. Number, type, and location of employers in the community:

_____

_____

_____

_____

3. Type of industry and employers (service, industrial):

_____

_____

_____

_____

4. Construction and renovation of commercial and residential buildings:

_____

_____

_____

_____

5. Retail sales in area:

_____

_____

_____

_____

6. Stability of banking and financial industry:

_____

_____

Major Employer Worksheet

The Major Employer Worksheet should be used to help identify the customers your program will target. For example, you may want to target employers by size, type of insurance (e.g., self-insured companies, specific insurance plans), industry, or type of occupation. The employer assessment may assist the program in developing projects, such as occupational medicine or behavioral medicine.

Major Employer Worksheet

	Company Name	Number of Employees	Location City	Current Insurance Plan/ Alliances/Coalitions
1				
2				
3				
4				
5				
6				
7				
8				
9				
10				
11				
12				
13				
14				
15				
16				
17				

Managed Care Organization/Insurance Worksheet

The purpose of the Managed Care Organization/Insurance Worksheet is to provide an assessment of the various payor sources available in the market. The degree of managed care penetration will also impact many of the projects within the program. Sources to assist the project team in completing the Managed Care Organization/Insurance Worksheet are:

- Direct interview of MCO/insurance personnel
- Research data sources
- Information received from physician prospects

Following the Managed Care Organization/Insurance Worksheet is an MCO Summary Table that can be used to summarize the managed care organizations/insurance companies in the market.

MANAGED CARE ORGANIZATION/INSURANCE WORKSHEET

Name of organization: _____

Address: _____

_____

Phone number: _____

Fax number: _____

For profit: _____

Physicians (primary care): _____

(Referring): _____

Number of hospitals: _____

Names of local hospitals: _____

_____

Areas served: _____

Average subscriber copayment: _____

- Primary care physician $ _____
- Prescription drugs $ _____
- Home health care $ _____
- Non-network physician $ _____
- Hospital emergency room $ _____
- Nursing home $ _____

Maximum number of days covered: _____

- Home health care: _____
- Nursing home: _____

Types of payment plans offered: _____

- Point of service: _____
- Discounted FFS: _____
- Capitated: _____
- Fee for service: _____
- Combination FFS & DFFS: _____

Average monthly fee per subscriber (employee plus employer contribution): _____

- Employee only (self): $ _____
- Medicare: $_____
- Employee and one family member: $ _____
- Employee and two family members: $ _____

Annual average deductible per subscriber:

- Employee only (self) $_____
- Medicare: $_____
- Employee and one family member: $ _____
- Employee and two family members: $ _____

Average claim compensation for fees charged:

- Physician fees: _____
- Hospital fees: _____

Qualifications needed to become a network hospital or nursing home:

- JCAHO accreditation: _____
- Medicare approved: _____
- Utilization review: _____
- Pre-admission certification: _____
- State license: _____
- Quality assurance program required: _____

Qualifications needed to become a network physician:

- Years of practice: _____
- Board certification: _____
- Pre-admission certification: _____

Peer review type:

- Utilization review: _____
- Case management: _____
- Second surgical opinion: _____

Employer references:

_____

_____

_____

_____

Subsidiaries:

_____

_____

_____

_____

Total number of patient complaints:

1995: _____

1994: _____

1993: _____

1992: _____

1991: _____

MCO Summary Table

Insurers	% Population	% of Patients Served	Payment Limitations	Coverage Patterns

Economic Environment Worksheet

Consider the present and future implications of the following factors.

1. Unemployed and employed rates:

_____

_____

_____

2. Number, type, and location of employers in the community:

_____

_____

_____

3. Type of industry and employers (service, industrial):

_____

_____

_____

4. Construction and renovation of commercial and residential buildings:

_____

_____

_____

5. Retail sales in area:

_____

_____

_____

6. Stability of banking and financial industry:

_____

_____

_____

Medical Practice Selection Matrix

The Selection Rating System Matrix is a subjective decision-making tool that may be used to narrow the list of prospects to targets. The criteria in the Selection Rating System Matrix is not meant to be all-inclusive of the possible considerations; however, it provides a continuum of factors that may be of assistance in selecting which physicians should be pursued further.

Selection Rating System Matrix

Rating	Rating Points (*)				
Criteria	1	2	3	4	5
Location Proximity of Practice to Hospital					
Loyalty Factor/Admissions Relationship to Hospital					
Physician Population/Qualifications (e.g., Board Certification)					
Physician Quality Assurance/Utilization Review Factors					
Pattern of Referral to Physician Specialists					
Managed Care Payor Relationships & Plan Participation					
Practice Life Cycle					
Receptiveness of Physician to Program					
Practice Patient Volume and Financial Viability					
RATING SUBTOTALS					
TOTAL SCORE					

*Note: 1 = Least Favorable, 5 = Most Favorable

Due Diligence Checklist

The following materials should be made available to allow us to proceed with the due diligence phase of our engagement. To assist us in our efforts on your behalf, we ask that you submit them to us as soon as possible. At your request, we will work with your accountant and staff to accomplish this.

I. CORPORATE

A. Copy of organizational chart of the company, trusts, partnerships, other entities, and all subsidiaries thereof, including fictitious business names owned or used by the selling corporation and its subsidiaries.

B. Copies of the charter, articles of incorporation and bylaws, and all amendments thereto, of the company(s), including dates of incorporation or partnership formation.

C. Copies of all shareholder, partnership, joint venture, and trust agreements as currently in effect.

D. Minute books of meetings and all actions taken without a meeting of the company's shareholders, board of directors, and committees of the board.

E. Stock books and stock transfer ledgers of the company(s) and subsidiaries. Comparable documents for all other entities.

F. A list of the states in which each entity is qualified to do business and copies of all certificates evidencing qualification to do business in each such state.

G. A list of states in which each entity files tax returns.

H. A list of names and addresses of each office location, and the nature of ownership or leasing thereof. Indicate planned locations at which operations have not yet begun.

I.   A list of all subsidiaries in which each entity holds, directly or indirectly, 5 percent or more of the outstanding shares of any class of stock or any comparable interest.

J.   List of all consultants of the various entities, including auditors, financial advisors, management consultants, and legal counsel used since inception, and a general listing of services rendered.

II. *SHARES AND STOCKHOLDERS: CORPORATE TRANSACTIONS*

A.   A list of the names and addresses of each stockholder, partner, beneficiary, or other owner of record or beneficiary, of each entity, the number of shares, partnership interests, or other equitable interests owned by each such person; and the dates on which the same were issued to each such person.

B.   Copies of all notes, loan or credit agreements, indentures, mortgages, deeds or trust, guaranties, security agreements, and other documents relating to outstanding obligations of each entity or its subsidiaries.

C.   Copies of any preincorporation, shareholder, voting, or comparable agreements.

D.   Copies of all stock purchase agreements and asset purchase agreements.

III. *MANAGEMENT AND EMPLOYEES*

A.   Organizational chart of management and employees with name and title. Physician/professional staff history/curriculum vitae.

   1. List any and all board/association/societies memberships.

   2. List any and all volunteer work.

   3. List any and all medical directorships.

      a. State where they are held.

      b. Do contracts exist?

      c. What are the terms of these contracts?

      d. What is the compensation?

   4. Staff appointments/special privileges.

      a. Where are the appointments/privileges held?

      b. When were the appointments made?

      c. What is extent and nature of these privileges?

      d. List the responsibilities involved.

      e. What is the compensation?

  5. Hospital privileges.

      a. List the hospital(s).

      b. List the extent and nature of these privileges at each hospital.

  6. Academic appointments.

      a. Where is each appointment?

      b. When was each appointment made?

  7. Board certification/recertification.

      a. List each and every specialty and subspecialty.

      b. For each professional, state whether he/she is board certified/qualified or otherwise designated.

      c. List all dates when certified and when recertified for each.

B. A list of key employees on whom important elements of the business depend, including curriculum vitae for each.

C. A list of the names and ages of current officers, directors, managing partners, trustees, etc., with terms of office and brief biographical sketch of each, and a brief description of any noncompetition or confidentiality agreements with other companies to which any officer or director is a party.

D. Copies of monthly or other periodic management reports for the last 12 months.

E. Copies of any documentation reflecting (1) transactions or series of similar transactions between any insiders of such entity or any affiliate; (2) any loans between such parties; and (3) any consulting agreements or other agreements between such parties. An insider shall mean (i) any person who at the time was an officer, director, partner, trustee, or nominee for the same, beneficiary, a stockholder of the company who beneficially owned more than 5 percent of the company's voting stock, or any member of the immediate family of any of the foregoing persons; (ii) any person who at the time was an officer, director, or general partner of an enterprise that owned 10 percent or more of any entity; or (iii) any entity who at the time had a common officer, director, partner, or trustee with any entity.

F. Copies of each employment contract, independent contractor agreement, and confidentiality and noncompetition agreement (or, if standard forms are used, a copy of the standard form with a list containing all variables of the current contracts).

G. Copies of all employee manuals, handbooks, and personnel policies, guides, or significant policy statements of the company.

H. Copies of all collective bargaining agreements with any unions or other organizations representing employees of any entity.

I. Copies of stock option plans, a list of the names and the number of options granted to each participant to date pursuant to the plans and documents relating to awards under the plans. Copies of any other options, warrants, or comparable rights.

J. Current information on employees, including date of hire, date of birth, job title, wage or salary rates, classification as full- or part-time. Also include information on employee turnover within the preceding five years.

K. Summary plan descriptions of all employee benefit and welfare plans, including profit sharing, deferred compensation/pension, defined benefit or contribution, stock ownership, retirement, welfare and other plans.

L. List of licensure status of all employees and independent contractors.

M. List of all employee training programs.

IV. OPERATIONS

A. Copies of contracts, management agreements, consulting agreements, medical director agreements, or provider agreements, and list of all major clientele and/or all other entities from which salaries or wages are earned.

B. Copies of all contracts made otherwise than in the ordinary course of business.

C. Copies of public relations and marketing materials, brochures, press releases, and articles appearing in print media in the past two years.

D. Copies of all leases, subleases, and installment payment contracts relating to real and personal property.

E. List of all tenants leasing or occupying space on company premises and monthly rental payments.

F. Copies of standard forms of agreements, including purchase orders, patient billing, invoices, etc.

G. A list of all trademarks, trade names, service marks, copyrights, or other intellectual property rights, or license agreements thereof, owned or used in the business, giving a brief description of use, registration number, and date of issuance of registration, name and address of any person to or from whom such time is licensed, and brief description of such arrangement.

H. A list of names and addresses of all local competitors and any information obtained concerning these competitors.

I. Copies of any membership agreements or other relationships with trade organization, membership or other agreements with groups or entities which engage in peer review, quality review, or rate review procedures.

J. Copies of any patient referral agreements and transfer agreements.

K. Patient information.

1. Source of patients and referrals.

   a. List the number of active patients (account activity) at present and within the past three years.

   b. What is the average number of patients seen per day at the office and at the hospital?

   c. What is the average number of new patients seen per week?

   d. Provide any and all referral sources (including percentages for each).

   e. Provide a breakdown of the average number of hours worked by each physician and physician extenders per week both at the office and at the hospital.

2. Patient mix.

   a. List the payor mix (i.e., percentages of self-pay, insurance, and third-party providers).

   b. Provide the level of capitation, if any.

   c. Provide the estimated age mix of patients at the practice.

   d. List all diagnoses and procedures.

3. Billing and claims resolution process.

   a. Provide the amount and frequency of all cash and currency receipts for medical services rendered, and the specific disposition of all cash receipts.

   b. List all staff responsible for billings and claims resolution procedures.

      (i.) Describe their daily responsibilities and periods of their employment for these tasks.

      (ii.) Provide the names of the staff who prepare deposits, accept payments, and make deposits at the bank.

      (iii.) Provide the frequency of these deposits.

    c. Provide a detail of all bank accounts (business and personal).

        (i.)   Provide date when each account was opened and at which bank.

        (ii.)   Explain the purpose of each account.

    d. Provide documentation explaining the collection policy and procedures at the practice.

    e. Provide the names of all staff responsible for the collection of payments for medical services rendered.

L.   Copies of all letters of intent, memorandums of understanding, and comparable documents.

M. Copies of all agreements relating to acquisitions, dispositions, or mergers that have been effected or proposed.

N. List naming and describing all furnishings, fixtures, and equipment owned by and/or used, including date and price of acquisition.

O. Detailed depreciation schedules from tax return or accountants' records, to verify schedule, if available.

P. Estimate of the number of days on hand of medical, lab, and office supplies as of date of valuation.

Q. Estimate of the number and type of major and minor procedures performed in the office and at the hospital within the immediate six months or one year prior to the date of valuation.

R. Copy of patient location/zip code distribution report (if available).

S. Copy of all quality control and safety policy/plans.

V. FINANCIAL INFORMATION

A. Copies of unaudited financial statements of the company and its subsidiaries subsequent to its last financial audit and all audited financial statements for the past three years.

B. Copies of all management letters issued by accountants in the past three years and responses thereto, and copies of auditors' inquiry letters to attorneys (and replies) for the past three years.

C. Copies of budgets adopted for the current fiscal year and budget for the next three fiscal years.

D. A detailed list of and copies of indenture, mortgage, promissory notes, loan or credit agreements, or other contracts or commitments relating to borrowing of money or line of credit by the selling corporation and its subsidiaries.

E. Documents relating to any intercompany type of operational charges, transactions/procedures, and total receipts by CPT code.

    F. Copies of all agreements or letters confirming available or outstanding lines of credit.

    G. Copies of all material correspondence with lenders, including all compliance reports submitted by any entity or its accountants.

    H. Copies of all feasibility studies and long-range strategic plans.

    I. Copies of the field tax returns of the company for the past three years, plus updates to most recent quarter or month prior to the date of the valuation.

    J. Accounts receivables.

       1. Provide percentage of accounts receivables aged less than 30 days (also between 31 and 60 days, between 61 and 90 days, and more than 90 days).

       2. List historical percent collectible for each aging category.

       3. List payment mix by payor.

       4. Set forth the procedures for posting charges to A/R.

          a. State method of posting of gross charges.

          b. State procedures for posting adjustments.

          c. State procedures for posting write-offs.

       5. State who at the practice receives the explanation of benefits (EOB) from third-party payors.

          a. State who processes the EOBs and where they are filed.

       6. State whether the EOBs are compared to and reconciled with A/R, patient billing statements, and appointment book(s). If not, what are the procedures for handling the reconciliations of services rendered to receipts in the practice?

VI. REIMBURSEMENT AND GOVERNMENT REGULATION

    A. Copies of contacts with preferred provider organizations, health maintenance organizations, and any other managed care entity or any other third-party payor.

    B. Copies of provider agreements, provider numbers, and any other documents related to participation in the Medicare and Medicaid programs. Same for CHAMPUS, if applicable.

    C. Copies of any health care and business licenses or any other permits necessary for operations, whether pending, in place, or expired.

D. Copies of any documentation relating to compliance with environmental, health, safety, and civil rights laws.

E. List of all professional or trade association memberships.

VII. LITIGATION AND CLAIMS

A. A list of case caption, cause, and date of filing of complaint, of any pending or threatened claim or litigation as to which, if any entity is a party, or by which the property, assets, or business of any entity is, or will be, adversely affected, whether as plaintiff or defendant, for the past three years.

B. A brief description of any outstanding judgements, orders, decrees and settlements, and other dispositions of legal proceedings against any entity.

C. A brief description of any pending or threatened disputes with Medicare, Medicaid, or CHAMPUS and of any such disputes occurring during the last three years.

D. A brief description of any actions or investigations threatened or taken by any state or federal department against any entity, its subsidiaries, or any of their operations over the past three years.

VIII. MISCELLANEOUS

A. A brief description of all insurance policies maintained by each entity, including the summary plan descriptions, the name of the carrier, the annual premium, the nature and amount of the coverage, the entity's claim experience for the past five years, and any outstanding claims (general liability, health, dental, malpractice, disability, workmen's compensation, unemployment compensation).

B. Copies of employee benefits handbook containing descriptions of all forms of insurance and other benefits.

C. A brief description of any plans for expanding the business into any other specialized health care areas or otherwise.

D. Copies of all notifications of pending audits and a list of all years in which any entity was required to file tax returns for which the statute of limitations, applicable to such entity's tax returns, has not expired.

1. Copies of analyses of any entity of the industry prepared by investment bankers, management consultants, accountants, or others, including other types of reports or memoranda relating to the broad aspects of the business of operations of any entity.

2. Copies of any material report filed with governmental agencies.
3. Copies of audit reports covering pension, retirement, or employee benefit plans of any entity.
4. Copies of any other material contracts not described above.
5. Copies of any real estate surveys, title reports, or appraisals made within the past three years.

Equipment Inventory Worksheet

The Equipment Inventory Worksheet is used to value the tangible assets of a medical practice, primarily in acquisition or consolidation projects. The Equipment Inventory Worksheet is usually completed by a staff member of the medical practice; however, a random verification should be completed during the site visit to insure accuracy of the valued assets.

Equipment Inventory Worksheet

Patient Waiting Room

#	Item	Approx. Acq. Date	Approx. Acq. Cost ($)	Leased or Owned?

Fixtures and Furnishings

#	Item	Approx. Acq. Date	Approx. Acq. Cost ($)	Leased or Owned?

Business/Reception Area

#	Item	Approx. Acq. Date	Approx. Acq. Cost ($)	Leased or Owned?

Fixtures and Furnishings

#	Item	Approx. Acq. Date	Approx. Acq. Cost ($)	Leased or Owned?

Office Equipment

#	Item	Approx. Acq. Date	Approx. Acq. Cost ($)	Leased or Owned?

Equipment Inventory Worksheet

Exam Room #1

#	Item	Approx. Acq. Date	Approx. Acq. Cost ($)	Leased or Owned?

Fixtures and Furnishings

#	Item	Approx. Acq. Date	Approx. Acq. Cost ($)	Leased or Owned?

Medical Equipment

#	Item	Approx. Acq. Date	Approx. Acq. Cost ($)	Leased or Owned?

Exam Room #2

#	Item	Approx. Acq. Date	Approx. Acq. Cost ($)	Leased or Owned?

Fixtures and Furnishings

#	Item	Approx. Acq. Date	Approx. Acq. Cost ($)	Leased or Owned?

Medical Equipment

#	Item	Approx. Acq. Date	Approx. Acq. Cost ($)	Leased or Owned?

Exam Room #3

#	Item	Approx. Acq. Date	Approx. Acq. Cost ($)	Leased or Owned?
Fixtures and Furnishings				
Medical Equipment				

Surgery/Procedures

#	Item	Approx. Acq. Date	Approx. Acq. Cost ($)	Leased or Owned?

Fixtures and Furnishings

#	Item	Approx. Acq. Date	Approx. Acq. Cost ($)	Leased or Owned?

Medical Equipment

#	Item	Approx. Acq. Date	Approx. Acq. Cost ($)	Leased or Owned?

10 *Equipment Inventory Worksheet*

MD Consult Office

#	Item	Approx. Acq. Date	Approx. Acq. Cost ($)	Leased or Owned?

Fixtures and Furnishings

#	Item	Approx. Acq. Date	Approx. Acq. Cost ($)	Leased or Owned?

Office Equipment

#	Item	Approx. Acq. Date	Approx. Acq. Cost ($)	Leased or Owned?

Lab

#	Item	Approx. Acq. Date	Approx. Acq. Cost ($)	Leased or Owned?

Fixtures and Furnishings

#	Item	Approx. Acq. Date	Approx. Acq. Cost ($)	Leased or Owned?

Medical Equipment

#	Item	Approx. Acq. Date	Approx. Acq. Cost ($)	Leased or Owned?

Sample Medical Practice Documents and Materials Request Form

The following materials should be available to allow us to proceed with consideration of the practice. To assist us in our efforts, we ask that you submit them to us as soon as possible. At your request, we will work with your accountant and staff to accomplish this.

1. Financial statements (including income and expense statements and balance sheets) and tax returns (including detailed attachments and supplemental information) for the last five full years, plus updates to most recent quarter, or month prior to the date of the valuation.

2. Fee schedules for office, hospital, and lab, current as of date of valuation, reflecting standard fee, medicare fee, and other prenegotiated fixed fee-for-service PPO fees.

3. Aged accounts receivable schedule with payor detail as of date of valuation.

4. Detailed inventory of medical equipment and office equipment (including furniture and fixtures) in use in practice as of date of valuation, with date and cost of acquisition. Detailed depreciation schedules should be included from tax return or accountants' records to verify schedule.

5. Estimate of the number of days of each category of supplies on hand (categorize by medical supplies, lab supplies, and office supplies) as of date of valuation.

6. Count of active patient charts which had experienced activity within the last one and a half to two years prior to the date of valuation.

Also, an estimate of the total patient charts with the practice as of date of valuation.

7. A CPT coded schedule of the number and type of major and minor procedures performed in the office and at the hospital; the number and type of lab and diagnostic tests and procedures performed in the office; and the number and type of office visits and other services provided within the practice for the immediate six months and one year prior to the date of valuation.

8. Summary and description of privileges at hospitals where staff privileges are held, and scheduling arrangement.

9. A description and list of referral sources as of the date of valuation.

10. A description of the call/coverage rotation schedule (if applicable).

11. Copy of all employment agreements, partnership agreements, shareholders agreements, buy/sell agreements, consulting agreements, management agreements, and income distribution plans in use in practice.

12. Copy of all agreements for past transactions involving the transfer of an equity or ownership interest in the practice, if any, prior to the date of valuation.

13. If applicable, a copy of any contracts, leases, or other agreements subject to transfer.

14. If applicable, a copy of any mortgage agreement related to any real property utilized within practice.

15. Curriculum vitae and board certification status of all professional providers in the practice.

16. Copy of declaration page (cover page) of malpractice insurance.

17. Patient location/zip code distribution report (if available).

18. Copies of all managed care contracts in use in practice.

Medical Practice Worksheet

The Medical Practice Worksheet is a valuable data-gathering tool that provides a broad understanding of a medical practice. The Medical Practice Worksheet is not a sufficient source of data to conduct extensive due diligence or valuation assignments, but will provide enough information to make an initial assessment or identify specific strengths or weaknesses of the subject practice. The Medical Practice Worksheet will be useful to most projects (e.g., practice acquisition, practice mergers) within the program.

MEDICAL PRACTICE WORKSHEET

DATE: ___ / ___ / ___

Name: _____ Specialty: _____

Address: _____ Sub-Spec: _____

City: _____ State: _____ Zip: _____ Office: (___) _____

Home: (___) _____ Other: (___) _____

Years at above location: _____ In community: _____

Legal structure of practice: Business Corp. ___ Professional Corp. ___
Sole Partnership ___ Unicorp. ___
Partnership _____

Owner(s)/Partners/Shareholders/Officers:

Name: _____ Interest: _____

Name: _____ Interest: _____

Name: _____ Interest: _____

Name: _____ Interest: _____

Academic affiliations: _____

Attorney's name: _____ CPA's name: _____

Attorney's firm: _____ CPA's firm: _____

Attorney's address: _____ CPA's address: _____

Attorney's phone: _____ CPA's phone: _____

Attorney's fax: _____ CPA's fax: _____

Current Office Hours

Day	Office Hours	Physician Hours
Monday		
Tuesday		
Wednesday		
Thursday		
Friday		
Saturday		

Describe your present backup/coverage arrangements:_____

Practice is: _____ % patient referred; _____ % physician referred

What is the primary drawing population of your practice?_____

How many physicians within your specialty in the area?   _____

Hospital Privileges Available At	Distance from Office	Number of Beds	Average Patient Census

What are the minimum requirements to acquire staff privileges for a qualified physician? _____

Other requirements or considerations: _____

Practice Personnel

Office Manager	Secretary	Medical Assistant
Business Manager	Medical Secretary	Registered Nurse
Receptionist	Transcriber	X-Ray Technician

Full Time

Name: _____ **Name:** _____
Resp: _____ Resp: _____
_____ _____

Salary: _____ Salary: _____

Benefits: _____ Benefits: _____
_____ _____
_____ _____

Tenure: _____ Tenure: _____

Staying: _____ Staying: _____

Name: _____ **Name:** _____
Resp: _____ Resp: _____
_____ _____

Salary: _____ Salary: _____

Benefits: _____ Benefits: _____
_____ _____
_____ _____

Tenure: _____ Tenure: _____

Staying: _____ Staying: _____

Name: _____ **Name:** _____
Resp: _____ Resp: _____
_____ _____

Salary: _____ Salary: _____

Benefits: _____ Benefits: _____
_____ _____
_____ _____

Tenure: _____   Tenure: _____

Staying: _____   Staying: _____

Part Time

Name: _____   **Name:** _____

Resp: _____   Resp: _____

_____   _____

Salary: _____   Salary: _____

Benefits: _____   Benefits: _____

_____   _____

_____   _____

Tenure: _____   Tenure: _____

Staying: _____   Staying: _____

Patient Base

Usual hospital census: _____

Is doctor accepting new patients? _____

Any walk-in trade? _____

How long do patients generally wait for an appointment? _____

Total patients' records: _____ Number active: _____

Income distribution: cash _____%; Medicaid/Medicare _____%;
Third party insurance _____%

Average number of patients per day seen in the office: _____

Average number of *new* patients per week seen in the office: _____

Average number of surgical procedures per week: Office _____
Hospital: _____

Charts are sorted: Annually _____ Two years _____ Other: _____

Those which have not experienced activity within _____ years are
removed to a storage area located: Within the practice location: _____
Other: _____

Patient records are primarily (check all that apply):
Hand written: _____ Dictated and transcribed: _____

Charts are (check all that apply): Color coded: _____
Alphabetized: _____ Computerized: _____

The age mix of the practice is estimated as follows:

Age	Approx. % Patient
—	%
—	%
Over	%

The aged accounts receivable for the practice is as follows:

Due Date	Amount
0–30 days	
31–60 days	
61–90 days	
Over 90 days	

Payor Mix

Payor	%	Capitated Yes/No	Number of Capitated Patients
Medicare			
Medicaid			
Blue Cross/Blue Shield			
Blue Choice			
GHI			
Champus			
Self Pay			
Other			
Other			

Strengths of your practice: _____

Threats to your practice: _____

Office Procedures

The approximate volume of procedures performed within practice for the last *6 months/1 year* and the current fee schedule are as follows:

Code	Procedure	Office/Hospital	Volume	Standard Fee

Description: _____

Number of square feet in office: _____   In building: _____

Nearest large city: _____   Distance: _____

Nearest colleges/medical schools: _____

Recreation/culture opportunities in area: _____

Real Estate (Please attach copy of mortgage, floor plan, and any appraisals)

Owned by: _____

Appraised value: _____

Date of appraisal: _____

Appraised by whom: _____

Reason for appraisal: _____

Mortgage amount: _____

Mortgage term: _____

Type of mortgage: _____

Holder of mortgage: _____

Monthly payment: _____

Assumable: _____

Building maintenance: _____

Must real estate be included in the sale?   Yes _____   No _____

Approximate fair market value: _____

Could it be leased?   Yes _____   No _____   Cost: _____

Leasehold (Please attach a copy of lease and floor plan if available)

Copy of lease: AVAILABLE _____ WILL SEND _____

Square feet leased: _____

Owned by:_____

Leased from: _____

Term of lease: _____

Transferable: _____

Subleasing allowed? _____

Monthly rent: _____

Utilities included: _____

Maintenance included: _____

Will lessor pay for improvements?_____

Rate for comparable space: _____

Is lease assumable at same rate? Yes _____ No _____

Expiration date of lease: _____

$/square foot: _____

Any renewal options? Yes _____ No _____

Total cost of leasehold improvements: _____

Number of days of supplies on hand: _____

Medical: _____ Lab: _____ Office: _____

Office Description

Geographic location within community: N ___ S ___ E ___ W ___

Type of neighborhood: Commercial ___ Residential ___
Professional ___ Mix ___

Street description: Number of lanes ___ On-Street Parking ___
Busy ___

Proximity to hospital: _____

Size (square feet/total number of rooms):_____

Floor plan available: _____

Description/decor (architecture/carpeting/air conditioning/disabled access/floor/walls/ceiling height/lighting): _____

Age of building: _____

Age of office (improvements/description/cost): _____

Reception/business area (number of people in area/files/equipment):

_____

Waiting room (number of chairs/access/play area/lavatory/special considerations): _____

Exam rooms (how many/features/in full use/identically equipped special uses/dressing area/lavatory): _____

Lavatories (number in whole facility/separate patient and staff):

_____

Physician's office (library/use for consultations/lavatory decor):

_____

X-ray (developing room/extremities/chest/back/full): _____

Laboratory (use/type): _____

Storage and closets (special uses/total number): _____

Basement or attic: _____

Pharmacy: _____

Employee's lounge: _____

Other: _____

Building Description

Size (freestanding/multi-story): _____

Style (architecture/general condition): _____

Type of construction (brick/stone/wood frame): _____

Parking facilities (adequate/number of spaces/reserved spaces):

_____

Disabled (access/lavatories/phones): _____

Other medical or professional use: _____

Medical Staff Description and Competitive Analysis

How strong is the practice compared to other specialist's practices?

_____

Could practice support two or more practitioners? _____

What would you expect the professional reception to be for someone assuming the practice? _____

Any other MDs of this specialty moving into the area? _____

Is anyone recruiting for this specialty? _____

Are there any programs being developed in hospitals (or other) that would have an impact on the practice? _____

How many MDs within this specialty are in the area? _____

How long have they been in the area? _____

Do they specialize? _____

What is their background? _____

Are any HMOs being developed in the area? _____

Are any PPOs being developed in the area? _____

History and Trends of the Practice

Is practice growing or declining? _____

Why? (Intentionally?) _____

How long in practice (and at this location)? _____

Physician referrals: _____%; patient referrals: _____%

Nonphysician referrals (pharmacists/optometrists): _____

Other referral patterns: _____

Past/present/future associations with other physicians: _____

Managed Care Environment

Discuss the impact of managed care on your practice during the past three years (i.e., impact on revenues, referral patterns):

_____

Discuss the general terms and conditions of the managed care contracts you currently participate in:_____

Discuss the managed care reporting capabilities of your practice (i.e., cost per procedure): _____

Practice positioning relative to an influx of managed care in the market:

_____

Discuss your willingness to participate in risk-sharing contracts:

_____

Issues/Concerns/Reasons to Affiliate with Other Physicians and/or Hospitals

Views of hospital: _____

Relationship with hospital: _____

Relationships with other physicians in community: _____

Relationships with PCPs in community: _____

_____

Concerns about affiliation: _____

_____

Desires/needs of affiliation arrangements (i.e., autonomy, leverage):

_____

Comfort levels regarding issue of autonomy versus leverage:

_____

Interests in a Management Services Organization
Discuss what type of physician integration model you believe to be appropriate and the extent of involvement you may desire for you and your practice:

Ownership:
Management consulting
Utilization mgt./Q.A.
A/R & A/P
Negotiate payor contracts
Negotiate vendor contracts
Operate information system
Marketing/public relations
Laundry services

Services:
Billing/collections
Physician recruitment
Supply ordering
Manage/employ staff
Operate payroll services
Financial services
Administer CME
Office management

Other: _____

Medical Practice Workbook

A Medical Practice Workbook is a comprehensive questionnaire used in gathering information on the practice, practice facilities, information systems, practice history, staff, competition, patients, hospital affiliations, credit and collection policies, and financial management of the subject practice. Some of the information included may be obtained through the Medical Practice Preliminary Worksheet and the document-requests forms found in the Appendices. If a site visit is conducted, the consultant may wish to bring this workbook to the site to complete and verify the information.

DESCRIPTION OF ENGAGEMENT—CONFIDENTIAL

Client company: _____

Contact name: _____

Project/contact name: _____

Proposed fee structure (indicate budget or client preference):_____

Retainer = $ _____

Entity: _____

Interest in the entity: 100% _____

Scope of engagement: _____

Areas to be assessed (check all that apply)

□ Operations Management

□ Financial Management

☐ Human Resources Management
☐ Strategic Planning
☐ Contracts for Service
☐ Organizational Assessment
☐ External and Internal Environment
☐ Other (as deemed appropriate by client)

Format of Report: _____ Other: _____

TABLE OF CONTENTS

I.	Practice Information	332
II.	Building and Lease Description	334
III.	Office Description	335
IV.	Management Information Systems/Reporting Systems	337
V.	History of Practice	340
VI.	Staff Description	341
VII.	Competitive Analysis	341
VIII.	Patient Base Information	343
IX.	Managed Care Environment	345
X.	Hospital Privileges and Facilities	346
XI.	Credit Policy and Collections	346
XII.	Financial Management	347
XIII.	Operational Assessment	350
XIV.	Summary	351

I. PRACTICE INFORMATION

Name: _____ Specialty: _____

Address: _____

Office phone: (   ) ___ - ___ _____Office fax: (   ) ___ - ___

Back office: (   ) ___ - _____Other: (   ) ___ - ___

Years at above location: _____ In community: _____

Legal structure of practice: _____

Shareholders: _____

Name	Specialty	Interest (%)

Describe any contingent liabilities, if applicable: _____

_____

_____

Attorney Information

Name: _____

Firm: _____

Address: _____

Phone: _____

Fax: _____

CPA Information

Name: _____

Firm: _____

Address: _____

Phone: _____

Fax: _____

Current Office Hours

Day	Office Hours	Physician Hours
Monday		
Tuesday		
Wednesday		
Thursday		
Friday		
Saturday		

Present backup/coverage/rotation arrangements: _____

Practice referrals are: patient referrals _____%;
physician referrals _____%

What is the primary drawing population of your practice? _____
_____
_____

Number of days of supplies on hand: Medical: _____   Lab: _____
Office: _____

Do doctors provide consultations? _____

For whom? _____

Is there a seasonal component to the practice: (e.g., ENT & AL summer; primary care, preschool, physicals; tourist seasons; etc.) _____
_____
_____

II. BUILDING AND LEASE DESCRIPTION

Geographic location within community: N ___   S ___   E ___   W ___;
Urban ___   Suburban ___   Rural ___

Type of neighborhood: Commercial ___   Residential ___
Professional ___   Mix ___   Other _____

Street description (number of lanes/on-street parking/busy): _____
_____

Proximity to hospital (distance in miles): _____

Nearest large city: _____   Distance: _____

Nearest colleges/medical schools: _____

Recreation/culture opportunities in area: _____

Size (freestanding/number of stories): _____

_____

Style (architecture/general condition): _____

_____

_____

Type of construction (brick/stone/wood frame): _____

Parking facilities (adequate/number of spaces/reserved spaces):_____

_____

Disabled (access/lavatories/phones): _____

_____

Other medical or professional use: _____

_____

_____

Age of building: _____

III. OFFICE DESCRIPTION

Leasehold (please attach a copy of lease and floor plan if available)

Do any of the owners of the practice have an interest in the leasing entity?   Yes ___   No ___

Is lease assumable at same rate?   Yes ___   No ___

Expiration date of lease: _____

$/square foot for comparable space in area: _____

Any renewal options?   Yes ___   No ___

Size (square feet/total number of rooms): _____

Floor plan available?   Yes ___   No ___

Description/decor (architecture/carpeting/air conditioning/disabled access/what floor/walls/ceiling height/lighting): _____

_____

_____

Age of office (improvements/description/cost): _____

_____

_____

_____

Reception/business area (number of people in area/files/equipment):

_____

_____

Waiting room (number of chairs/access/play area/lavatory/special considerations): _____

_____

_____

Exam rooms (how many/features/in full use/identically equipped special uses/dressing area/lavatory):_____

_____

_____

Lavatories (number in whole facility/separate patient and staff): _____

_____

_____

Physicians' offices (number/library/use for consultations/lavatory decor):

_____

_____

X-ray (developing room/extremities/chest/back/full): _____

_____

_____

Laboratory (use/type): _____

_____

_____

Storage and closets (special uses/total number): _____

_____

_____

Basement or attic: _____

Pharmacy: _____

Employee's lounge:_____

Other:_____

_____

IV. MANAGEMENT INFORMATION SYSTEMS/REPORTING SYSTEMS

Who has responsibility for information systems in the practice? What is the administrator's role?

_____

_____

_____

_____

Does the practice have an in-house computer system of any capacity or shared computer services? How long has the current system been in place? Are there any plans to update the current system?

_____

_____

_____

_____

What type of systems, hardware and software, are currently in place? (If planning for a new system, what type?)

_____

_____

_____

What was the cost of the current information system? Operational and maintenance cost?

_____

_____

_____

List functions performed by the current information system (e.g., type of reports generated, frequency of the reports, etc.).

_____

_____

_____

_____

Inventory of Reports Generated

Reports	Is a report prepared by or for your group?	How often is a report prepared?		Who sees the report?					Is report information used to change goals, policies, procedures, or services? (specify)
		Monthly	Yearly	Administration	Governances body	Physicians	Others		
Budget									
Balance Sheet									
Statement of Cash Flow									
A/R									
Payroll									

Sick Time Absenteeism						
Referrals (to/from group)						
Utilization Rates						
Volume of Diagnostics (by number of procedures & revenue)						
Volume of Lab Services (by number of procedures & revenue)						
Quality of Care						
Others						

V. HISTORY OF PRACTICE

Date practice founded, by whom: _____

First location, subsequent moves: _____

_____

_____

Complete the following table indicating the average number of FTE physicians in the practice for each year (1.0 FTE = 2,080 hours/year).

Year	1991	1992	1993	1994	1995	1996
TOTAL # OF FTE PHYSICIANS						

Date and Names of physicians entering and leaving practice (as employees or partners)

Name	Age	Date Started/Left Practice	Employment Status (W-2 or 1099) When Started	Board Certification Status	Date Buy-in Completed

VI. STAFF DESCRIPTION

Describe the present nonphysician staff: the employment basis (FT/PT), tenure, and salary for each position.

Last Name/Position	FTE Basis	Tenure	Salary

VII. COMPETITIVE ANALYSIS

Are there any programs being developed in hospitals (or elsewhere) that have an impact on the practice?

_____

_____

_____

Is practice growing or declining?
Why? (Intentionally?)

_____

_____

Past/present/future associations with other physicians:

_____

_____

_____

_____

How do you feel the practice distinguishes itself from its competition (competitive advantages)?

_____

_____

_____

_____

Other strengths of the practice:

_____

_____

_____

_____

Threats to the practice:

_____

_____

_____

_____

Office Procedures

The approximate volume of procedures performed within practice for the past 12 months and the current fee schedule are as follows.

Code	Procedure	Office/Hospital	Volume	Standard Fee

Is fee schedule comparable to other practices in area? _____

_____

How have the volumes/types of procedures changed over the past ___ months/years? _____

_____

_____

_____

_____

VIII.   PATIENT BASE INFORMATION

Usual hospital census (number of patients per week): _____

The practice refers approximately _____ outpatient procedures per week

Total patients' records: _____   Number active: _____

Income distribution: cash ____%; Medicaid/Medicare ____%; third-party insurance ____%

Average number of patients per day seen in the office: _____

Average number of *new* patients per week seen in the office: _____

Charts are sorted: Annually: _____   Two years _____   Other: _____

Inactive charts are held for: _____ years

Inactive charts are held: Within the practice location: _____ Other: _____

Patient records are primarily (check all that apply): Hand written: _____ Dictated and transcribed: _____

Charts are (check all that apply): Color coded: _____ Alphabetized: _____   Computerized: _____

The age mix of the practice is estimated as follows.

Age	Approximate % of Patients
Under 18	%
18–54	%
Over 55	%

Payor Mix

Payor	%	Capitated Yes/No	Number of Capitated Patients
Medicare			
Medicaid			
Blue Cross/Blue Shield			
GHI			
Champus			
Self Pay			
Other: Commercial Insurance, PPOs			
Other:			

Average number of hours spent by each physician in patient care activities per week.

Physician Name	Hours in Patient Care Activities per Week

How long do patients generally wait for an appointment? _____

How has this changed during the past three years? _____

IX. MANAGED CARE ENVIRONMENT

Discuss the impact of managed care on your practice during the past three years (i.e., impact on revenues, referral patterns): _____

_____

_____

_____

Discuss the general terms and conditions of the managed care contracts you currently participate in:_____

_____

_____

_____

Discuss the managed care reporting capabilities of your practice (i.e., cost per procedure, IBNR): _____

_____

_____

_____

Practice positioning relative to an influx of managed care in the market:

_____

_____

_____

_____

Discuss your willingness to participate in risk-sharing contracts:

_____

_____

_____

_____

Are services provided at any long-term care facilities? _____

_____

_____

Who provides internal/external lab testing? _____

_____

_____

Is dispensing provided through the practice?
Drugs: _____   Lenses: _____   Hearing Aids: _____   Other: _____

If Applicable

Number of surgeries performed: _____

Major (% or number per week): _____

Minor: (% or number per week): _____

Surgery regularly scheduled: _____

X.   HOSPITAL PRIVILEGES AND FACILITIES

Hospital Privileges Available At	Distance from Office	Average Weekly Patient Census

What are the minimum requirements to acquire staff privileges for a qualified physician? _____

_____

Other requirements or considerations: _____

_____

XI.   CREDIT POLICY AND COLLECTIONS

Basic billing/payment policy/procedures: _____

_____

_____

_____

Do you use a collection agency? How often ? _____

_____

_____

Do you accept assignments? _____

_____

Other sources of revenue (directorships, honorariums, etc.): _____

_____

_____

_____

_____

_____

The aged accounts receivable for the practice is as follows (As Of _____).

Due Date	Amount	Historical Collection %
0–30 days		
31–60 days		
61–90 days		
Over 90 days		

XII. FINANCIAL MANAGEMENT

Cash Flow/Cash Management Analysis

Are cash receipts recorded and deposited daily? ☐ Yes ☐ No

Is cash adequately protected from theft and fraud? ☐ Yes ☐ No

Are book cash balances monitored on a daily basis? ☐ Yes ☐ No

Are bank accounts reconciled monthly? ☐ Yes ☐ No

If not, how often are they reconciled? _____

Is there a clear separation of duties between those who have access to cash and those who have access to the accounting records? ☐ Yes ☐ No

Do you have any credit lines with banks? ☐ Yes ☐ No

If yes, what is the interest rate? _____

Do you have any credit lines with any hospitals or health systems? ☐ Yes ☐ No

If yes, what is the interest rate? _____

Are copayments collected at the time of the office visit? ☐ Yes ☐ No

What actions are taken to improve and monitor cash flow? _____

_____

_____

_____

_____

Accounts Payable/Accounts Receivables Management

What are the internal controls to ensure timely payment of A/P? _____

_____

_____

_____

_____

What (if any) is the frequency of late fees that are paid by the practice?

_____

_____

_____

_____

Are discounts for prompt payment utilized?   ☐ Yes   ☐ No

Are the persons responsible for purchasing separate   ☐ Yes   ☐ No
from the persons authorized to sign checks?

Please explain responsibilities:_____

_____

_____

_____

_____

Financial Planning and Budgeting Process

Is the financial planning process: ☐ Formal   ☐ Informal

Please explain the financial planning process:

_____

_____

_____

Are there specific goals and objectives set?   ☐ Yes   ☐ No

Which of the following are key factors that drive the financial planning process?

☐ Future personal income   ☐ Changes in productivity

☐ Changes in work hours   ☐ Changes in staffing levels

☐ Changes in style of practice

Describe the budgeting process: _____

_____

_____

_____

_____

Who is responsible for the budgeting process? _____

_____

_____

What types of budgets are prepared?

☐ Operating   ☐ Cash

☐ Capital expenditures   ☐ Statement of financial position

Is the budget broken down by service area?   ☐ Yes   ☐ No

Are budgets regularly updated?   ☐ Yes   ☐ No

How often: _____

How are managed care contracts accounted for in the budgeting process?

_____

_____

_____

_____

What cost-accounting methods are used?

_____

_____

_____

Are fixed and variable costs identified?   ☐ Yes   ☐ No

Do any administrative/management personnel have   ☐ Yes   ☐ No
compensation arrangements that are tied to budget
performance?

(If yes, explain): _____

_____

_____

_____

Are financial statements available and analyzed comparing budgeted to actual performance? ☐ Yes ☐ No

XIII. OPERATIONAL ASSESSMENT

Governance

How is the practice structured? _____

_____

_____

_____

_____

_____

How is the governing board elected? _____

_____

_____

_____

_____

What types of committees (i.e., contracting, finance, compensation, executive.) does the organization have? _____

_____

_____

_____

_____

Does the governing board review and assess the following?
☐ Organization/group performance   ☐ Individual physicians
☐ Staff   ☐ Committees

Task Responsibility Checklist

Responsibility	Governing Board	Physicians or Medical Director	Administration/ Management	Task Not Performed
Utilization Review				
Physician Credentialing				
Administration of CME program				
Determination of Physician Income				
Conflict Resolution				
Staff Performance Review				
Staff Recruitment				
Outcomes Measurement				
Case Management				
Reimbursement				

XIV. SUMMARY

What are your three biggest concerns/issues or frustrations relative to your present practice environment (internal/external)? _____

_____

_____

_____

_____

_____

_____

_____

_____

What are the three biggest advantages or potential benefits of continuing practice in the present environment? _____

_____

_____

_____

_____

_____

_____

_____

_____

Relationships with other physicians in community: _____

_____

_____

_____

_____

_____

_____

_____

_____

Relationships with PCPs (or specialists if applicable) in community:

_____

_____

_____

What issues have we not discussed that you would like to address?

_____

_____

_____

_____

_____

_____

_____

Notes: _____
_____
_____
_____
_____
_____
_____

Completed by: _____   Date: _____

Sample Income Distribution Plan

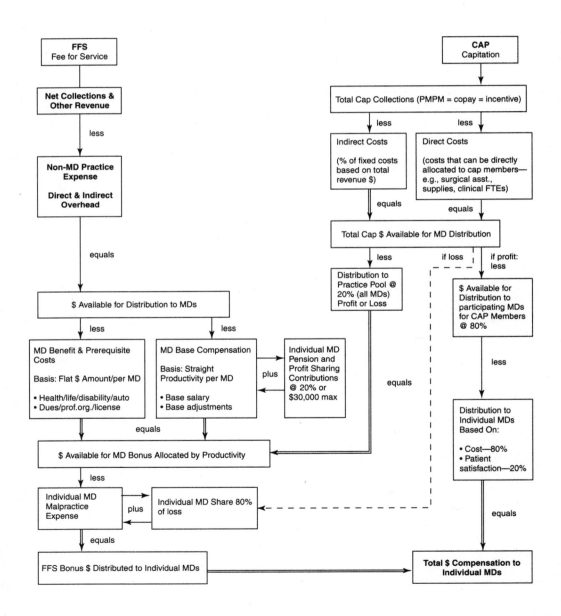

Analysis of Compensation Package

The Analysis of Compensation Package, which can be found on the next few pages, illustrates the financial impact of an acquisition on both the acquiror and the practice being acquired. The user of this model can construct different scenarios of an acquisition by changing the variables in the input section. In this model, it is assumed that the provider (whose practice is being acquired) will be employed by the acquiror entity and he/she will be paid a guaranteed compensation component as a certain percentage (52 percent in this example) of his/her prior year's net provider benefit.[1] This amount of guaranteed compensation will consist of a base salary, continuing medical education allowance, deferred compensation, and professional liability insurance. There will be additional compensation for any production above the number of "floor encounters," which is also an input variable (as a percentage of the number of projected encounters).

The lower portion of the model sets forth the calculations to arrive at the return to the acquiror. This model takes into account the current overhead factor, the guaranteed compensation to the provider, and the amortization of the purchase price of the practice. It then calculates the threshold of revenues that would allow the provider to be paid additional compensation above the guaranteed compensation. With different inputs, the user can generate different scenarios as to the incentive (in dollars) that will be paid to the provider with different productivity levels achieved.

---

[1]*Net provider benefit* is calculated as the net profit plus all non-cash charges, nonrecurring and discretionary expenses.

The last page is the abbreviated version of the model, which can be used during negotiations with the provider. It has all the elements which can facilitate these discussions without belaboring the mathematical aspects of amortization and other issues.

Analysis of Compensation Package

	Description			Provider
(A)	Net Provider Benefit, '94 Actual	(A)	i-1	$378,498
(B)	Net Provider Benefit, '95 Projected	(B)	i-2	$416,348
(C)	% Total Guaranteed Compensation Component	(C)	i-3	52%
(D)	$ Total Guaranteed Compensation Component (1)	(D)	c	$216,001
(E)	Base Salary	(E)	c	$162,501
(F)	CME Allowance (2)	(F)	i-4	$5,000
(G)	Deferred Compensation (3)	(G)	i-5	$10,000
(H)	Professional Liability Insurance (4)	(H)	i-6	$6,000
(I)	% Benefits and Pension as % of Base Salary	(I)	i-7	20%
(J)	$ Benefits	(J)	c	$32,500
(K)	Projected '95 Patient Encounters	(K)	i-8	3,000
(L)	% Floor for Base Salary	(L)	i-9	70%
(M)	Floor Encounters for Base Salary (5)	(M)	c	2,100

Productivity Incentive Component Compensation Calculation

	Description			Provider
(N)	Projected '95 Net Collections	(N)	i-10	$498,666
(O)	% Current Overhead Factor (as shown on C/S)	(O)	i-11	24.1%
(P)	Post-Acquisition Practice Overhead Factor	(P)	i-12	30.0%
(Q)	% Available for Provider Compensation, Incentive, Amortization, and Profit	(Q)	c	70.0%
(R)	Less: Total Guaranteed Compensation per (C) Above	(R)	c	($216,001)
(S)	$ Net Revenue after Guaranteed Compensation	(S)	c	$282,666
(T)	Less: $ Current Overhead Expenses (as shown on C/S)	(T)	c	($120,179)
(U)	$ Net Revenue after Compensation and Overhead Expenses	(U)	c	$162,487
(V)	Number of Years Amortization of Purchase Price	(V)	i-13	10.00
(W)	% Interest—Cost of Acquisition Purchase Money Capital	(W)	i-14	9.0%
(X)	$ Purchase Price	(X)	i-15	$255,000
(Y)	$ Annual Amortization of Purchase Price (principal only)	(Y)	c	$25,500
(Z)	Amortization as % of Gross Collections	(Z)	c	5.11%
(AA)	$ Net Revenue after Compensation, Overhead Expenses, and Amortization	(AA)	c	$136,987
(AB)	Threshold of Revenues before Incentive to Provider	(AB)	c	$345,002
(AC)	Increment over Threshold	(AC)	c	$153,664

Productivity Incentive Component Compensation Calculation

	Description			Provider
(AD)	Less: $ Current Overhead Expenses on Increment (line AC)	(AD)	c	($37,033)
(AE)	$ Increment over Threshold less Current Overhead Expenses Available for Incentive	(AE)		$116,631
(AF)	$ Amount of Incentive Required for Provider Break-Even	(AF)	c	$200,347
(AG)	% of Amount Available Required for Provider Break-Even	(AG)	c	171.78%
(AH)	% of Increment over Threshold Available as Incentive	(AH)	c	70.00%
(AI)	% of Increment over Threshold as Incentive (input)	(AI)	i-16	60%
(AJ)	$ Incentive to Be Paid to Provider	(AJ)	c	$92,199
(AK)	Total Provider Compensation	(AK)	c	$308,200
(AL)	Variance from Previous Year's Total Net Benefit to MD	(AL)	c	($70,298)
(AM)	Total Revenue after Provider Compensation	(AM)	c	$190,466
(AN)	Total Practice Overhead (post-acquisition) plus Amortization of Purchase Price	(AN)	c	$175,100
(AO)	$ Post-Acquisition Profit/(Loss)	(AO)	c	$15,366
(AP)	% Post-Acquisition Return	(AP)	c	3.08%

i-# = input item-Line#   c = calculated figure

i   Inputs

	Line		Provider
A			
1	1994 Actual Net Provider Benefit	(A)	$378,498
2	1995 Projected Net Provider Benefit	(B)	$380,000
3	% Total Guaranteed Compensation Component	(C)	51.88%
4	CME Allowance (2)	(F)	$5,000
5	Deferred Compensation (3)	(G)	$10,000
6	Professional Liability Insurance (4)	(H)	$6,000
7	% Benefits and Pension as % of Base Salary	(I)	20%
8	Projected '95 Patient Encounters	(K)	3,000
9	% Floor for Base Salary	(L)	70%
10	Projected '95 Net Collections	(N)	$498,666
11	% Current Overhead Factor (as shown on C/S)	(O)	24.1%
12	Post-Acquisition Practice Overhead Factor	(P)	30.0%
13	# Years Amortization of Purchase Price	(V)	10.00
14	% Interest—Cost of Acquisition Purchase Money Capital	(W)	9.0%
15	$ Purchase Price	(X)	$255,000
16	% of Increment over Threshold as Incentive (input)	(AI)	60%

Equations

A	input #1	'94 Actual
B	input #2	'95 Projected
C	input #3	% Total Guaranteed Compensation Component
D	= B*C	$ Total Guaranteed Compensation Component (1)
E	= D – F – G – H – J	Base Salary
F	input #4	CME Allowance (2)
G	input #5	Deferred Compensation (3)
H	input #6	Professional Liability Insurance (4)
I	input #7	% Benefits and Pension as % of Base Salary
J	= E * I	$ Benefits
K	input #8	Projected '95 Patient Encounters
L	input #9	% Floor for Base Salary
M	= K * L	Floor Encounters for Base Salary (5)
N	input #10	Projected '95 Net Collections
O	= –1 * D	% Current Overhead Factor (as shown on C/S)
P	= N + O	Post-Acquisition Practice Overhead Factor
Q	input #11	% Available for Provider Compensation, Incentive, Amortization, and Profit
R	= –1 * (N * Q)	Less: Total Guaranteed Compensation per (C) Above
S	= P + R	$ Net Revenue after Guaranteed Compensation
T	– N * O	Less: $ Current Overhead Expenses (as shown on C/S)
U	= S + T	$ Net Revenue after Compensation and Overhead Expenses
V	input #13	Number of Years Amortization of Purchase Price
W	input #14	% Interest—Cost of Acquisition Purchase Money Capital
X	input #15	$ Purchase Price
Y	X/V	$ Annual Amortization of Purchase Price (principal only)
Z	= Y / N	Amortization as % of Gross Collections
AA	= U – Y	$ Net Revenue after Compensation, Overhead Expenses, and Amortization
AB	= (–D – Y)/(P – 1)	Threshold of Revenues before Incentive to Provider
AC	= N – AB	Increment over Threshold
AD	= –O * AC	Less: $ Current Overhead Expenses on Increment (line AC)
AE	= AC + AD	$ Increment over Threshold less Current Overhead Expenses Available for Incentive
AF	= B – D	$ Amount of Incentive Required for Provider Break-Even
AG	= AD / AE	% of Amount Available Required for Provider Break-Even
AH	= 1 – P	% of Increment over Threshold Available as Incentive
AI	input #16	% of Increment over Threshold as Incentive (input)
AJ	= AC * AI (=0 if AE<0)	$ Incentive to Be Paid to Provider
AK	= D + AE	Total Provider Compensation
AL	= AK – A	Variance from Previous Year's Total Net Benefit to MD
AM	= N – AF	Total Revenue after Provider Compensation

AN	= (N * P) + Y	Total Practice Overhead (post-acquisition) plus Amortization of Purchase Price
AO	= AM − AN	$ Post-Acquisition Profit/(Loss)
AP	= AO/N	% Post-Acquisition Return

Notes:

(1) Total guaranteed component = % of projected 1995 provider net benefits as determined by acquiring party.

(2)–(4) These amounts per acquiring (input lines F, G, and H).

(5) To the extent that patient encounters fall below the estimated threshold, then the provider's base salary shall be proportionally reduced at the end of the year.

Analysis of Compensation Package

Description	Pay 1
Projected '95 Net Collections	$498,666
$ Annual Amortization of Purchase Price (principal only)	$25,500
Net Provider Benefit, '94 Actual	$378,498
Net Provider Benefit, '95 Projected	$416,348
Base Salary	$162,501
CME Allowance	$5,000
Deferred Compensation	$10,000
Professional Liability Insurance	$6,000
$ Benefits	$32,500
$ Total Guaranteed Compensation Component	$216,001
Productivity Incentive Component Compensation Calculation	
Post-Acquisition Practice Overhead Factor	30.0%
Threshold of Revenues before Incentive to Provider	$345,002
% of Increment over Threshold as Incentive (input)	60%
$ Incentive to Be Paid to Provider	$92,199
Total Provider Compensation	$308,200
$ Post-Acquisition Profit/(Loss) to Acquiror	**$15,366**
% Post-Acquisition Return to Acquiror	**3.08%**

Exit Strategies Worksheet

1. What are the exit strategies in terms of the following?
   - Will written notice be given?   ☐ Yes ☐ No
   - Is there a grievance resolution process?   ☐ Yes ☐ No
   - What is the method of valuation or price?   ☐ Yes ☐ No
   - Will capital contribution be repaid?   ☐ Yes ☐ No
   - What are the terms of repayment of ownership interest (e.g., a third at withdrawal, another third at the first anniversary of withdrawal, and the final third on the second anniversary of withdrawal)?

   _____

   _____

2. Does the company desire to impose a covenant not to compete on its members/shareholders and employees?   ☐ Yes ☐ No
   If so, what activities, geographic scope, and duration will be included?

   _____

   _____

   _____

   _____

3. What remedy against a member/shareholder who breaches a covenant not to compete? _____

   _____

   _____

   _____

4. Will covenants survive the termination of the bylaws/operating agreement?   ☐ Yes ☐ No

5. Will all amendments to bylaws/operating agreement be in writing?
☐ Yes ☐ No

6. Will members/shareholders have a right to assign any of their rights under the bylaws/operating agreement without the prior written consent of the other members/shareholders or the company?
☐ Yes ☐ No

7. May any member/shareholder offer to transfer his/her interest at any time to another physician member/shareholder or to a physician who is not a member/shareholder of the LLC/corporation but who meets the professional criteria for admission to the LLC/corporation, except that such interest must first be offered to the LLC/corporation? ☐ Yes ☐ No

8. Any member/shareholder who dies, retires, becomes disabled, or whose employment agreement is not renewed shall be obligated to offer to sell his/her portion of interest to the following parties:

a. To physician member/shareholders or qualified physician(s) practicing at the same practice site

b. To all other physician member/shareholders collectively

c. To the LLC/corporation

Is the above order acceptable? ☐ Yes ☐ No

If no, please rank in the preferred order of priority:

1. _____

2. _____

3. _____

9. How shall the purchase price of a withdrawing member/shareholder's interest be calculated?

☐ Member/shareholder's capital account only?

☐ Average annual "net revenue" of the LLC/corporation for ___ prior years multiplied by a factor?

☐ Combination of the above?

☐ Fair market value appraisal by certified appraiser

☐ Other: _____

10. Shall the payment terms of a member/shareholder's interest be restricted according to how long the member/shareholder holds an interest in the LLC/corporation (i.e., the longer a member/shareholder holds an interest, the more the member/shareholder receives of his/her interest)? ☐ Yes ☐ No

11. Shall a physician who is an employee of the LLC/corporation but is not a member/shareholder be allowed to acquire an interest in the LLC/corporation by making a cash contribution in installments or making a contribution by taking a reduction in any bonus or regular salary over a certain period of time?   ☐ Yes ☐ No

12. Shall a qualified physician who is not a member/shareholder be allowed to acquire an interest in the LLC/corporation by contributing his/her assets and/or cash?   ☐ Yes ☐ No

13. The following events will trigger dissolution of the LLC/corporation.

    a. A unanimous decision by all member/shareholders to dissolve?
       ☐ Yes ☐ No
    b. The expiration of the LLC/corporation's term of existence?
       ☐ Yes ☐ No
    c. The sale or disposition of all assets?   ☐ Yes ☐ No
    d. The occurrence of an involuntary withdrawal of a member/shareholder?   ☐ Yes ☐ No
    e. When so required in accordance with other provisions of the agreement?   ☐ Yes ☐ No

14. Upon dissolution, the LLC/corporation will commence liquidation and wind up its affairs; consequently shall the proceeds from the liquidation and winding-up of affairs be applied in the following order of priority.

    a. Creditors (including member/shareholders who qualify as such)
    b. Reserves
    c. Member/shareholders in return for their capital contributions
    d. Any withdrawing member/shareholder
    e. The balance to member/shareholders in accordance with their positive capital account balances

    Is the above order acceptable?   ☐ Yes ☐ No

    If no, please rank in the preferred order of priority:

    1. _____
    2. _____
    3. _____
    4. _____
    5. _____

15. If a member/shareholder has a negative balance in his/her capital account upon liquidation of the LLC/corporation, will such member/shareholder be obligated to make an additional capital contribution to the LLC/corporation to make up for this deficit?   ☐ Yes ☐ No

Governance Checklist

1. How many classes of stock or ownership will there be? _____

   Do you anticipate having outside investors (e.g., hospitals, lay investors)that will not participate in management?

   ☐ Yes ☐ No

   How will recent graduates of their medical residency be handled? Associateship arrangements?): _____

2. How many managers will there be? _____ (only one member per group)

   Will you allow nonproviders to participate?   ☐ Yes ☐ No

3. Must managers be restricted to only members?   ☐ Yes ☐ No

   If no, would you consider having outsiders, (e.g., independent professionals, accountants, consultants) participate on the board?

   ☐ Yes ☐ No

   Outsiders participate only as owners?   ☐ Yes ☐ No

4. May managers be removed?   ☐ Yes ☐ No

   With or without cause?   ☐ Yes ☐ No

   Who may remove them? _____

5. Where will annual meetings be held?_____

   Will the annual meetings only be held at the registered place of business?   ☐ Yes ☐ No

   Within the city/county limits?   ☐ Yes ☐ No

   Who determines where the meetings are held? _____

6. How many days' notice will be required for a board of managers meeting? _____

7. How many days' notice will be required for a meeting of the membership/shareholders? _____

8. Can members participate in meetings by telephone? ☐ Yes ☐ No (This may be desirable when issues arise requiring super-majority voting or a majority of the members/shareholders.)

9. Will managers and members be allowed to vote by proxy?
   ☐ Yes ☐ No
   If yes, what sort of format will be used? _____
   Will the proxies be revocable? ☐ Yes ☐ No
   Under what circumstances? _____
   _____

10. May special meetings of members or managers be called?
    ☐ Yes ☐ No
    What circumstances/issues will allow for special meetings? _____
    _____
    Who is authorized to call a special meeting? _____
    How many members/shareholders are required to call/authorize a special meeting? _____

11. Will written notice be required for special meetings of managers?
    ☐ Yes ☐ No
    Members? ☐ Yes ☐ No

12. How much notice is required for special meetings? (BOM, 48 hrs.; general membership, 7 days)
    ☐ 24 hrs. ☐ 48 hrs. ☐ 7 days ☐ 30 days ☐ Other: _____

13. May notice be waived? ☐ Yes ☐ No
    If a member is in attendance, will that serve as proper notice?
    ☐ Yes ☐ No
    Must waiver of notice be in writing? ☐ Yes ☐ No

14. Must purpose of the meeting be stated in notice? ☐ Yes ☐ No
    Does a formal agenda need to be included with the notice?
    ☐ Yes ☐ No

15. Must officers be members? ☐ Yes ☐ No
    If there are different classes of members, which classes may be officers? _____
    _____
    _____

16. What officers and board do you envision the organization having? The term of each?

- [ ] President   [ ] 1 yr. [ ] 2 yr. [ ] 3 yr. [ ] Other: ____
- [ ] Vice President   [ ] 1 yr. [ ] 2 yr. [ ] 3 yr. [ ] Other: ____
- [ ] Treasurer/Secretary   [ ] 1 yr. [ ] 2 yr. [ ] 3 yr. [ ] Other: ____
- [ ] Asst. V.P. of _____   [ ] 1 yr. [ ] 2 yr. [ ] 3 yr. [ ] Other: ____
- [ ] Asst. V.P. of _____   [ ] 1 yr. [ ] 2 yr. [ ] 3 yr. [ ] Other: ____

(The number and composition of officers should be representative yet of a workable number—i.e., probably should not exceed five officers. The term of each office should be a balanced structure that will allow for new ideas, interests, and representations, yet will not create stagnation.)

17. Will terms be staggered?   [ ] Yes [ ] No

(Staggered terms may prevent disruption by having short-term consistency on the executive committee/board.)

18. Can officers and members be elected using cumulative voting?

     [ ] Yes [ ] No

(Would certain members gain an inequitable advantage? Consider what effect the largest group(s) could have on elections if cumulative voting is allowed. Could monopoly powers exist on the board? Among the officers?)

19. What percentage of members will constitute a quorum?

Board of Managers: _____%   Members: _____%

Should there be different percentages for the board versus the members? What percentage is required?   [ ] 51% [ ] 66%? [ ] 75%?

20. Will officers be compensated?   [ ] Yes [ ] No   Amount? $ _____

Certain officers (e.g., the president) may spend considerable time on administrative/management tasks resulting in fewer hours devoted to patient care activities. What level of compensation is reasonable? $ _____

21. May officers be removed?   [ ] Yes [ ] No (same as board)

With or without cause?   [ ] Yes [ ] No

Who may remove them? _____

22. Must officers be bonded?   [ ] Yes [ ] No

(Consider the need based on the authority given to each officer—e.g., president, treasurer.)

23. What committees will the entity have? How many members will sit on each committee?

☐ Finance   # _____   ☐ Payor Contracting   # _____

☐ Executive   # _____   ☐ Governance   # _____

☐ Planning   # _____   ☐ Human Resources   # _____

☐ CQI   # _____   ☐ Provider Relations   # _____

☐ _____   # _____   ☐ _____   # _____

24. Will membership interest be held by?

☐ Individual physicians   ☐ practices

Other comments: _____

_____

_____

_____

_____

_____

Completed by: _____   Date: _____

Operational Compliance Worksheet

1. Will the company include language in its bylaws/operating agreement which evidences its intent to comply with:

   - Fraud and abuse statute?   ☐ Yes ☐ No
   - State self-referral law and the Stark Act?   ☐ Yes ☐ No
   - An antitrust code of compliance?   ☐ Yes ☐ No

2. Does the company wish to include in its bylaws/operating agreement a statement that evidences its intent to comply with hospital or other bylaws or religious ethical directives?   ☐ Yes ☐ No

3. Will the company provide services to:

   - Indigents?   ☐ Yes ☐ No
   - Medicare?   ☐ Yes ☐ No
   - Medicaid?   ☐ Yes ☐ No

4. Will the company provide or arrange for health care services?   ☐ Yes ☐ No

5. Will the Company be registered as a:

   - PPO?   ☐ Yes ☐ No
   - PSO?   ☐ Yes ☐ No
   - HMO?   ☐ Yes ☐ No

6. Will the company or its members assume any liability incurred by the other members prior to the date of the bylaws/operating agreement?   ☐ Yes ☐ No

7. Will the company indemnify the managers/directors, members/shareholders, and committees from any and all claims asserted against them?   ☐ Yes ☐ No

8. Must members/shareholders offer a right of first refusal to the company to participate in specified related business opportunities?
☐ Yes ☐ No

9. Will members/shareholders provide certain services to the company?
☐ Yes ☐ No

If yes, what services will they provide?
- Management? ☐ Yes ☐ No
- Leasing? ☐ Yes ☐ No
- Will member/shareholder consent be required? ☐ Yes ☐ No

10. Will the company be acquiring the assets of practices (as capital contributions or through purchase) to begin operations? ☐ Yes ☐ No

11. Does the company plan to lease office space or equipment from any other practice or individual member/shareholder? ☐ Yes ☐ No

12. Will the company have other compensation relationships with any of its members/shareholders? ☐ Yes ☐ No

13. If applicable, how will company bill for its management services?
- Percentage of gross revenues? ☐ Yes ☐ No
- Percentage of collections? ☐ Yes ☐ No
- By full-time physicians? ☐ Yes ☐ No
- Cost plus basis? ☐ Yes ☐ No
- Flat Fee? ☐ Yes ☐ No

14. Will management agreements be exclusive? ☐ Yes ☐ No
- Long-term? ☐ Yes ☐ No

15. What insurance will be maintained (and if so, what type and in what amount)?
- Malpractice? ☐ Yes ☐ No Amount: $ _____
- Office? ☐ Yes ☐ No Amount: $ _____
- Health? ☐ Yes ☐ No Amount: $ _____
- Workers' Comp.? ☐ Yes ☐ No Amount: $ _____
- Stop-Loss? ☐ Yes ☐ No Amount: $ _____
- Life? ☐ Yes ☐ No Amount: $ _____
- Disability? ☐ Yes ☐ No Amount: $ _____
- Liability? ☐ Yes ☐ No Amount: $ _____

16. Where will the company establish its bank account?_____

17. Do members/shareholders have the right to solicit offers from third parties to acquire substantially all of the assets or interests in the company? ☐ Yes ☐ No

18. Will members/shareholders have the right to withdraw at any time? ☐ Yes ☐ No

Capital Contribution Worksheet

1. What constitutes a capital contribution?
   ☐ a. Cash?
   ☐ b. Fair market value of property?
   ☐ c. Value of services rendered?
   ☐ d. All of the above, net of liabilities.

2. Will members/shareholders be required to loan the LLC/corporation additional capital? ☐ Yes ☐ No

3. Will members/shareholders be allowed to make additional capital contributions or voluntary loans to the LLC/corporation?
   ☐ Yes ☐ No

4. Will members/shareholders be paid interest on their capital contributions? ☐ Yes ☐ No

5. If a member/shareholder defaults on his/her obligation to make additional capital contributions to the LLC/corporation, is there a trigger event for involuntary withdrawal? ☐ Yes ☐ No

6. Who should have the right to buy out the member/shareholder who involuntarily withdrew?
   ☐ LLC/corporation?
   ☐ Another member/shareholder?
   ☐ Any qualified physician?
   ☐ Other: _____

7. Will a member/shareholder who defaults on making an additional capital contribution still retain voting rights during the default period? ☐ Yes ☐ No

8. Will the LLC/corporation or its members/shareholders assume any liability incurred by other members/shareholders prior to the date of the operating agreement/bylaws? ☐ Yes ☐ No

9. Will members/shareholders be entitled to withdraw any portion of their capital contribution? ☐ Yes ☐ No

10. How will members/shareholders be entitled to receive a return of their capital contribution?

    ☐ a. Cash distribution?

    ☐ b. Notes?

    ☐ c. Property?

    ☐ d. Combination of the above?

11. If a member/shareholder withdraws from the LLC/corporation in violation of its operating agreement, shall the member/shareholder be entitled to a return of his/her capital contribution? ☐ Yes ☐ No

12. Will member/shareholder interest in the LLC/corporation be defined in proportion to member's/shareholder's initial capital contributions or simply by decision?

    ☐ a. Capital contribution

    ☐ b. Decision

13. Will a charter (or founding) member/shareholder get a greater proportion of the LLC/corporation's per capita contribution? ☐ Yes ☐ No

14. Profits and losses shall be allocated in accordance with:

    ☐ The percentage interest each member/shareholder holds in his/her capital accounts

    ☐ Membership/ownership class

    ☐ A combination of the above

15. Shall net cash from operations be distributed as follows?

    a. To repay principal and interest to persons other than members/shareholders who have lent funds to the LLC/corporation.

    b. To repay principal and interest to members/shareholders who have lent funds to the LLC/corporation.

    c. To members in accordance with the percentage interest each member/shareholder holds in his/her capital account.

    Is the above order acceptable? ☐ Yes ☐ No

If no, please rank in the preferred order of priority:

1. _____

2. _____

3. _____

16. When shall net cash from operations be distributed after the fiscal year? Not later than:

☐ 60 days?

☐ 75 days?

☐ 90 days?

Physician Contact/ Interview Summary

The Physician Contact/Interview Summary is used as a synopsis of the conversations or interviews that have been conducted relative to a particular project. This is most often used in projects involving:

- Several physicians
- A degree of uncertainty regarding the ultimate outcome of the new entity
- A situation in which there are many other groups or competing entities in the market

Physician Contact/Interview Summary—Sample

Name	Professional Title	Specialty	Phone (555)	Contact	ABC IPA	XYZ MSO	BC/BS	Comments/Possible Affiliations
Adams	MD	PD	687-0193	PC	✔			She cancelled two meetings, says she's interested. Need to follow up.
Brown	MD	OTO/PS	520-5777	PC				Not interested in meeting as of 6/95.
Cardinal	MD	GS/VS	686-8724	PC				Not interested in meeting as of 6/95.
Drake	MD	GS	687-0181	PC	✔	✔		Met with 6/95. Possible affiliation interest.
Evans	MD	OTO	687-1981	PC			✔	Met with 7/95. Not interested in discussion presently.
Franko	MD	NL/PDNL	686-7803	PC		✔		Met with 6/95. Possible MSO interest.

Voting Checklist

Issue	Governing Body									Vote Required	
	Board of Managers	Members	Officers	Executive Comm.	Finance Comm.	Other Comm.	Site Location	Medical Specialty	Individual Doctor	Simple Majority	Super Majority (% vote required)
Amendment of articles of organization											
Amendment of operating agreement											
Appointment or election, and removal of officers											
Appointment or election, and removal of manager											
Adoption of the budget											
Addition of new members											
Participation, including renewal of agreements, in networks, affiliations, joint ventures, mergers, or acquisitions											
To determine (and enter into) the types of risk-sharing agreements the company will enter into											
Capital expenditures greater than $5,000											
Capital expenditures greater than $20,000											

Capital expenditures greater than $100,000									
Adjustment to management fee, if applicable									
Distribution of profits									
Additional capital calls/contributions									
Incurring any debt or liability greater than $10,000									
Executing any bond in company's name, except in the ordinary course of business									
Making loans on behalf of the company, requesting a loan from the members, or causing the company to guarantee the obligations of others									
Changing company's purposes or services that materially alter the operation of the company									
Pleading or encumbering any company asset as security for an obligation of a member									
Commingling any company fund or capital with the funds of any other person									

Issue	Governing Body									Vote Required	
	Board of Managers	Members	Officers	Executive Comm.	Finance Comm.	Other Comm.	Site Location	Medical Specialty	Individual Doctor	Simple Majority	Super Majority (% vote required)
Filing a voluntary petition for bankruptcy, debtor relief, or insolvency											
Making an assignment of the company's assets for the benefit of creditors, or appointing (or consenting to the appointment of) a receiver for the assets of the company for the benefit of creditors											
Determining the amount of reserves required by the company											
All actions taken as the liquidation trustee											
Acquiring property/services/goods from any person that a manager or member is directly or indirectly affiliated, connected, or related to											
Purchasing liability and other insurance to protect the company property and business											

Managers or members holding and/or owning any company real and/or personal properties in the name of the company							
Investing company funds temporarily in time deposits, short-term governmental obligations, commercial paper, or other investments							
Selling or disposing of all or substantially all of the company's assets in a single transaction							
Executing on behalf of company all instruments and documents							
Determining (and instituting) the types of cost-containment objectives and programs the company will implement							
Developing a business plan for company							
Exploring (and implementing) a plan that will lead to a reduction of certain administrative services							

Issue	Governing Body									Vote Required	
	Board of Managers	Members	Officers	Executive Comm.	Finance Comm.	Other Comm.	Site Location	Medical Specialty	Individual Doctor	Simple Majority	Super Majority (% vote required)
Determining the manner in which claims will be collected and the manner in which revenues relating to services will be allocated if the company evolves to direct contracting											
Employing accountants, legal counsel, managing agents, consultants, or other experts to perform services for the company and to compensate them from company funds											
Hiring, firing, and evaluating site-specific clinical personnel											
Hiring, firing, and evaluating site-specific front office personnel											
Hiring, firing, and evaluating site-specific back office personnel											
Allocating site-specific fixed expenses											
Allocating site-specific variable expenses											

Allocating specialty aggregate fixed expenses						
Allocating specialty aggregate variable expenses						
Allocating doctor-specific fixed expenses						
Allocating doctor-specific variable expenses						
Other: _____						
Other: _____						

Exit Strategies

Consequences ⇑ ⇑ ⇑ ⇑ ⇑ ⇑

Triggering Events ⇒ ⇒ ⇒ ⇒ ⇒	Written Notice	Grievance Resolution Process	Rest of Bus. Corp Doctors Remain	Rest of Bus. Corp Doctors Leave	Individual Doctors Remain with PLLP	Individual Doctors Leave PLLP	Notes
Individual doctor quits bus. corp.	Yes	Yes—internal for group					
Individual doctor quits PLLP							
Individual doctor is involuntarily terminated by bus. corp.							
Several doctors quit bus. corp.			Yes		Yes		
Several doctors quit PLLP							
Entire bus. corp. splits up							
Entire bus. corp. quits PLLP							
Failure to make a properly requested capital contribution							They are out of organization (can't use bankruptcy).
Improper transfer of shares							
Termination of employment agreement							
Bankruptcy or dissolution of a doctor							
Suspension, exclusion, or debarment from Medicare or state health care program of a partner						Yes	
Conviction of a doctor of a felony						Yes	
Providing proper notice of withdrawal	Yes						

*Must change shares to successor in interest clause

Database Fields Sample

Database development is an important initial step in many projects within the program. The purpose of developing a database is to have a collection of all possible suspects in the relevant market. The sample fields are some of the basic information you may want to compile before evaluating the suspects. Depending on the nature of the project, you may want to look at other items, such as medical specialty, type of practice, etc.

DATABASE FIELDS—SAMPLE

First name: _____

Middle initial: _____

Last name: _____

Professional title: _____

Salutation: _____

Company name 1: _____

Company title: _____

Work address 1: _____

Work address 2: _____

Work city: _____

Work state: _____

Work zip: _____

Work phone 1: _____

Work phone 2: _____

Work fax: _____

Cell phone: _____

Ownership status: _____

Type: _____

Classification: _____

Memo: _____

Employee Insurance/
Resource Worksheet

Practice: _____

	Name	Title	Status	(Date Started) Tenure	Date of Birth	Sex	FT/PT	Hrs/Wk	Salary/Year Wage/Hr	Vacation (weeks)	Qtr. and YTD per employee	Sick Time
1												
2												
3												
4												
5												
6												
7												
8												
9												
10												

Insurance Benefits Assessment

Practice Name: _____

Benefits:　　☐ Yes　☐ No

Please indicate dollar amounts deducted per pay period for each insurance benefit per employee.

Name	A	B	C	D	E	F	G

Appendix **26**

Employer and Employee Insurance Expenses

1. Health Insurance

Single

Employer contribution/
month: $_____

Employee contribution/
payroll period: $_____

Health insurance carrier: _____

Comments: _____

Family

Employer contribution/
month: $_____

Employee contribution/
payroll period: $_____

2. Dental Insurance

Single

Employer contribution/
month: $_____

Employee contribution/
payroll period: $_____

Carrier: _____

Family

Employer contribution/
month: $_____

Employee contribution/
payroll period: $_____

3. Life/AD&D Insurance

Amount of life insurance benefit per MD: $_____

Amount of life insurance benefit per employee: $_____

Life Insurance Carrier: _____

AD&D coverage: ☐ Yes   ☐ No

Dependent life option: ☐ Yes   ☐ No

4. Disability Insurance: ☐ Yes ☐ No
   If yes:
   Employer contribution: $_____
   Employee contribution: $_____
   Disability Carrier: _____

5. Flexible Spending Accounts: ☐ Yes ☐ No
   Medical: _____
   Dependent care: _____
   A. Health Insurance
   B. Dental
   C. Life
   D. Disability
   F. Pension/Profit Sharing
   G. Tuition Reimbursement
   If you answered yes to A and/or B above, please also fill in type of coverage:
   E = Employee
   S = Spouse
   C = Child(ren)

Summary of Practice Services Worksheet

Service/Task	Service Provided Internally	Service Provided Externally	Service Not Provided
Management Consulting Services			
• Billing/Collections • Claims Resolution			
• Utilization Management/Review • Quality Assurance			
Physician/Provider Recruitment			
Administration of CME			
• Accounts Receivable/Payable Management			
Group Purchasing • Clinical Supplies • Office Supplies • Pharmaceutical			
Group Insurance • Malpractice • Health • Office			
Vendor Contract Management/Negotiation			

(continued)

Service/Task	Service Provided Internally	Service Provided Externally	Service Not Provided
• Centralized Payroll • Worker's Compensation • Employee Benefit Accounts			
Managed Care Contracting			
• Marketing • Public Relations			
Financial Services • Accounting • Tax • Financial Planning			
Human Resources/Personnel Services			
Management Information Systems			
• Medical Records Management • Chart Maintenance/Filing			
Transcription			
Appointment Scheduling			
Diagnostic Activities • Imaging • Laboratory			
Facilities Planning and Management			

Sample Management Status Assessment and Operational Review: Practice Contracts Summary

Practice Name/Legal Structure	Physician	Type of Contract/Agreement	Terms					
			Effective Date	Exp. Date	Renew	Services	Signatories	Fee Basis
Peak Medical Group, P.A., 4000 West Highway, Othercity, USA	All Association Members	Management, Services & Facility Agreement	10/1/91	7/31/94	Automatic upon same terms & conditions for successive one-year periods	Provide medical office, equipment, management services & administration, supplies, utilities, patient records, billing & collection, staffing, strategic planning & practice consulting	Life Hospitals, Inc., general partner of BNJ Hospitals of Anystate, Ltd. & Peak Medical Group, P.A. & all but two association members	53% of net collections, but only 22.5% of net collections generated by any new physicians employed by association after effective date of the agreement
Peak Medical Group, P.A., 4000 West Highway, Othercity, USA	All Association Members	Amendment 1 to Management, Services & Facility Agreement	1/1/93	(n/a)	(n/a)	Provide medical office, equipment, management services & administration, supplies, utilities, patient records, billing & collection, staffing, strategic planning & practice consulting	BNJ Hospitals of Anystate, Ltd., d/b/a Fields Hospital & Peak Medical Group, P.A. Not Signed	53% of net collections minus facility fee of $21,833 & equipment fee of $15,673, but only 22.5% of net collections re: any new physicians employed by association after effective date of the agreement

Appendix **29**

Sample Management Status Assessment and Operational Review: Synopsis/Timeline of Recommendations

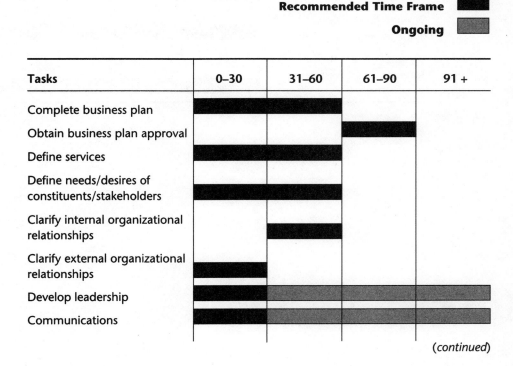

| | Recommended Time Frame ■ |
| | Ongoing ▩ |

Tasks	0–30	31–60	61–90	91 +
Complete business plan	■	■		
Obtain business plan approval			■	
Define services	■	■		
Define needs/desires of constituents/stakeholders	■	■		
Clarify internal organizational relationships		■		
Clarify external organizational relationships	■			
Develop leadership	■	▩	▩	▩
Communications	■	▩	▩	▩

(continued)

395

	Recommended Time Frame ■
	Ongoing ▨

Tasks	0–30	31–60	61–90	91 +
Assess practice patterns and life cycles	■	■		
Review/standardize practice arrangements (pricing/fees)	■	▨	▨	▨
Assess geographic disparity	■	■		
Address employee morale		■	▨	▨
Evaluate practice employees			■	
Distinguish between practice and corporate activities		■	▨	▨
Review MIS and develop new policies	■	▨	▨	▨
Implement CBO	■	▨	▨	▨
Evaluate PPI I/S staffing	■	▨	▨	▨
Develop financial management procedures	■	■	▨	▨
Conduct review of all agreements and regulatory compliance	■	▨	▨	▨

Sample Management Status Assessment and Operational Review: Summary of Issues and Concerns

Issue/Concern	Number Reporting a Problem	Percent Reporting a Problem	General Comments
Financial reporting	14	82%	Not received, not timely, not of use to a physician
A/R management & collections	14	82%	A/R has increased since joining UPI; concern about how collections are handled and timeliness
Lack of leadership, management turnover, unfulfilled promises	12	70%	Never know who is in charge; unfulfilled promises; no continuity
Don't know anything about ABC	9	52%	Have not met anyone with ABC; would like information on ABC
Communication	8	47%	Physicians not properly informed about practice changes

(continued)

Issue/Concern	Number Reporting a Problem	Percent Reporting a Problem	General Comments
Computers & ONEMED system	8	47%	Not enough terminals available, staff not properly trained, limited support, useful reports not generated and distributed
Managed care contracting	8	47%	Need support, analysis of contracts; can't participate because ABC hospital is not a preferred facility
Policies & procedures	7	41%	No formal policies on collections, coding, reporting relationships
Staff training	7	41%	Staff not sufficiently trained to optimize coding, use computers, appropriately handle patient grievances
Supply ordering	6	35%	More expensive through ABC/UPI; slow response and delivery
Increasing expenses	5	29%	Expenses have increased since joining UPI, overhead increasing substantially due to new benefit package
Coding	5	29%	Lack of confidence in whether coding is being optimized; problems with lab charges
Human resources issues	5	29%	Lack of support, appropriate orientation, no job descriptions, understaffed practices

Sample Management Status Assessment and Operational Review: Format for Specific Recommendations

STRATEGIC PLANNING INITIATIVES

A. Business Plan

Observations & Findings: Strategic goals and objectives for UPI are not clearly defined; no business plan (short- or long-term) exists for the company. The lack of a business plan that has been thoughtfully developed and communicated to all constituents/stakeholders has caused confusion within UPI.

Analysis & Conclusions: To be successful, UPI needs to develop a strategic business plan to be used as a game plan to delineate financial, operational, affiliation, and marketing objectives for the entity.

Recommendations: The stakeholders of UPI and ABC Physician Management Services should develop a business plan for a 3–5 year period to include the following features.

- Mission statement
- Goals/objectives for the entity
- An analysis of the internal strengths/weaknesses and external opportunities/threats (SWOT analysis)

- Product/service identification
- Pro forma financial statements, including working capital and capitalization requirements
- Marketing/sales tactics

Timeframe: Begin by developing key underlying assumptions and conducting interviews with key constituents/stakeholders to obtain input. Complete plan within 60 days. Obtain appropriate sign-offs within 30 days after the plan has been submitted for approval.

Sample Management Status Assessment and Operational Review: Medical Practice Site Visit Summary

OTHER PRACTICES

Ronald Bower, M.D. (GP)—Site Visit 7/20/94

Dr. Bower indicated a need to add a staff member to assist/coordinate patient flow issues for his primary care practice. Office is small with limited storage space. He wants to have ONEMED installed in his office and have his staff trained on the system.

Salient Practice Features

- FTEs: 3.0.
- Visits: 5,926.
- Family practice, located in strip mall. Contract has expired and now is on a month-to-month basis.
- Interested in signing new contract. Should increase OH rate to 52 percent.
- Full-body X-ray equipment in his office.
- Increase in visits could occur because he is on more managed care plans. Dr. Bower does a lot of Breath Analyzer Tests.

Other Practice Issues

- Averages 18–20 patients/day.
- Participating in capitated plans as a primary care physician with managed care organizations.
- Office located in Biz building.

Information System Vendor Key Business Selection Criteria

1. Experience providing practice management information system solutions within an organization comprising multiple locations. Minimum of five implementations with over five locations each. At least one implementation with over 10 locations.

2. Experience providing information system solutions within an MSO environment. Minimum of five MSO implementations.

3. Experience providing information system solutions within an MSO environment with multiple locations. Minimum of two MSO implementations with over 15 locations.

4. Commitment to their industry and client base through participation in a product user's organization.

5. Commitment to industry longevity. Minimum of five years existence in the healthcare I/S industry.

6. Ability to support electronic claims submission.

Medical Management Software: Annual Maintenance Cost Comparison

	SYSTEM A		SYSTEM B			
Hardware	$11,120	$11,120	$4,628	$4,628	$4,628	$4,628
Application Software Base Product	$55,462		(4) $36,650		(5) $21,990	
Optional Software	(3) $1,800		(2) $24,585		$14,751	
		$57,262		$61,235		$36,741
Data Conversion Detail	0					
Bal. Fwd.			0			
Scratch Pad		0	0	0		0
Implementation Services	0	0	0	0		0
Initial Total		$68,382		$65,863		$41,369

New Client Server Product

	SYSTEM A		SYSTEM B			
Software	0		$24,800		$14,880	
Implementation	0		0		0	
Database License	0	0	(1) $11,520	$36,320	(1) $11,520	$26,400
New Product Total		$68,382		$102,183		$67,769
Estimate 10 Additional Practices	0	0	$15,000	$15,000		$9,000

(1) Vendor insists no database license. Not logical, estimate same database license as comparable system.

(2) Estimate includes referral and report writer, advanced appointment scheduler, and laser forms generator; no estimate provided for G/L interface.

(3) Optional software estimate includes G/L interface and report writer.

(4) Software maintenance estimated for System B at 20% of software license fee for like comparison with System A. Discounted support to be negotiated.

(5) Software Maintenance at 12% of the software license fee, reduced service.

Medical Management Software: Pricing Comparison

All Pricing Based on 128 Concurrent Users

	SYSTEM A		SYSTEM B	
Hardware	$150,014	$150,014	$60,847	$60,847
Application Software Base Product Optional Software	$387,380 (4) $23,000	$410,380	$183,250 (3) $122,925	$306,175
Data Conversion Detail Bal. Fwd. Scratch Pad	(8) $84,000	$84,000	(5) $140,000 (6) $ 42,000	$182,000
Implementation Services	$227,000	$227,000	$135,000	$135,000
Total Pre New Product		$871,394		$684,022

New Client Server Product

	SYSTEM A		SYSTEM B	
Software	0		$124,000	
Implementation	0		(1) $ 60,000	
Database License	0	0	(2) $ 96,000	$280,000
Total		$871,394		$964,022

Estimate 10 additional Practices—

	SYSTEM A		SYSTEM B	
Base Software	0		(7) $75,000	
Conversions	(8) $60,000	$60,000	(5)(6) $130,000	$205,000
Total With New Product & 10 Additional Practices		$931,394		$1,169,022

(1) Vendor provided no figure. Estimate 50% of initial implementation for installation and training.

(2) Vendor insists no database license. Not logical; estimate same database license as comparable system.

(3) Estimate includes referral and report writer, advanced appointment scheduler, and laser forms generator; no estimates provided for G/L interface.

(4) Optional software estimate includes G/L interface and report writer.

(5) Estimate for bal. fwd. conversion $10,000 per practice.

(6) Estimate for detail scratch pad at $3,000 per practice.

(7) Each additional practice requires dataset creation at $7,500 per practice.

(8) Demographic and modified detail at $6,000 per practice.

Practice Management Information Systems Request for Information

TABLE OF CONTENTS

I. Background

     A. Mission Statement
     B. History and Governance
     C. Infrastructure Requirements
     D. Current Applications

II. Information Systems Planning and Vendor Selection Methodology

     A. Information Systems Philosophy
     B. The Vendor Selection Process
     C. Project Calendar
     D. Vendor Selection Criteria
     E. Administrative Matters

III. Application Profiles

     A. General Information
     B. Application Profile: Patient Appointment Scheduling
     C. Application Profile: Patient Registration
     D. Application Profile: Patient Billing/Receivables Management

IV. Vendor Instructions

     A. Reply Instructions
     B. Materials Request
     C. Vendor Questions Requiring Response

I. BACKGROUND

A. Mission Statement

Company strives to provide superior management services utilizing appropriate technologies.

B. History, Governance, and Direction

COMPANY is a Management Service Organization (MSO) owned and managed by the clinic membership of the MSO. The formation of COMPANY is the result of initial integration efforts by these medical specialty practices in the region. The MSO expects to continue its growth in the next year.

Continued expansion, competition, and polarization of the existing health systems in the area generated an atmosphere which required the physicians to take action to protect their professional interests and capabilities. Our member practices recognized that only through mutual cooperation and commitment would they be able to continue providing the excellent level of medical care synonymous with the region.

COMPANY is managed by a board of managers elected by the membership of the MSO. The managers are all physician owners of the MSO. Officers of the MSO are elected from this board of managers.

Direction and control of the MSO is further distributed to the membership of the organization through participation in governing committees. Current MSO committees include:

- Finance
- Planning
- Human Resources
- CQI
- Grievance
- Payor Contracting
- Provider Relations
- Insurance
- Practice Advisory

COMPANY provides management services to its independent member clinics. The initial level of services provided to our member clinics includes:

- Accounting and Financial Services
- Billing, Claims Resolution, and Collection Services

- Transcription and Medical Records Management
- Managed Care Contracting
- Information Technology Assistance

In order to support these levels of service, a technology infrastructure must be defined, developed, and implemented. This RFI document is the first step in establishing the basic infrastructure for capturing, maintaining, and reporting information from which all future services are directed.

C. Infrastructure Requirements

In order to properly support managed care contracting and prepare for a capitated environment in the area, COMPANY will require that billing and claims resolution be performed in a centralized business office for all MSO member organizations. COMPANY requires a central repository of all financial, billing, payment, and claim resolution data for all members. The key to this repository will be the ability to maintain separate and distinct receivables and files for each of the member groups, while providing the ability to "roll up" the figures to generate total MSO statistics.

The first step in establishing this repository of data is the selection of a clinic receivables management system, which will support the central business office. The applications that will be required to support the clinic receivables management system include:

- Appointment Scheduling
- Patient Registration
- Guarantor and Insurance Billing
- Accounts Receivable Management

Other applications that will be of interest include:

- Medical Records Management
- Patient Clinical Management

Connectivity is a key concern for the MSO. A centralized business office supporting the practice management/clinic receivables applications for distinct practices requires high-speed on-line, real-time processing capabilities. A number of industry options are available which include:

- Dial Up Lines
- ISDN Lines
- LAN and WAN Technologies
- Internet Communications

Independence and security are key issues for each of our individual practices. Each vendor will be requested to address options and alternatives in response to the connectivity challenge for the MSO.

D. Current Applications

Each of the practices maintains an independent practice management system to support its billing and patient accounts management. Approximately eight different vendor products provide practice-management support to MSO member clinics. Our membership includes a wide variety of practices, from the solo practitioner to clinics with many physicians. As a result, hardware platforms supporting the variety of vendor products vary widely from AS/400 and RISC-based systems to PC-based DOS and Windows applications.

II.   INFORMATION SYSTEMS PLANNING AND VENDOR SELECTION METHODOLOGY

A. Information Systems Philosophy

In this section we provide key concepts that have guided the information systems planning process to date, and will continue to guide the vendor selection and system implementation process.

- The system must support each practice independently, while allowing a roll-up capability to maintain and report MSO-wide statistics.
- A single host system is preferred; use of independent hardware platforms is not acceptable.
- The system must be an on-line, interactive system utilizing a Windows-based environment.
- The decision is hardware independent, though the proposed solution will require top-line support in the market.
- It is essential that the information system selected support a powerful, user-friendly report-writing capability. COMPANY expects that any information input into the system will be readily accessible and reportable without the need of high-level technical staff interaction.
- Supporting the future healthcare needs of the region are of paramount importance to the information systems processing capabilities of any system selected by COMPANY. The technical infrastructure of any system selected by COMPANY must support an open architecture model which will provide and support connectivity with third-party organizations.

- Senior management will continue to dedicate sufficient time and resources to the information systems function because information is a valuable resource.
- COMPANY will continue to be successful and meet future challenges utilizing information as a resource for operational, financial, and administrative management. Therefore, its systems vendors' commitment to support, keeping pace with regulatory changes, and timely response to a changing healthcare delivery environment is critical.
- Management will generally take a conservative approach to vendor selection. For example, all application software must be demonstrated as operational in a similar technical environment as proposed.

B. The Vendor Selection Process

This request for information is different from the standard request for proposal process in that the system vendor does not have to respond to a lengthy checklist of functions/features, complete cost estimates, etc., at this stage of the process. Instead, the vendors receiving this document are requested to respond to a short list of questions and supply product and client information pertaining to their experience and capability to provide a solution to our needs.

Upon the review of the requested information, as well as the vendor's response to the short list of questions, three to four vendors will be requested to continue in our selection process.

Utilizing the information in this document as background, the remaining vendors will present their solution to management's information systems issues and needs via discussion, "blackboard presentations," and scenario-based product demonstration.

During later steps, when only one or two system vendors remain under consideration, each vendor will be required to document functionality, as identified in the application profiles, software configuration, costs, implementation workplans, etc., for contractual purposes.

In this section we describe the process management will utilize to select the "best fit" vendor. This section also describes the responsibilities of the COMPANY management and staff, the systems vendors and Health Capital Consultants. (In the next section the process is summarized in calendar format.)

Distribute Request for Information to Vendor Community

Review Vendor Response Information and Establish Short List of Vendors

Prepare and Conduct Intensive Vendor Interviews and Product Demonstration

Each vendor requested to participate will present their company, appropriate products, and key management and staff during a one-day intensive session. The day is divided into two distinct sections: vendor/solution interview and product demonstration.

Management's objectives for these interviews on COMPANY's site are to:

- Quickly reveal the vendor's capability for meeting the systems requirements for selected applications.
- Identify potential areas of benefit compared to other vendors/products.
- Enable the vendor to describe a solution utilizing its products.
- Provide the COMPANY staff with an understanding of the products proposed and the degree of success other MSO organizations in a similar environment have achieved.
- Meet key vendor management, implementation staff, support staff, and so forth who would be responsible for contract negotiations, implementation, and ongoing support should a contract be awarded.

COMPANY will select a core group of MSO members to conduct these interviews. They will be fully prepared to determine how each vendor's product can be a solution to their needs. Their concerns are defined in the application profiles section of this request for information. They will rate each vendor's application group with a preformatted scorecard they will prepare to enable an objective evaluation.

The group's preparation will consist of each person reviewing the application profiles' functions/features and technological requirements sections to determine the eight to twelve questions that are critical to understanding the following about the vendor's product(s).

- How are the databases updated with accurate and complete data in a timely and efficient manner?
- How are the databases accessed? On-line or via reports?
- How does the vendor support contract management needs, specifically multiple receivables and fee schedules, and cost accounting for managed care contracting.

During the afternoon each vendor will be requested to provide a demonstration of its product. The product demonstration will encompass situational scenarios that will be provided by COMPANY in advance of the demonstration. Management's objectives for the demonstration are to:

- Observe the vendor's solution to the COMPANY requirements utilizing scenarios.
- Provide the COMPANY staff the opportunity to observe the interaction and operational complexity of the product.

Conduct Management Meeting

Following all applicable vendor demonstrations, the selection group will meet. They will review their objective ratings and impressions and make recommendations for elimination of vendors from further consideration.

As a result of this effort, management desires to have no more than two vendors remaining for consideration.

Prepare for and Conduct Contract Negotiations

Management is willing to expend the time and effort to commence contract negotiations with more than one systems vendor concurrently. The remaining vendors will:

- Receive detailed cost schedules for completion.
- Document operational functions, features, and data flow.
- Furnish detailed implementation and staffing plans.

C. Project Calendar

Week	Action
1	Forward request for information to vendors.
3	Receive and evaluate vendor responses.
4	Management meeting to review and establish vendor short list.
4	Notify vendors of results of elimination meeting.
4	Schedule short-listed vendors for interviews and product demonstrations.
4	Distribute demonstration scenarios.
6 & 7	Intensively interview and witness product demonstrations by prospective vendors.
7	Management meeting to review and eliminate vendors.
7	Notify vendors of results of elimination meeting and initiate contract discussions with selected vendor.

Management wishes to the remaining internal timeplan of the approval process to be flexible. We therefore have not imposed any target dates or commencement and conclusion of contract negotiations, etc.

D. Vendor Selection Criteria

Management has defined the following minimal business selection and application support criteria for the practice management system vendor.

- Must provide referenceable, fully installed practice management applications for an MSO environment.
- Must provide referenceable, fully installed applications that support the three application groupings: patient appointment scheduling, patient registration, billing and accounts receivable management.
- Must display a committed presence to the industry through:
  - Significant MSO Base
  - Significant Research and Development Budget
  - Significant Support Organization
- Must have at least one referenceable, installed site with both a corporate structure and application software configuration like that desired by COMPANY.

E. Administrative Matters

Interim Questions and Responses. During the vendor's preparation period, the chief operating officer will be available to answer questions. Questions and responses will be distributed to all vendors if they contain material information not included in this request for information.

Confidentiality of Information. Information provided by COMPANY as part of the request for information process must be considered confidential, proprietary information of COMPANY and cannot be used outside of the scope of this request for information process. All copies of the request for information and all other information gathered subsequent to the issuance of the request for information must be returned to COMPANY once a selection is made.

Site Visits/References. The vendor may be asked to identify one or more sites currently using the system proposed. As travel costs for these site visits will be the responsibility of COMPANY, every effort should be made to identify meaningful sites that can be visited at minimal expense. It will also be *mandatory* to provide sufficient references, when requested, in order to allow COMPANY to perform a telephone screening to validate that the selected site is appropriate for its needs.

Costs. All costs incurred by the vendor in developing the responses and/or attending meetings directly or indirectly related to this request for information are entirely the responsibility of the vendor and may not be charged to COMPANY or Health Capital Consultants either as a separate charge or as part of services provided.

News Releases. Vendors will make no public statement explicitly or implicitly indicating a service relationship with COMPANY or its agent unless written permission is provided.

Forwarding of Materials and Visiting PRN. Vendor representatives may contact the chief operating officer to deliver any documents for review prior to the intensive interviews. However, the documents should not be marketing materials. Only documents that provide background material on the vendor's products will be accepted.

III. APPLICATION PROFILES

A. General Information

The application profiles are a result of interviews with management. Three primary application profiles were developed.

1. Patient Appointment Scheduling

2. Patient Registration

3. Patient Billing and Accounts Receivable

Within each application profile are the following categories.

- Name of the Application
- Narrative Description of Application
- Desired Application Features and Functions Summary
- Desired Reporting Capabilities
- Technological Support Desired

Other applications may be available from the respective system vendor, and may be introduced but at present these are the applications upon which a decision will be based.

B. Application Profile: Patient Appointment Scheduling

1. **Name of Application:** Patient Appointment and Resource Scheduling

2. **Narrative Description of Application:** The patient appointment scheduling application provides COMPANY member practices with the capability to independently develop a template of available appointment hours for each applicable member physician. Patient appointments will be scheduled on the defined provider templates. Patient appointment history will be maintained for statistical reporting requirements for each member physician and practice.

3. **Desired Application Features and Functions Summary:** This section describes those capabilities important to COMPANY. They include the following.

   - The application must provide the ability to schedule patients across the spectrum of the MSO. Staff within one MSO practice should be allowed to schedule patients in another member practice.
   - The application should support the gathering of patient referral information during the appointment scheduling function.
   - The development of physician schedule templates must be performed for either a single date or range of dates.
   - The scheduling clerk must be able to review online the availability of multiple providers or resources, by type of service, simultaneously for a particular appointment target.
   - The scheduling clerk must be able to review a range of potential appointment dates for a single provider/resource.
   - The system should generate an encounter form (fee ticket) on demand for scheduled patients within a defined date or range of dates.
   - The system should support automatic coordination of appointments for related visits to multiple providers on the same day.
   - The system should support and identify appointment conflict control and resolution.
   - Encounter forms will be generated with applicable procedure and diagnosis codes, based on the provider or department of service.

- The system should provide the ability to maintain the status for each appointment—completed, canceled, missed, etc.—and provide statistics by patient, facility, and provider. This data would be integrated with the registration module.
- The system should support both centralized and decentralized patient appointment scheduling.

4. **Desired Reporting Capabilities:** This section describes those application reporting capabilities important to the COMPANY membership. They include the following.

- The system should provide a listing, on demand, of appointments scheduled for a particular date or range of dates. This listing may be by provider, resource, facility, or a combination thereof.
- The system should provide a mechanism for return patients to review current demographic and insurance data on file and notate any changes or updates.
- The system should generate a medical record "pull list" for any established patient with a scheduled appointment with a defined date or range of dates.
- The system should provide an ad hoc report generator to create user-defined listings and statistical reports of appointment activity by member facility, member provider, resource, payor, or other defined category.

5. **Technological Support Desired:**

- Online, real time data input, update, and inquiry.
- No scheduled downtime during member clinic hours.

C. Application Profile: Patient Registration

1. **Name of Application:** Patient Registration

2. **Narrative Description of Application:** The patient registration application provides the cornerstone for the proper gathering of patient demographic and financial information. This data is shared with the billing application to generate third-party and guarantor billing statements.

3. **Desired Application Features and Functions Summary:** This section describes those capabilities important to COMPANY. They include the following:

- The system should provide COMPANY with the flexibility to define the required registration fields of data, based on alternate criteria established by member practices.

- The system should provide the ability to set up either family or individual billing accounts at the discretion of the COMPANY member practice.

- The system should provide the capability to differentiate patient encounters for insurance billing alternatives, such as workers' compensation or accidents, employee physicals, and standard care.

- The system should allow the capability to update all applicable patient demographic records from one root file-update transaction.

- The system should provide a mechanism to record inpatient admissions and respective discharge dates for a patient.

- The system should provide the ability to make an account inquiry by account number, social security number, or name.

- The system should provide the capability to purge history data to a retrievable medium based on user-defined criteria.

- The system should support the ability to generate prescription cards.

- The system should maintain month-to-date and year-to-date summary of activity for comparison purposes.

4. **Desired Data Elements Maintained:** This section describes those application data elements important to COMPANY. They include the following.

- The system should provide the ability to individually record the social security number of both the patient and guarantor.

- The system should provide for the recording of employer data to include address and phone number for the patient, guarantor, and spouse, if applicable.

- The system should provide the ability to record international addresses, as applicable for the foreign clientele of COMPANY.

- The system should provide free-form comment fields to record registration notes or special instructions.

5. **Desired Reporting Capabilities:** This section describes those application reporting capabilities important to the COMPANY members. They include the following.

- The system should provide a report, based on a user-defined volume of days, of discharged inpatients without corresponding charges applied to the account.

- The system should provide a report, based on a user-defined volume of days, of clinic patient encounters without corresponding charges applied to the account.

- The system should provide an ad hoc report generator for demographic statistical reporting by user-defined dictionaries.

6. **Technological Support Desired:**
   - Online, real-time data input, update, and inquiry.
   - No scheduled downtime during member clinic hours.

D. Application Profile: Patient Billing and Accounts Receivable

1. **Name of Application:** Patient Billing and Accounts Receivable
2. **Narrative Description of Application:** The patient billing and accounts receivable application provides COMPANY with the ability to generate applicable third-party and guarantor billing statements for professional services rendered. The application will also support the proper posting and reporting of service revenue, payments, and adjustments by provider, member practice, and/or facility.
3. **Desired Application Features and Functions Summary:** This section describes those capabilities important to COMPANY. They include the following.
   - The system should maintain a minimum of three iterations of pricing history per service item, to include price and effective date. Rebilling or retroactive service charge application should automatically apply the proper price based on effective date and date of service.
   - The system should support the ability to generate automatic pricing adjustments based on user-defined criteria, (i.e., insurance plans, financial type, etc.) and post adjustments at the time of billing to the patient's account.
   - The system should support the ability to generate an adjustment based on an insurance payment amount and the amount approved. This adjustment may be posted automatically at the time of insurance payment.
   - The system should support all third-party billing requirements for the generation of the HCFA 1500 claim form as required by the fiscal intermediaries representing Medicare and Medicaid. Examples include:
     - Support CPT-4 procedure code reporting formats
     - Support ICD9-CM diagnosis code reporting formats
     - Support ADA coding requirements
   - The system should support family account–based statement generation, based on the guarantor's account.

- The system should support multiple user-defined cycle billing parameters (i.e., monthly, weekly, etc.) based on financial type, location, clinic, and insurance.
- The system should support an on-line bill edit/claim form review function prior to third-party claim generation.
- The system should support on-line specific account bill selection capabilities for the generation of both third-party and guarantor billings.
- The system should support a rebill capability for third-party claim form generation.
- The system should support an automatic secondary insurance claim form generation function.
- Dunning messages and collection letters will be user defined.
- The system should support the creation and status reporting of "contract accounts" for time-payment plans.
- The system should support multiple account write-off capabilities based on user-defined insurance plan, financial type, or employer criteria.
- The system should support the application of payments to a specific item of service or encounter.
- The system should support a method of on-line charge entry that eliminates repetitive keystroke entry, such as account number, date, etc.
- The system should support both direct account, on-line charge entry and a transaction facility for the batch entry of charges.
- The system should support the capability to post third-party payments based on a bill claim number generated at the time of billing.
- The system should support the capability to inquiry a patient account on-line.
- The system must support the capability to automatically integrate all patients account transaction activity to the general ledger.

4. **Desired Reporting Capabilities:** This section describes those application reporting capabilities desired by COMPANY. They include the following.

- The system must provide billing, payment, and adjustment reporting based on user-defined criteria—i.e., provider, facility, member group.
- An ad hoc report generator with user-defined data element dictionary should be provided for miscellaneous statistical reporting.

- The system should provide user-defined aged trial balance reports based on payor, dollar balance, financial type, or other defined status coding.
- Provider activity reports should be generated.
- Audit trails should be supported which identify missing charges or charge tickets.
- Revenue, payment, and adjustment control reports must be generated which validate system balancing procedures.
- Payment posting reports must be generated which validate cash deposits.

5. Technical Support Desired:

- On-line data input, update, and review
- Minimum scheduled downtime.

IV. VENDOR INSTRUCTIONS

A. Reply Instructions

1. We request that all vendors receiving this document respond by fax transmission indicating whether or not they intend to participate. Please respond to our fax number, by *Tuesday of week 2.*

2. All participating vendor responses, product information, and client data are due by *5:00 P.M.* on *Friday, week 2.* Responses should be directed to:

Chief Operating Officer

Company

Address

City, State Zip

B. Materials Request

1. Provide product information pertaining to the features and functions of the applications being proposed.

2. Provide complete list of currently installed clients.

3. Provide a generic implementation plan pertaining to the implementation of your product.

C. Vendor Questions Requiring Response

1. Do you provide a Windows-based application solution?

2. Is there a product users group? Is this users group supported by your company?

3. How many installed clients does your organization currently support? How many of your installed clients have over five locations using the software?

4. How many installed clients are MSO organizations? How many of these MSO organizations support over 15 separate locations?

5. How long has your organization provided information system solutions to the healthcare industry? How long in practice-management applications?

6. Can you support electronic claims submission for all payors?

7. What is your product's preferred hardware configuration?

Healthcare Executive Search

Overview of Conducting a Search for a Healthcare Executive

The sections below provide an overview for conducting a search for a healthcare executive for an ORGANIZATION TYPE.

I. CANDIDATE PROFILE/JOB DESCRIPTION

The candidate profile/job description for the healthcare executive includes all job functions, criteria required for the successful candidate, as well as the relationship of the position with all parts of the organization. Recommendations are welcomed from the executive and human resources committees of the Organization's governing board, and interested physicians.

A. Experience

A healthcare executive should have an operations background and hands-on practice-management experience. Many organizations fail because their administrators lack vision and detailed knowledge necessary to execute a strategic plan.

1. Experience in physician group practice management is often required. Preferably, this experience would be with a relatively large clinic or clinics.

2. Experience as a healthcare administrator in a managed care environment is also valuable.

B. Qualifications

Clearly, the healthcare executive must be able to work well with physicians, on both operational and strategic issues. The healthcare executive will also have to be a jack of all trades to some extent; he or she must understand legal, financial, contracting, and operational dimensions of medical group practice. In short, the healthcare executive must be a planner as well as a firefighter.

In organizations with multiple sites, developing a common culture and common operating procedures can be a challenge. Therefore, in such circumstances, a healthcare executive should have excellent organizational development skills and the ability to work with multiple, diverse physicians towards common objectives.

Specific competencies include the following.

1. Knowledge of or experience with medical information systems is important.
2. Thorough understanding of and skill in negotiating risk-sharing contracts (including capitation) is valuable.
3. Overall ORGANIZATION TYPE operations knowledge—including billing, collections, strategic planning, contracting, quality analysis, utilization review, and human resources—is an aid in success in such a position.
4. Excellent communications, interpersonal, and promotional skills required.

C. Education

1. A bachelor's degree in business, accounting, finance, or health administration is required.
2. A master's degree in business administration or health administration is preferred.

II. AVENUES FOR ADVERTISING/RECRUITING

A. Healthcare Administration Journals/Publications

Examples:

1. *Medical Economics*
2. *Modern Healthcare*
3. *Medical Group Management Update*

B. Placement Services

> Example: MGMA Placement Service

C. Executive Search Firms

> Example: Cejka & Company—Administrators, Medical and Executive Directors

III. EQUAL EMPLOYMENT OPPORTUNITY/FAIR HIRING PRACTICES (REFER TO APPENDICES FOR ADDITIONAL INFORMATION)

A. Preemployment Inquiries

> Employers may not make inquiries that would disproportionately disadvantage persons based on their race, color, religion, sex, national origin, height, weight, marital status, number of children, provision for child care, English language skill, education, friends or relatives working for employer, arrest records, conviction records, discharge from military service, age, citizenship, economic status, or availability for work on weekends or holidays *unless* this information can be demonstrated to be a valid predictor of job performance or may be justified by "business necessity."[1]

B. Americans with Disabilities Act

> Employers may not ask questions concerning disability or require medical examinations until an applicant has been given a conditional job offer. Employers may however ask about applicants abilities to perform job functions and may ask candidates to describe or demonstrate how they would perform job functions.[2]

IV. SALARY

> Average salary and benefits for ORGANIZATION TYPE healthcare executives should be researched. Sources of salary information for healthcare executives include:

---

[1]"Pre-employment inquiries and equal employment opportunity law." EEOC, Office of Public Affairs, 1981.

[2]"ADA Enforcement Guidance: Preemployment Disability-Related Questions and Medical Examinations." EEOC, 1995.

1. "Compensation Report: Management Employees in Hospital, Nursing Home, and Home Health Management Companies" (annual). Hospital & Health Care Compensation Service, P.O. Box 376, Oakland, NJ 07436; (201) 616-5722.

2. "Group Practice Physician Compensation Trends and Productivity Correlations Survey" (annual). American Medical Group Association, 1422 Duke Street, Alexandria, VA 22314; (703) 838-0033.

3. "Health Care Strategic Executive Compensation Survey" (annual). Center for Healthcare Industry Performance Standards, 1550 Old Henderson Road, Suite S-277, Columbus, OH 43220-3626; (800) 859-2447.

4. "Hospital Salary & Benefits Report" (annual). Hospital & Health Care Compensation Service, P.O. Box 376, Oakland, NJ 07436; (201) 616-5722.

5. "Management Compensation Survey" (annual). Medical Group Management Association, 104 Inverness Terrace East, Englewood, CO 80112-5306; (303) 799-1111.

This type of information should be used as a guide in determining the appropriate salary and benefit levels.

Process Outline

Phase 1: Definitions and Process Infrastructure		Assigned To:
1.	Develop needs assessment for position.	ORGANIZATION/ CONSULTANTS
2.	ORGANIZATION's executive and HR committee and CONSULTANTS assigned task of recruiting a healthcare executive for ORGANIZATION.	ORGANIZATION'S governing board
3.	Develop candidate profile/job description.	ORGANIZATION/ CONSULTANTS
Phase 2: Recruiting for "Suspects"		
1.	Determine advertising vehicle.	CONSULTANTS
2.	Create advertisement.	CONSULTANTS
3.	Publish advertisement.	CONSULTANTS

(continued)

Phase 3: Screening for "Prospects"		Assigned To:
1.	Gather resumes.	CONSULTANTS
2.	Review and determine qualified candidates.	ORGANIZATION/ CONSULTANTS
3.	Initiate contact with qualified candidates and arrange telephone interviews.	CONSULTANTS

Phase 4: Interviewing for "Targets"		
1.	Conduct telephone interviews and evaluate candidates.	ORGANIZATION/ CONSULTANTS
2.	Determine qualified applicants.	ORGANIZATION/ CONSULTANTS
3.	Arrange and conduct first on-site interview and tour.	ORGANIZATION/ CONSULTANTS
4.	Determine qualified applicants.	ORGANIZATION/ CONSULTANTS
5.	Arrange and conduct final interview.	ORGANIZATION/ CONSULTANTS
6.	Prioritize candidates and make final decision.	ORGANIZATION/ CONSULTANTS

Phase 5: Hiring for a Successful Candidate		
1.	Develop compensation and benefits package.	ORGANIZATION/ CONSULTANTS
2.	Extend offer.	ORGANIZATION/ CONSULTANTS
3.	If accepted, project complete; if not, negotiate or go to second choice.	ORGANIZATION/ CONSULTANTS

Healthcare Executive Candidate Profile/Job Description

Position Title: Healthcare Executive

Reports to: Executive committee of ORGANIZATION's governing board.

Supervises: All administrative staff

Functions: Responsible for the nonmedical administration of the organization. Works to implement the policies established by the governing board as assigned through the executive committee.

DUTIES

Organizing: Establishes procedures to effectively manage and administer the business functions of the organization.

- Responsible for working with the governing board on strategic planning initiatives.
- Works to create administrative procedures and systems.

Coordinating/Facilitating: Coordinates the work of the administrative staff in order to effectively accomplish the daily administrative functions of the organization. Acts as a liaison between the governing board, the administrative staff, and physicians.

- Organizes the agenda for meetings of the governing board.
- Oversees and maintains administrative procedures and systems, WHICH MAY INCLUDE: billing, collections, human resources, medical information, quality assurance (QA), continuing quality improvement (CQI), utilization review (UR), and other ORGANIZATION TYPE functions.
- *May* participate in the identification, solicitation, analysis, and negotiation of risk-sharing contracts.

Professional Image: Acts as a spokesperson and works to promote ORGANIZATION directly and through overall professionalism.

Team Participation: Works, where appropriate, as a team leader or member and generally supports an atmosphere of participation and team/organizational goals.

Other Duties: MAY INCLUDE Marketing of ORGANIZATION's services to physicians and groups.

POSITION REQUIREMENTS

Knowledge: Must have knowledge of ORGANIZATION TYPE operations, WHICH MAY INCLUDE: billing, collections, contracting, strategic planning, medical information systems, QA, CQI, UR, and HR.

Abilities: Excellent interpersonal skills are required, including the ability to communicate clearly and professionally, verbally and in writing. Must have the ability to work well independently, within a team, and under the direction of the governing board as well as with administrative staff and physicians. Strong organizational and leadership skill are necessary.

Education: Bachelor's degree in business or health administration, MHA or MBA preferred.

Experience: NUMBER OF YEARS experience in physician practice-management for large groups, ORGANIZATION TYPE management experience a plus. MAY REQUIRE experience in the analysis and negotiation of risk-sharing contracts, including capitation.

Healthcare Executive's Working Relationship with the Constituencies within the ORGANIZATION TYPE

	Duties and Responsibilities	Percent of Time
Governing Board	The healthcare executive operates under the executive committee and reports to the committee for assignment of duties. The healthcare executive relates to the governing board through the executive committee on administrative matters.	XX%
Officers	The healthcare executive will generally report to the executive committee, who will in turn report to the officers and governing board as a whole.	XX%
ORGANIZATION Members	The healthcare executive and administrative staff will work with physicians on a regular basis concerning the administration of the organization.	XX%
ORGANIZATION Staff	ORGANIZATION/DEPARTMENT staff report to and are directed by the healthcare executive.	XX%

Advertisement for ORGANIZATION TYPE Healthcare Executive

Healthcare Executive—ORGANIZATION TYPE: ORGANIZATION located in CITY, STATE, is seeking a healthcare executive. Applicants must have a bachelor's degree in business or health administration, MHA or MBA preferred. Candidates should have NUMBER or more years experience in physician practice management for large groups or hospital management. ORGANIZATION TYPE management desirable. Successful candidates should [MAY NEED TO] have experience in the analysis and negotiation of risk-sharing contracts, including capitation. Knowledge of ORGANIZATION TYPE operations, WHICH MAY INCLUDE billing, collections, contracting, strategic planning, medical information systems, QA, CQI, UR, and HR. Applicants should submit resume and salary history to: ORGANIZATION, Attn: CONTACT, ADDRESS. EOE.

Telephone Interview Questions

The telephone interview serves as a secondary screen to eliminate unqualified candidates (consultants will conduct a preliminary resume screen). The purpose of this interview is to ascertain the candidate's professional experience, personal characteristics, and level of interest in the position. This evaluation should give the interviewer a good indication of how well the person is able to respond to an impromptu interview and present information in a clear and concise manner. The telephone interview should only take about 30 minutes; two more interviews follow for successful candidates.

After an initial background discussion (regarding the city area, ORGANIZATION, healthcare executive position overview, and relationship to governing board), the interviewers should proceed with the questions that follow. The interviewers should rate the candidate by using the attached Telephone Interview Rating Form.

TELEPHONE INTERVIEW QUESTIONS

1. Walk us through your resume: What has led you to this point in your career where you are now considering this opportunity?
2. Are there any potential conflicts of interest, covenants not to compete, or other restraints that would hinder your ability to accept this position?
3. Describe a professional situation in which you have had to exert leadership to unite various people or organizations with different agendas.
4. Given your knowledge of ORGANIZATION, what are the major strategic issues facing this organization? Operational issues?
5. If you were a competitor of ORGANIZATION, whether a hospital or physician group, how would you attack us?
6. Do you enjoy working in close contact with physicians? Clinical staff? Clerical staff?
7. Describe your management style.

Telephone Interview Rating Form

Candidate's Name: _____ Date: _____
Telephone #: _____ Time: _____

	Interviewer Rating	
Professional Experience	Excellent	Poor
Undergraduate educational background—appropriate to position, accomplishments	☐ ☐ ☐ ☐ ☐	
Graduate educational background—appropriate to position, accomplishments	☐ ☐ ☐ ☐ ☐	
Work experience—relevance to position, depth and breath, successes	☐ ☐ ☐ ☐ ☐	
Professional certifications—relation to requirements of position	☐ ☐ ☐ ☐ ☐	
Other experience—relation to requirements of position	☐ ☐ ☐ ☐ ☐	
References—relation to candidate, professional level	☐ ☐ ☐ ☐ ☐	
Personal Characteristics		
Intelligence—perceptiveness, understanding, alertness	☐ ☐ ☐ ☐ ☐	
Initiative—ambition, appropriateness, energy	☐ ☐ ☐ ☐ ☐	
Communication—clarity, organization, listening	☐ ☐ ☐ ☐ ☐	
Preparation for Interview/Interest in Job		
Relevant knowledge—organization, local market, other	☐ ☐ ☐ ☐ ☐	
Overall Rating	☐ ☐ ☐ ☐ ☐	

Comments: _____

_____

_____

Interviewer: _____

Second Telephone Interview Questions

The second telephone interview serves as a measure of screening the initial telephone interview. Its form is primarily scenario-based, which is used to further evaluate the candidate's ability to respond to possible situations in any organization. This telephone interview should last approximately 20 minutes. Successful candidates will move on to the first in-person interview.

SECOND TELEPHONE INTERVIEW QUESTIONS

1. How do you plan to keep abreast of all the changes in the market?
2. How would you look to monitor new insurance products entering the marketplace?
3. When physician groups are interested in joining the ORGANIZA-TION, what characteristics would you consider?
4. What do you foresee as your interaction with the operations of all the ORGANIZATION's practices?
5. How do you foresee your interaction with ORGANIZATION board of managers?
6. What visions or plans do you hope to bring to ORGANIZATION for its success?
7. Scenario: One of the hospitals in AREA has pressured one or two of its employed physicians to stop referring patients to some of ORGA-NIZATION's physicians. Those physicians come to you looking for help in deterring the hospital and its employed physicians from discontinuing their referrals. What would you do in this scenario?

Second Telephone Interview Rating Form

Candidate's Name: _____ Date: _____
Telephone #: _____ Time: _____

Professional Experience	Interviewer Rating Excellent Poor				
Undergraduate educational background—appropriate to position, accomplishments	☐	☐	☐	☐	☐
Graduate educational background—appropriate to position, accomplishments	☐	☐	☐	☐	☐
Work experience—relevance to position, depth and breath, successes	☐	☐	☐	☐	☐
Professional certifications—relation to requirements of position	☐	☐	☐	☐	☐
Other experience—relation to requirements of position	☐	☐	☐	☐	☐
References—relation to candidate, professional level	☐	☐	☐	☐	☐

(continued)

	Interviewer Rating	
Professional Experience	Excellent	Poor

Personal Characteristics

Intelligence—perceptiveness, understanding, alertness	☐	☐	☐	☐	☐
Initiative—ambition, appropriateness, energy	☐	☐	☐	☐	☐
Communication—clarity, organization, listening	☐	☐	☐	☐	☐

Preparation for Interview/Interest in Job

Relevant knowledge—organization, local market, other	☐	☐	☐	☐	☐

Scenario-Based Questions

Analysis—problems, organization, hierarchy	☐	☐	☐	☐	☐
Creativity—approach, analysis, solution	☐	☐	☐	☐	☐
Overall Rating	☐	☐	☐	☐	☐

Comments: _____

_____

_____

Interviewer: _____

First In-Person Interview Questions

The first in-person interview further assesses the general knowledge and professional experience of the candidate. The interview questions consist of an assessment of information systems, financial management, practice management, and personnel management. The interviewer should volunteer as many details as possible about the job to see which details elicit a response or can be tied to relevant factors in the candidate's background. This interview should take 1 to 1.5 hours. The interviewers should rate the candidate by using the attached First In-Person Interview Rating Form.

1. Background Discussion
   - CITY area, ORGANIZATION, healthcare executive position overview, relationship to governing board.
2. Educational Background
   - Describe what educational experience you have that is relevant to this position.
   - Were you involved with any special projects, fellowships, or internships that provided pertinent experiences?

3. Work Experience
   - Describe each of the positions listed on your resume and tell how those experiences relate to this position.

4. Practice Management Questions
   A. Computer Systems
      (i) What medical management computer systems have you worked with?
      (ii) Detail your experience and use of these systems.
   B. Financial Management Experience
      (i) What do you feel are the greatest challenges and issues involved with operational budgeting and financial planning?
      (ii) How did you address these issues in planning and how effective were you in dealing with them? How close to budget have you been?
      (iii) What tactics did you use to adjust expenses and also budget more effectively in future?
   C. Operational Management
      (i) What methods and techniques have you used to improve materials management and purchasing?
      (ii) Patient satisfaction?
      (iii) Continuous quality improvement or other quality-management techniques?
      (iv) Utilization review?
      (v) Billing/collections?
   D. Personnel Management Skills
      (i) Describe your management style and philosophy.
      (ii) What type of positions have you managed and how did your management technique apply to each?
      (iii) How many physicians have you managed and what were their specialties?
      (iv) Describe your relationship with these physicians.
      (v) Explain how you have handled grievances with staff and with physicians.
      (vi) What do you consider your greatest strengths? Weaknesses?

5. References

   May we contact your references? Are there any other people, supervisors, or managers we may contact for additional references?

First In-Person Interview Rating Form

Candidate's Name: _____ Date: _____

Telephone #: _____ Time: _____

Professional Experience	**Interviewer Rating** Excellent Poor
Undergraduate educational background—appropriate to position, accomplishments	☐ ☐ ☐ ☐ ☐
Graduate educational background—appropriate to position, accomplishments	☐ ☐ ☐ ☐ ☐
Work experience—relevance to position, depth and breath, successes	☐ ☐ ☐ ☐ ☐
Professional certifications—relation to requirements of position	☐ ☐ ☐ ☐ ☐
Other experience—relation to requirements of position	☐ ☐ ☐ ☐ ☐
References—relation to candidate, professional level	☐ ☐ ☐ ☐ ☐

Personal Characteristics

Intelligence—perceptiveness, understanding, alertness	☐ ☐ ☐ ☐ ☐
Initiative—ambition, appropriateness, energy	☐ ☐ ☐ ☐ ☐
Communication—clarity, organization, listening	☐ ☐ ☐ ☐ ☐

Preparation for Interview/Interest in Job

Relevant knowledge—organization, local market, other	☐ ☐ ☐ ☐ ☐

Practice Management Competencies

Computer systems	
Knowledge	☐ ☐ ☐ ☐ ☐
Proficiency	☐ ☐ ☐ ☐ ☐
Financial management	
Knowledge	☐ ☐ ☐ ☐ ☐
Proficiency	☐ ☐ ☐ ☐ ☐
Operational management	
Knowledge	☐ ☐ ☐ ☐ ☐
Proficiency	☐ ☐ ☐ ☐ ☐
Personnel management skills	
Knowledge	☐ ☐ ☐ ☐ ☐
Proficiency	☐ ☐ ☐ ☐ ☐
Overall Rating	☐ ☐ ☐ ☐ ☐

Comments: _____

_____

_____

Interviewer: _____

References/Background Form

Confirmation of Information Provided

Background Information	Agrees with Resume (Check)	Comments
Position Title		
Work Location		
Work Dates		
Supervisor/Title		
Number of People Supervised		
Responsibilities		
Accomplishments		

If possible, briefly describe healthcare executive position and ask the following questions:

1. Do you believe this candidate would thrive in this position in our organization?
2. What do you consider this individual's greatest assets? Weaknesses?
3. Do you have a reason not to recommend this individual?

Final Interview Questions

The final set of interviews are designed to further assist the interviewers in determining the talents of the candidates. Specifically, it assesses the candidate's ability to handle the operational and strategic issues that are expected to arise within ORGANIZATION. The candidate's compensation requirements are also be discussed. This interview should take about two hours and should be followed by a tour of the community, hospitals, and clinics. The interviewers should rate the candidate by using the attached Final Interview Rating Form.

1. Marketing and Negotiation
   A. What is your experience with advertising, promotion, and/or marketing of physician groups or networks to the community, hospitals, managed care organizations, and other physicians and groups?
   B. Did you negotiate the contracts, obtain financing, and structure the terms of the business relationship?
   C. How would you approach a physician group interested in affiliating with ORGANIZATION?
2. Strategic Planning
   A. How do you handle organizational change?
   B. Explain how you feel strategic financial and operational planning can most effectively be used by organizations?
   C. What role do you feel physicians should have in the planning and design process?
   D. Overall, how do you feel physicians fit in with the organization?
   E. Have you utilized incentives to increase productivity? If so, how?
3. Fulfillment of Job Description
   A. After a brief discussion of the job description, what contributions will you make towards this organization?
   B. What will be some of your strategies toward gaining the trust of the physicians within ORGANIZATION?
4. Case Analyses

   Case analyses to observe the candidate's problem solving processes: If you were the healthcare executive of ORGANIZATION, how would you respond to the following scenarios?

   Scenario 1—Operational Problem Solving: ORGANIZATION is at the stage in the development of a Management Services Organization where the medical practice administrative staff will be employed by the ORGANIZATION. During the transitional phase many nonclinical staff within the practices are upset because they believe other nonclinicians who do exactly the same thing and have the same title and experience but are already employed by ORGANIZATION are making more money. They have frustrated physicians and office managers in their respective practices with their complaints and want to come to the next ORGANIZATION board meeting to discuss the issue. You are concerned that this issue may escalate drastically if immediate action is not taken. What do you do?

   Scenario 2—Strategic Problem Solving: Two years from now, everything at ORGANIZATION has gone even better than you could have imagined: Physicians love working with each other, patient satisfaction is through the roof, internal staff couldn't be happier with the management, and even the other healthcare organizations and insurers think ORGANIZATION is doing great things for the community. However, you believe that ORGANIZATION should develop its own insurance product to complement its current services delivery function to its current member providers. How do you test your idea to make sure it is viable? How do you sell the physician leadership of ORGANIZATION on your plan?

5. Compensation Requirements

    A. What is your compensation history?

        (i)   Salary

        (ii) Benefits

        (iii) Perquisites

        (iv) Family Benefits

        (v) Title

        (vi) Exit

    B. What are your current compensation requirements?

Final In-Person Interview Rating Form

Candidate's Name: _____ Date: _____

Telephone #: _____ Time: _____

Professional Experience	Interviewer Rating	
	Excellent	Poor
Work experience—relevance to position, depth and breath, successes	☐ ☐ ☐ ☐ ☐	
Other experience—relation to requirements of position	☐ ☐ ☐ ☐ ☐	
References—relation to candidate, professional level	☐ ☐ ☐ ☐ ☐	
Personal Characteristics		
Intelligence—perceptiveness, understanding, alertness	☐ ☐ ☐ ☐ ☐	
Initiative—ambition, appropriateness, energy	☐ ☐ ☐ ☐ ☐	
Communication—clarity, organization, listening	☐ ☐ ☐ ☐ ☐	
Preparation for Interview/Interest in Job		
Relevant knowledge—organization, local market, other	☐ ☐ ☐ ☐ ☐	

Practice Management Competencies	Interviewer Rating	
	Excellent	Poor
Marketing and negotiation		
Knowledge	☐☐☐☐☐	
Proficiency	☐☐☐☐☐	
Strategic planning		
Knowledge	☐☐☐☐☐	
Proficiency	☐☐☐☐☐	
Fulfillment of job description		
Knowledge	☐☐☐☐☐	
Proficiency	☐☐☐☐☐	
Case analyses		
Knowledge	☐☐☐☐☐	
Proficiency	☐☐☐☐☐	
Overall Rating	☐☐☐☐☐	

Comments: _____

_____

_____

Interviewer: _____

Candidate Evaluation Form

The Candidate Evaluation Form tabulates the candidate's overall interview performance. Each evaluator should enter his or her ratings from the telephone interview, the first in-person interview, and the final interview. The box on the lower right yields an overall rating. This form will quantitatively summarize the interview experience for all finalists and will provide a valuable tool for making a decision on whom to extend an offer.

CANDIDATE EVALUATION FORM

Date: _____

Candidate: _____

Interviewer: _____

Rate from 1 (excellent) to 5 (poor)

	Professional Experience	Interest in Position	Personal Characteristics	Strategic Planning	Marketing/ Negotiation Skills	Practice Management Skills	Case Analyses Problem Solving
Telephone Interview Rating							
Second Telephone Interview Rating							
First In-Person Interview Rating							
References Comments							
Final Interview Rating							
General Comments							
Overall Rating							

Confidentiality and Stand Still Agreement

DATE

PHYSICIAN NAME
ADDRESS
CITY, STATE, ZIP CODE

Re: Confidentiality and Stand Still Agreement

Dear Dr. PHYSICIAN LAST NAME:

Thank you for your expression of interest in our preliminary discussions related to the potential affiliation of your specialty practice with other practicing TYPE OF SPECIALIST. Because of the confidential nature of our discussions, and the information regarding your practice that we will need to review, it is necessary that prior to our continued discussions both parties agree to and be bound by the following.

1. **Access and Due Diligence:** PHYSICIAN FULL NAME and CONSULTANT, as authorized representatives of the TYPE OF SPECIALTY group, shall be afforded, from and after the date hereof, reasonable opportunity to inspect the books, records, and assets of the medical practice of LEGAL NAME OF PRACTICE. This proposal is expressly contingent upon and subject to review by CONSULTANT of the books and records, assets, agreements, licenses, and facilities of PRACTICE, and any other due diligence deemed reasonably necessary by CONSULTANT, all to the satisfaction of and in the sole and absolute discretion of _____.

2. **Confidentiality:** Parties agree that they will keep confidential (except for such disclosure to attorneys, consultants, lenders, bankers, investors, etc., as may be appropriate in the furtherance of the negotiations or transactions contemplated by this letter) all information of a confidential nature, including, without limitation, the provisions of this letter and any definitive agreements, obtained by it from the other party in connection with the negotiations or transactions contemplated by this letter, and, in the event that such transactions are not consummated, will return to the other party all documents and other materials obtained from the other party in connection therewith. Paragraph 2 shall not apply to information to the extent:

   A. The information is or becomes generally known to the public other than by breach of this letter.

   B. Disclosure is lawfully required in a judicial or administrative proceeding.

   C. Disclosure is necessary for purposes of obtaining approvals by licensing, accreditation, or similar agencies.

   D. The information is known by a party before disclosure from the other party.

   E. The information is or becomes known to a party from a source other than the other party to this letter.

3. **Exclusive Negotiations:** Physician agrees that until NUMBER days after execution of this letter by parties, or on such earlier date that the parties hereto mutually determine that they are unable to enter into the agreements contemplated by this letter, PHYSICIAN NAME or any of his/her agents, or any shareholders of, or any person or entity on his/her behalf, shall not offer or seek to offer, or negotiate, entertain, or discuss any offer to combine the assets or capital stock of PRACTICE, or any part thereof, nor shall PRACTICE permit its shareholders or partners to offer or seek to offer, or negotiate, entertain, or discuss any offer to combine any of their stock, assets, or practice interests, to any other person or entity. The individual who executes this letter on behalf of PRACTICE represents and warrants that he/she is authorized to execute this letter on behalf of PRACTICE.

4. **Press Release:** Partners shall jointly prepare, and determine the timing of, any press release or other announcement to the public relating to the execution of this letter or any transaction arising therefrom. No party hereto will issue any press release or make any other public announcement relating to the transactions contemplated by this letter

without the prior written consent of each other party hereto, except that any party may make any disclosure required to be made by it under applicable law if it determines in good faith that it is appropriate to do so and gives prior notice to each other party hereto.

5. **Binding and Nonbinding Provisions:** Except for Paragraphs 2, 3, and 4, which shall be legally binding in accordance with their terms, this letter is not intended to, and shall not, constitute or create a binding legal obligation or obligation to reach a binding obligation on the part of either PRACTICE, and the understanding set forth herein is subject to execution of the agreements contemplated by this letter. All documents and agreements to be developed pursuant to this letter shall be subject to the mutual agreement of the parties in their sole and absolute discretion. This letter is written with the understanding that definitive agreements shall control matters contemplated herein, which agreements and their precise wording shall be mutually negotiated and shall include items described in this letter and such additional items as negotiated and shall include items described in this letter and such additional items as to which the parties may mutually agree. Neither the expenditure of funds nor the undertaking of actions consistent with this letter shall be regarded as the partial performance of a binding agreement or entitle the party expending funds or taking action to assert claims for reimbursement or damages against the other party relating to such expenditure of funds or actions.

Please indicate your acceptance of the terms and conditions of this letter by signing in the space provided below. This proposal shall expire NUMBER days from DATE OF EXECUTION OF AGREEMENT, without any further action by _____, if not earlier executed by PRACTICE. This letter may be signed in counterparts, all of which taken together shall constitute one instrument, and any of the parties hereto may execute this letter by signing any such counterpart. This letter shall become effective upon execution by all parties hereto.

Signed by:

_____   _____
_____   _____
_____   _____
_____   _____
_____   _____
_____   _____

BY: _____   BY: _____
      President and CEO   PHYSICIAN NAME, M.D.

Letter of Intent A: Employment with Practice Acquisition

DATE

PHYSICIAN'S FULL NAME, M.D.
ADDRESS
CITY, STATE, ZIP CODE

Re: Affiliation Arrangement with Sample Hospital

Dear Dr. PHYSICIAN LAST NAME:

We are pleased with your interest in an affiliation with SAMPLE HOSPI-TAL (SH) or an affiliate thereof and stand ready to assist you toward this end. We look forward to providing an arrangement which will be mutually beneficial to both you and our patients and which allows you to concentrate on the practice of medicine while meeting your personal needs and career goals.

In summary of our preliminary conversations and to assist each of us in making our definite plans and agreements, we have committed to writing the following points, which describe the terms of a relationship that would be acceptable to SH and, we hope, acceptable to you. We propose the following.

Practice Acquisition

1. The practice assets to be acquired by SH in this transaction will be acquired at fair market value as determined by a qualified third-party appraiser.

2. We anticipate that an asset purchase agreement and other required documents for concluding this transaction will be entered into no later than DATE, with the closing and transfer to be no later than DATE, or at some other mutually agreed upon time.

3. In keeping with the patient needs of SH (e.g., senior care, community need), you will maintain your current practice location during a transition period to be mutually agreed upon by the parties.

-OR-

In keeping with the (e.g. senior care, community need) mission of SH, the current practice site will be maintained. SH will handle all maintenance and other occupancy-related items.

Employment Agreement

1. You will agree to be directly employed by SH or an affiliate thereof at (e.g., SH Senior Health Center). An employment agreement for your services will be available for a period of five (5) years renewable for an additional NUMBER years with a base compensation component in the amount of $DOLLAR AMOUNT. The base salary will be adjusted annually according to the Consumer Price Index (CPI) plus one percent (1.0%).

2. In addition to the base compensation component, an incentive compensation component will be available, based on your personal productivity and other goals to be agreed upon.

3. Additional employment benefits will include the availability of the SH pension plan, health insurance (for you and your family), and life insurance package of benefits as is made available to all employees of SH, as described on the attached schedule.

4. An amount not to exceed $DOLLAR AMOUNT will be provided as an expense account for reasonable and necessary professional expenses to be allocated at your discretion for continuing medical education, dues and subscriptions, travel and meetings, and similar expense items.

5. Deferred compensation in the amount of $DOLLAR AMOUNT will be payable to you upon completion of the full NUMBER-year term of the employment agreement, subject to the terms of the SH deferred compensation plan.

6. In keeping with the community-based and geriatric care mission of SH, you will practice from SH Senior Center and maintain your med-

ical staff privileges with SAMPLE HOSPITAL. You will spend approximately fifty percent (50%) of your time seeing patients in the SH Senior Center. You will maintain your medical directorship at Sample Nursing Home and will work closely with other physicians in seeing patients at other nursing homes. Approximately fifty percent (50%) of your time will be spent in following patients in the various area nursing homes with which the hospital has an arrangement.

7. You will receive four (4) weeks of vacation each year and one (1) week each year for continuing medical education.

8. An on-call arrangement will be available in which you will share the responsibilities with at least two (2) other physicians.

9. The billing and administrative aspects related to your practice will be handled by the hospital.

10. The cost of required professional liability insurance acceptable to SH will be provided by SH.

11. You will agree not to practice medicine or provide services related to the medical field within NUMBER miles of the hospital and practice site for a period of NUMBER years following the termination of this agreement.

12. You will be required to join the SH Independent Practitioner Association (IPA).

It is our understanding that you are currently employed at (associated with) PRESENT EMPLOYER. Although we have never attempted to persuade you to breach any existing written employment contract or other agreement to which you are a party in order to affiliate with SH, we are pleased that you have indicated an interest in pursuing an affiliation relationship with SH. We believe that SH's patients would benefit from this relationship.

The terms contained in this letter are intended as summaries of our proposed affiliation and are subject to more detailed provisions, which will be specified in the formal agreements between you and SH. If a conflict exists between the terms of this letter and the terms of the formal agreements, the latter documents will control.

From and after the date of execution by all parties of this letter until the closing date, you agree not to solicit, negotiate, discuss, continue, encourage, or accept any other proposal or offer relating to a transaction similar to the transactions contemplated herein.

If you understand and agree to the above proposal, I would appreciate your signing and returning one copy of this letter to me. Should you have any questions or have any additions or changes, please call me at your earliest convenience so that we might adjust this letter in a mutually satisfactory fashion. When I have received a signed version of this letter from you, I will immediately cause the asset purchase agreement, employment agreement, and other required documents for closing to be prepared.

It is our hope that we might conclude our arrangement soon and enjoy a long and mutually beneficial relationship. I will look forward to hearing from you at your earliest convenience. Thank you again for your continuing cooperation and interest in this matter.

Sincerely,

Sample Hospital of Anytown, Inc.

BY: _____

    John Doe
    President & Chief Executive Officer

I have read the above letter and it accurately represents my understanding regarding the sale of my practice and my subsequent employment agreement with SAMPLE HOSPITAL.

_____   Date: _____

PHYSICIAN'S FULL NAME, M.D.

Letter of Intent B: Option A = Employment and Option B = Affiliation

DATE

PHYSICIAN'S FULL NAME, M.D.
ADDRESS
CITY, STATE, ZIP CODE

Re: Affiliation Arrangement

Dear Dr. PHYSICIAN'S LAST NAME:

It has been a pleasure discussing with you your interest in pursuing a closer affiliation of your practice with SAMPLE HOSPITAL (SH). We look forward to providing an arrangement that will be mutually beneficial to both parties while meeting your needs and career goals.

It is our understanding that you are currently employed at (associated with) PRESENT EMPLOYER. Although we have never attempted to persuade you to breach any existing written employment contract to which you are a party in order to affiliate with SH, we are pleased that you have indicated an interest in pursuing an affiliation relationship with SAMPLE HOSPITAL. We believe that SH's patients would benefit from this relationship.

The terms contained in this letter are intended as summaries of our proposed affiliation and are subject to more detailed provisions, which will be specified in the formal agreements between you and SH. If a conflict exists between the terms of this letter and the terms of the formal agreements, the latter documents will control. In summary of our conversations and to assist each of us in making our definite plans and agreements, we have committed to writing the following points, which describe the terms of a relationship that we believe would be acceptable to SH and, we hope, acceptable to you. We propose the following two (2) options.

Option A

1. You will agree to be directly employed by SH at SH Senior Health Center. An employment agreement for your services will be available for a period of five (5) years with a guaranteed base compensation component based on the fair market value of your services in the local market and reflecting your experience and capabilities in the annual amount of $120,000.00. The base salary will be adjusted annually according to the Consumer Price Index (CPI) plus one percent (1.0%).

2. An incentive compensation component will be based on your personal productivity and other goals we have agreed upon.

3. Additional employment benefits will include the availability of the SH pension plan, health insurance for you and your family, and life insurance package of benefits that is made available to all employees of SH.

4. An amount not to exceed $DOLLAR AMOUNT will be provided as an expense account for professional expenses to be allocated at your discretion for continuing medical education, dues and subscriptions, travel and meetings, and similar expense items.

5. Deferred compensation in the amount of $DOLLAR AMOUNT will be set aside annually, during the term of the employment agreement, payable upon completion of the full five-year (5-year) term of the employment agreement.

6. In keeping with the community-based and geriatric care mission of SH, you will practice from SH Senior Center in Acme Plaza and maintain your medical staff privileges with SAMPLE HOSPITAL. You will spend approximately fifty percent (50%) of your time seeing patients in the SH Senior Center. You will maintain your medical directorship at Sample Nursing Home and will work closely with other physicians in seeing patients at other nursing homes. Approximately fifty percent (50%) of your time will be spent in following patients in the various area nursing homes with which the hospital has an arrangement.

7. You will receive four (4) weeks of vacation each year and one (1) week each year for continuing medical education.

8. An on-call arrangement will be available in which you will share the responsibilities with at least two (2) other physicians.

9. The billing and administrative aspects of your practice will be handled by the hospital.

10. Professional liability insurance comparable to your current policy will be provided.

11. You will be required to sign a covenant not to compete that stipulates you will not practice medicine or provide services related to the medical field within NUMBER miles of the hospital or practice site for a period of NUMBER years following the termination of this agreement.

12. You will be required to join the SH Independent Practitioner Association (IPA).

Option B

1. To assist you in maintaining an independent private practice, SH will be pleased to assist you in the transition from your current practice setting into an individual private practice.

2. SH will help identify potential practice office locations, provide insight into the real estate market conditions, and assist you in obtaining and setting up offices for your practice.

3. Billing and claims resolution services, accounting, and management services will be provided for your new practice at favorable market rates.

4. SH will arrange for a practice assessment engagement to enhance operations.

5. You will become affiliated with the SH Independent Practitioner Association (IPA), which will provide assistance to your practice in the negotiation of managed care contracts.

6. Computer linkage to the hospital will be established, which will allow up-to-date test results and other pertinent patient information.

7. Marketing studies will be provided to assist your practice in identifying patient needs in your specific service area.

8. Assistance in the hiring, interviewing, training, and retention of employees will be made available to the practice.

9. You will be included in the SH group purchasing network which will ease the burden and cost of acquiring medical supplies.

From and after the date of execution by all parties of this letter until the closing date, you agree not to solicit, negotiate, discuss, continue, encourage, or accept any other proposal or offer relating to a transaction similar to the transactions contemplated herein.

If you understand and agree to one (1) of the two (2) set forth options, I would appreciate your signing and returning one copy of this letter to me with your indication below as to which option you wish to pursue. Should you have any questions or have any additions or changes, please call me at your earliest convenience so that we might adjust this letter in a mutually satisfactory fashion. When I have received a signed version of this letter from you, I will immediately begin the process of developing the necessary documentation for the transaction.

I look forward to concluding an arrangement soon and developing a long and bountiful relationship between you and SH. I will look forward to hearing from you at your earliest convenience. Thank you again for your continuing cooperation and interest in this matter.

Sincerely,

_____

John Doe
President & Chief Executive Officer

I have read the above letter and it accurately represents my understanding regarding the affiliation of my practice with Sample Hospital.

_____   Date: _____
PHYSICIAN'S FULL NAME, M.D.

Option A _____   Option B _____

Letter of Intent C:
Employment—
No Practice Acquisition

DATE

PHYSICIAN'S FULL NAME, M.D.
ADDRESS
CITY, STATE, ZIP CODE

Re: Affiliation Arrangement

Dear Dr. PHYSICIAN'S LAST NAME:

It has been a pleasure discussing with you your interest in pursuing a closer affiliation of your practice with SAMPLE HOSPITAL (SH). We look forward to providing an arrangement that will be mutually beneficial to both parties while meeting your needs and career goals.

In summary of our conversations and to assist each of us in making our definite plans and agreements, we have committed to writing the following points, which describe the terms of a relationship that we believe would be acceptable to SH and, we hope, acceptable to you. We propose the following.

1. You will agree to be directly employed by SH or an affiliate thereof at (e.g., SH Senior Health Center). An employment agreement for your services will be available for a period of five (5) years renewable for an additional five (5) years with a base compensation component in the amount of $DOLLAR AMOUNT. The base salary will be adjusted

annually according to the Consumer Price Index (CPI) plus one percent (1.0%).

2. In addition to the base compensation component, an incentive compensation component will be available, based on your personal productivity and other goals to be agreed upon.

3. Additional employment benefits will include the availability of the SH pension plan, health insurance (for you and your family), and life insurance package of benefits as is made available to all employees of SH as described on the attached schedule.

4. An amount not to exceed $DOLLAR AMOUNT will be provided as an expense account for reasonable and necessary professional expenses to be allocated at your discretion for continuing medical education, dues and subscriptions, travel and meetings, and similar expense items.

5. Deferred compensation in the amount of $DOLLAR AMOUNT will be payable to you upon completion of the full five-year (5-year) term of the employment agreement, subject to the terms of the SH deferred compensation plan.

6. In keeping with the community-based and _____ (e.g., geriatric care) mission of SH, you will practice from _____ (e.g., SH Senior Center) and maintain your medical staff privileges with SAMPLE HOSPITAL. You will spend approximately _____ (e.g., fifty percent) of your time seeing patients in the _____ (e.g., SH Senior Center). You will _____ (e.g., maintain your medical directorship at Sample Nursing Home and will work closely with other physicians in seeing patients at other nursing homes). Approximately _____ (e.g., fifty percent) of your time will be spent _____ (e.g., in following patients in the various area nursing homes with which the hospital has an arrangement).

7. You will receive four (4) weeks of vacation each year and one (1) week each year for continuing medical education.

8. An on-call arrangement will be available in which you will share the responsibilities with at least two (2) other physicians.

9. The billing and administrative aspects related to your practice will be handled by the hospital.

10. The cost of required professional liability insurance acceptable to SH will be provided by SH.

11. You will agree not to practice medicine or provide services related to the medical field within NUMBER miles of the hospital and practice site for a period of NUMBER years following the termination of this agreement.

12. You will be required to join the SH Independent Practitioner Association (IPA).

13. Should there be assets related to your current arrangement that will need to be sold or disposed of, we will be pleased to either assist you in the transaction or assist you in transitioning out of your current practice.

It is our understanding that you are currently employed at (associated with) PRESENT EMPLOYER. Although we have never attempted to persuade you to breach any existing written employment contract or other agreement to which you are a party in order to affiliate with SH, we are pleased that you have indicated an interest in pursuing an affiliation relationship with SAMPLE HOSPITAL. We believe that SH's patients would benefit from this relationship.

The terms contained in this letter are intended as summaries of our proposed affiliation and are subject to more detailed provisions, which will be specified in the formal agreements between you and SH. If a conflict exists between the terms of this letter and the terms of the formal agreements, the latter documents will control.

From and after the date of execution by all parties of this letter until the closing date, you agree not to solicit, negotiate, discuss, continue, encourage, or accept any other proposal or offer relating to a transaction similar to the transactions contemplated herein.

If you understand and agree to the above proposal, I would appreciate your signing and returning one copy of this letter to me. Should you have any questions or have any additions or changes, please call me at your earliest convenience so that we might adjust this letter in a mutually satisfactory fashion. When I have received a signed version of this letter from you, I will immediately cause the employment agreement and other required documents for closing to be prepared.

It is our hope that we might conclude our arrangement soon and enjoy a long and mutually beneficial relationship. I will look forward to hearing from you at your earliest convenience. Thank you again for your continuing cooperation and interest in this matter.

Sincerely,

Sample Hospital of Anytown

BY: _____
John Doe
President & Chief Executive Officer

I have read the above letter and it accurately represents my understanding regarding the sale of my practice and my subsequent employment agreement with SAMPLE HOSPITAL.

_____   Date: _____
PHYSICIAN'S FULL NAME, M.D.

Letter of Intent D: Affiliation Arrangement

DATE

PHYSICIAN'S FULL NAME, M.D.
ADDRESS
CITY, STATE, ZIP CODE

Re: Affiliation Arrangement

Dear Dr. PHYSICIAN'S LAST NAME:

It has been a pleasure discussing with you your interest in pursuing a closer affiliation of your practice with Sample Hospital (SH). We look forward to providing an arrangement which will be mutually beneficial to both parties while meeting your needs and career goals.

It is our understanding that you are currently employed at (associated with) PRESENT EMPLOYER. Although we have never attempted to persuade you to breach any existing written employment contract to which you are a party in order to affiliate with SH, we are pleased that you have indicated an interest in pursuing an affiliation relationship with SAMPLE HOSPITAL. We believe that SH's patients would benefit from this relationship.

The terms contained in this letter are intended as summaries of our proposed affiliation and are subject to more detailed provisions, which will be specified in the formal agreements between you and SH. If a conflict exists between the terms of this letter and the terms of the formal agreements, the latter documents will control. In summary of our conversations and to assist each of us in making our definite plans and agreements, we have committed to writing the following points, which describe the terms of a relationship that we believe would be acceptable to SH and, we hope, acceptable to you. We propose the following.

1. To assist you in maintaining an independent private practice, SH will be pleased to assist you in the transition from your current practice setting into an individual private practice.

2. SH will help identify potential practice office locations, provide insight into the real estate market conditions, and assist you in obtaining and setting up offices for your practice.

3. Billing and claims resolution services, accounting, and management services will be provided for your new practice at favorable market rates.

4. SH will arrange for a practice assessment engagement to enhance operations.

5. You will become affiliated with the SH Independent Practitioner Association (IPA), which will provide assistance to your practice in the negotiation of managed care contracts.

6. Computer linkage to the hospital will be established, which will allow up-to-date test results and other pertinent patient information.

7. Marketing studies will be provided to assist your practice in identifying patient needs in your specific service area.

8. Assistance in the hiring, interviewing, training, and retention of employees will be made available to the practice.

9. You will be included in the SH group purchasing network, which will ease the burden and cost of acquiring medical supplies.

From and after the date of execution by all parties of this letter until the closing date, you agree not to solicit, negotiate, discuss, continue, encourage, or accept any other proposal or offer relating to a transaction similar to the transactions contemplated herein.

If you understand and agree to the above and are prepared to move forward, I would appreciate your signing and returning one copy of this letter to me. Should you have any questions or have any additions or changes, please call me at you earliest convenience so that we might adjust this letter in a mutually satisfactory fashion. When I have received a signed version of this letter from you, I will immediately begin the process of developing the necessary steps for the implementation of this arrangement.

I look forward to concluding an arrangement soon and developing a long and successful relationship between you and SH. I will look forward to hearing from you at your earliest convenience. Thank you again for your continuing cooperation and interest in this matter.

Sincerely,

_____

John Doe
President & Chief Executive Officer

I have read the above letter and it accurately represents my understanding regarding the affiliation of my practice with SAMPLE HOSPITAL.

_____   Date: _____
PHYSICIAN'S FULL NAME, M.D.

Consulting Engagement Pre-Engagement Acceptance Form

Prospective Client: _____

Completed by: _____ Date: _____

INSTRUCTIONS: This form should be completed for a prospective new client or a prospective engagement for an existing client. The person completing this checklist need only complete those parts of the form that apply to the proposed engagement.

I. PROSPECTIVE CLIENT DATA

[The following data should be obtained for the prospective client (the person or company that will be engaging the consultant). That client may not be the subject of the consulting engagement. Accordingly, a separate section of the form is designed for documenting information about the subject entity.]

Prospective Client's Name: _____ Phone No.: _____

Fax No.: _____

Business Address:_____

_____

Referral Source (how the consultant became aware of the potential engagement): _____

_____

Is the prospective client the subject entity?

_____ Yes   Proceed to Section II of this form (Consulting Services Subject Entity). The remaining portion of Section I does not need to be completed.

_____ No   Complete the remaining portion of Section I before proceeding to Section II

Briefly explain the prospective client's relationship to the subject entity (e.g., the client's ownership interest in the entity, if any; whether the entity is a proposed acquisition candidate of the entity, etc.): _____

_____

_____

Professional references of the prospective client. (This is optimal information. Some consultants may desire to obtain the names of the proposed client's attorney, CPA, and other business references.)

Reference Name: _____ Occupation: _____

Address: _____ Phone No.: _____

_____

Reference Name: _____ Occupation: _____

Address: _____ Phone No.: _____

_____

Reference Name: _____ Occupation: _____

Address: _____ Phone No.: _____

_____

II. SUBJECT ENTITY FOR CONSULTING SERVICES

(If the prospective client and the subject entity are the same, it is not necessary to repeat the data obtained in the preceding section of this form.)

Name of Subject Entity:_____

Type of Legal Entity (Corp., S Corp., LLC, Partnership, Proprietorship, etc.): _____

Business Address: _____

_____

Phone No.: _____ Fax No.: _____

Contacts at the entity with whom we would work (state name and title):

_____

_____

Brief description of the entity's business: _____

_____

_____

_____

_____

Entity's Accounting firm: _____

Address: _____

Phone No.: _____Contact: _____

Entity's Primary Attorney: _____

Address: _____

Phone No.: _____Contact: _____

Other References (optional): _____

Address: _____Phone No.: _____

III. SCOPE OF THE ENGAGEMENT

Briefly describe the purpose of the engagement (e.g., management assessment, operational review, physician integration/affiliation consulting, MIS assessment or implementation, valuation of a company for a proposed sale or acquisition, etc.).

_____

_____

Entity: _____

Describe any specific research data lacking which could affect the assessment of the financial or operational background and trends of the company.

_____

_____

Describe any other issue which will affect the scope of the engagement.

_____

_____

Describe the scope and nature of the report:
- [ ] Financial
- [ ] Managerial
- [ ] Operational
- [ ] Market Assessment
- [ ] Other

_____

_____

_____

Format of Report:
- [ ] Oral Presentation
- [ ] Informal or Interim Report
- [ ] Comprehensive, Formal Narrative Report
- [ ] Draft
- [ ] Other _____

What is the intended distribution of a written report? (check one)

_____ It will be restricted to internal use.

_____ It will be distributed to third parties.

Will historical or prospective financial statements be included in a written report? (check one) _____ Yes _____ No

Based on your knowledge of the subject entity, what methods appear to be appropriate for the engagement?

_____

_____

IV. ACCEPTANCE CONSIDERATIONS

	Yes	No
1. Are we aware of any independence problems or conflicts of interest?	_____	_____
2. Are we aware of any potential fee collection problems?	_____	_____
3. Is the expertise necessary to perform the engagement beyond our capabilities?	_____	_____

4. Is the staffing commitment required by the engagement beyond our capabilities?   _____   _____

5. Do the terms of the proposed engagement, including fee arrangements, violate applicable professional standards?   _____   _____

6. If there anything about the engagement that subjects us to undue legal risk or causes us to be uncomfortable about being associated with the engagement?   _____   _____

COMMENTS: A "yes" answer does not necessarily indicate that the prospective engagement should be rejected. However, for any "yes" answers, explain the steps that we plan to take to mitigate the situation—e.g., closer supervision, a substantial fee deposit before work can start, or use of specialists.

_____

_____

_____

_____

_____

_____

V. CONCLUSION

We should accept _____ not accept _____ the engagement.

Completed by: _____Date: _____

Approved by:* _____Date: _____

---

*If required by firm policy.

Bibliography

EMERGING HEALTHCARE ORGANIZATIONS SOURCES

Alexander, Jeffrey M. *Integrated health care delivery systems: a guide to successful strategies for hospital and physician collaboration.* New York, NY: Thompson Publishing Group, 1993.

Amatayakul, Margaret. *Managing integration and operations: a guide to quality health care systems.* Washington, D.C.: Thompson Publishing Group, 1995.

American Hospital Association. *Transforming health care delivery toward community care networks.* Chicago, IL: American Hospital Association Services, 1993.

Barnett, Albert E., et al. *Integration issues in physician/hospital affiliations.* Englewood, CO: Medical Group Management Association, 1993.

Becker, Scott. *Physician's managed care success manual: strategic options, alliances, and contracting issues.* St. Louis, MO: Mosby Year Book, 1999.

Brown, Montague, ed. *Physicians and management in health care.* Gaithersburg, MD: Aspen Publishers, 1992.

Capital survey of emerging healthcare organizations. Los Angeles, CA: Integrated Healthcare Report, Medical Group Management Association, and Ziegler Securities, 1994.

Coddington, Dean C.; Chapman, Cary R.; Pokoski, Katherine M. *Making integrated health care work: case studies.* Englewood, CO: Center for Research in Ambulatory Health Care Administration, 1996.

Coddington, Dean C.; Moore, Keith D.; Fischer, Elizabeth A. *Making integrated health care work.* Englewood, CO: Center for Research in Ambulatory Health Care Administration, 1996.

———. *Integrated health care: reorganizing the physician, hospital and health plan relationship.* Englewood, CO: Center for Research in Ambulatory Health Care Administration, 1994.

The corporation of health care delivery: the hospital-physician relationship. [S.1.]: American Hospital Association Services, 1986.

Deloitte & Touche. *U.S. hospitals and the future of health care: a continuing opinion survey.* 7th ed. 1998.

Developing ambulatory healthcare facilities: for medical groups, hospitals, and integrated delivery systems: a practical guidebook. Madison, WI: Marshall Erdman & Associates, 1996.

Directory of physician groups & networks: covering IPAs, PHOs, MSOs, PPMCs, and large group practices. Irvine, CA: Center for Healthcare Information, 1998.

Engstrom, Paul; Droste, Therese M. *Building effective medical networks: medical network strategy report 1996 yearbook.* Santa Barbara, CA: COR Healthcare Resources, 1996.

Evans, Christopher J.; DePorter, F. Gene; Wilson, Robert L. *Integrated community healthcare: next generation strategies for developing provider networks.* The HFMA Healthcare Financial Management Series. New York, NY: McGraw Hill, 1997.

Freeman, Beth. *The IPA financial operations manual.* 1st ed. Oakland, CA: National IPA Coalition, 1997.

Gammel, J. D. *The internist's guide to practice integration.* (Strategies for Success in Managed Care.) Washington, D.C.: American Society of Internal Medicine, 1995.

Goldstein, Douglas. *From physician bonding to alliances: building new physician-hospital relationships.* Alexandria, VA: Capitol Publications, 1992.

Gorey, Thomas M. *Management services organizations: cases and analysis.* Spotlight Series. Chicago, IL: Health Administration Press, 1997.

———. *Physician organizations: cases and analysis.* Spotlight Series. Chicago, IL: Health Administration Press, 1997.

Hospital-affiliated integrated delivery systems: formation, operation, and contracts handbook. AAHA Practice Guide Series, Volume 2. Chicago, IL: American Hospital Association Services Inc., 1995.

Kaluzny, Arnold D., et al. *Partners for the dance: forming strategic alliances in health care.* Ann Arbor, MI: Health Administration Press, 1995.

Key strategies and trends shaping the growth of PPMCs. Washington, D.C.: Atlantic Information Services, 1998.

Korenchuk, Keith M. *Management services organizations.* (Integration document design and analysis.) Englewood, CO: Medical Group Management Association, 1994.

———. *Physician-Hospital Organizations.* (Integration document design and analysis.) Englewood, CO: Medical Group Management Association, 1994.

———. *Transforming the delivery of health care: the integration process.* Englewood, CO: Medical Group Management Association, 1994.

Kovner, Anthony R.; Nenhauser, Duncan, eds. *Health services management: a book of cases.* 5th ed. Chicago, IL: Health Administration Press, 1997.

McCall-Perez, Fred. *Physician equity groups and other emerging entities: competitive organizational choices for physicians.* The HFMA Healthcare Financial Management Series. New York, NY: McGraw Hill, 1997.

A national initiative: the survey of hospital sponsored management services organizations. Cleveland, OH: Medimetrix, 1997.

O'Neil, Brooks G.; Manderfeld, T. Brett. *Physician practice management: searching for value.* Minneapolis, MN: Piper Jaffray, 1997.

———. *Physician practice management: just what the doctor ordered.* Minneapolis, MN: Piper Jaffray, 1995.

Peters, Gerald R. *Healthcare integration: a legal manual for constructing integrated organizations.* NHLA Focus Series. Washington, D.C.: National Health Lawyers Association, 1995.

Physician group practice joint ventures: survey results. [S.1.]: Ernst & Whinney, 1987.

PPMC yearbook. North Wales, PA: Sherlock Company, 1998.

Reich, Janet, ed. *Hospital/physician organizations: models for considerations.* Flagstaff, AZ: Reich Consulting, 1992.

Renz, Anne M. *Integration strategies for the medical practice: the physician's handbook to integration alternatives.* (Practice Success.) Norcross, GA: Coker Publishing, LLC, 1996.

Shih, Bruce John. *Healthcare transactions: a guide to mergers, acquisitions, & integration.* American Health Lawyers Association Cornerstone Series. Washington, D.C.: American Health Lawyers Association, 1998.

Sneed, James H.; Marx, David Jr. *Antitrust: challenge of the health care field.* NHLA Focus Series. Washington, D.C.: National Health Lawyers Association, 1990.

Strategic alignment: managing integrated health systems. Ann Arbor, MI: AUPHA Press/ Health Administration Press, 1994.

Stromberg, Ross E.; Boman, Carol R. *Joint ventures for hospitals and physicians: legal considerations.* Chicago, IL: American Hospital Association Services, 1986.

Unland, James J. *Physician/hospital transactions: the complete guide to planning, structuring and negotiating physician transactions.* Chicago, IL: Irwin Professional Publishing, 1994.

INTEGRATED DELIVERY SYSTEMS BIBLIOGRAPHY

"Antitrust laws: considerations but not barriers to integration." *Health care law newsletter,* Vol. 8, no. 10 (Oct. 1993), p. 20–27.

"Are IDSs paying too much for PCPs?: look again, expert survey says." *Healthcare systems strategy report,* Sept. 15, 1995, p. 7–9.

"Are the new integrated delivery networks working?" *St. Louis commerce,* Vol. 7, no. 11 (Nov. 1994), p. 25.

"Biggest HMO deals." *Jenks healthcare business report,* June 24, 1994, p. 2–3.

"Building the new health care delivery alliance." *Hospitals,* Vol. 68, no. 9 (May 5, 1994), p. 28–30, 32, 34.

"Capital cost indicators." *Pulse,* 1995.

"Capital survey of emerging healthcare organization." *Ziegler securities,* 1994, p. 1–26.

"Capitation, integration, and managed care lessons from early experiments." *Journal of the American Medical Association,* Mar. 27, 1996.

"Changes in the HMO industry." *Interstudy competitive edge 5.2 Part I: HMO directory.* InterStudy Publications, Aug. 1995, p. viii–xii.

"The 'clinics without walls' controversy." *Integrated healthcare report,* Aug. 1993, p. 1–9.

"Consolidation mania: major healthcare deals surge to record high of $60 billion." *Jenks healthcare business report,* Vol. 5, no. 8 (Jan. 24, 1995), p. 1–4.

"Coventry Corp." *Jenks healthcare business report,* Nov. 24, 1994, p. 8.

"Forming risk-bearing PSOs one option for rural providers." *BNA's managed care reporter,* Vol. 2 (Mar. 13, 1996), p. 257–258.

"Full-risk contracting is the goal for Connecticut's newest delivery system." *Health care capitation report,* Vol. 3, no. 12 (Apr. 1997), p. 1–4.

"Garvey group finds Florida physicians ready to form, fund own HMO." Sept. 11, 1995.

"Have valid reasons for forming or joining 'clinic without walls.' " *Professional practice today,* Sept. 1993, p. 4, 6.

"Health Systems International to acquire Greater Atlantic, a Philadelphia-area HMO, and other for-profit subsidiaries of Graduate Health System, for $100 million in cash and notes." *Business Wire,* July 11, 1995.

"Healthcare shares are mostly mixed: Coram plunges." *Jenks healthcare business report,* Sept. 9, 1995, p. 3.

"Healthsource announces a letter of intent to purchase PACC HMO and PACC health plans and enter the northwest." July 26, 1995.

"Healthsource announces closing of its acquisition of Provident's group health business for $23.1 million and receives its HMO license in North Texas." *Business Wire,* June 1, 1995.

"The HMO picture: more consolidation, more growth, more government business." *Jenks healthcare business report,* Vol. 5, no. 13 (Apr. 9, 1995), p. 1–3.

"HMO purchased." *Caribbean update,* May 1995.

"Horizontal integration urged as first rural IDS step." *Physician manager,* Vol. 6, no. 10 (May 19, 1995).

"HSI to acquire HMO in Pennsylvania." Aug. 14, 1995, p. 40.

"Integrated delivery systems begin to emerge." *HMO/PPO directory,* 1995.

"An integrated delivery systems review: common problems to be addressed." *Health care law newsletter,* Vol. 10, no. 1 (Jan. 1995), p. 3–7. Matthew Bender & Co., Inc.

"Investment consideration: who will control the profit margin in healthcare."

"IRS breakthrough for foundations." *Integrated healthcare report,* Vol. 1, no. 2 (Feb. 1993), p. 1–4.

"Legal pitfalls too often ignored by wall-less groups." *Physician's advisory,* Vol. 93, no. 8 (Aug. 1993), p. 3.

"A look at the group practice without walls: a MOM mini seminar." *Medical office manager,* Vol. 8, no. 3 (Mar. 1994), p. 6–7.

"Managed care licensure, tax issues threaten IDS development." *BNA health care daily,* Nov. 7, 1995.

"Market needs influence network structure: integration efforts slowed by tradition, inexperience, consumer choice." *Integrated health care delivery systems,* Vol. 4, no. 2 (Oct. 1996), p. 1–2.

"Medical practice mergers." *Mechanics of merger appraisals,* p. 121–129.

"Medical practice valuation, IDS update feature in IRS continuing education text." *The bureau of national affairs,* Vol. 4, no. 35 (Aug. 31, 1995), p. 1336–1338.

"New Mexico 'clinic without walls.'" *Integrated healthcare report,* Vol. 1, no. 2 (Feb. 1993), p. 12–13.

"Pacificare Health Systems Inc." *Jenks healthcare business report,* May 9, 1995, p. 8.

Prepared statement of Gail Warden, president, Henry Ford Health System, Detroit, Michigan, and chairman of the American Hospital Association before the House Committee on Ways and Means on saving Medicare. Sept. 22, 1995.

"Profiting from consolidation the big theme at Alex Brown seminar." *Health alliance alert,* Vol. 10, no. 10 (May 26, 1995).

"Protective Life announces agreement to acquire dental HMO." *Business Wire,* Oct. 30, 1995.

"Ramsey-HMO Inc. and Pacificare Health Systems Inc." *Jenks healthcare business report,* Jan. 9, 1994, p. 8.

"Regional news (St. Paul)." *Modern healthcare,* Aug. 19, 1996, p. 22.

"Rochester, Minnesota." *Modern healthcare,* Mar. 10, 1997, p. 64.

"Seattle PPO nabs HMO license, to form new dental subsidiary." *Managed care week,* Vol. 5, no. 5 (Jan. 30, 1995). Atlantic Information Services, Inc.

"Seen one? you haven't seen 'em all." *Medical economics,* Jan. 27, 1997, p. 36.

"Self-assessment of integrated system boards." *Health system leader,* Vol. 1, no. 3 (May 1994), p. 15–17.

"Sharp Healthcare: Six years after the foundation." *Integrated healthcare report,* Aug. 1992, p. 8–9.

"Stephen M. Shortell: do integrated healthcare systems add value?" *Integrated healthcare report,* Sept. 1996, p. 3–7.

"Temblors in lotus land: lessons for other markets abound in this vast laboratory of system change." *Hospitals health networks,* Vol. 69, no. 15 (Aug. 5, 1995), p. 58.

"Texas hospital forming nation's first pediatric HMO." *Managed care week,* Vol. 5, no. 32 (Sept. 11, 1995).

"Texas: Houston hospital to form first children's HMO." *Health line,* Sept. 6, 1995.

"Tips on how to avoid the pitfalls of a group practice without walls." *Medical staff strategy report,* Vol. 2, no. 9 (Sept. 1993), p. 2–4.

"United Healthcare Corp." *Jenks healthcare business report,* Sept. 24, 1994, p. 8.

"United Healthcare's latest deal may signal new round in managed care consolidation." *Jenks healthcare business report,* Vol. 5, no. 19 (July 9, 1995), p. 1–2.

"University hospital blurs Richmond, VA, battle lines." *Modern healthcare,* Vol. 26, no. 17 (Apr. 22, 1996), p. 40–41.

"Virginia doctors create an HMO of their own; Medical Society of Virginia forming PHP Virginia Inc. health maintenance organization." Vol. 96, no. 3 (July 1995), p. 16.

" 'Virtual capitation' is future of managed care payment." *BNA's managed care reporter,* Vol. 2 (Aug. 28, 1996), p. 843.

"Wall-less groups, PHOs and MSOs: much talk but little action." *Physician's advisory,* Vol. 94, no. 3 (Mar. 1994), p. 3–4.

Aseltyne, William J.; Peters, Gerald R. "Tax exemption and integrated delivery systems." *Topics in health care financing,* Vol. 20, no. 3 (Mar. 22, 1994), p. 46.

Bader, Barry S. "Physician involvement in the governance of integrated systems." *Health system leader,* Vol. 1, no. 3 (May 1994), p. 4–14.

Barnett, Albert E. "The integration of health care as a model for the future." *Medical group management journal,* Vol. 38, no. 4 (July/Aug. 1991), p. 16, 18.

Bazzoli, Fred. "Market pressures will continue to fuel networking." *Health data management,* Dec. 1996, p. 181.

Beck, Leif C. "A 'group without walls': sounds great but will it work?" *Physician's advisory,* Vol. 91, no. 12 (Dec. 1991), p. 8.

Bohlmann, Robert C. "Health care delivery in the 1990s—putting the pieces together." *Medical group management journal,* Vol. 38, no. 4 (July/Aug. 1991), p. 64–65, 67.

Broccolo, Bernadette M. "IDS planning: tax, fraud and abuse and Stark implications." *American Academy of Healthcare Attorneys,* June 25–28, 1995, p. 9, 78–79.

Bromberg, Robert S. "MSOs & 'clinic without walls.' " *Integrated healthcare report,* Vol. 1, no. 9 (Sept. 1993), p. 12–17.

Campos-Outcalt, Doug. "Occupational health epidemiology and objectives for the year 2000." *Occupational health,* Vol. 21, no. 2 (June 1994), p. 213–223.

Cerne, Frank. "Are your integration efforts all talk and little action?" *Hospitals,* Vol. 68, no. 12 (June 20, 1994), p. 29.

Chase, Brett. "Blue Cross eyes future of Iowa's insurance." *Business dateline,* Vol. 89, no. 3 (Jan. 18, 1993), p. 1.

Cimasi, Robert James. "Planning for successful practice integration." *Physician recruiter,* Dec. 1995, p. 24–26, 47.

Coddington, Dean C.; Moore, Keith D.; Fischer, Elizabeth A. "Integrated health care systems: the key characteristics." *Medical group management journal,* Vol. 40, no. 6 (Nov./Dec. 1993), p. 76–78, 80.

Coddington, Dean C.; Moore, Keith D.; Fischer, Elizabeth A. "Optimizing primary care services." *Making integrated health care work,* p. 37–41, 45–55.

Cohen, Richard L. "Clinic without walls improves physician satisfaction." *Healthcare marketing report,* Vol. 9, no. 6 (June 1991), p. 19–21.

Coile, Russell C. "Assessing healthcare market trends and capital needs: 1996–2000." *Healthcare financial management,* Aug. 1995, p. 60–62, 64–65.

Collins, Hobart; Johnson, Bruce A. "How to save distressed IDS-physician marriages: a case study." *Healthcare financial management,* Apr. 1998, p. 29–31.

Cummings, Elizabeth. "3 area hospital systems form new type of HMO." *Central Penn business journal,* Vol. 11, no. 8 (Apr. 7, 1995), p. 6.

Davis, Gary Scott; Holmquest, Donald L. "IDS implementing agreements." *Critical steps in managed care contracting: a looseleaf guide,* p. 34–44.

De Lollis, Barbara. "Pacificare acquires big Valley presence; Valucare, the HMO affiliated with Saint Agnes, is second only to Kaiser Permanente in the Valley." *Fresno bee,* Apr. 4, 1995, p. A1.

deGuzman, Meg Matheny. "Are specialists staging a comeback?" *Health system leader,* Apr. 1997, p. 4–13.

DeMuro, Paul R. "Management services organizations (DeMuro)." *Topics in health care financing,* Vol. 20, no. 3 (Spring 1994), p. 19–27.

DeMuro, Paul R.; Owens, James F. "Special Medicare reimbursement and fraud and abuse considerations for management services organizations, medical foundations, and integrated delivery systems." *Topics in health care financing,* Vol. 20, no. 3 (Spring 1994), p. 54–60.

Desmond, Kathryn J. "Provider-based integrated systems not yet profitable." *BNA's managed care reporter,* Vol. 2 (Aug. 14, 1996), p. 782–784.

DeWitt, John. "Managed care comes to outland; small hospitals form rural HMO." *Arizona business gazette,* Aug. 17, 1995, p. 1.

Dowell, Michael A. "Legal issues affecting integrated delivery systems—a primer." *Group practice journal,* May/June 1995.

Downs, Peter. "Acquisitive hospitals want to integrate." *Medical business journal,* Oct. 1996, p. 1, 4.

Downs, Peter. "Intangibles make the difference." *Medical business journal,* Vol. 9, no. 7 (Jan. 1997), p. 1, 4–7.

Eskin, Evelyn. "The ABCs of management services organization." *Health network alliance sourcebook,* 1997, p. 101–106.

Forster, Robert J. "Putting together a 'group practice without walls.'" *Internist,* Vol. 29, no. 9 (Oct. 1988), p. 12–15.

Freudenheim, Milt. "Doctors, on offensive, for H.M.O.'s." *New York times,* Mar. 7, 1995, p. 1.

Gillies, Robin R., et al. "Conceptualizing and measuring integration: findings from the health systems integration study." *Hospital health services administration,* Vol. 38, no. 4 (Dec. 22, 1993), p. 467.

Glenn, John K. "Hospitals and the 'ecology' of primary care." *Hospital health services administration,* Vol. 34, no. 3 (Fall 1989), p. 371–384.

Graham, Judith. "Health systems ready to acquire east coast HMO." *Denver post,* Jul. 12, 1995, p. C1.

Green, Jason; Barnett, Rebecca. "A physician's perspective on capitation." *Physician executive,* Vol. 21, no. 7 (July 1995), p. 5.

Greene, Jay. "Clinical integration may not be needed for system growth—study." *Modern healthcare,* Vol. 26, no. 10 (Mar. 4, 1996), p. 48.

Griggs, Ted. "Franciscans acquire 50% of HMO." *The advocate,* Sept. 20, 1995, p. 12A.

Harris, Richard M. "Models for medical practice integration." *Physician executive,* Vol. 20, no. 8 (Aug. 1994), p. 18–24.

Hastings, Douglas A.; Leopold, Ann. "Developing integrated delivery systems: an era of change in hospital-physician relationships." *Physician executive,* Vol. 18, no. 6 (Nov./Dec. 1992), p. 18–21.

Heavenrich, Adam. "Seeking a strong partner: a guide to practice affiliations and mergers." *Family practice management,* Vol. 2, no. 7 (July/Aug. 1995), p. 54–63.

Hilgers, David W. "Legal obstacles to medical communities' full participation in managed care: hospitals versus physicians: who will control managed care contracting?" *Journal of health care finance,* Vol. 21, no. 3 (Mar. 22, 1995), p. 9.

Hiltzik, Michael A. "HMO acquisition shows there's still big money in medicine." *Los Angeles times,* Apr. 5, 1995, p. 1.

Hitchner, Carl H. "IDS panel: the formation of integrated delivery systems." *American Academy of Healthcare Attorneys,* Jun. 25–28, 1995, p. 111, 126, 128.

Hodapp, Thomas E. "Physician practice management and the wave to integrated delivery systems." 1993. Robertson Stephens & Company: San Francisco, CA.

Howatt, Glenn. "Allina retooling to unify services." *Star tribune,* Dec. 2, 1995, p. 1D.

Howatt, Glenn. "Burgeoning health: have health-care reforms wrought a company with too much power?" *Star Tribune,* Jul. 11, 1994, p. 1D.

Hudson, Terese. "A Model for integration: group practices without walls offer unique problems and possibilities." *Hospitals health networks,* Vol. 68, no. 10 (May 20, 1994), p. 52, 54–56.

Hull, Brenda. "Do integrated delivery systems add value: research findings indicate: not yet." *Medical group management update,* Dec. 1996.

Ingram, Richard. "The make or buy decision for finance, administration, and data management support services." *Managing the IDS: finance, data systems, and benefits administration,* p. 4–24.

Jaklevic, Mary Chris. "Doctors try to own managed care: fed up with big for-profit HMOs, physicians across the nation are forming their own plans." *Modern healthcare,* Apr. 24, 1995, p. 63.

James, Cal. "Lessons learned from 10 years of MSO development." *Healthcare financial management,* Sept. 1996, p. 36, 38.

Japsen, Bruce. "Creation of new HMOs picks up steam, fueled by reform, market forces." *Modern healthcare,* Jun. 13, 1994, p. 45–46.

Johnson, Bruce A. "The legal issues of integrated delivery systems." *Medical group management journal,* Jan./Feb. 1995, p. 17–18, 20, 22.

Johnson, Bruce A.; Schryver, Darrell L. "Positioning for vertical integration through clinics 'without walls.' " *Medical group management journal,* Vol. 41, no. 3 (May/June 1994), p. 80, 82, 84.

Jordan, John F. "The physician organized delivery system empowers physicians." *Group practice journal,* Jan./Feb. 1997, p. 32, 35–36.

Kenkel, Paul J. "The systematic approach: physician-hospital collaborations increase, work to capture managed-care contracts." *Modern healthcare,* Apr. 4, 1994, p. 59–60, 62, 64–65.

Levick, Diane. "Norwalk company to acquire HMO firm." *Hartford courant,* Mar. 31, 1995, p. F1.

Lumsdon, Kevin. "Framing the issues: corralling the clinical integration beast." *Hospitals,* Vol. 68, no. 1 (Aug. 5, 1994), p. 48–49.

Lutz, Sandy. "Eight New Orleans hospitals team up against for-profits." *Modern healthcare,* Vol. 26, no. 17 (Apr. 22, 1996), p. 25.

Lutz, Sandy. "Tax-exempts in New Orleans aim to compete via alliance." *Modern healthcare,* Vol. 26, no. 17 (Apr. 22, 1996), p. 42, 44.

Mangan, Doreen. "The rapidly changing world of clinics without walls." *Medical economics,* p. 3–7.

McCormick, Brian. "Law thwart physician networks." *American medical news,* Vol. 38, no. 33 (Sept. 4, 1995), p. 1.

McKinney, Leigh. "Group practice without walls: FPs find strength in numbers." *Family practice management,* Vol. 1, no. 4 (Apr. 1994), p. 54–62.

Mjoseth, Jeannine. "Insurance regulation: NAIC creates body of regulation to address managed care entities." *BNA health care daily,* Oct. 5, 1995.

Montague, Jim. "Can purchasing alliances adapt?" *Hospitals health networks,* Vol. 69, no. 16 (Aug. 20, 1995), p. 30.

Morrissey, John. "HMO acquisition in N.H. gets antitrust ok with strings." *Modern healthcare,* Oct. 23, 1995, p. 6.

Naisbitt, John. " 'Clinic without walls' a futuristic model." *Integrated healthcare report,* Dec. 1992, p. 1–7.

Niederman, Gerald A.; Johnson, Bruce A. "Integrated provider networks—a primer." *Medical group management journal,* Vol. 41, no. 6 (Nov./Dec. 1994), p. 62, 64, 66, 68.

Olmos, David R. "Rival companies duel to acquire health net." *Los Angeles times,* Dec. 1994, p. 1.

Ottensmeyer, David J. "Governance of the integrated health care system: a new governance issue for group practice." *Group practice journal,* Jan./Feb. 1993.

Owens, James F. "Miscellaneous legal issues affecting integrated delivery systems, foundations, and management services organizations." *Topics in health care financing,* Vol. 20, no. 3 (Spring 1994), p. 61–69.

Pallarito, Karen. "Babes in managed-care land: provider-sponsored networks are stepping cautiously into risk contracting." *Modern healthcare,* Nov. 18, 1996, p. 34–36, 38, 40.

Riddick, Frank A.; Davidson, Richard J. "Physicians and hospitals join forces for the future." *Group practice journal,* Jan./Feb. 1993.

Robinet, Jane-Ellen. "Tri-state health system might create Medicaid HMO." *Pittsburgh business times,* Vol. 15, no. 5 (Sept. 4, 1995), p. 4.

Rynne, Terrence J. "Bringing an integrated system to market." *Healthcare forum,* Vol. 38, no. 6 (Nov./Dec. 1995), p. 52–59.

Schieble, Mark T.; Driscoll, Thomas L. "Tax exemption criteria for integrated delivery systems." *Health care law newsletter,* Vol. 8, no. 10 (Oct. 1993), p. 14–19.

Schryver, Darrell L.; Niederman, Gerald A.; Johnson, Bruce A. "Clinics 'without walls'—from concept to reality." *Group practice journal,* Jan./Feb. 1993.

Schupp, Meg. "Matching the occupational health product to the employer's needs." Mar. 1998, p. 1–36.

Scott, James L. "Integrated delivery system message is spreading throughout the nation." *Report on physician trends,* June 1994, p. 8–9.

Scott, Lisa. "4th Colorado hospital network formed." *Modern healthcare,* Apr. 1, 1996, p. 22.

Scott, Lisa. "Communities ask, 'what's in it for us?': systems will confront more lawsuits, questions about the value of integration." *Modern healthcare,* Jan. 6, 1997, p. 39.

Selby, Stephen E. "Management services organization for group practices." *Journal of ambulatory care management,* July 1996, p. 81–85.

Selis, Sara. "14 rural hospitals form consortium to run HMO." *Business first–Columbus,* Vol. 12, no. 8 (Oct. 23, 1995), p. 4.

Shinkman, Ron. "Health Systems International files for stock offering to acquire HMO." *Los Angeles business journal,* Vol. 16, no. 49 (Dec. 12, 1994), p. 8.

Simmons, Janice C. "Integrated delivery systems need to be alert to fraud and abuse." *Managing integration operations,* Dec. 1996, p. 4–5.

Slater, Pam. "Doctors to form their own HMO." *Sacramento bee,* Apr. 19, 1995, p. G1.

Sneider, Julie. "EyeCare One affiliate forms insurance plan for vision care." *Business journal–Milwaukee,* Vol. 10, no. 17 (Jan. 30, 1993), p. 2–3.

Valiant, Carrie. "Checklist: Stark II and anti-kickback issues in IDS." Aug. 1994, p. 43–46.

Weinstein, Matthew; Edley, Richard S. "Whither the solo and the group practice: IDS and the future of public sector initiatives." *Behavioral healthcare tomorrow,* Feb. 1997, p. 39–43.

White, Suzanne; Lamm, Richard. "Adam Smith reshapes Colorado's health care." *Denver post,* Nov. 11, 1995, p. B7.

Zablocki, Elaine. "The economics of managing healthcare delivery systems by service lines." *Health system leader,* July 1997, p. 4–12.

INDEPENDENT PRACTICE ASSOCIATIONS BIBLIOGRAPHY

"Affiliation 101: a crash course for PRPs." *Physician relations advisor,* Vol. 2, no. 1 (Jan. 1993), p. 1–4.

"Capitation, integration, and managed care lessons from early experiments." *Journal of the American Medical Association,* Mar. 27, 1996.

"DOJ, FTC announce new guidelines superseding previous guidance." *The Bureau of national affairs,* Vol. 3 (Sept. 29, 1994), p. 1344–1345.

"East bay medical network: a contracting entity for physicians and hospitals." *Medical staff strategy report,* Vol. 3, no. 7 (July 1994), p. 2–4.

"Expanded health care guidelines, from 6 to 9, with changes in between." *FTC watch,* Oct. 10, 1994.

"Financial controls and reporting." *Financial controls & reporting,* July 1995, p. 1–2, 5–7, 11–18, 23–25, 31–35, 41–44, 53–60, 65–70.

"FTC: IPA-owned PPO won't violate law by negotiating hospital fees." *Managed care week,* Vol. 1, no. 18 (Sept. 30, 1991).

"Inability to share financial risk would subject IPA to attack, FTC says." *BNA s health law reporter,* July 20, 1995.

"Increase in federal investigations predicted : Key issues discussed." *The Bureau of national affairs,* Vol. 3 (Dec. 8, 1994), p. 1744–1746.

"Independent practice association vs. integrated practice organization: a comparison." *Medical staff strategy report,* Vol. 3, no. 9 (Sept. 1994), p. 2–3.

"Law firm warns of FTC's and DOJ's increased focus on messenger models." *The Bureau of national affairs,* Vol. 4, no. 16 (Apr. 20, 1995), p. 603–604.

"Managed care survey results: chiropractors reject trends." *Chiropractic economics,* Nov. 1997, p. 34–36.

"Managed care usually means changing your income-sharing formulas." *Conomikes reports,* Vol. 14, no. 2 (July 1994), p. 4–5.

"Medpartners affiliates with Long Beach Memorial IPA." *Integrated healthcare report,* Oct. 1996, p. 15.

"'Messenger model' go-between too involved, FTC warns Nevada providers." *Healthcare systems strategy report,* Aug. 18, 1995, p. 5.

"Multi-provider networks." *Health law reporter,* Oct. 6, 1994, p. 19–20.

"NHLA seminar predicts increase in federal probes and focus on key issues." *The bureau of national affairs,* Vol. 67, no. 1693, p. 697.

"Observers say FTC/DOJ guidelines offer clearer roadmap for providers." *Health care policy report,* Oct. 10, 1994.

"Pennsylvania supreme court rules IPA structured HMO is not a professional healthcare provider, so its peer review records are not stautorily immune from discovery in negligence suit." *Health law digest,* Vol. 25, no. 2 (Feb. 1997), p. 47.

"Percentage or revenue from individual practice arrangements (IPAs) per physician, among physicians with IPA contracts, 1994." *Physician marketplace statistics,* 1994, p. 131.

"Physician reimbursement through an IPA network." *Billing,* Vol. 3, no.1 (Jan. 1995), p. 3, 7.

"The PO: sort of an IPA, but the doctors control the entire operation." *Medical office manager,* Vol. 9, no. 10 (Oct. 1995), p. 9–10.

"Pricing by physician network." *BNA s health law reporter,* Vol. 4, no. 15 (Apr. 13, 1995), p. 557–558.

"Union IPAs no different from others." *Primary care weekly,* Vol. 2, no. 24 (June 10, 1996), p. 4.

"Year of the consumer." *Integrated healthcare report,* Mar. 1997, p. 1–12.

Aeschleman, Marcia; Koch, Alma. "Independent practice associations: risk contracting, financial controls, and processes." *Medical group management journal,* Vol. 40, no. 4 (July/Aug. 1993), p. 70, 72, 74, 76–78, 80, 82, 84.

Alexander, Walter. "A Urology IPA." *Oncology issues,* Mar./Apr. 1995, p. 14–16.

Aluise, John J.; Konrad, Thomas R.; Buckner, Bates. "Impact of IPAs on fee-for-service medical groups." *Health care management review,* Vol. 14, no. 1 (Winter 1989), p. 55–63.

Anderson, Suzanne T. "Networks: is an IPA the right strategy for you?" *Academic clinical practice,* Vol. 3, no. 8 (Nov. 1995), p. 19–20.

Appleby, Jean M. "Top 25 IPA-model plans." *Managed healthcare,* Sept. 1996, p. 64.

Azevedo, David. "Will capitation unite or kill this IPA?" *Medical economics,* Vol. 72, no. 24 (Dec. 26, 1995), p. 34–36, 38, 40, 43.

Brown, Harriet Press; Shinto, Richard. "Making physician networks work: why it's important to educate physicians about managed care." *Health care strategic management,* Vol. 14, no. 4 (Apr. 1996), p. 21–23.

Clousson, Jerry P. "Forming an independent physicians organization: a checklist." *The internist,* June 1993, p. 29–30.

Crowley, Leo T. "Integrated delivery systems under increased antitrust scrutiny." *New York law journal,* Mar. 9, 1995.

deGuzman, Meg Matheny. "Are specialists staging a comeback?" *Health system leader,* Apr. 1997, p. 4–13.

Dolan, John R. "IPAs—the managed care road of the future." *Group practice journal,* Jan./Feb. 1993, p. 1–2.

Dowell, Michael A. "Legal issues affecting integrated delivery systems-a primer." *Group practice journal,* May/June 1995.

Ettinger, David A. "How PHOs can avoid price-fixing charges." *Healthcare financial management,* July 1996, p. 72–76.

Gabel, Jon. "Ten ways HMOs have changed during the 1990s." *Health affairs,* Vol. 16, no. 3 (May/June 1997), p. 134–145.

Gardner, Jonathan. "Antitrust changes should ease minds of IPA managers." *Modern physician,* Oct. 1996, p. 6.

Goldstein, Douglas. "Organizing physician equity alliances for aggressive growth and capitation." *Group practice journal,* May/June 1995.

Gotts, Ilene Knable. "Health care joint ventures and the antitrust laws: a guardedly optimistic prognosis." *Journal of contemporary health law & policy,* Spring 1994.

Harding, Jonathan. "Risk management in an IPA setting—part I." *Physician executive,* Vol. 20, no. 5 (May 1994), p. 32–37.

Harding, Jonathan. "Risk management in an IPA setting—part II." *Physician executive,* Vol. 20, no. 6 (May 1994), p. 21–24.

Harris, David G.; Smith, Paul J.; Benedetti, Sherry A. "The transformation and progression of physician organizations." *Medical group management journal,* Vol. 39, no. 5 (July/Aug. 1992), p. 76–78.

Harris, Richard M. "Models for medical practice integration." *Physician executive,* Vol. 20, no. 8 (Aug. 1994), p. 18–24.

Hepps, S. A. "Beware: hospital control or ownership of medical groups." *Medical group management journal,* Vol. 42, no. 3 (May/June 1995), p. 62–64.

Jaklevic, Mary Chris. "The New clout of IPAs." *Modern physician,* Oct. 1996, p. 4–5.

Johnson, Donald E. L. "Hospital and physician joint venture IPAs threaten HMOs." *Health care strategic management,* Vol. 8, no. 2 (Feb. 1990), p. 2–3.

Johnsson, Julie. "Antitrust guides explain messenger-model." *American medical news,* Sept. 23–30, 1996, p. 5–6.

Kertesz, Louise. "California IPA sues Cedars-Sinai over patient 'feeding frenzy.'" *Modern healthcare,* Vol. 26, no. 25 (June 17, 1996), p. 48.

King, Jeffrey P. "Legal issues affecting IPA formation." *Healthcare financial management,* Nov. 1995.

Knox, Wyck A.; Epstein, Daniel M. "Legal implications of managed care arrangements." *Physician executive,* Vol. 20, no. 9 (Sept. 1994), p. 22.

Kopit, William G. "DOJ and FTC demonstrate continued commitment to health care antitrust enforcement guidance." *The bureau of national affairs,* Nov. 21, 1994.

Lowes, Robert L. "The second-generation IPA: will it save independent practice?" *Medical economics,* Aug. 11, 1997, p. 183–186, 189–191.

McKinney, Leigh. "The building blocks of successful IPAs : family physicians highlight the benefits and point out the pitfalls of forming an IPA." *Family practice management,* Vol. 1, no. 9 (Oct. 1994), p. 35–39.

Meyer, Harris; McCormick, Brian. "Florida doctors' union tests bargaining limits: federation of physicians and dentists." *American medical news,* Vol. 37, no. 45 (Dec. 5, 1994), p. 1.

Miller, Jeremy N. "Forming a specialty IPA." *California physician,* Dec. 1993.

Miller, Joel E. "Successful chiropractic managed care programs showcased at national conference." *Journal of American Chiropractic Association,* Sept. 1996, p. 35–40.

Mjoseth, Jeannine. "Justice charges, settles with Conneticut, Missouri providers over impeding managed care." *The bureau of national affairs,* Vol. 4 (Sept. 21, 1995), p. 1399–1400.

Mootz, Robert D.; Hess, Jennifer A.; McMillin, Austin D. "Resource-based relative value scales: impacts and recommendations relative to chiropractic practice." *Journal of manipulative and physiological therapeutics,* Vol. 18, no. 5 (June 1995), p. 271–284.

Murata, Steve. "IBNR—the second most dangerous acronym in medicine today." *Medical economics,* Dec. 12, 1994, p. 8.

Nemes, Judith. "Creditors see life in bankrupt physicians group bid by Reese Hospital, U of C venture." *Crains' Chicago business,* Jan. 23, 1995, p. 3.

Niederman, Gerald A.; Johnson, Bruce A. "Integrated provider networks—a primer." *Medical group management journal,* Vol. 41, no. 6 (Nov./Dec. 1994), p. 62, 64, 66, 68.

Oloroso, Arsenio. "Physicians group prescribes overhaul to cure its chapter 11 ills: unpredictable revenue flow at heart of problems." *Crain's Chicago business,* May 30, 1994, p. 11.

Pokryfki, John P. "Carefully negotiated IPA contracts strengthen an HMO's relationship." *Contract healthcare,* Vol. 2, no. 17 (Aug. 1988).

Pretzer, Michael. "The managed-care juggernaut: explosive growth nationwide." *Medical economics,* Vol. 73, no. 7 (Apr. 15, 1996), p. 64–66, 69–70, 73–74.

Schwartz, Burton; Signorelli, Timothy F. "Forming a multispecialty IPA." *Oncology issues,* Vol. 10, no. 2 (Mar./Apr. 1995), p. 12–13.

Shenkel, Roger C. "Rural IPA formation: nothing like what the city slickers do." *Family practice managment,* Vol. 1, no. 9 (Oct. 1994), p. 10–11.

Shenkin, Budd N. "The independent practice association in theory and practice." *Journal of the American Medical Association,* Vol. 273, no. 24 (June 28, 1995), p. 1937–1942.

Shenkin, Budd N. "Models of managed care: the potential power of the IPA." *Managed care quarterly,* Vol. 4, no. 4 (Autumn 1996), p. 68–74.

Shouldice, Robert G. "HMOs: four models profiled." *Medical group management journal,* Vol. 33, no. 3 (May/June 1986), p. 8–9, 33.

Stocker, Michael A. "Quality assurance in an IPA." *HMO practice,* Vol. 3, no. 5 (Sept./Oct. 1989), p. 183–187.

Sulger, Jack F. "Establishing reserves for capitation contracts." *Healthcare financial management,* July 1996, p. 52–54, 56, 58.

Szilagyi, Peter G., et al. "The effect of independent practice association plans on use of pediatric ambulatory medical care in one group practice." *Journal of the American Medical Association,* Vol. 263, no. 16 (Apr. 25, 1990), p. 2198–2203.

Tan, J. Sim. "Quality assurance in an IPA setting." *Physician executive,* Vol. 17, no. 3 (May/June 1991), p. 43–45.

Terry, Ken. "You can thrive under managed care." *Medical economics,* Apr. 7, 1997, p. 12–14, 17–18, 21–22, 24–25.

Valentine, Steven T. "Independent practice associations: are they viable?" *Topics in health care financing,* Vol. 20, no. 2 (Winter 1993), p. 65–67.

Vogel, David E. "The secret of failure in physician organizations." *Family Practice Management,* Vol. 1, no. 5 (May 1994), p. 40–44.

Walker, Lauren M. "How IPAs fail." *Medical economics,* Dec. 12, 1994, p. 60–65, 68, 70.

Waterman, Robert A.; Bonham, M. Lawrence. "Case study: the integration of a medical foundation and an independent practice association." *Topics in health care financing,* Vol. 20, no. 3 (Spring 1994), p. 80–85.

Weissburg, Carl. "Minimizing antitrust and corporate liability risks." *Health progress,* Apr. 1987, p. 68–73.

Welch, W. Pete. "IPAs emerge on the HMO forefront." *Business and health,* Vol. 5, no. 4 (Feb. 1988), p. 14–15.

MANAGEMENT SERVICES ORGANIZATIONS BIBLIOGRAPHY

"Advisory board gives equity models an 'A+'; staff models get an 'A.'" *Report on physician trends,* July 1994, p. 7–8.

"Beware the hospital-directed MSO." *Physician's advisory,* Vol. 93, no. 12 (Dec. 1993), p. 5–6.

"Capitation's new middleman: management service organizations lighten providers' administrative load." *Capitation medical practice,* Vol. 1, no. 11 (May 1995), p. 1–3.

"A Case study of 'town & gown' integration." *Integrated healthcare report,* Vol. 2, no. 1 (Jan. 1994), p. 10–13.

"Cautious commitment: before you sign with a management service organization, make sure it fits needs—and can deliver." *American medical news,* Vol. 37, no. 3 (Sept. 26, 1994), p. 17–19.

"Checklist: what to consider before establishing a management services organization." *Allan Fine's trends in integrated health care,* Vol. 5, no. 8 (Mar. 1996), p. 4.

"The 'Clinics without walls' controversy." *Integrated healthcare report,* Aug. 1993, p. 1–9.

"East Bay Medical Network: a contracting entity for physicians and hospitals." *Medical staff strategy report,* Vol. 3, no. 7 (July 1994), p. 2–4.

"Equity MSO offers strategic alternative for hospitals." *Medical network strategy report,* Vol. 6, no. 5 (May 1997), p. 1–4.

"Have valid reasons for forming or joining 'clinic without walls.'" *Professional practice today,* Sept. 1993, p. 4, 6.

"Information system helps MSO pull practices out of the red." *Health data management,* Vol. 6, no. 1 (Jan. 1998).

"Legal pitfalls too often ignored by wall-less groups." *Physician's advisory,* Vol. 93, no. 8 (Aug. 1993), p. 3.

"A look at the group practice without walls: a MOM mini seminar." *Medical office manager,* Vol. 8, no. 3 (Mar. 1994), p. 6–7.

"Management service organization (MSO) capital profile." *Capital survey of emerging healthcare organizations,* 1994, p. 20.

"Management services organization (MSO)." *Journal of health hospital law,* Vol. 29, no. 2, p. 88–96, 106.

"Management services organizations offer a way to develop solid hospital/physician partnerships." *Medical staff strategy report,* Vol. 1, no. 1 (Nov. 1992).

"The MSO: better contracts, new management services, but a loss of home rule." *Medical office manager,* Vol. 7, no. 11 (Nov. 1993), p. 7–8.

"The MSO model." *Integrated healthcare report,* Vol. 1, no. 1 (Spring 1992).

"MSO uses information system to attract physicians." *Sponsored supplement,* p. 7–9, 11, 13–14.

"New Mexico 'clinic without walls.'" *Integrated healthcare report,* Vol. 1, no. 2 (Feb. 1993), p. 12–13.

"The "physician equity" model." *Integrated healthcare report,* Vol. 1, no. 9 (Sept. 1993), p. 1–4.

"Planning and implementing a management services organization." *Allan Fine's trends in integrated health care,* Vol. 5, no. 9 (Mar. 1996), p. 1–3.

"Practice efficiencies increase through open system communication." *Health data management,* Vol. 6, no. 1 (Jan. 1998).

"Statewide MSO network finds successful integration tool." *Health data management,* Vol. 6, no. 1 (Jan. 1998).

"Survey shows continued interest in PHOs, MSOs: some supplanting IPAs." *Report on physician trends,* Aug. 1994, p. 4–5.

"This could be the year of the MSO." *Report on physician trends,* Jan. 1996, p. 3–4.

"Tips on how to avoid the pitfalls of a group practice without walls." *Medical staff strategy report,* Vol. 2, no. 9 (Sept. 1993), p. 2–4.

"Wall-less groups, PHOs and MSOs: much talk but little action." *Physician's advisory,* Vol. 94, no. 3 (Mar. 1994), p. 3–4.

Beck, Leif C. "A 'Group without walls': sounds great but will it work?" *Physician's advisory,* Vol. 91, no. 12 (Dec. 1991), p. 8.

Beckham, J. Daniel. "New wave equity." *Hospitals health networks,* July 5, 1995, p. 28, 30–31.

Benedict, Gerry; Feorene, Brent. "An MSO at work—for physicians." *American medical news,* vol. 40, no. 40 (Oct. 27, 1997), p. 13–14.

Benedict, Gerry; Feorene, Brent. "The PPM phenomenon (and the MSO alternative)." *American medical news,* Vol. 40, no. 38 (Oct. 13, 1997), p. 13–14.

Bernstein, William S. "Business and legal issues affecting the development of management service organizations." ACHE annual conference on healthcare administration, 1995.

Braun, Joseph L. "MSOs: key to PHOs and community-based health care systems." *Physician executive,* Vol. 21, no. 2 (Feb. 1995), p. 28–29.

Broccolo, Bernadette M. "IDS planning: tax, fraud and abuse and stark implications." *American Academy of Healthcare Attorneys,* June 25–28, 1995, p. 9, 78–79.

Bromberg, Robert S. "MSOs & 'clinic without walls.'" *Integrated healthcare report,* Vol. 1, no. 9 (Sept. 1993), p. 12–17.

Burcham, Michael R. "Single-specialty networks, carve-outs, and consolidations." *Managed care quarterly,* Vol. 5, no. 2 (1997), p. 34–43.

Campbell, Bert. "Mergers and acquisitions: physician practice transactions and management services organizations." *GFP notes,* Vol. 7, no. 2 (Spring 1994), p. 23–26.

Campbell, Bert L. "Financing an integrated delivery system." *National Health Lawyers Association health law update and annual meeting,* June 7–9, 1995, p. 19–21.

Carpenter, Russell B. "Management services organizations: capitalizing on an unconventional solution to fund raising." *Group practice journal,* Jan./Feb. 1988.

Coddington, Dean C.; Moore, Keith D.; Fischer, Elizabeth A. "Extent of physician-hospital integration." *Intergrated health care: reorganizing the physician, hospital and health plan relationship,* p. 10, 42–45.

Coddington, Dean C.; Moore, Keith D.; Fischer, Elizabeth A. "Integrated health care systems: the key characteristics." *Medical group management journal,* Vol. 40, no. 6 (Nov./Dec. 1993), p. 76–78, 80.

Cohen, Richard L. "Clinic without walls improves physician satisfaction." *Healthcare marketing report,* Vol. 9, no. 6 (June 1991), p. 19–21.

Cross, Margaret Ann. "Management services organizations make the most of information technology." *Health data management,* Apr. 1997, p. 87–88, 90, 92.

Davis, Gary Scott; Holmquest, Donald L. "IDS implementing agreements." *Critical steps in managed care contracting: a looseleaf guide,* p. 34–44.

Dechene, James C.; O'Neill, Karen P. "'Stark II' and state self-referral restrictions." *Journal of health hospital law,* Vol. 29, no. 2, p. 65–87.

Deily, Mary Ellen. "Choosing the right MSO requires up-front planning." *Report on physician trends,* Vol. 4, no. 12 (Dec. 1996), p. 1–3.

DeMuro, Paul R. "Management service organizations." *Topics in health care financing,* Spring 1994, p. 19–27.

DeMuro, Paul R. "Management services organizations (MSOs)." *The finanical manager's guide to managed care and integrated delivery systems,* p. 93–103.

DeMuro, Paul R.; Owens, James F. "Special medicare reimbursement and fraud and abuse considerations for management services organizations, medical foundations, and integrated delivery systems." *Topics in health care financing,* Vol. 20, no. 3 (Spring 1994), p. 54–60.

Dial, William F. "MSOs a stepping stone to a higher level of integration." *Group practice managed healthcare news,* Vol. 11, no. 9 (Sept. 1995), p. 20L.

Dowell, Michael A. "Legal issues affecting integrated delivery systems—a primer." *Group practice journal,* May/June 1995.

Enders, Robert J. "Antitrust law in 1995: mixed messages for providers." *Health systems review,* Mar./Apr. 1996, p. 39–40, 44, 46–47.

Eskin, Evelyn. "The ABCs of management services organizations." *Health network alliance sourcebook,* 1997, p. 101–106.

Forster, Robert J. "Putting together a 'group practice without walls.'" *Internist,* Vol. 29, no. 9 (Oct. 1988), p. 12–15.

Goldstein, Douglas. "Management service organization." *From physician bonding to alliances: bonding new physician-hopsital relationships,* p. 26–31.

Goldstein, Douglas. "Organizing physician equity alliances for aggressive growth and capitation." *Group practice journal,* May/June 1995.

Golembesky, Henry; Harrison, Dean; Muller, Ralph. "Primary care networks: the Chicago-Meyer model for community medical practice: university medical center forms MSO with private physician group." *GFP notes,* Vol. 6, no. 4 (Fall 1993), p. 19–23.

Groner, P. Campbell. "Legal aspects of practice mergers." *Medical practice management news,* Nov./Dec. 1994, p. 111–115.

Harris, Richard M. "Models for medical practice integration." *Physician executive,* Vol. 20, no. 8 (Aug. 1994), p. 18–24.

Hepps, S. A. "Beware: hospital control or ownership of medical groups." *Medical group management journal,* Vol. 42, no. 3 (May/June 1995), p. 62–64.

Hill, John; Mullen, Paddy. "Exploring practice management options." *Healthcare financial management,* Jan. 1996, p. 22–23.

Hitchner, Carl H. "IDS panel: the formation of integrated delivery systems." *American Academy of Healthcare Attorneys,* June 25–28, 1995, p. 111, 126, 128.

Hitchner, Carl H. "Survey of organization models." *Wake Forest law review,* 1994, p. 9–13.

Hudson, Terese. "A Model for integration: group practices without walls offer unique problems and possibilities." *Hospitals health networks,* Vol. 68, no. 10 (May 20, 1994), p. 52, 54–56.

Hudson, Terese. "MSOs: calculated risks." *Hospitals health networks,* Sept. 20, 1994, p. 38–41.

Jaeger, Linda L. "Physician sovereignty brings quality and control." *Group practice journal,* July/Aug. 1988.

Jaklevic, Mary Chris. "MSO model is new favorite among docs." *Modern healthcare,* Aug. 19, 1996, p. 29.

James, Cal. "Lessons learned from 10 years of MSO development." *Healthcare financial management,* Sept. 1996, p. 36, 38.

Johnson, Bruce A.; Waddington, Bette. "How to build a specialty MSO," p. 1–9.

Johnson, Bruce A. "The legal issues of integrated delivery systems." *Medical group management journal,* Jan./Feb. 1995, p. 17–18, 20, 22.

Johnson, Bruce A.; Schryver, Darrell L. "Positioning for vertical integration through clinics 'without walls.'" *Medical group management journal,* Vol. 41, no. 3 (May/June 1994), p. 80, 82, 84.

Kelly, Marshall. "Financing a management services organization." *Creating physician driven managed care networks,* Jan. 24–26, 1996.

Kepner, John C. S.; Thornton, D. McCarty. "Management services organization issues." *National Health Lawyers Association healthcare fraud and abuse,* Oct. 11–13, 1995, p. 8–9.

LaPenna, A. Michael; Kimble, James A. "Investigate MSOs to cope with environmental changes." *Professional practice today,* p. 4–5.

Larrimer, Sharon. "MSOs help cut costs, streamline operations and standardize MIS." *Report on physician trends,* Jan. 1996, p. 10.

Mangan, Doreen. "The rapidly changing world of clinics without walls." *Medical economics,* p. 3–7.

Matyas, David. "HCFA issues final stark I rules." *Physician executive,* Vol. 21, no. 11 (Nov. 1995), p. 44–45.

McKell, Douglas C. "Organizing doctors is the physician relations of the '90s." *Report on physician trends,* Aug. 1994, p. 3–4.

McKinney, Leigh. "Group practice without walls: FPs find strength in numbers." *Family practice management,* Vol. 1, no. 4 (Apr. 1994), p. 54–62.

Miller, John L. "MIS priorities for MSO's & clinics without walls." *Integrated healthcare report,* Vol. 2, no. 1 (Jan. 1994), p. 7–9.

Mitka, Mike. "You pay for what you get: management firms offer physicians capital and administrative help—at a price." *American medical news,* Vol. 36, no. 3 (Aug. 23–30, 1993), p. 3, 15.

Naisbitt, John. "'Clinic without walls' a futuristic model." *Integrated healthcare report,* Dec. 1992, p. 1–7.

Niederman, Gerald A.; Johnson, Bruce A. "Integrated provider networks—a primer." *Medical group management journal,* Vol. 41, no. 6 (Nov./Dec. 1994), p. 62, 64, 66, 68.

O'Hare, Patrick K. "Understanding the 'physician-equity model.'" *Healthcare financial management,* Vol. 49, no. 7 (July 1995), p. 20.

Oloroso, Arsenio. "On health reform's front lines: synergy and RX for Meyer Group." *Crain's Chicago business,* Oct. 4, 1993, p. 51.

Owens, James F. "Miscellaneous legal issues affecting integrated delivery systems, foundations, and management services organizations." *Topics in health care financing,* Vol. 20, no. 3 (Spring 1994), p. 61–69.

Perry, Kristie. "Would an MSO make your life easier?" *Medical economics,* Apr. 10, 1995, p. 1–8, 127–130, 133–134.

Peters, Gerald R. "Fixing the quick fixes to physician relations." *Healthcare financial management,* Nov. 1991.

Peters, Gerald R. "Management services organizations." *Healthcare integration: a legal manual for constructing integrated organizations,* p. 297–333.

Reich, Janet. "Hospital-group models emerging in group practice arena." *Medical group management update,* Vol. 31, no. 1 (Jan. 1992), p. 8.

Rosenfield, Robert H. "Replacing the workshop model." *Topics in health care financing,* Vol. 20, no. 4 (Summer 1994), p. 1–15.

Saalwaechter, John J. "MSO—the new kid on the block." *Physician executive,* Vol. 18, no. 4 (July/Aug. 1992), p. 50–51.

Schryver, Darrell L.; Niederman, Gerald A.; Johnson, Bruce A. "Clinics 'without walls'—from concept to reality." *Group practice journal,* Jan./Feb. 1993.

Scott, Ronald S. "MSO's: a medical entity that endangers physicians and patients." *Administrative radiology journal,* Vol. 14, no. 10 (Oct. 1995), p. 50, 52.

Selby, Stephen E. "Management services organization for group practices." *Journal of ambulatory care management,* July 1996, p. 81–85.

Terry, Ken. "The many pluses of investing in your own MSO." *Medical economics,* Apr. 10, 1995, p. 136, 139, 143–144, 146, 151.

Todd, Maria K. Chapter 6, "Credentialing issues and guidelines." *IPA, PHO & MSO devleopment strategies: building successful provider alliances.* McGraw-Hill, 1997.

Tokarski, Cathy; Larkin, Howard. "Partners in practice." *American medical news,* Sept. 9, 1996, p. 15–16.

Waxman, J. Mark. "Mergers and affiliations: key issues in a managed care environment." *Group practice journal,* Jan./Feb. 1994.

Waxman, J. Mark. "The MSO-group practice tie: a basic managed care building block." *Group practice journal,* Nov./Dec. 1994.

Zirkle, Thomas E.; Peters, Gerald E. "How to develop a management services organization." *Healthcare commentaries: almanac of essential facts,* 1993, p. 137–141.

PHYSICIAN HOSPITAL ORGANIZATIONS BIBLIOGRAPHY

"Advisory board gives equity models an 'A+'; staff models get an 'A.'" *Report on physician trends,* July 1994, p. 7–8.

"Affiliation 101: a crash course in new practice models." *Physician relations advisor,* Vol. 2, no. 1 (Jan. 1993), p. 5–9.

"Antitrust, doctors, hospitals charged with impeding entry of managed care plans into market." *Daily report for executives,* Sept. 15, 1995.

"Antitrust rulings set PHO limits." *Modern healthcare,* Sept. 18, 1995, p. 2, 12.

"AOA and contact lens manufacturers face more charges of antitrust." *Review of optometry,* Jan. 15, 1997, p. 4, 6.

"Avoiding contract dilemmas in a 'super' PHO." *Integrated health care delivery systems,* p. 7.

"Connecticut, Missouri hospitals resolve competitive concerns of division, states." *Antitrust and trade regulation report,* Vol. 69, no. 1730 (Sept. 21, 1995), p. 338.

"Delayed limits on HMO doctor incentives: what signal is the government sending?" *Health alliance alert,* Vol. 11, no. 13 (July 12, 1996), p. 1–2.

"Does your physician network violate antitrust law?" *Medical economics,* Oct. 14, 1996, p. 68, 70, 73–76, 79.

"Federal trade commission will not challenge formation and operation of Billings, Montana multispecialty physician network joint venture." *Health law digest,* Vol. 25, no. 6 (June 1997), p. 15.

"Justice department will not challenge formation of rural hospital network in Wisconsin." *Health law digest,* Vol. 24, no. 12, p. 17.

"Justice to issue antitrust policy on physician-hospital organizations." *The bureau of national affairs,* Vol. 3 (Jan. 27, 1994), p. 109–110.

"Merger of two hospital chains requires asset divestitures to gain FTC approval." *BNA's health law reporter,* Vol. 6 (Feb. 6, 1997), p. 211–212.

"Physician-hospital organizations and antitrust." *New York law journal,* Sept. 27, 1995, p. 3.

"Physician-hospital organizations: low level of integration helps doctors handle managed care contracts." *Medical staff strategy report,* Vol. 2, no. 4 (Apr. 1993), p. 1–5.

"POs, information systems key to successful PHOs." *Report on physician trends,* Vol. 2, no. 8 (Aug. 1994), p. 1–2, 11–12.

"Survey shows continued interest in PHOs, MSOs: some supplanting IPAs." *Report on physician trends,* Aug. 1994, p. 4–5.

"Transitioning PHOs to the next stage: key ingredients: risk management, quality, leadership, customers." *Integrated health care delivery systems,* Vol. 3, no. 11 (July 1996), p. 5–6.

"Use messenger model to avoid antitrust problems with POs." *Professional practice today,* Vol. 6, no. 8 (Sept. 1995), p. 4, 7.

"Wall-less groups, PHOs and MSOs: much talk but little action." *Physician's advisory,* Vol. 94, no. 3 (Mar. 1994), p. 3–4.

"Year of the consumer." *Integrated healthcare report,* Mar. 1997, p. 1–12.

Bennett, Tom; Gerber, Randy S.; Mueller, Donald G. "Making sense of antitrust policy: its application to physician directed networks." *Missouri medicine,* Vol. 94, no. 4 (Apr. 1997), p. 180–184.

Benvenuto, John A.; Stark, Michael J.; Radoccia, Richard A. "Group practice/hospital alliances: the key to regaining lost income and control: from 12 solo practices to a hospital-based LMSG in 100 easy steps." *Medical group management journal,* Vol. 38, no. 4 (July/Aug. 1991), p. 84, 86, 88, 90, 92.

Berger, Ernest L. "Specialty physician networks in managed care." *Health care innovations,* Vol. 5, no. 3 (July/Aug. 1995), p. 16, 18, 37–38.

Bohlmann, Robert C. "Health care delivery in the 1990s—putting the pieces together." *Medical group management journal,* Vol. 38, no. 4 (July/Aug. 1991), p. 64–65, 67.

Burda, David. "Antitrust rulings set PHO limit." *Modern healthcare,* Sept. 18, 1995, p. 2.

Carlstone, Linda Mae. "Health care report: new care choice in doctor groups." *Crain's Chicago business,* June 5, 1995, p. 16.

Cleary, Allison. "Kid-sized care: pediatric PHOs and children's networks emerge, but will they play?" *Hospitals health networks,* Aug. 5, 1994, p. 101–103.

D'Antuono, Robert. "PHO physician contracting options." *GFP notes,* Vol. 6, no. 3 (Summer 1993), p. 7–8.

Dial, William F. "MSOs a stepping stone to a higher level of integration." *Group practice managed healthcare news,* Vol. 11, no. 9 (Sept. 1995), p. 20L.

Dowell, Michael A. "Legal issues affecting integrated delivery systems—a primer." *Group practice journal,* May/June 1995.

Ettinger, David A. "How PHOs can avoid price-fixing charges." *Healthcare financial management,* July 1996, p. 72–76.

Garry, Tom. "How OB/GYN networks can put the power back into your hands." *OBG management,* Nov. 1995, p. 29–31, 34, 36, 38.

Giffin, Robert B. "PHOs: the past or the future of physician alliance strategies?" *Health care strategic management,* Vol. 11, no. 12 (Dec. 1993), p. 20–24.

Grady, Kevin. "1996 revised antitrust policy statements: building a bridge to network competition." *Health law digest,* Vol. 24, no. 10, p. 3.

Harris, Richard M. "Models for medical practice integration." *Physician executive,* Vol. 20, no. 8 (Aug. 1994), p. 18–24.

Hastings, Douglas A.; Leopold, Ann. "Developing integrated delivery systems: an era of change in hospital-physician relationships." *Physician executive,* Vol. 18, no. 6 (Nov./Dec. 1992), p. 18–21.

Hepps, S. A. "Beware: hospital control or ownership of medical groups." *Medical group management journal,* Vol. 42, no. 3 (May/June 1995), p. 62–64.

Holm, Craig. "Primary care networks: choose your physicians wisely." *Physician executive,* Vol. 22, no. 5 (May 1996), p. 29–30.

Hudson, Terese. "What PHOs know: read this and you won't have to feel your way in the dark any longer." *Hospitals health networks,* Sept. 5, 1996, p. 54, 56, 58.

Johnsson, Julie. "FTC slams doctor network, PHO: Montana physicians deny blocking managed care." *American medical news,* Vol. 39, no. 42 (Nov. 11, 1996), p. 1, 28.

Johnsson, Julie. "Justice department squelches Baton Rouge PHO." *American medical news,* May 13, 1996, p. 3, 33.

Kauffman, Bruce A. "Message from Jacksonville: don't threaten the blues with your PHO." *Medical economics,* Apr. 14, 1997, p. 111–112, 118, 120, 126–128.

Kenkel, Paul J. "The systematic approach: physician-hospital collaborations increase, work to capture managed-care contracts." *Modern healthcare,* Apr. 4, 1994, p. 59–60, 62, 64–65.

Kleiman, Mitchell A. "Provider integration: PO versus PHO." *Healthcare financial management,* June 1995.

Larrimer, Sharon. "PHOs cannot manage capitation without adequate infrastructure." *Report on physician trends,* June 1996, p. 7–9.

Lueck, Thomas J. "Illegal price-fixing charged in Danbury hospital lawsuit." *The New York times,* Sept. 14, 1995, p. 6.

MacDonald, Andrew S. "Integrating management of physician groups and hospitals." *Topics in health care financing,* Vol. 20, no. 4 (Summer 1994), p. 48–54.

McCall-Perez, Fred. "The physician-hospital organization (PHO): an emerging competitive health care delivery system." *Medical practice management news,* Nov./Dec. 1994, p. 132–137.

McCormick, Brian. "Firing a warning on PHOs: antitrust settlements a 'shot across the bow' by feds." *American medical news,* Vol. 38, no. 37 (Oct. 2, 1995), p. 3.

McManis, Gerald L.; Stewart, Jerrie A. "Hospital physician alliances: building an integrated medical delivery system." *Healthcare executive,* Mar./Apr. 1992, p. 18–21.

Miller, Polly. "How are doctors adjusting?: very well thank you." *Medical economics,* Vol. 73, no. 7 (Apr. 15, 1996), p. 77–78, 81–82, 84, 90, 94.

Mjoseth, Jeannine. "Two petitions for antitrust immunity approved by Washington's health board." *The bureau of national affairs,* Vol. 5, no. 4 (Jan. 25, 1996), p. 105–106.

Moore, J. Duncan. "Missouri antitrust probe focuses on PHO. . . ." *Modern healthcare,* Vol. 26, no. 9 (May 6, 1996), p. 6.

Niederman, Gerald A.; Johnson, Bruce A. "Integrated provider networks—a primer." *Medical group management journal,* Vol. 41, no. 6 (Nov./Dec. 1994), p. 62, 64, 66, 68.

O'Gara, Nellie. "Charging forward: hospital-physician relations in managed care." *Healthcare executive,* Vol. 7, no. 2 (Mar./Apr. 1992), p. 22–25.

O'Gara Nellie; Marren, John P. "Forming PHOs for direct contracting." *Medical group management journal,* Sept./Oct. 1991, p. 56, 58, 60.

O'Malley, Sharon. "Changing antitrust prospects for hospital mergers." *Health system leader,* Jan. 1997, p. 4–12.

Ogden, David F. "Physician/hospital organizations in managed care contracting." *Medical group management journal,* May/June 1993, p. 12, 17.

Pallarito, Karen. "Testing antitrust boundaries: N.Y. hospital merger probe may break new ground." *Modern healthcare,* Mar. 17, 1997, p. 12.

Preston, Susan Harrington. "Deal a hospital a minority stake in your doctor group: these physician groups swapped a limited voice in governance for seed money." *Medical economics,* Apr. 14, 1997, p. 46, 48–49.

Pretzer, Michael. "The managed-care juggernaut: explosive growth nationwide." *Medical economics,* Vol. 73, no. 7 (Apr. 15, 1996), p. 64–66, 69–70, 73–74.

Rosenfield, Robert H. "Replacing the workshop model." *Topics in health care financing,* Vol. 20, no. 4 (Summer 1994), p. 1–15.

Sarfati, Joy. "Friend or PHO." *CFO,* Nov. 1996, p. 16.

Scott, Lisa. "Iowa antitrust case dismissed." *Modern healthcare,* Mar. 24, 1997, p. 24.

Shartel, J. Stratton. "PHO chief suggests strategies for responding to physician incentive regulations: limiting bonuses may circumvent stop-loss requirement." *Capitation medical practice,* Vol. 3, no. 8 (Feb. 1997), p. 1–2.

Straley, Peter F.; Ryan, J. Bruce. "Developing a physician-hospital organization." *Topics in health care financing,* Vol. 19, no. 3 (Spring 1993), p. 24–31.

Straley, Peter F. "PHO planning, marketing and the development of the business plan." June 1994.

Taulbee, Pamela. "Correct pricing is critical for successful PHO development." *Report on physician trends,* Vol. 2, no. 6 (June 1994), p. 1–2, 12.

Teach, Randy L. "Antitrust policy revised for provider networks: Allows for networks that promote competition, benefit consumers." *MGMA directory,* p. 1, 3.

Todd, Maria K. Chapter 6, "Credentialing issues and guidelines." *IPA, PHO & MSO devleopment strategies: building successful provider alliances.* McGraw-Hill, 1997

Unland, James. "Hospitals versus physicians, POs versus PSOs: the providers' struggle for control of managed care contracting." *Journal of health care finance,* Vol. 21, no. 3 (Spring 1995), p. 17–36.

Unland, James. "POs can help maintain independence in new era of managed care." *Professional practice today,* Vol. 5, no. 9 (Oct. 1994), p. 1, 5, 7.

Unland, James J. "Physician-directed managed care efforts in the United States." *Medical practice management news,* Vol. 11, no. 4 (Jan./Feb. 1996), p. 163–173.

Waterman, Robert A. "Nonprofit medical care foundations." *Topics in health care financing,* Vol. 20, no. 3 (Spring 1994), p. 13–18.

PHYSICIAN PRACTICE MANAGEMENT COMPANIES BIBLIOGRAPHY

"Caution required when considering PPMCs: strategy offers advantages, but advisers say beware of pitfalls." *Physician practice options,* June 1998, p. 1, 7–8.

"Cautious commitment: before you sign with a management service organization, make sure it fits needs—and can deliver." *American medical news,* Vol. 37, no. 3 (Sept. 26, 1994), p. 17–19.

"Coastal physician considers sale." *Medical industry today,* Sept. 25, 1996.

"The Effect of PPMC characteristics on capital costs." *Physician Practice Management Companies PPMC,* Oct. 1996.

"Equity MSO offers strategic alternative for hospitals." *Medical network strategy report,* Vol. 6, no. 5 (May 1997), p. 1–4.

"Feds hit PPMC with anti-kickback violation." *Physicians payment update,* June 1998, p. 100–101.

"FHP international, Ultralink and Allianz Life Insurance." *Modern healthcare,* Apr. 15, 1996, p. 14.

"FPA and AHI Healthcare announce merger." *Integrated healthcare report,* Oct. 1996, p. 14–15.

"FPA Medical Management Inc." *The Wall Street journal,* July 2, 1996.

"FTC OKs urology network: shows antitrust fears persist." *Healthcare business legal strategies,* Feb. 21, 1996.

"FTC sees Medicare risk market sufficiently competitive for now." *BNA's managed care reporter,* Vol. 3 (Feb. 19, 1997), p. 173–174.

"Future physician management giants can be good news for payers." *Capitation risk contracting,* Vol. 2, no. 10 (July 1996), p. 1–2.

"Industry notes." *Pulse,* p. 2–3.

"Industry notes (1996)." *Pulse,* Apr. 1996, p. 2.

"Industry notes (PPMC)." *Physician Practice Management Companies PPMC,* May 1996, p. 2–4.

"Learn answers to doctors' top questions about IOMCs." *Report on physician trends,* Vol. 4, no. 2 (Feb. 1996), p. 9–10.

"Management of physician practices a major market opportunity." *BNA's managed care reporter,* Vol. 2, no. 20 (May 15, 1996), p. 480–481.

"Medpartner's latest acquisition." *BNA's managed care reporter,* Vol. 2 (July 10, 1996), p. 671.

"Medpartners affiliates with Long Beach Memorial IPA." *Integrated healthcare report,* Oct. 1996, p. 15.

"Medpartners and Cardinal Healthcare." *Modern healthcare,* Vol. 26, no. 9(May 6, 1996), p. 32.

"Medpartners/Mullikin." *Modern healthcare,* Vol. 26, no. 31 (July 29, 1996), p. 12.

"Medpartners' purchase of Inphynet makes dominant PPM firm even bigger." *BNA's managed care reporter,* Vol. 3 (Jan. 29, 1997), p. 109.

"Medpartners, Team Health and Emergency Physician Associates." *Modern healthcare,* July 8, 1996, p. 16.

"MedPartners to pay $200 million for troubled Talbert Medical Management." *BNA's managed care reporter,* Vol. 3 (Aug. 20, 1997), p. 796–797.

"Pacificare Health Systems." *Modern healthcare,* Aug. 26, 1996, p. 4.

"PCA to sell Florida medical centers to FPA." *Modern healthcare,* May 13, 1996, p. 29.

"Phycor's Georgia, Colorado purchases." *BNA's managed care reporter,* Vol. 2 (July 10, 1996), p. 671.

"Physician-practice firms: if you don't join 'em, buy 'em." *Medical economics,* Jan. 9, 1995, p. 140.

"Physician practice management company formed in northwest." *BNA's managed care reporter,* Vol. 2, no. 29 (July 17, 1996).

"Physician practice management: the road ahead." *Medical industry today,* Sept. 30, 1996.

"Physician Reliance Network named defendant in class action." *Medical industry today,* Sept. 23, 1996.

"Practice management." *Medical economics,* July 29, 1996, p. 226–227.

"Primary care practice management companies." *Physician Practice Management Companies PPMC,* Feb. 1997.

"So you want to join a physician practice management company. . . ." *Report on physician trends,* Vol. 4, no. 9 (Sept. 1996), p. 1–3.

"U.S. medical alliance has acquired 5 businesses since April." *Medical industry today,* Aug. 26, 1996.

"Will Medpartners be supermagnet for nationwide physician practices net?" *Health alliance alert,* p. 2.

Bachrach, David J. "Developing physician leaders in academic medical centers." *Medical Group Management Journal,* Nov./Dec. 1996, p. 35–38, 40, 44, 46, 48, 50.

Benedict, Gerry; Feorene, Brent. "The PPM phenomenon (and the MSO alternative)." *American medical news,* Vol. 40, no. 38 (Oct. 13, 1997), p. 13–14.

Berry, Kate. "Pediatrix profit is expected to hit forecast." *The Wall Street journal,* June 15, 1998.

Burkholder, Steve. "Accounting/disclosure questions posed in physician practice acquisition arena." *BNA's health law reporter,* Vol. 6 (Feb. 6, 1997), p. 209–210.

Burton, Thomas M.; Blackmon, Douglas A. "Medpartners-Caremark pact is likely to fuel a debate: do patients suffer when more and more doctors practice under one roof?" *The Wall Street journal,* Vol. 127, no. 149 (May 15, 1996).

Dobrzynski, Judith H. "Physician management merger deal." *New York times,* Aug. 16, 1995, p. 1.

Falk, Scott. "'PPM pac-mana': new firms proliferate as industry's big players consolidate." *BNA's managed care reporter,* Vol. 3 (May 21, 1997), p. 484–487.

Fleckenstein, Loren. "California doc aims to take firm nationwide." *Modern healthcare,* Vol. 26, no. 18 (Apr. 29, 1996), p. 88, 90.

Foster, Mary Jane. "FPA fattens coffers with more IPAs." *Medical industry today,* July 18, 1996.

Freedman, Eric. "Michigan doctors' group enlists management firm." *American medical news,* Aug. 5, 1996, p. 5.

Gilkison, Mary J. "Physician practice management organizations are here to stay." *BNA's managed care reporter,* June 5, 1996, p. 558–559.

Goldstein, Douglas. "Group practice revolution: leading the way in restructuring health care delivery." *Group practice journal,* Jan./Feb. 1997, p. 12–14, 16–18, 20, 22–23, 26, 30, 31.

Hudson, Terese. "Ties that bind: doctors want to hand their hassles to practice managers, but corporate life can have a dark side." *Hospitals health networks,* Mar. 5, 1997, p. 20, 22, 24, 26.

Jaeger, Linda L. "Physician sovereignty brings quality and control." *Group practice journal,* July/Aug. 1988.

Jaklevic, Mary Chris. "3 Oregon medical groups to merge into management firm." *Modern healthcare,* July 8, 1996, p. 12.

Jaklevic, Mary Chris. "Doc practice management set to explode: with HMOs, hospitals facing difficulties organizing physicians, independent firms see a huge opportunity." *Modern healthcare,* Aug. 14, 1995, p. 26–28, 30–31.

Jaklevic, Mary Chris. "FHP spins off doc unit as deals lag." *Modern healthcare,* July 22, 1996, p. 8.

Jaklevic, Mary Chris. "FPA to buy doc assets of Foundation Health." *Modern healthcare,* Vol. 26, no. 28 (July 8, 1996), p. 12.

Jaklevic, Mary Chris. "Investor passion for doc management firms fades." *Modern healthcare,* June 24, 1996, p. 134, 136.

Jaklevic, Mary Chris. "Issues of control: some docs disillusioned with their PPM experience." *Modern healthcare,* Mar. 24, 1997, p. 44.

Jaklevic, Mary Chris. "Medpartners adds Inphynet to acquisition list." *Modern health-care,* June 27, 1997, p. 22.

Jaklevic, Mary Chris. "Partnering with a PPM: New York's Beth Israel, Phymatrix agree to form MSO." *Modern healthcare,* Apr. 28, 1997, p. 8.

Jaklevic, Mary Chris. "Physician practice management issues of control: some doctors disillusioned with their PPM experience." *Medical business journal,* Vol. 10, no. 2 (Aug. 1997), p. 1, 6.

Jaklevic, Mary Chris. "PPMs look to academia: faculty practices targeted despite cultural, legal gaps." *Modern healthcare,* May 19, 1997, p. 38.

Jaklevic, Mary Chris. "Reining in doctors: tougher accounting rules urged for physician practice management firms." *Medical business journal,* Vol. 10, no. 2 (Aug. 1997), p. 1, 3.

Jaklevic, Mary Chris. "Starting your own PPM: nine midwest groups unite to cut costs, stay competitive." *Modern healthcare,* Apr. 21, 1997, p. 42.

Kendall, Melissa. "More doctors form networks to get managed care contracts." *Orlando business journal,* Vol. 11, no. 20, p. 3.

Kornreich, Edward S.; Moskowitz, Ellen H. "HHS IG advisory opinion on PPMC percentage contracts raises questions." *Health law reporter,* Vol. 7, no. 20 (May 14, 1998), p. 804–806.

Krohn, Richard W. "Making risk contracting work in specialty networks." *Medical group management journal,* Jan./Feb. 1997, p. 13–16, 18, 20.

Larkin, Howard. "Is bigger better?" *American medical news,* Sept. 23–30, 1996, p. 13–15.

Larkin, Howard. "The Gold Standard." *American medical news,* Sept. 9, 1996.

Lowes, Robert L. "Will low tide for coastal leave doctors beached?" *Medical economics,* Vol. 73, no. 14 (July 29, 1996), p. 30–34, 36, 41, 46.

Martin, James P. "Physician practice management companies—a good deal or not?" *Medical business journal,* Feb. 1997, p. 12–13.

Morrissey, John. "OrNda deal in Massachusetts near completion." *Modern healthcare,* Vol. 26, no. 36 (Sept. 2, 1996), p. 22.

Murata, Stephen K. "Merger mania: this is the year it will reach you." *Medical economics,* Mar. 7, 1994, p. 29–31, 33, 36.

Pallarito, Karen. "Flow of IPOs ebbs: but '97 market looks hot for physician practice management, assisted living." *Modern healthcare,* Feb. 10, 1997, p. 43, 47.

Pallarito, Karen. "IntegraMed acquires four women's health firms in Florida." *Modern healthcare,* July 8, 1996, p. 52.

Pallarito, Karen. "PPM buys a PPO: deal expands New York company's reach to Conneticut, N.J." *Modern healthcare,* June 23, 1996, p. 24.

Rovner, Julie. "Physician management companies: are they a good choice for doctors?" *Health system leader,* July 1995, p. 4–12.

Scott, Kathryn J. "Medpartners/Mullikin-Caremark merger will create huge practice management company." *BNA's managed care reporter,* Vol. 2 (May 22, 1996), p. 506–507.

Sellmeyer, Sheri. "Fight brewing over control of Coastal Physician Group." *BNA's managed care reporter,* Vol. 2 (Aug. 28, 1996), p. 840–841.

Shepherd, Gary. "Doctors, not just hospitals, now takeover targets: practice management groups allow physicians to concentrate on health care, not paperwork." *Tampa Bay business journal,* Vol. 15, no. 28 (July 14, 1995), p. 16–17.

Shinkman, Ronald. "Salick Healthcare signs to provide specialty cancer care for HMO." *Los Angeles business journal,* Vol. 16, no. 29, p. 13.

Terry, Ken. "The many pluses of investing in your own MSO." *Medical economics,* Apr. 10, 1995, p. 136, 139, 143–144, 146, 151.

Tokarski, Cathy. "Medical express: physician practice management is one of the hottest fields in health care—but can those riding the wave manage the undertow?" *Hospitals health networks,* Dec. 5, 1995, p. 39–40.

Tokarski, Cathy. "Not selling out." *American medical news,* Vol. 39, no. 38 (Oct. 14, 1996), p. 25–28.

Tokarski, Cathy; Larkin, Howard. "Partners in practice." *American medical news,* Sept. 9, 1996, p. 15–16.

Tomsho, Robert. "Texas doctors learn the perils of linking fate to a corporation: firm that bought practice got sold, leaving them at mercy of marketplace." *The Wall Street journal,* May 1, 1998, p. A1, A10.

Treadwell, Janet E.; Richards, Melissa A. "Caring for your practice: maximizing quality and effectiveness through practice management services." *Missouri medicine,* Vol. 91, no. 2 (Feb. 1994), p. 78–80.

Waxman, J. Mark. "Practice management agreements: the core of the MSO–group practice alliance." *Healthcare financial management,* Dec. 1996, p. 65–68, 70.

Glossary of Healthcare Terms

ACTIVE INVESTOR: One who holds an investment interest, is responsible for day-to-day entity management, and who holds liability, as a general partner or as an agent acting within the scope of an employment contract.

ADMINISTRATIVE PROCEEDING: An adjudication by any administrative agency.

ADVISORY OPINION: A formal opinion by a court or administrative agency having no precedential force.

ALTERNATIVE DELIVERY SYSTEMS (ADS): Healthcare delivery techniques that directly finance or provide delivery of services in innovative ways designed to improve and/or contain costs.

ANTITRUST: In 1993, 1994, and 1996, the Justice Department and the Federal Trade Commission issued "Statements of Antitrust Enforcement Policy in Health Care" describing the legal standards for prosecution for anticompetitive actions related to hospital mergers and joint ventures, physician networks, multi-provider networks, and other groups. The statements include descriptions of safety zones or "Safe Harbors," criteria for determining compliance. The 1996 statements expanded the "Rule of Reason" for physician networks, which provides an overall approach to determining anticompetitiveness.

ANY WILLING PROVIDER: This describes state laws requiring that managed care networks accept any physician who meets their membership criteria, is willing to accept their reimbursement rates, and accepts their utilization standards.

ASSIGNMENT: A process where the patient requests that the third-party payor forward payment directly to the provider.

ASSIGNMENT OF BENEFITS: A written authorization by a subscriber permitting payment of benefits directly to a provider.

AT RISK: The state of being subject to some uncertain event occurring that causes loss or difficulty.

AVERAGE LENGTH OF STAY (ALOS): Number of inpatient days per admission (total days/total admissions).

BALANCE BILLING: Patient is billed by the physician for the difference between the physician's charge and the amount reimbursed by a third-party payor.

BUNDLED BILLING: An inclusive package price or global fee for all services required for a specific procedure (usually includes professional and institutional services).

BUSINESS COALITION: A group of employers in a community that form a cooperative to purchase healthcare services at a lower cost for their employees.

CAPITATION: Payment for healthcare services where the physician/provider receives a fixed amount per enrollee for a fixed period of time for specified services.

CARVE-OUT: A system in which a health maintenance organization (HMO), specifically an individual practice association (IPA), makes all mental health referrals to a specific group practice rather than to independent practitioners. This group practice is often under a capitation or other managed care contract.

CASE MANAGEMENT: A systematic approach to the treatment of patients that attempts to optimize efficiency, quality, and cost savings based on the patient's total experience from admission to discharge planning.

CASE-MIX: The diagnosis-specific makeup of a health program's acuity level. A case-mix directly influences the intensity, length of stay, cost, and scope of the services provided by a hospital or other health program.

CHAIN ORGANIZATION: A group of two or more healthcare facilities that are leased, owned, or controlled by a single organization.

CLINIC WITHOUT WALLS: An entity legally combining independent physicians or medical practices in order to create centralized management and decision-making structures and to share services such as administrative, billing, and purchasing costs. The organization has multiple practice sites. Physicians and medical practices retain their independence by maintaining their private office and practice styles. Under this arrangement assets are not merged.

CIRCUMVENTION SCHEME: Any arrangement (prohibited by the Stark Bill) in which physicians located in different cities transfer the ownership of their facilities and cross-refer patients.

CIVIL EXCLUSION: An act barring a provider from receiving funds from a federal health program.

CLOSED-PANEL PPO: A Preferred Provider Organization (PPO) that requires patients to utilize only member providers in order to receive benefits (also called Closed-Panel Provider or Exclusive Provider Organization).

COINSURANCE: The portion of covered expenses, beyond the deductible, to be paid by the insured party.

COMMUNITY RATING: A method of establishing premiums for health insurance in which the premium is based on the average cost of actual or anticipated healthcare used by all subscribers in a specific geographic location, which does not vary for different groups or with variables such as demographics.

COMPETITIVE MEDICAL PLAN (CMP): Any alternative healthcare delivery plan.

CONTRACT RATES: Rates reduced from a physician's or other health service fee schedule components that result from the contractual agreement between a PPO and a provider.

CONVERSION FACTOR: A standard dollar value that converts relative value units (RVUs) to dollar amounts. A fee schedule is derived from multiplying the RVUs for each service by the conversion factor.

COPAYMENT: A type of cost sharing whereby the insured or covered person pays a fixed amount per unit of medical service or unit of time and the insurer pays the remaining cost.

COST-BASED REIMBURSEMENT: A method of payment for medical care by third parties, typically by government agencies or Blue Cross plans. In cost-related systems, the amount of the payment is based on the costs to the provider of delivering the service.

COST SHIFTING: Occurs when costs not paid by one consumer result in higher charges to another consumer.

CURRENT PROCEDURAL TERMINOLOGY (CPT): A publication of the American Medical Association standardizing procedure coding for the purpose of providing a uniform language to describe healthcare services.

CUSTOMARY, PREVAILING, AND REASONABLE (CPR): Describes a fee based on past rates and what other physicians in the area charge.

DAYS PER 1,000: The number of inpatient hospital days per one thousand persons in a particular population group.

DIAGNOSIS RELATED GROUP (DRG): A classification system of patients by surgical procedure or diagnosis into major diagnostic categories for the purpose of Medicare reimbursement of hospitalization costs.

DISCOUNTED FEE-FOR-SERVICE: A payment arrangement where a provider agrees to render services on a fee-for-service basis but whose fees are discounted relative to the provider's customary charges.

DME: Durable Medical Equipment.

ENCOUNTER: A face-to-face contact between a patient and a healthcare provider during which dental, social, medical, or family-planning services are provided and documented in the patient's health record.

ENROLLEE: One who enrolls in a prepaid health program for health services. The terms of enrollment are understood to mean that the health delivery program provides, or contracts for, an agreed-upon list of health services for a given period of time in return for a fixed payment or premium.

EMERGING HEALTHCARE ORGANIZATIONS (EHO): Hospitals, physicians, and/or payors that are merging, affiliating, or integrating in response to changes in the healthcare environment.

ERISA: The Employee Retirement Income Security Act was enacted in 1974 and sets federal requirements for pension and employee benefit plans' inclusion of employer health plans.

EXCLUSIVE PROVIDER ORGANIZATION (EPO): A type of PPO in which the patient must utilize only member providers in order to receive benefits.

EXCLUSIVITY CLAUSE: Prohibits physicians from contracting with more than a single PPO or HMO.

EXPERIENCE RATING: A method of establishing premiums that are based on the average cost of anticipated or actual healthcare used by various groups and subgroups of subscribers, or using variables such as demographics.

EXTERNAL AUDIT PROGRAM: A program instituted by a healthcare insurer where a portion of the claims are examined to verify that service was rendered and payment was received by the proper party.

FALSE CLAIM: A fraudulent or incorrect claim.

FEE-FOR-SERVICE (FFS): A method of reimbursing on the basis of services rendered.

FISCAL AGENT: Any organization under contract with a state agency that receives, processes, and pays claims under the Medicaid program.

FRAUD ALERT: Published by the Office of the Inspector General (OIG), this warning to providers informs them of arrangements that violate fraud and abuse laws.

FRAUD AND ABUSE: The violation of federal Medicare and Medicaid fraud and abuse laws, the Stark Law and Stark II, the Internal Revenue Code, and various state laws. These laws prohibit remuneration for referrals of any kind and for services not rendered. Stark and Stark II prohibit physician referrals to entities in which they or an immediate family member have a financial interest. Abuse may be described as the delivery of excessive, unnecessary, harmful, or poor-quality healthcare.

FREESTANDING FACILITY: Usually applied to an ambulatory care facility that has no physical connection with a hospital or other healthcare unit.

GATEKEEPER: May be a primary care physician or another specialist or physician extender to whom a defined insured population is assigned and who is required either to provide all healthcare or to authorize care from other specialists, if necessary, for the assigned individuals.

GLOBAL BUDGET: A national cap on healthcare spending that would be determined by the National Health Board. President Clinton included caps as part of his healthcare reform proposal.

GROUP MODEL: An HMO that contracts with physicians in an existing group practice. Physicians are usually paid on a salary-plus-incentive basis.

GROUP PRACTICE MODEL: A medical group that contracts with an HMO to provide medical services on a capitated basis. Physicians share common facilities and staff, and practice income is pooled together and distributed according to an agreed-upon plan.

HEALTH CARE FINANCING ADMINISTRATION (HCFA): The federal agency responsible for administering Medicare laws.

HEALTH MAINTENANCE ORGANIZATION (HMO): Any organization that, through an organized system of healthcare, provides or ensures the delivery of an agreed-upon set of comprehensive health maintenance and treatment services for an enrolled group of persons under a capitation or prepaid fixed sum arrangement.

HEALTH PLAN EMPLOYER DATA AND INFORMATION SET (HEDIS): Standardized performance measures developed by the National Committee for Quality Assurance to allow for the comparison of managed healthcare plans.

HOLDBACK: A portion of a clinician's fee held by an HMO in a risk agreement. Periodically, there is a financial return to the clinician based on the cost-containment performance of the organization.

HEALTH PROFESSIONAL SHORTAGE AREA (HPSA): Areas that are federally designated as having shortages of healthcare providers.

INCURRED BUT NOT REPORTED (IBNR): An accounting term that refers to potential liabilities resulting from service delivery that were not reported in the current report.

INDEMNITY BENEFITS: The arrangement of benefits on the basis of a set number of dollar allowances for covered services. Usually, the indemnity insurance contract defines the maximum amounts that will be paid for the covered services.

INDIVIDUAL PRACTICE ASSOCIATION (IPA): An organization of independent physicians and providers created to conduct managed care contracting activities.

INTEGRATED DELIVERY SYSTEM (IDS): A combination of hospitals, medical services, physicians, and other providers to provide coordinated, continuing ambulatory and tertiary care to a defined population or group of enrollees.

INTERNATIONAL CLASSIFICATION OF DISEASES, 9TH EDITION, CLINICAL MODIFIERS (ICD-9-CM): A standardized categorization of morbidity and mortality information for the purpose of indexing statistical data.

LENGTH OF STAY (LOS): The length of an inpatient's stay in a hospital, reported as the number of days spent in a facility per admission or discharge.

MANAGED CARE: Method of providing healthcare services within a network of selected providers who are given the responsibility to provide cost-effective healthcare while maintaining quality.

MANAGED CARE ORGANIZATION (MCO): An organization that provides managed healthcare services.

MANAGEMENT SERVICES ORGANIZATION (MSO): A separate legal entity that provides a variety of assets, administrative support, and practice-management services to one or more medical practices. These assets and services may include office space, medical equipment, management information, billing, accounting, and other administrative services. An MSO provides a forum to effectively pursue and negotiate managed care contracts and to provide practice-management services to physicians in an effort to improve and support practice operations.

MEDICAID: The federal program, administered by the states, that provides medical care to the indigent.

MEDICAID FRAUD: Any act whereby a person claims or receives funds he/she is not entitled to as deemed by federal and/or state laws, rules, or provisions from a state Medicaid program, or its agents, by way of a false claim, kickback, bribe, rebate, or deliberate concealment of a fraudulent scheme.

MEDICARE: The federal program which ensures sufficient healthcare services for the aged.

MEDICARE AND MEDICAID PATIENT AND PROGRAM PROTECTION ACT OF 1987: The federal law which enacts criminal penalties against persons and/or entities that participate in Medicare or Medicaid and that knowingly offer, pay, solicit, or receive payment in order to encourage a service or item for which payment is made by these programs.

MEDICARE PART A: The Medicare program that compensates hospitals and/or related institutions for inpatient care.

MEDICARE PART B: The Medicare program that provides remuneration for doctor services and other services not covered by Medicare Part A.

MEDICARE RISK CONTRACT: A contract between a managed care plan and Health Care Finance Administration to provide services to Medicare beneficiaries for a fixed monthly payment and that requires all services to be provided on an at-risk basis.

NATIONAL COMMITTEE ON QUALITY ASSURANCE (NCQA): A not-for-profit organization that performs accreditation review of managed care plans.

NETWORK MODEL: An HMO that contracts with many independent multispecialty group practices.

OFFICE OF THE INSPECTOR GENERAL (OIG): An unconstrained unit within the Department of Health and Human Services appointed to investigate suspected fraud and abuse cases, perform audits and inspections of department programs, collect data, and analyze and conduct special studies.

OPEN PANEL: An HMO that allows benefits to be received outside of its provider network, usually subject to an additional out-of-pocket payment.

OUTCOMES MEASUREMENT: Formal process for evaluating the effectiveness of medical treatment and patient satisfaction with treatment results.

PASSIVE INVESTOR: Any investor who does not manage an entity.

PAYMENT REVIEW PROGRAM: A program developed to discover and preclude fraud and abuse by reviewing providers and practitioners.

PEER REVIEW ORGANIZATION (PRO): An organization under a federal program that processes data concerning healthcare services provided to Medicare beneficiaries and intervenes when data indicates the services have been provided inappropriately, unnecessarily, or with inadequate quality.

PENETRATION: The percentage of possible subscribers in a service area who have in fact contracted for benefits.

PER CAPITA: Payment for healthcare services based on the number of enrollees regardless of the number who actually receive services.

PER DIEM: Total reimbursement payment based on a set rate per day rather than on charges.

PER MEMBER PER MONTH (PMPM): Reimbursement based on the ratio of service or cost divided by the number of enrollees per month in a particular group.

PHYSICIAN HOSPITAL ORGANIZATION (PHO): A joint venture between a hospital and its medical staff for the purpose of negotiation with HMOs.

PHYSICIAN PAYMENT REVIEW COMMISSION (PPRC): Created by Congress in 1986 to recommend changes in current physician Medicare reimbursement procedures.

PHYSICIAN PRACTICE MANAGEMENT COMPANY (PPMC): Company specializing in physician practice management with the goal of earning a profit. PPMCs often purchase or affiliate with physicians, offering capital, management experience, economies of scale, and economic security. Leading national PPMCs are PhyCor, Coastal, and Pacific Physician Services. (Also referred to as Practice Management Companies or PMCs).

POINT OF SERVICE: This product combines aspects of both an HMO and a PPO. It allows members to either use providers within the network or, by paying additional fees, use a provider outside the network.

PREFERRED PROVIDER ORGANIZATION (PPO): An entity through which healthcare providers contract with insurers to provide fees based on a schedule. Plan members are encouraged to use the services of "preferred providers." If plan members use a provider other than one in the plan, the insured might be liable for a certain share of the charges.

PREPAID GROUP PRACTICE: A group of physicians that contracts to provide a specific set of services, at a prepaid fixed sum, to a health plan enrollee (also called a group model HMO).

PREPAID HEALTH PLAN (PHP): Contract between an insurer and a group of subscribers whereby the plan agrees to provide certain health services for a prepaid fixed sum.

PRIMARY CARE: The first and most basic level of outpatient medical service (as opposed to surgery, heart transplants, tertiary care, etc.). Encompasses the physician specialties of general/family practice, pediatrics, internal medicine, and obstetrics/gynecology.

PRIMARY CARE NETWORK: A group or list of primary care physicians, under contract to care for a defined population, that restricts patients' access to specialty care by acting as gatekeepers.

PRIVATE INUREMENT: The payment for services, other than reasonable reimbursement for services rendered or goods provided, at the expense of tax-exempt entities (e.g., a 501(c)3 community or charitable hospital).

PROSPECTIVE PAYMENT SYSTEM (PPS): The federal medical system that reimburses hospitals for Part A Medicare services based on Diagnosis Related Groups (DRGs).

PROSPECTIVE REIMBURSEMENT: Any method of payment to a healthcare organization by which rates of payment are established in advance regardless of the actual costs incurred by the organization.

PROVIDER AGREEMENT: A contractual agreement between a provider and insurer that outlines requirements of the insurance programs that providers must adhere to when providing services and billing patients.

QUALITY ASSURANCE: Activities and programs that are designed to ensure quality of care in a medical setting.

REINSURANCE: An insurance plan purchased by some managed care companies to cover the risks pertaining to individual stop-loss, aggregate stop-loss, out-of-area, and insolvency protection.

RELATIVE VALUE SCALE (RVS): A guide used to establish fee schedules that attempts to quantify the relative values of medical procedures by evaluating components such as the physician's work, malpractice costs, and office expenses required to perform each procedure. Usually these values are multiplied by a conversion factor to derive a dollar value.

RELATIVE VALUE UNIT (RVU): A numeric value placed on a service that is derived from the skill required in delivering the service, the legal risk to the physician, and the severity of the patient's condition.

RESOURCE BASED RELATIVE VALUE SCALE (RBRVS): The relative value scale used by the government to reimburse physicians for Medicare and Medicaid patients. It is based on the necessary resources used to perform a medical service: overhead, malpractice insurance costs, and physicians' work.

RISK: Any chance or possibility of loss.

RISK POOL: Money that is set aside to cover defined expenses. Those managing risk will receive a refund of some or all of the money that is not used in a particular year.

RISK SHARING: An agreement between program administrator and provider whereby any funds remaining at the end of the year will be shared, as will shortages when spending exceeds the budgeted amount.

SAFE HARBOR: A payment practice that is always acceptable and will not be in violation of the fraud and abuse laws under regulations dictated by the OIG of HHS.

SELF-INSURANCE: An entity itself instead of an insurance company, managed care organization, or other third party, assumes the risk of medical costs.

SERVICE AREA: The geographic area served by a healthcare organization.

SHELL LABORATORY: A laboratory, also known as a storefront laboratory, that refers tests to another laboratory and bills the referring physician for the tests. The referring physician usually has an ownership interest.

SKILLED NURSING FACILITY (SNF): A facility (freestanding or not) with an organized professional staff that provides medical, continuous nursing, and various other health and social services to patients who are not in an acute phase of illness but require subacute and/or rehabilitative care on an inpatient basis.

SLIDING SCALE MODEL: A discounted fee schedule that is based on a customer's ability to pay.

STAFF MODEL: An HMO in which physicians are retained as salaried employees.

STARK BILL: The federal statute that keeps physicians from referring Medicare reimbursable services under Medicare to an entity in which they or their immediate family have a vested financial interest.

STOP-LOSS: Insurance provided by a third party that insures an unexpected financial loss to a healthcare plan or provider.

TERTIARY CARE: Subspecialty care that requires extensive diagnostic and treatment capabilities.

THIRD-PARTY PAYOR: Any organization that pays or insures medical benefits on behalf of a beneficiary. It is the third-party payor that is ultimately responsible for payment of services to the provider.

TOTAL QUALITY MANAGEMENT (TQM)/CONTINUOUS QUALITY IMPROVEMENT (CQI): A systematic method for improving quality and efficiency by analyzing systems and data. TQM/CQI is a step-by-step process that includes analyzing data, determining causes of problems, and implementing solutions on a continuous basis. Quality is defined through measurable customer satisfaction feedback, input, and process and outcomes measures, and is used to continuously assess and improve quality of care.

UNBUNDLING: Billing separately for the components of a service previously included in a single fee.

USUAL, CUSTOMARY, AND REASONABLE (UCR): Physician's full charge may be reimbursed by a health insurance plan if it does not exceed his usual charge or exceed the amount customarily charged by other physicians in the area, or is reasonable.

UTILIZATION: The patterns, frequencies, or rates of use of a medical service.

UTILIZATION REVIEW (UR): Evaluates the necessity, appropriateness, or efficiency of the use of medical services. Specifically examines the appropriateness of admissions, length of stay, and ancillary services ordered.

VERTICALLY INTEGRATED NETWORKS (VIN): An alliance of providers encompassing a continuum of healthcare services used for meeting the needs of managed care contracts.

WITHHOLD: The "at risk" portion of the monthly capitation payment to physicians withheld by an HMO until the end of a specified time period. Serves as a financial incentive to lower utilization.

Index

Accounting, 4
 cash versus accrual accounting, 196
 cost accounting, 175–176
Acquisitions, *see* Practice acquisitions
Allied health providers, 32
Anti-kickback, 20, 70–72, 129. *See also*
 Self-referral
Antitrust, 70–71, 130, 174
 Clayton Act, 131
 Sherman Act, 130–131
 Statements of Antitrust Enforcement
 in Healthcare, 22, 131
"Any willing provider" laws, 129–130
Appraisal, *see* Valuation
Archiving, *see* Records management
Autonomy, 116–117, 158

Benchmarking, *see* Consulting,
 analysis
Blue Cross and Blue Shield Association,
 12
Business Planning, 108–111, 230–231,
 233, 238, 241, 267, 272–275
 competitors, 201
 customers, 109, 200
 services, 201
 SWOT analysis, 201

Capitation, 4, 11, 13, 16, 26, 87, 175,
 237–238. *See also* Managed care
Centralized services, 131–133, 177–178,
 182

Clinical Laboratory Improvement Act
 of 1988 (CLIA), 20
Clinics Without Walls, *see* Group
 Practices Without Walls
 (GPWWs)
Communication, 181, 186, 189,
 217–218
Consensus building, 110, 115, 117,
 128, 158, 169
Consulting, 91–92, 112. *See also*
 Business planning; Research;
 Strategic planning
 analysis, 99–100, 239, 241–267
 engagement process, 102–104,
 180–181
 knowledge and experience, 92,
 140–141
 management status assessments,
 180–182, 191–192, 226–228
 methods and processes, 91
 operational reviews, 180, 182,
 185–186, 189–191, 227–228
 opportunities and market for
 services, 1–2, 5, 9
 presentation and reporting, 100, 184,
 275
 professional fees, 104–105
 project planning, 93, 111–112, 140,
 143–148, 168–169
 milestone chronologies, 93–94,
 110, 153
 process outlines, 93–95, 153–155

Consulting (*cont.*)
    timetables of events, 93, 95–97,
      156
    proposals, 98
    records management, 100, 112–113
Corporate practice of medicine laws,
    72, 129
Current Procedural Terminology (CPT),
    165–166

Designated Health Services, 18
Diagnostic Related Groups (DRGs), 5,
    165
Downsizing, *see* Right-sizing
Due diligence, 102, 229–230, 272–275

Emerging Healthcare Organizations
    (EHOs), *see also* Specific types
    (MSOs, IPAs, etc.)
    costs, 141
    general definition and classification,
      3, 7, 33–36, 117, 159
    licensure, state, 129
    start-up, 106, 111–116, 136, 171–172
    statistics, 8–9
    strategy, 136, 157–159, 178–179
Employer coalitions, 122
Employment Retirement Income
    Security Act of 1974 (ERISA),
    135
Equity, physician, 61–62, 64–65, 67, 74,
    117

Fee-for-service, 11
Financial management, 183, 191–200
Fraud and abuse, 17, 128. *See also*
    Specific types
Fully Integrated Medical Groups
    (FIMGs), 120–121, 163
    costs, 79
    definition, 78
    functions, 80–81
    objectives, 78
    organizational structure, 79–80

Gatekeeper system, *see* Managed care,
    gatekeeper system

Group practices, *see* Physician practices
Group Practices Without Walls
    (GPWWs), 15, 119, 161
    advantages and disadvantages, 77,
      81, 119
    costs, 76
    definition, 75
    functions, 77
    future, 77–78
    organizational structure, 76

Health Insurance Portability and
    Accountability Act of 1996, 22
Health Maintenance Organizations
    (HMOs), 25
Healthcare, *see* Industry, healthcare;
    Specific topics
HMO Act of 1973, 5, 37
Hospitals, 122
Human Resources, 182, 203–204,
    210–211, 215, 218–220. *See also*
    Right-sizing
    benefits planning, 135, 212
    hiring, orientation and training, 211
    performance reviews, 206–208, 216
    policies, 211, 214–215, 216–217

Incentives, physician, 21, 89, 172,
    174–175
Income distribution plans, 174–177
Independent Practice Associations
    (IPAs), 118, 159–160
    advantages and disadvantages, 118,
      159–160
    costs, 40
    definition, 36–37
    functions, 41
    history, 37–38
    managed care contracting, 38–39
    mergers and acquisitions, 41–43
    organizational structure, 40
    services, 38–39
    specialty mix, 41
    valuation, 40
Industry, healthcare, 10, 24, 26, 29–30,
    140, 178–179, 233–238, 274
    costs, 4, 6, 12, 14

consolidation, 2, 6, 28, 116, 158, 179.
    See also Integration
Information Systems/Technology
    (IS/IT), *see also* Management
    Information Systems (MIS)
networking, 185
Insurance, indemnity, 11–12
Integrated Delivery Systems (IDS), 28
    advantages and disadvantages, 89
    capitation, 87
    definition, 81–82
    functions, 87–89
    future, 90
    governance, 86
    history, 85
    incentives, physician, 89–90
    management information systems
        (MIS), 87
    medical management, 85
    objectives, 83–84
    organizational structure, 83, 85–86
    risk sharing, 88
    strategy, 84
    transfer prices, 88
    vertical integration, 82
Integration:
    economies of scale, 3
    horizontal, 3, 34
    phases of integration, 101, 113–116,
        149, 153
    physician, 3, 100–101, 106–107,
        111–117, 128, 137–139, 143–149,
        157, 169–170, 178–179
    vertical, 3, 34, 82
Inurement, private, 19
IRS code and tax law, *see* Nonprofit
    organizations

Leadership, 107, 111, 181, 207
Leverage, negotiating, 3, 116–117, 158

Major Diagnostic Category (MDC),165
Managed care, 12, 25, 27–28. *See also*
    Medicare and Medicaid
    contracting, 26, 135–136, 197–198.
        See also Leverage, negotiating
    enrollment, 12–13, 25, 28, 116, 234

gatekeeper system, 26, 32, 231,
    233–237
withholds, 4
Managed Care Organizations (MCOs),
    122–123. *See also* Specific types
    (Health Maintenance
    Organizations, etc.)
Management, *see* Consulting,
    management status assessment;
    Specific topics
Management Information Systems
    (MIS), 87, 109, 133, 182, 185–187
    computerized patient records (CPR),
        186
    functions, 134, 187
    objectives, 134, 185
Management Services Organizations
    (MSOs), 120, 162–163, 180,
    183–185, 227–228
    advantages and disadvantages,
        68–69, 120, 163
    antitrust, 70–71
    costs, 63–65, 163
    definition, 56
    fraud and abuse, 70–73
    governance, 66, 74
    history, 59
    integration, 59
    Management Services Bureaus
        (MSBs), 63, 119–120, 161–162
    objectives, 59
    organizational structure, 66–67, 72
    ownership, 60–62, 66
    practice management services, 57–58,
        162–163
    profitability, 65
    strategy, 73–75
    types, 57, 63, 66–67
Medical management, 85
    continuum of care, 85
    outcomes management, 4, 84
Medical practices, *see* Physician
    practices
Medical records, *see* Patient records
Medical Service Organizations, *see*
    Management Services
    Organizations (MSOs)

Medicare and Medicaid, 5, 23, 123
Medicare and Medicaid Patient and
	Program Protection Act of 1987
	(MMPPA), 21
Medicare Part C or Medicare + Choice,
	6, 13, 15, 29
Medicare Payment Advisory
	Commission (MEDPAC), 14
Mission statements, *see* Strategic
	planning

Nonprofit organizations, 18–19, 130.
	See also Inurement, private
Nurse practitioners, *see* Allied health
	providers

Office of the Inspector General (OIG),
	130
Omnibus Budget Reconciliation Acts
	(OBRA), 14–15
Open access specialty-driven panels,
	32
Operations, *see* Consulting, operational
	reviews
Outcomes management, *see* Medical
	management
Outsourcing, 132

Patient records, 186, 188–189. *See also*
	Management Information
	Systems (MIS), computerized
	patient records (CPR)
Physician Hospital Organizations
	(PHOs), 118, 160–161
	advantages and disadvantages, 55,
		118–119
	contracting, 53
	costs, 53–54
	definition, 51
	functions, 55
	future, 56
	objectives, 53
	open versus closed, 54–55
	organizational structure, 54
	ownership, 51–52
	practice management, 160–161

Physician Payment Review
	Commission, *see* Medicare
	Payment Advisory Commission
	(MEDPAC)
Physician Practice Management
	Companies (PPMCs), 42, 44–45,
	229–233, 238–241, 267
	affiliation models, 46
	Coastal Physician Group (case study),
		50–51
	definition, 42
	disadvantages, 49
	IPA acquisitions, 43
	management fees, 47–48
	objectives, 42
	organizational structure, 45, 232
	physician practice acquisitions, 44
	practice management, 49, 232
Physician practices, 2, 4, 8
Physician Services Network, *see*
	Management Services
	Organizations (MSOs)
Physician specialties, 233–238
Physician supply, 7, 29–31
	balance of specialists and primary
		care physicians, 31–32. *See also*
		Physician specialties
Physician's Assistants (PAs), *see* Allied
	health providers
Planning, *see* Specific types
Practice acquisitions, 174. *See also*
	Thornton letter; Valuation
	costs, 141–143
	planning, 137–139, 143–148,
		150–151, 171–172
	process flow model, 151–152,
		166–168, 174
	targets, 127–128, 166–168, 170
Practice Asset Organization, *see*
	Management Services
	Organizations (MSOs)
Practice Management Companies, *see*
	Physician Practice Management
	Organizations (PPMCs)
Preferred Provider Organizations
	(PPOs), *see* Managed care;

Managed Care Organizations (MCOs)
Primary Care Physicians (PCPs), *see* Physician specialties
Prospective Payment Systems (PPS), 5
Provider Sponsored Organizations (PSOs), 15, 17, 23, 107

Recruiting, physicians, 127–128, 137, 166–170, 204, 231, 267–275
Regulation, *see* Specific types
Reimbursement, 4–6, 11. *See also* Specific types
Research, 99, 220–221
    benchmarking, 241. *See also* Consulting, analysis
    competitors/local providers, 127, 140, 166, 222–223
    customers/patients, 124–125
    demographics, 123–124
    economics, local, 123, 125, 166
    employers and coalitions, 122, 125
    hospitals and healthcare facilities, 122
    internal (specific to subject entity), 127, 139, 221

managed care, 122–123, 126, 157–158
markets, local, 116, 121, 164, 220
utilization demand, 164–165
Resource Based Relative Value Scales (RBRVS), 5, 13, 15–16, 236–237
Right-sizing, 134–135
Risk, business, 3, 88, 117, 274

Safe harbors, 21–22
Self-referral, 18, 21–22, 71, 129, 173. *See also* Designated health services
Specialists, *see* Physician specialties
Staffing, *see* Right-sizing
Stark laws, *see* Self-referral
Strategic planning, 182, 200–203
    strategic initiatives, 97–98, 139
    tactical plans, 97–98
    vision statements, 97–98, 108

Tax-exempt entities, *see* Nonprofit organizations
Thornton letter, 19, 173

Valuation, 142, 167